5,500 QUILT
BLOCK
DESIGNS

Edited by Nancy E. Sherman

Library of Congress Cataloging-in-Publication Data Available

10 9 8 7 6 5 4 3 2 1

Published by Sterling Publishing Co., Inc.
387 Park Avenue South, New York, NY 10016
© 2003 by Maggie Malone
Distributed in Canada by Sterling Publishing
C/o Canadian Manda Group, One Atlantic Avenue, Suite 105
Toronto, Ontario, Canada M6K 3E7
Distributed in Great Britain by Chrysalis Books
64 Brewery Road, London N7 9NT, England
Distributed in Australia by Capricorn Link (Australia) Pty. Ltd.
P.O. Box 704, Windsor, NSW 2756, Australia

Sterling ISBN 0-8069-7749-3

Maggie Malone

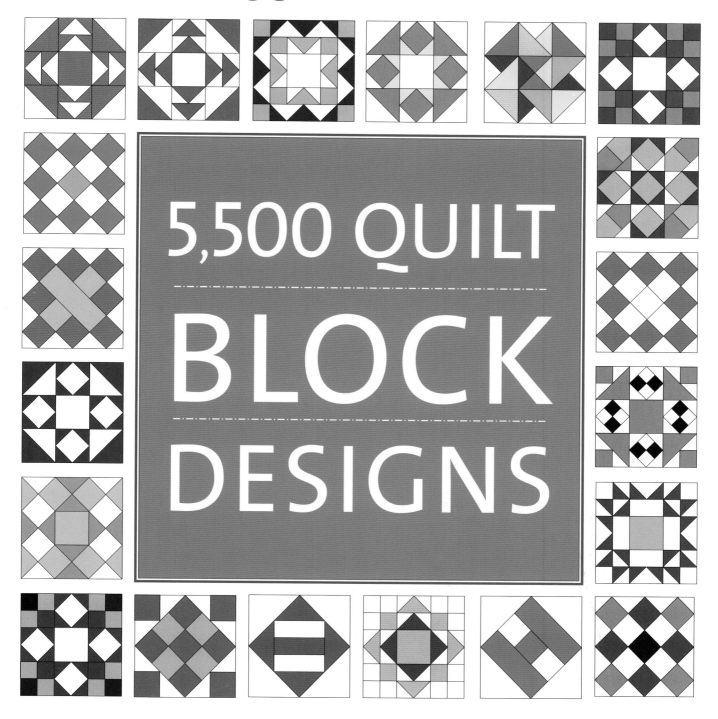

5,500 QUILT
BLOCK
DESIGNS

Sterling Publishing Co., Inc.
New York

Key

AB	Alice Brooks		MLM	Mary Lee Moynihan
AG	Alice Gammell		MM	Maggie Malone
AK	Aunt Kate		MoM	Mountain Mist
AMS	Aunt Martha Studios		NC	Nancy Cabot
CAM	Cincinnati Art Museum		NCS	Needle Craft Supply
CaS	Carlie Sexton		NM	Needlecraft Magazine
CG	Country Gentleman		NP	Nancy Page
CoM	Comfort Magazine		OCS	Old Chelsea Station
CR	Caroline Reardon		OF	Ohio Farmer
CS	Clara Stone		OJF	Orange Judd Farmer
CW	Capper's Weekly		PAG	Patchwork Accessories & Gifts
EH	Ernie Haight		PF	Progressive Farmer
FF	Farm and Fireside		PP	Prudence Penny
FJ	Farm Journal		PQ	Patchwork Quilts
GB	Georgia Bonesteel		qac	quilting.about.com
GC	Grandmother Clark		QC	Quilt Craft
GD	Grandma Dexter		QEQ	Quick & Easy Quilting
GH	Golden Hands		QM	Quiltmaker
GLB	Godey's Lady's Book		QN	Quilter's Newsletter
HaM	Harriet Moore		QT	Quilting Today
HAS	Home Art Studios		QW	Quilt World
HH	Hearth & Home		QWB	Quilter's Workbook
HHA	Household Arts		QWO	Quilt World Omnibook
HHJ	Household Journal		RD	Roy Daniel
HM	Household Magazine		RF	Robert Frank
HMD	H.M. Designs		RM	Ruby McKim
IS	Indianapolis Star		RMS	Ruth M. Swasey
JM	Judy Martin		SD	Susan Dague
KCS	Kansas City Star		SSQ	Stitch 'n Sew Quilts
LAC	Ladies Art Company		TFW	The Farmer's Wife
LBC	Lockport Batting Company		TQ	Traditional Quiltworks
LCPQ	Ladies' Circle Patchwork Quilts		TQr	Traditional Quilter
			VJ	Victoria Johnson
LHJ	Ladies' Home Journal		VS	Virginia Snow
LR	Lou Rathjen		WB	Workbasket
LS	Lois Smith		WBM	Workbasket Magazine
LW	Laura Wheeler		WC	Woman's Century
MD	Mrs. Danner		WD	Woman's Day
MJ	Michael James		WW	Woman's World

Table of Contents

I clipped my very first quilt pattern in 1958 from *McCall's Needlework and Crafts* magazine. It was called Lone Star, a five point star set in a pieced circle. I made one block and decided I'd never live long enough to complete a quilt by hand. Nevertheless, quilts continued to catch my eye and I clipped many more patterns. I didn't really start to quilt though until the early 1970s, when I read Barbara Johannah's book, *Quick Quilting*. That book made it begin to seem that it might not take a lifetime to make a quilt after all.

The first quilt I completed was an Ohio Star I made for my brother-in-law. It took only about two weeks to finish. After that, I was hooked. Every quilt pattern I came across was added to my collection, as well as every picture of one. By 1980, I had stacks of magazines everywhere. And I could never remember which magazine it was that contained the pattern I needed. So I began removing the patterns from magazines, organizing them by the number of squares in a block, and filing each type by name in alphabetical order. The file boxes proliferated, but so did the new magazines I bought. I just wasn't gaining on the problem.

As I became more proficient at quilting, I realized I didn't need the entire pattern, just a sketch of it. That was the basis for *1,001 Patchwork Patterns*, but those sketches were all hand drawn and it seemed like an awful lot of time-consuming work to draw pictures of every new pattern I happened upon. As I collected and filed them, I also became aware that some patterns went by more than one name, sometimes as many as five or ten.

Then came the computer. Once I found a decent drawing program, it was child's play to draw the patterns and save them to disk. I got rid of tons of paper. The end result is the book you now hold in your hands.

The patterns are drawn on a grid showing the number of squares to the block. The most basic and most common pattern is the nine patch, a block that is 3 squares by 3 squares. Patterns progress from there to blocks that are 6 squares by

6 squares, 9 squares by 9 squares, and so on. This arrangement also makes it easy to mix and match patterns if desired, as they all draft to the same size block.

To draft a pattern, draw a square the size you want the finished block to be. Divide it into the appropriate number of squares and draw in the lines.

If possible, find grid paper for circles and hexagons. These designs are so much easier to draft when you have the proper grid. You'll find that many octagonal patterns are easier to draw on a circular grid.

If you feel uncomfortable about drawing your own patterns, take this book to a copy shop and have them enlarge your selected pattern. Be aware that there may be some distortion in the enlarging process. Draw a grid over the enlarged pattern, then adjust any lines that do not line up with the grid.

This book gives the name (or names) of each pattern, as well as some of the publications in which the patterns first appeared and the name of the creator, where known (see key on p. 4). Some of the patterns are very old and are copied from holdings in museum collections. Other old patterns were passed along from friend to friend and were not actually published until the 1890s or later. Most of the patterns published in the *Kansas City Star* fall into this category. Readers sent in patterns for publication that had been in their families for 50, 60, even a 100 years. Other publications, designers, and editors relied heavily on patterns from the Ladies Art Company catalogs. The oldest catalog I have was published in 1892 and many of the designs appearing in it have become classics.

I hope you enjoy this book and find it useful for many projects and many, many years.

—Maggie Malone

NINE
PATCH
PATTERNS

3 X 3 GRID

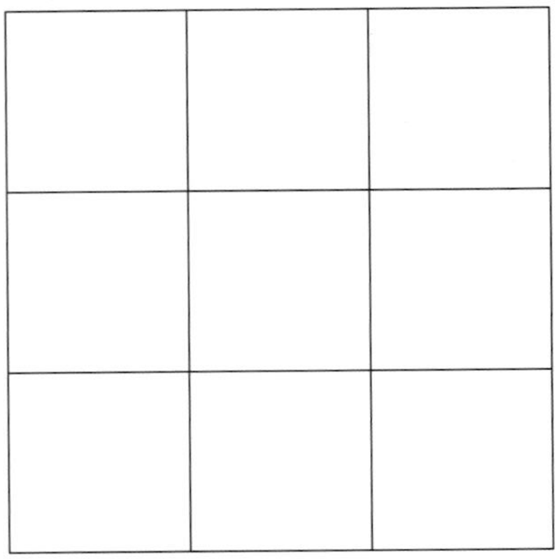

6 X 6 GRID

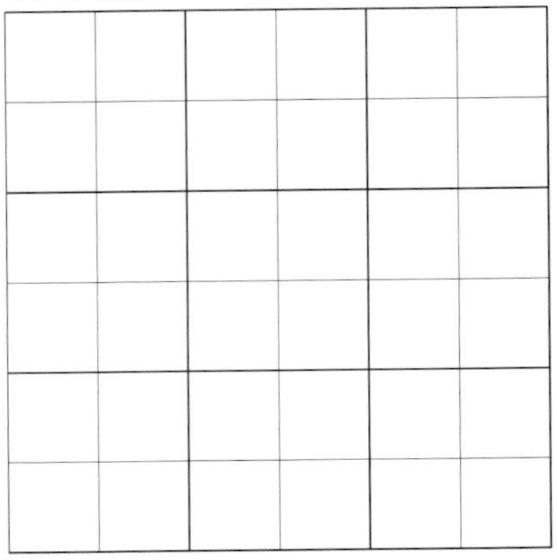

A NINE PATCH PATTERN IS MADE ON A GRID OF 3X3 SQUARES
THESE PATTERNS ARE EASILY SCALED TO ANY BLOCK SIZE DIVISIBLE BY 3

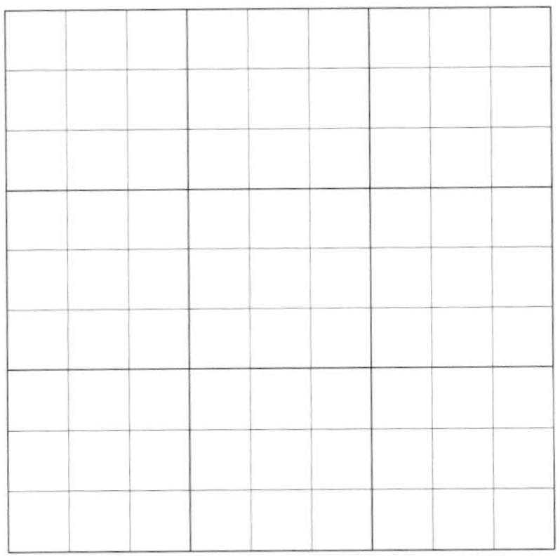

9 X 9 GRID

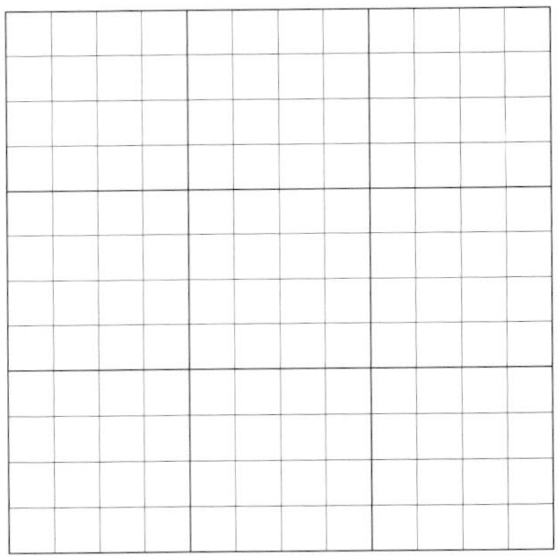

12 X 12 GRID

1 Nine Patch, *OF, 1896*
   Simplex Star, *HH*
   Checkerboard Design,
      1931
   Double Nine Patch

2 Nine Patch
   Patience Nine Patch
   Easy Quilt

3 Red Cross

4 Patience Nine Patch

5 H-Square
   Blocks in a Box

6 Bright Hopes
   Twist

7 Hourglass

8 Calico Puzzle, *KCS, 1930*

9 Snowball

10 Snowball Variation

11 Split Nine Patch

12 Split Nine Patch

13 Big O

14 Octagon, *KCS*
    Calico Snowball
    Hour Glasses
    The Marble Floor, *KCS*
    Rob Peter to Pay Paul,
       CaS
    Snowballs, *NC*

15 Hourglass

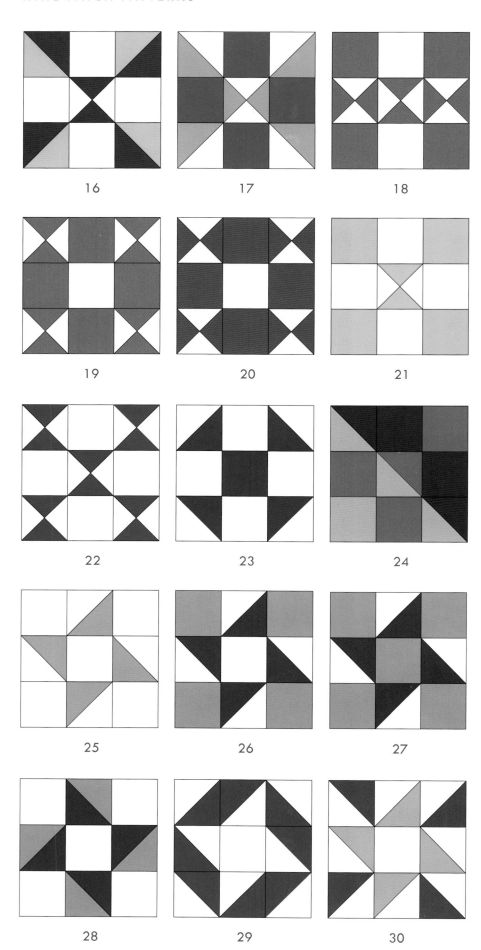

16 Practical Orchard, *LAC*

17 Hour Glass, *CS*

18 Triplet, *KCS*

19 Letter X, *LAC*

20 At the Square, *LAC*

21 Practical Orchard, *LAC*
   Practical Orchard, *NC*,
   1934

22 Clown's Choice

23 Shoofly, *LAC*
   Eight Cornered Box,
   1896
   Fifty Four Forty or
   Fight, *NC*
   Simplicity, *OCS*
   Fence Row Quilt, *KCS*
   Hole in the Barn Door

24 Straight Furrow
   Nine Patch Variation
   Perkomen Valley

25 Friendship Star

26 The Pinwheel, *KCS*
   Simplex Star, *HH*
   Wings in a Whirl, *KCS*

27 The Lost Goslin', *KCS*

28 New Home

29 Ribbon Star, *NP*

30 Nine Patch Star

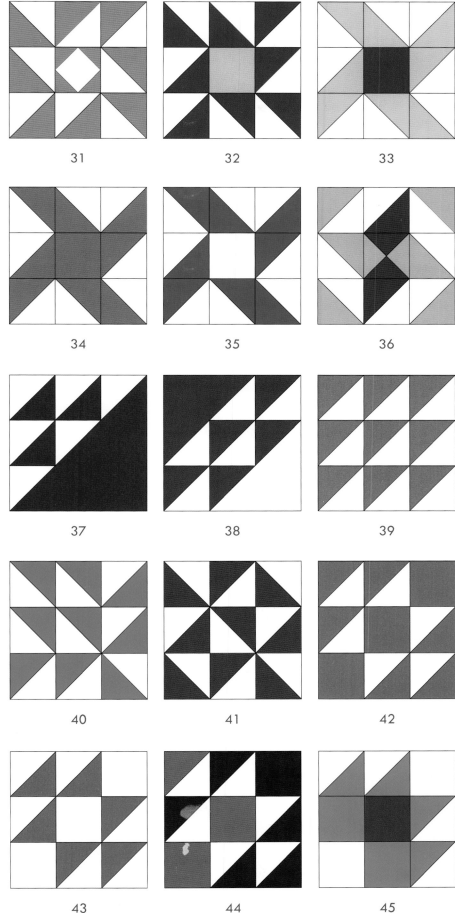

31

32

33

34

35

36

37

38

39

40

41

42

43

44

45

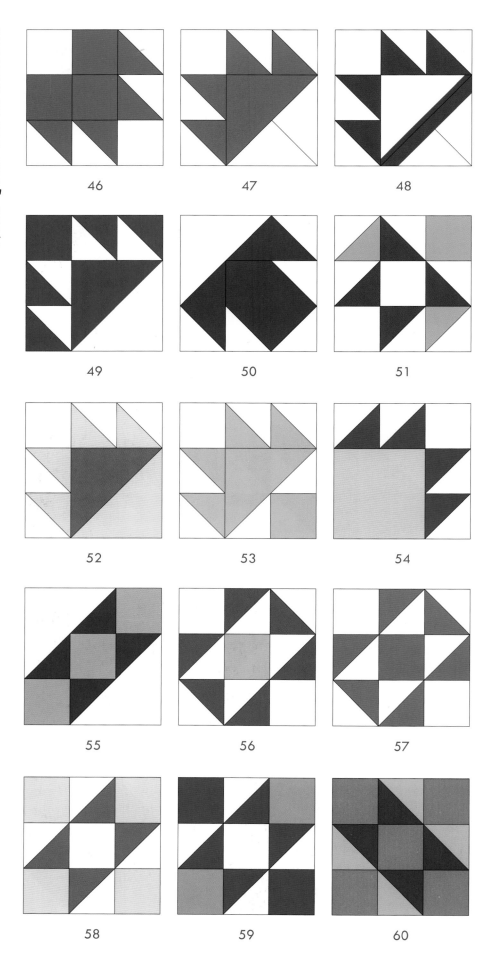

46 Tea Leaf
    Bear Tracks, *NC, 1937*
    Duck's Foot in the
     Mud, *NC*
    Maple Leaf Quilt
    Tea Leaves, *NC*

47 Maple Leaf, *CS*
    Album
    Autumn Leaf, *LW*
    Magnolia Leaf, *CS*
    Poplar Leaf
    Tea Leaves

48 Sawtooth

49 Cactus Bud

50 Tin Soldier "T" Quilt
    Boxed T, *LAC*

51 Darting Birds, *NP*

52 Cake Stand

53 Old Bear's Paw

54 Bear Paw

55 Road to California

56 Split Nine Patch

57 Split Nine Patch

58 Double Hour Glass, *NC,*
    1933

59 Contrary Wife, *KCS*

60 Contrary Wife

61 Attic Window
   Garret Window, *NC*

62 Autumn Trails, *MM*

63 Slanted Diamonds, *NC*

64 Spool
   Empty Spool, *NC*
   Love Knot

65 Malvina's Chain, *LAC*
   Aunt Melvernia's
      Chain, *NC*

66 Friendship Name
      Chain, *KCS*

67 Sailboat Block, *KCS*
   Lost Ship, *LAC*
   Victory Boat
   West Wind, *NP*

68 Cobwebs

69 Green River, *NP*

70 Calico Spools

71 Zig Zag Path, *SD, 1999*

72 Sailboat

73 Northwind

74 Birds in the Air

75 Attic Window
   Shadow Box

61

62

63

64

65

66

67

68

69

70

71

72

73

74

75

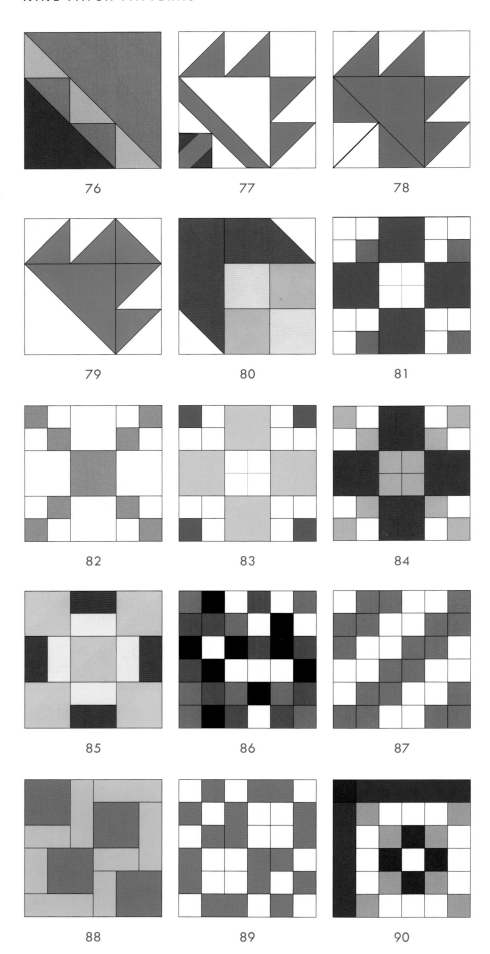

76 Golden Stairs

77 Texas Flower, *LAC*

78 Apple Leaf, *KCS*
   Maple Leaf

79 Double T, *NP*
   Mixed T, *NP*

80 Beginner's Choice

81 Pussy in the Corner,
   GC, 1931
   Puss in the Corner, *NC,*
   1932

82 Pennsylvania, *NP*
   Criss Cross Quilt, *NP*
   Simple Cross
   Single Irish Chain, *NC*

83 Homeward Bound

84 Thrifty, *KCS*

85 Unknown

86 Postage Stamp

87 Streak of Lightning

88 Patience Corners

89 Domino
   Chained Dominos

90 Nine Patch Plaid

91 Nine Patch

92 Antique Tile Block, *NC*, *1938*

93 Interlocked Squares, *KCS*
Four Part Striped Block, *KCS*
Spin Wheel

94 Zig Zag

95 Spirit of St. Louis, *NC*, *1934*
Tricolor Block, *NC*

96 Basket Weave

97 London Stairs, *KCS*
Virginia Worm Fence
Endless Stairs, *HH*
Endless Stair, *NC*

98 Roman Square

99 Four H, *KCS*

100 Unknown

101 Edna's Choice

102 Confetti, *TQ*

103 Color Ways

104 Interlocked Squares

105 Roman Squares
Fence Posts
Three by Three, *CG*

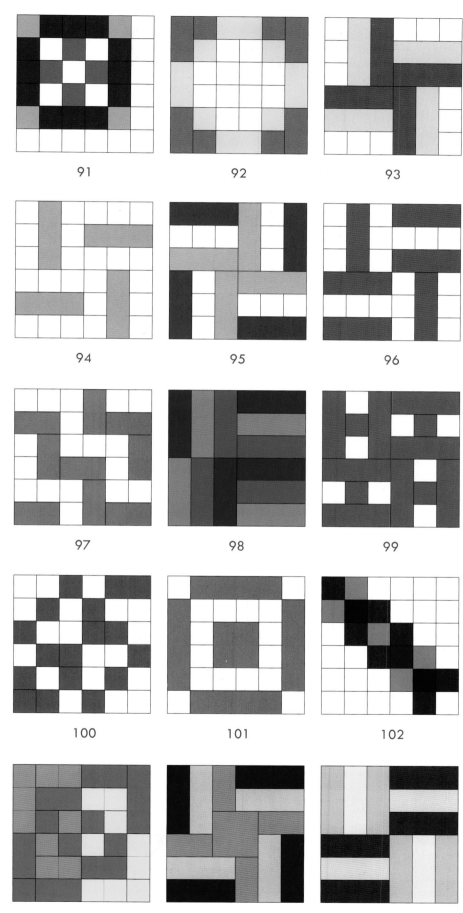

91

92

93

94

95

96

97

98

99

100

101

102

103

104

105

5,500 QUILT BLOCK DESIGNS

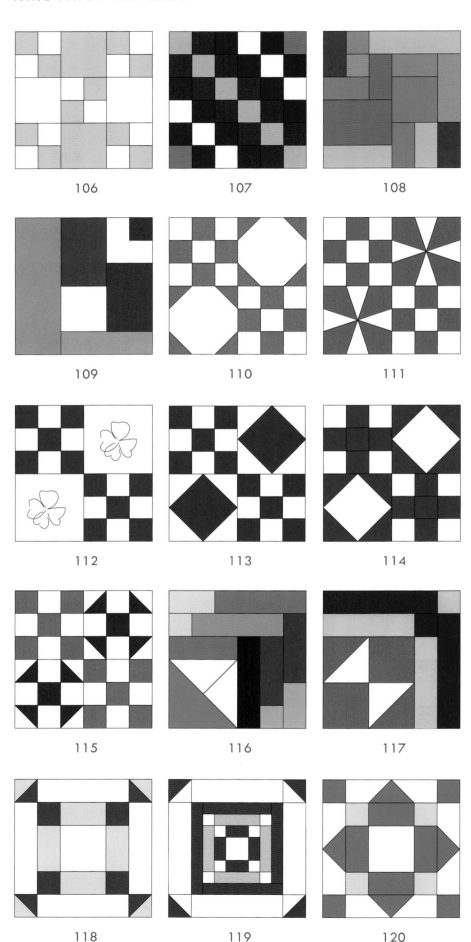

106

107

108

109

110

111

112

113

114

115

116

117

118

119

120

121 Fair and Square, *KCS*

122 Boxes

123 Churn Dash, *RM*
   Broken Plate, *NC*
   Double Monkey
     Wrench
   Double T, *HH*
   Dragon's Head, *WW*
   Fisherman's Reel
   Hens and Chickens
   Hole in the Barn Door
   Indian Hammer
   Joan's Doll Quilt
   Lincoln's Platform
   Love Knot
   Ludlow's Favorite
   Old Mill Design, *TFW*
   Picture Frame
   Puss in the Corner
   Quail's Nest
   Sherman's March, *CW*
   Shoo Fly, *NC*
   Wrench

124 Churn Dash

125 Grecian Design, *LAC*
   Grecian Square, *WW*
   Grecian
   Greek Square, *NC*

126 Greek Cross

127 Prairie Queen
   True Blue, *HH*

128 Chained Nine Patch

129 Cups and Saucers, *KCS*

130 Illinois, *HH*

131 Eddystone Light

132 Hidden Star

133 Card Trick

134 No Name Patch

135 Arbor Window

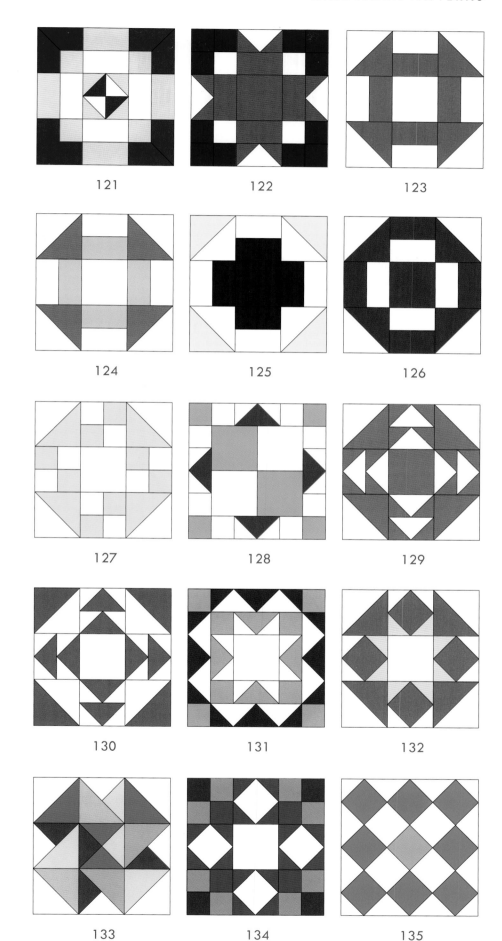

121

122

123

124

125

126

127

128

129

130

131

132

133

134

135

5,500 QUILT BLOCK DESIGNS

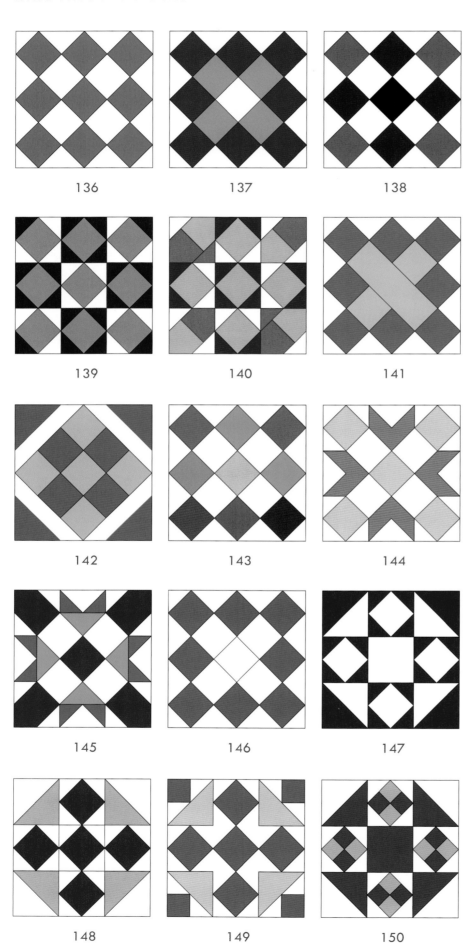

136

137

138

139

140

141

142

143

144

145

146

147

148

149

150

136 Nine Patch

137 Courthouse Square
   Grandmother's Pride,
   HAS

138 Checkerboard

139 Montpelier Quilt Block

140 Patchwork Bedspread

141 Album, *KCS*
   Arbor Window, *GC*
   Courthouse Square
   The Cross Patch
   Odd Fellow's Quilt, *OJF*

142 Mayor's Garden, *NC*
   Modern Broken Dish,
   KCS

143 Checkerboard
   Nine Patch
     Checkerboard
   Old Mail, *WC*
   The Queen's Favorite,
   CW

144 Joy Bells
   Eight Hands Around
   Swing in the Center, *NC*
   Turkey in the Straw, *NC*

145 Swing in the Center,
   LAC
   Dumbbell Block
   Mrs. Roosevelt's
     Favorite
   Roman Pavement
   Swinging in the
     Center, *NC*

146 Beggar Block

147 Sawtooth Patchwork,
   LAC
   Mrs. Brown's Choice

148 Sawtooth Patchwork
   Five Diamonds

149 Five Spot, *NC*

150 The Pinwheel Quilt,
   KCS

151 Cross and Chains, *KCS*

152 Richmond
Aunt Vina's Favorite
Butterfly Quilt Block, *NC*
Lucy's Four and Nine

153 Jefferson City, *HH*

154 No Name Patch

155 Creole Puzzle, *NC*

156 Fresh Start, *RMS, SSQ, 1983*

157 Robbing Peter to Pay Paul

158 Arizona, *NP*

159 Crossroads to Jericho, *HH*

160 Union Squares

161 Double Anchor, *KCS*

162 Mrs. Bryan's Choice

163 Cracker

164 H Quilt

165 Jewel

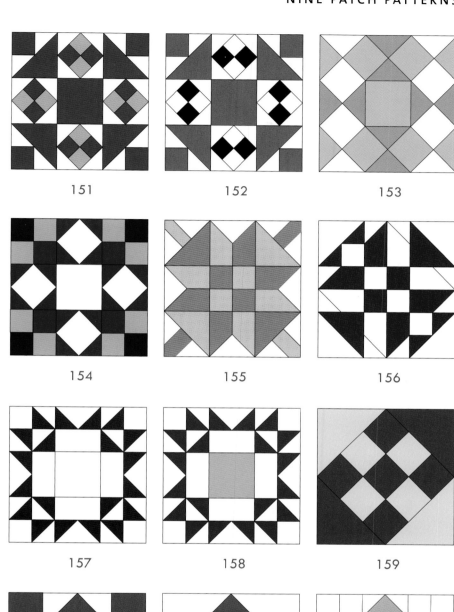

151 152 153
154 155 156
157 158 159

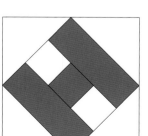

160 161 162

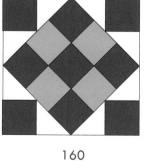
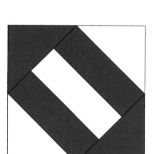
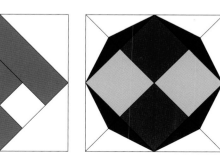

163 164 165

166

167

168

169

170

171

172

173

174

175

176

177

178

179

180

166 Union Square, *NC*
   Beacon Light, *NC*

167 Ladies' Aid, *LAC*

168 Carol's Scrap Time
   Quilt

169 Storm Signal, *NC*
   Hail Storm, *NC*

170 Four Ships Sailing,
   LCPQ

171 Wheeling Triangles

172 Trees in the Park

173 Weathervane Pinwheel

174 Nine Patch Frame

175 Twisting Star

176 Merry-Go-Round

177 Cornerstone, *KCS*

178 Turnabout Variation

179 Turnabout, *QN*

180 Squares and Diamonds

181 Vines at the Window,
     NC

182 Nine Patch Frame

183 The Village Green, *1930*

184 Diamond Star, *LAC*
     A Quilt Mosaic, *KCS*

185 Mother's Choice, *CS*
     Dove at the Windows,
       MD
     Fringed Square, *NC*
     Laurel Wreath, *CW*

186 Sandhills Star, *KCS*
     Blossoming Cactus, *NC*

187 A Quilt Mosaic, *KCS*

188 Aunt Sukey's Choice,
     LAC

189 Hopscotch, *KCS*

190 Christmas Star, *KCS*

191 Turkey's Dilemma,
     RMS, SSQ, 1982

192 Indian Puzzle, *KCS*

193 Love in a Mist

194 Best of All

195 Housewife Quilt Block

181

182

183

184

185

186

187

188

189

190

191

192

193

194

195

196

197

198

199

200

201

202

203

204

205

206

207

208

209

210

196 All Hallows

197 Castle Tower

198 Shaded Compass

199 Cups and Saucers, *KCS*

200 Autumn Maze

201 Diamond Star, *AMS*

202 Weathervane Variation

203 Garden Path

204 Shaded Trail, *KCS*

205 Arrowhead Star, *KCS*
      Laurel Wreath, *GC*
      Many Pointed Star, *NC*
      Michigan Beauty, *CS*
      Modern Star, *GC*
      Star of Many Points,
        LAC

206 Sailboat Block

207 Ohio Star
      Eastern Star
      Eight Point Design, *LAC*
      Eight Point Star
      Lone Star
      Shoofly
      Star
      Texas
      Texas Star
      Tippecanoe and Tyler,
        Too

208 Variable Star
      Henry of the West, *NP*
      Lone Star, *NP*
      Star of Hope, *NP*
      Star of the West, *NP*
      Star Spangled
      Texas

209 Flying Crow, *FJ*

210 Mosaic
      Star of Virginia
      Variable Star
      Happy Home, *HH*

211 Four X Quilt
Four X's

212 Unknown Star

213 Mosaic

214 Squares and
Diamonds, *KCS*

215 Mosaic, *NP*

216 Silent Star, *KCS*
Star X
Old Tippecanoe

217 Swamp Angel, *NC*

218 Midnight Star Block

219 Star X, *NC*

220 Combination Star, *LAC*
Ornate Star

221 Mystery Flower
Garden, *AMS*

222 Variable Star
Aunt Eliza's Star, *HH*
Ohio Star
Star of Hope, *NP*

223 Country Farm

224 Braced Star

225 Braced Star

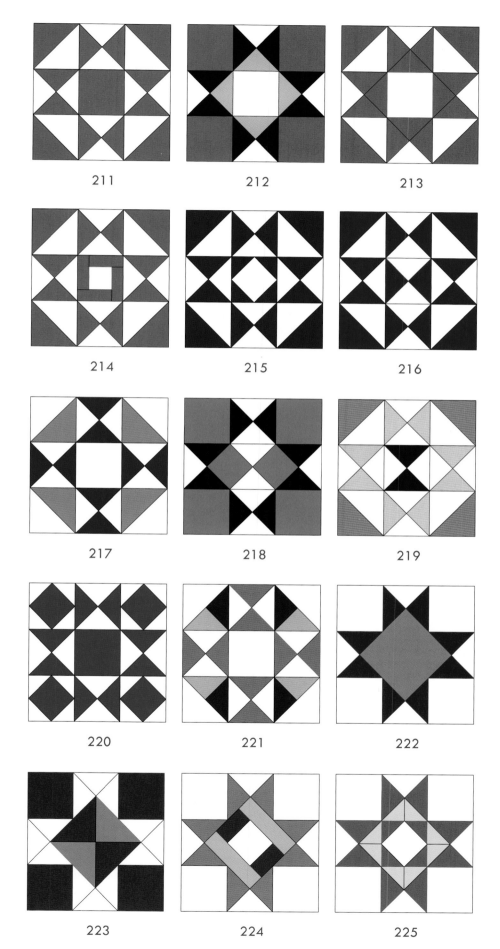

211 212 213

214 215 216

217 218 219

220 221 222

223 224 225

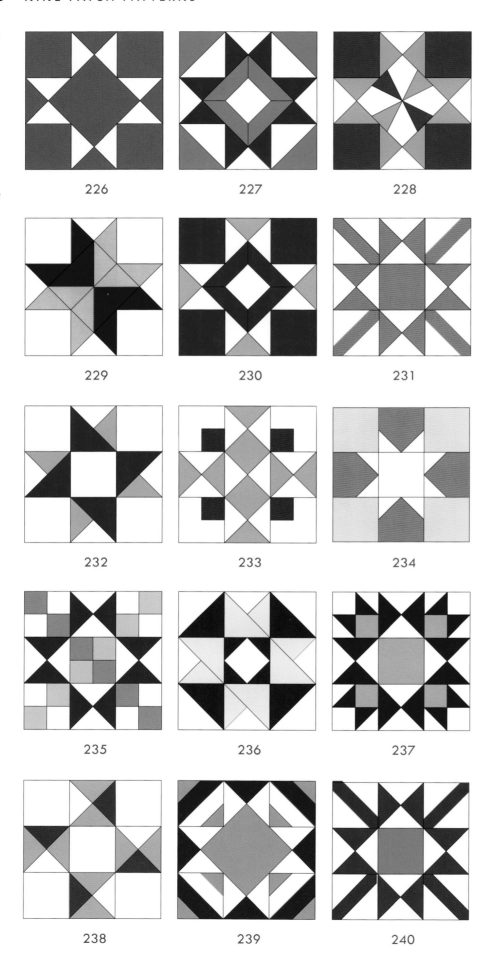

226

227

228

229

230

231

232

233

234

235

236

237

238

239

240

226 Aunt Eliza's Star, *LAC*
Aunt Lottie's Star, *NC*
Texas Star

227 Card Basket

228 Sparkling Star Block

229 Right Hand of
Fellowship, *HH*

230 Friendship Star, *HH*
Braced Star, *LAC*
Eliza's Star

231 Turnabout T

232 Twin Star

233 Four Corners

234 Morning Star

235 Chained Star,
Margaret Huckeby,
QN, 2000

236 Air Castle, *LAC*
Towers of Camelot, *NC*

237 Honeymoon

238 Stellie

239 Jackknife
Treasure Chest, *OCS*
Night and Noon

240 Old Snowflake, *NC*

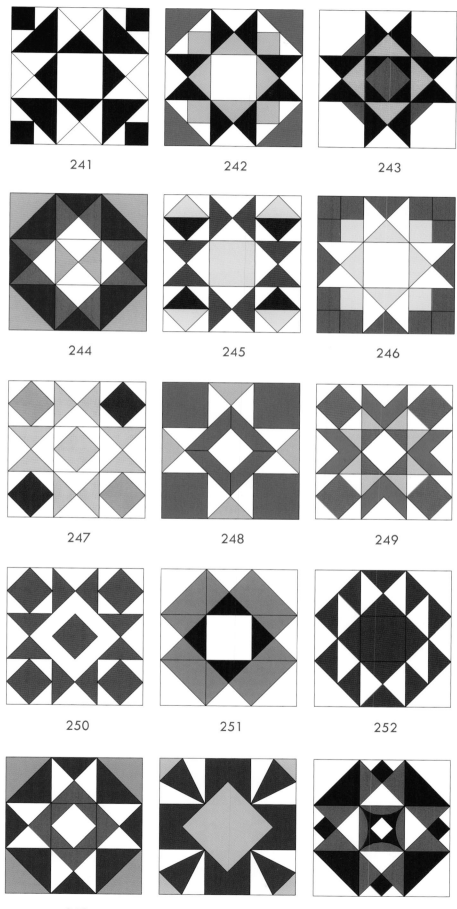

241

242

243

244

245

246

247

248

249

250

251

252

253

254

255

5,500 QUILT BLOCK DESIGNS

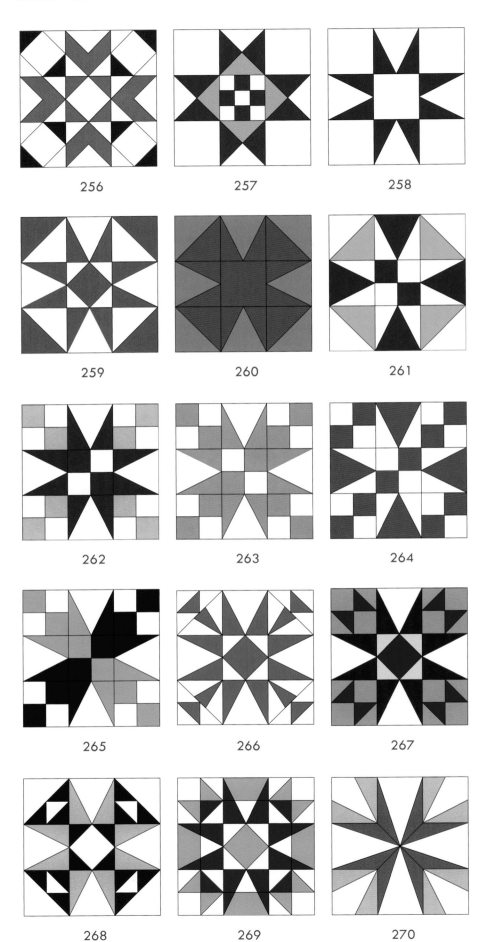

256

257

258

259

260

261

262

263

264

265

266

267

268

269

270

256 Salem

257 Dolly Madison's Star

258 Sun Rays Quilt, *KCS*

259 Doris' Delight, *FJ*
    Storm at Sea

260 Eight Pointed Star

261 Judy in Arabia, *Beth
    Gutcheon*

262 Fifty-Four Forty or
    Fight

263 Fifty-Four Forty or
    Fight, *KCS*
    Grandma's Star
    Nine Patch Star Quilt
    Railroad Quilt

264 Garden Walk, *KCS*
    Garden Patch
    Texas, *NP*
    An Old-Fashioned
    Pinwheel

265 Bird of Paradise

266 Rosebuds

267 Rose Mosaic

268 Panama Star

269 Scattered Points

270 Lily Palm

271 Claws

272 Pineapple

273 Double Z

274 Mayflower

275 Maltese Star

276 1941 9-Patch

277 Eight Pointed Star

278 Straight and Narrow,
   Beth Schwartz, SSQ

279 Big T

280 Garden Square

281 Capital T, *LAC*
   Double T, *NP*
   Cut the Corners, *1910*

282 Friendship Quilt, *KCS*

283 Capital T, *HM*
   Double T

284 Imperial T, *LAC*
   Big T, *Dakota Farmer,*
   1927
   Capital T
   Tea for Four, *NP*

285 Double T, *NP*
   Four T Square, *NC*

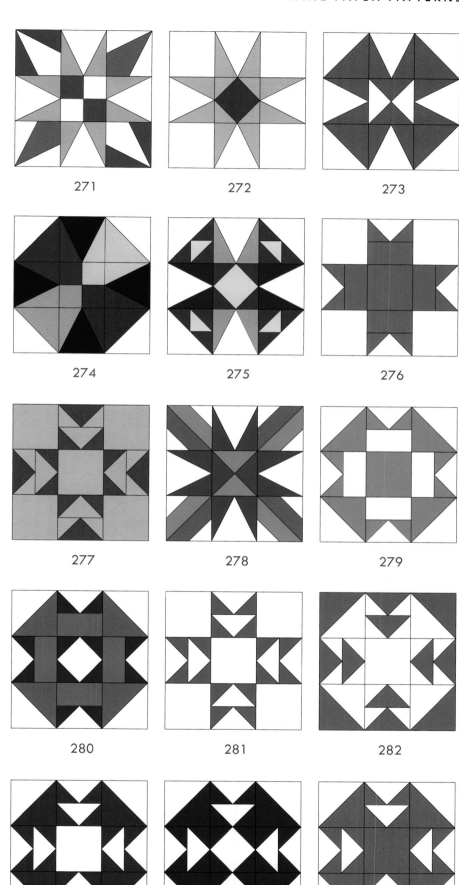

271   272   273

274   275   276

277   278   279

280   281   282

283   284   285

5,500 QUILT BLOCK DESIGNS

286

287

288

289

290

291

292

293

294

295

296

297

298

299

300

286 Imperial T, *KCS*

287 Boxes

288 Gentleman's Fancy, *LAC*
Mary's Block, *NC*
Twenty-four Triangles, *FJ*
Unnamed, *OF*, *1894*

289 Handy Andy

290 Treasure Box

291 Queen's Petticoat, *1979*

292 A Dandy

293 The Dandy Quilt Block, *1910*

294 Amish Star

295 Prairie Home, *QM*, *1994*

296 Tennessee Waltz

297 Eight Point Star

298 Arkansas Star, *KCS*
Bursting Star, *HAS*
Morning Sun, *KCS*

299 Star Geese

300 Country Farm

301 T-Squares

302 Pershing, *NP*

303 Morning Star, *LAC*
Rosebud, *NC*
Virginia, *HH*

304 South Carolina Star

305 Maltese Cross

306 State of Virginia, *HH*

307 Crowning Glory

308 Kansas Star, *KCS*
Crystal Star, *KCS*

309 Lover's Lane

310 Traditional T

311 Sawtooth

312 Sawtooth
Kansas Troubles

313 Lost Ships

314 Lost Ships

315 Tangled Briars

301

302

303

304

305

306

307

308

309

310

311

312

313

314

315

5,500 QUILT BLOCK DESIGNS

316

317

318

319

320

321

322

323

324

325

326

327

328

329

330

316 London Square, *NC*
City Square

317 Birthday Cake

318 Four Crowns

319 Lady of the Lake, *NC*
Galahad's Shield, *PF*

320 Star of Spring, *LW*

321 City Park, *QN*
Crossroads America
Flower Fields
Galaxy
Night Watch
Under Blue Mountain
Skies

322 F Patchwork, *1900*

323 Utility Block, *OF, 1896*

324 Pyramids, *NC*

325 Navajo, *LAC*
Indian Mats, *NC*

326 Mother's Choice

327 Kansas, *HH*

328 Lindy's Plane

329 Union Star

330 Triangles

331

332

333

334

335

336

337

338

339

340

341

342

343

344

345

346 King's Crown

347 Joyce's Mystery Block

348 Silver Lane

349 Buzz Saw Charm, *LS, QN, 1991*

350 Bride's Puzzle
    Twelve Crowns, *FJ*
    Wedding March,
    Women's Comfort

351 Square Dance

352 Large Star Pattern

353 King's Crown

354 Frame

355 Friendship Block

356 Framed Squares, *NP*

357 Star Gardner

358 Union Square, *CW*
    Four Crowns, *KCS, 1933*
    Union, *LAC*
    Union Block, *NC*

359 Maple Leaf

360 Four Crowns

361

362

363

364

365

366

367

368

369

370

371

372

373

374

375

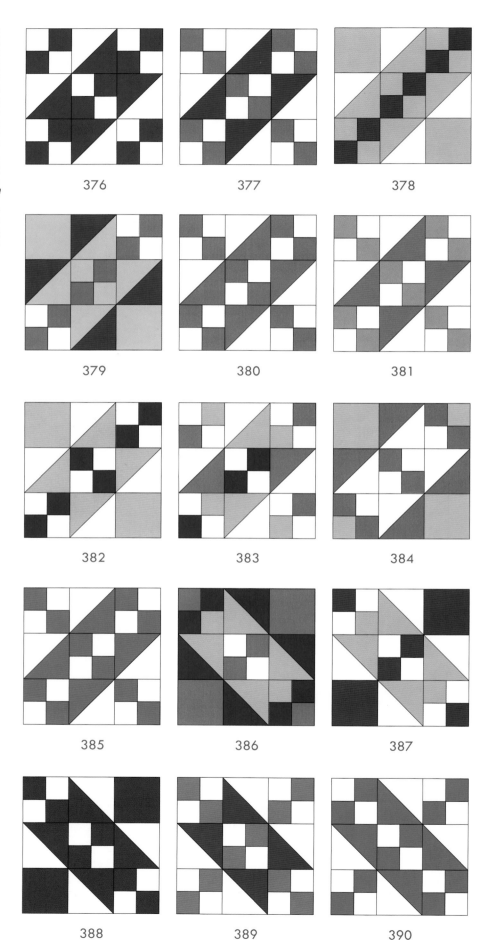

376
377
378
379
380
381
382
383
384
385
386
387
388
389
390

376 Road to Arkansas

377 Jacob's Ladder
Double Hour Glass, *GC*
Stepping Stones
Tail of Benjamin's Kite
Trail of the Covered
Wagon
Underground Railroad
Wagon Tracks

378 Road to the White
House

379 Road to the White
House

380 Going to Chicago, *NP*
Golden Stairs, *NC*
Jacob's Ladder
Off to San Francisco,
NP
Railroad
Road to California
Susie's Fancy

381 Jacob's Ladder

382 Rocky Road to
California

383 Unknown Silk Block

384 Broken Sugar Bowl,
KCS
Road to the White
House, *FJ*

385 Railroad

386 Broken Sugar Bowl
Rocky Road to
California

387 Broken Sugar Bowl

388 Rocky Road to
California

389 Jacob's Ladder

390 Jacob's Ladder

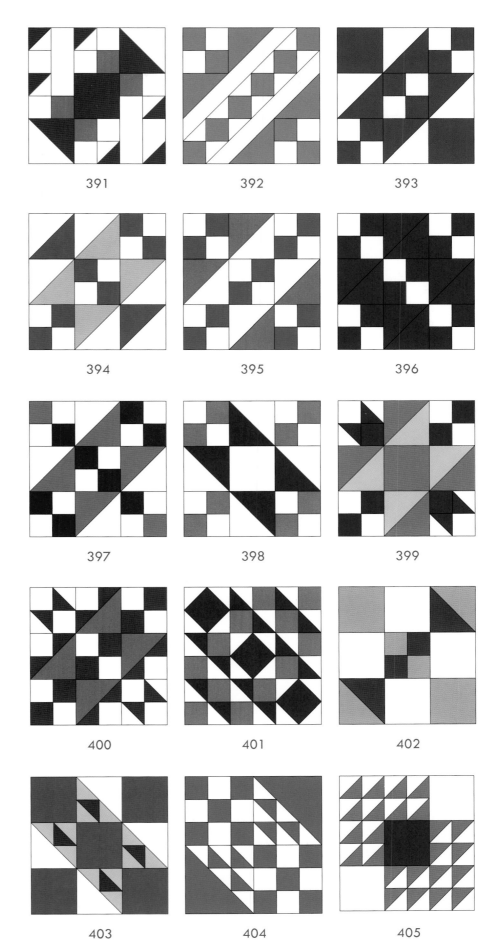

391   392   393

394   395   396

397   398   399

400   401   402

403   404   405

406 Cut Glass Dish, *LAC*
Golden Gates
Prism Block
Winged Square

407 Birds in the Air
Flight of Swallows, *NC*
Flock of Geese
Flying Birds

408 Cat's Cradle
Dove at the Window,
CoM
Double Pyramids, *MD*
Flying Birds, *NP*
Harrison, *Dakota
Farmer, 1929*
Harrison Rose, *1930*
Harrison Quilt
Hour Glass, *NP*
Wandering Lover, *HH*

409 Yellow Ribbon, *Cindy
Erwin*

410 Garden Path
Flower Garden Path

411 Spider Legs

412 Wood Lily, *KCS*
Indian Head, *KCS*
St. Elmo's Fire, *NC*

413 Cats and Mice, *LAC*

414 St. George's Cross

415 Linoleum

416 Golgotha
Cross Upon Cross
The Three Crosses

417 Mrs. Fay's Favorite
Friendship Block, *HH*

418 Merry Kite, *LAC*

419 An Arrangement of
Small Pieces, *KCS*

420 Four Squares

421 Aunt Dinah

422 The Chinese Quilt
   Block, *KCS*
   Broken Dishes, *NM*

423 Mystery Block

424 Friendship Block

425 Weathervane, *NC*

426 Owl, *KCS*

427 Ranger's Pride

428 Friendship Quilt, *KCS*

429 Morning

430 Summer Winds, *NP*

431 Welcome Hand

432 Follow the Leader

433 Whirlpool

434 Dove in the Window

435 Broken Wheel
   Block Circle
   Johnnie Round the
     Corner
   Single Wedding Ring
   Squirrel in a Cage
   Wheel

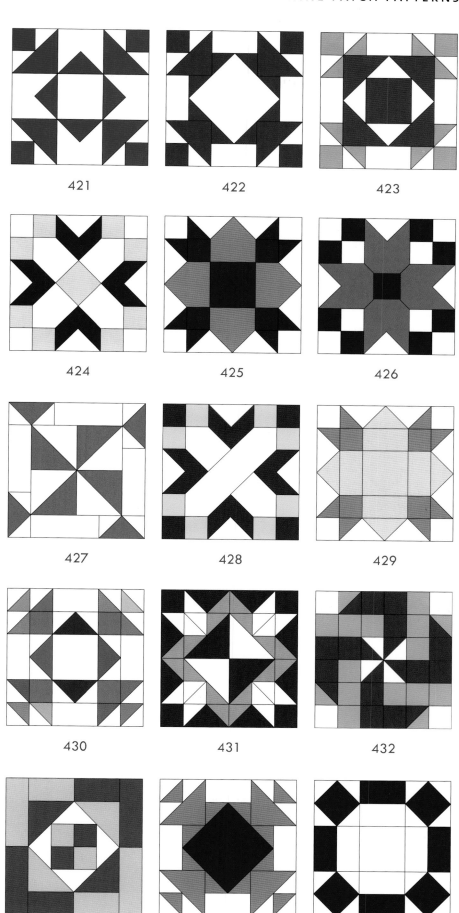

421   422   423

424   425   426

427   428   429

430   431   432

433   434   435

5,500 QUILT BLOCK DESIGNS

436

437

438

439

440

441

442

443

444

445

446

447

448

449

450

436 Squirrel in a Cage

437 Broken Wheel, *CS*
Mrs. Miller's Favorite

438 Rolling Stone, *LAC*
Letter O, *Dakota Farmer*
Wedding Ring

439 Friendship Quilt

440 New Hampshire Granite Block

441 Rolling Squares

442 Friendship Quilt, *HH*

443 Square and Half Square, *KCS*
Chinese Coin, *AMS*
Crosses and Losses, *QN*
Friendly Hand, *CoM*
Indian Puzzle, *AMS*
Indiana Puzzle, *KCS*
Milky Way, *LAC*
Monkey Wrench, *AMS*
Pinwheels, *NC*

444 Water Wheel

445 Chinese Coin

446 Waterwheel

447 Mississippi, *HH*

448 Sunflower, *QN*

449 Quartered Star

450 Waterwheel

451 Dancing Pinwheels, *NC*

452 Amish Star

453 T Quilt, *LAC*

454 Rolling Pinwheel

455 Mrs. Morgan's Choice, *LAC*
　　Spinning Wheel

456 Rolling Pinwheel, *NC*
　　Pinwheel Star
　　Whirling Pinwheel, *KCS*

457 Tunnels

458 Corn and Beans, *LAC*

459 Arkansas Snowflake, *KCS*
　　Arkansas Star, *KCS*
　　The Kite Quilt, *KCS*
　　Star Kites, *NC*

460 Carnival, *NC*

461 Mill and Stars

462 No Name

463 No Name

464 President Carter, *QW, 1977*

465 Optical Illusion

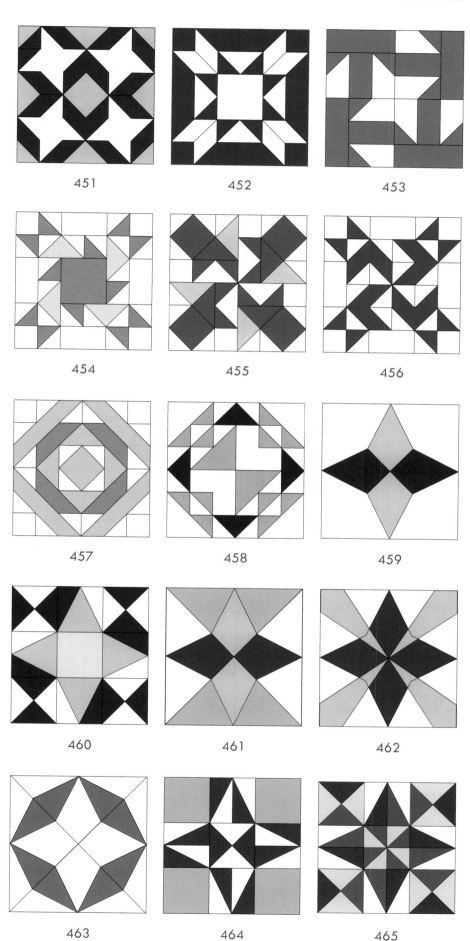

451

452

453

454

455

456

457

458

459

460

461

462

463

464

465

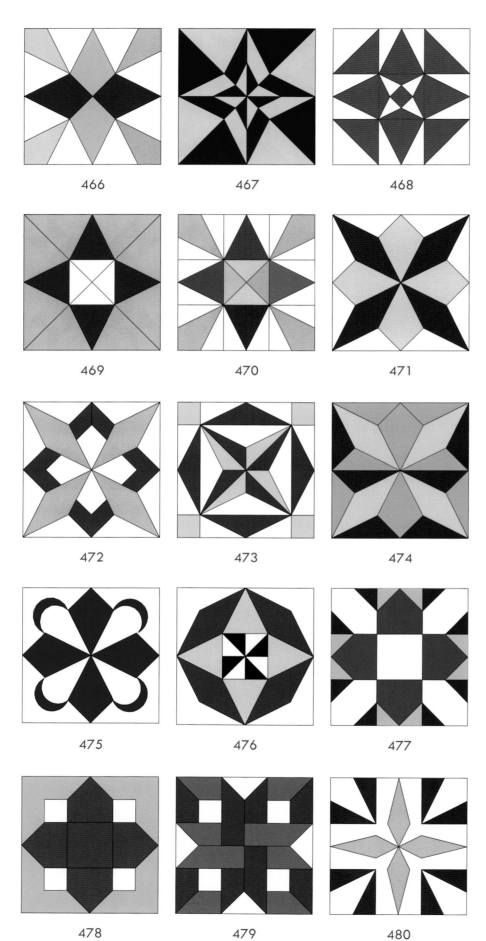

466
467
468

469
470
471

472
473
474

475
476
477

478
479
480

466 Time and Tide
Four Pointed Star, *KCS*
Twinkling Stars, *CoM*

467 Night and Day

468 Little Rock Block, *LAC*
Arkansas Star, *NC*
Butterfly Block, *NC*
Sea Star, *NC*
Star of the Sea, *NC*

469 The Star of Alamo, *KCS*

470 Japanese Scrap Quilt,
QT

471 Skyrocket

472 Barbara Bannister Star

473 Wintery Reflections

474 Century of Progress,
KCS

475 Star and Crescent

476 Rolling Pinwheel

477 Prairie Flower, *NC*

478 Grandmother's Own

479 Endless Ribbon, *SSQ*

480 Guiding Star, *KCS*

481 Victorian Square, *MLM, SSQ, 1982*

482 Lucky Clover, *AMS*

483 Betty's Delight

484 Double Necktie, *LAC*

485 Spools, *LAC*

486 California Chimney

487 Beginner's Choice

488 Oklahoma Twister, *AK*

489 Love and Kisses

490 Tulip Lady Fingers, *LAC*

491 Steps to the Altar, *LAC*
Dish of Fruit, *1896*
Flatiron Patchwork
Strawberry Basket

492 Nosegay, *KCS*

493 Galaxy Star

494 Firecrackers and Skyrockets

495 Maple Leaf

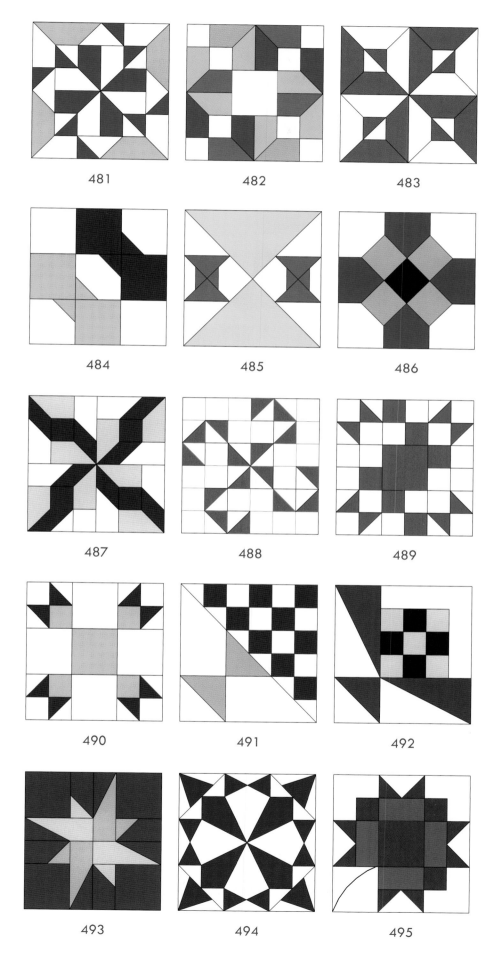

481

482

483

484

485

486

487

488

489

490

491

492

493

494

495

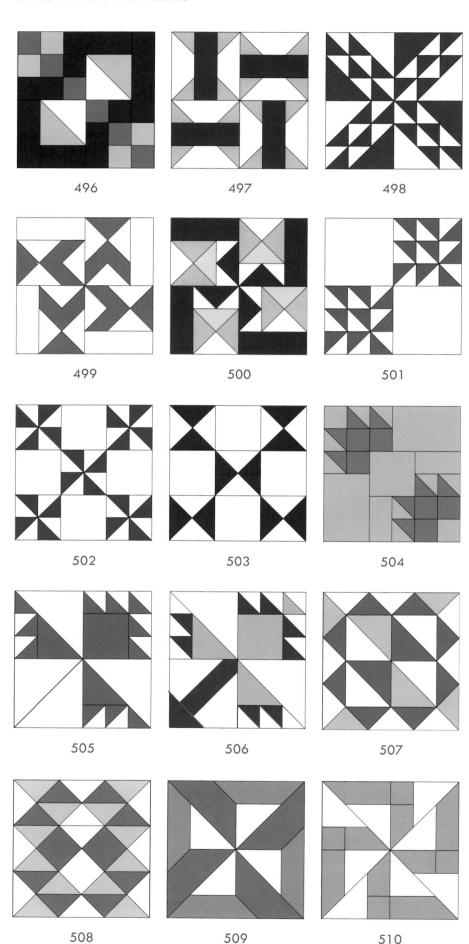

496   Hay's Corner

497   Arkansas Traveller, *LAC*

498   Mosaic

499   Flying Dutchman, *LAC*

500   Flying Dutchman, *NP*

501   Windmill

502   Windmill, *LHJ, 1903*
       Clover Leaf
       Flutter Wheel, *LAC*
       Pin Wheels

503   Flying X

504   Tea Leaf

505   Historic Oak Leaf

506   English Ivy

507   Grandma's Hopscotch,
       KCS

508   Buckwheat

509   Unnamed

510   Good Luck

511 Indian Mats, *NC*

512 Mosaic

513 Colonial Rose

514 Sweet Gum Leaf, *LAC*

515 Love Knot

516 Maggie's Double
Pinwheel

517 Wedding Bouquet

518 Cats and Mice, *LAC*

519 T-Quartette, *LAC*
Boxed T, *LAC*
Mixed T
Tete-a-Tete

520 Builder's Block, *KCS*

521 Contrary Wife

522 Cedars of Lebanon

523 Mosaic

524 Battlegrounds

525 Rosebud, *LAC*
Bright Star, *NC*
Crow's Foot
Hummingbird, *CoM*
Maple Leaf, *NC*

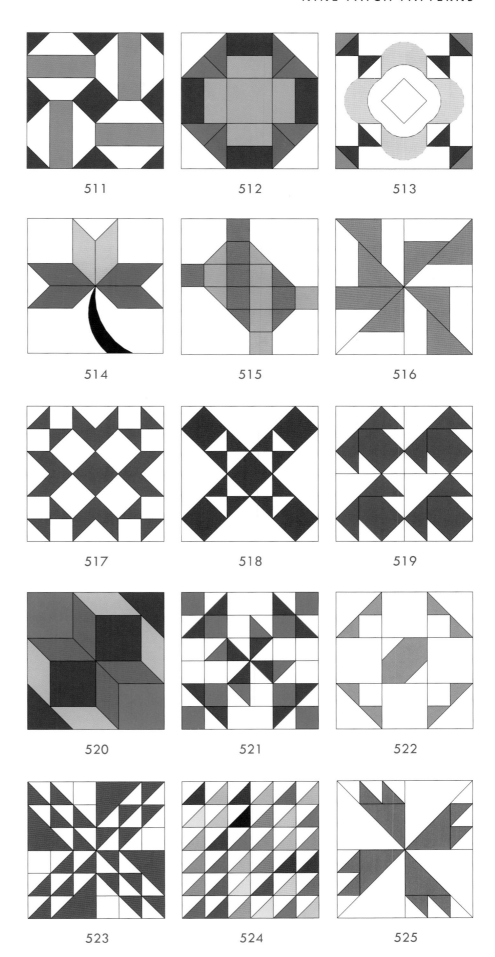

511

512

513

514

515

516

517

518

519

520

521

522

523

524

525

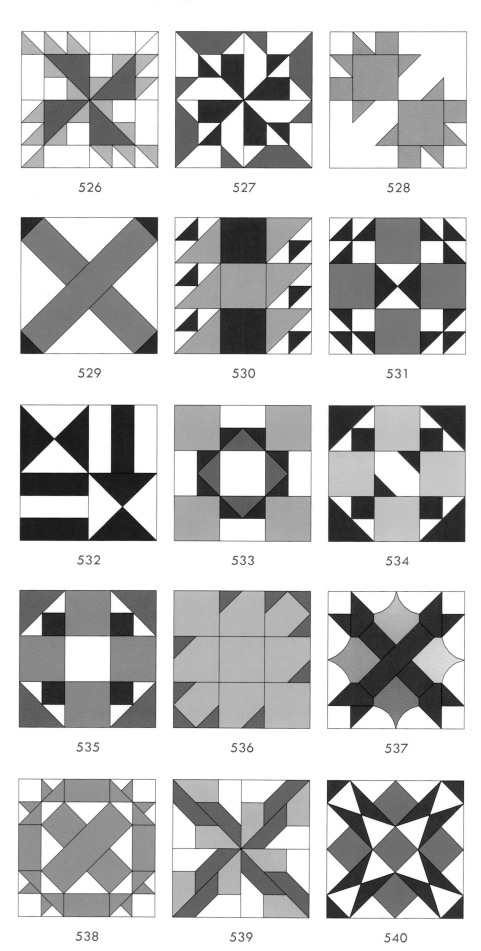

526

527

528

529

530

531

532

533

534

535

536

537

538

539

540

526 Straw Flowers

527 Victoria Square

528 Ozark Maple Leaf, *NP*
Broad Arrow, *FJ*
Maple Leaf Design, *LHJ*
Broad Arrows, *NC*
Arabic Latticework, *QN*
Fig Leaf, *QN*

529 Crosspatch

530 Wampum, *NC*

531 Peaceful Evening

532 Chain and Hourglass

533 Ladies Aid Album, *LAC*

534 New Album, *KCS*
Cedars of Lebanon, *HH*

535 Album

536 Flying Leaves, *NC*

537 Pathfinder

538 Easy Ways

539 Christmas Cheer

540 Augusta, *HH*

541 Gardener's Prize

542 Cookies and Milk,
    HaM, SSQ, 1983

543 Japanese Lantern

544 Sparkler

545 Dover, *HH*
    Dover Quilt Block, *LAC*

546 Patch as Patch Can,
    AMS

547 Double Tulip

548 Double Pinwheel

549 Whirlaround, *KCS*

550 The Mayflower, *LAC*
    Hard Times Block, *NC*

551 Butterfly

552 Hill and Valley

553 Weathervane and
    Steeple, *NC*

554 Square within Squares

555 Evening's Last

541

542

543

544

545

546

547

548

549

550

551

552

553

554

555

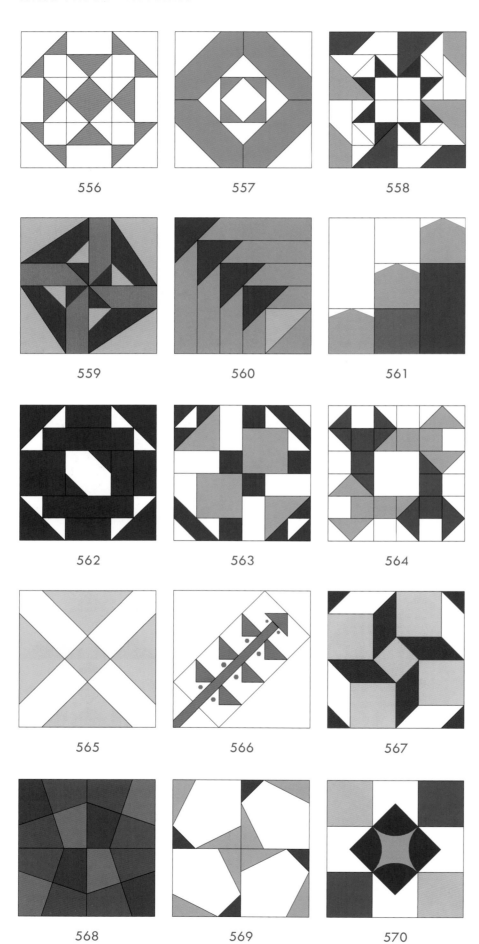

556 State Fair, *NC*

557 A Striped Plain Quilt, *KCS*

558 Rolling Pinwheel

559 My Mistake, *MM*

560 Chicago Geese

561 American Homes, *QW*

562 Cedars of Lebanon, *KCS*

563 Indian Mat, *NC*

564 Crab Claws

565 St. Andrew's Cross

566 Fernberry

567 Whirlaround

568 Broken Rainbows, *NC*

569 Unnamed, *QN*

570 Window Square

571 Shooting Star, *SSQ, 1989*

572 Patchwork Bedspread

573 Double L

574 Ballot Box

575 The Wind Wheel Quilt Block

576 Tandi Whirl Quilt

577 Pennsylvania, *HH*

578 Gretchen

579 Patch as Patch Can

580 Union Star

581 The Sprite, *AMS*

582 Kite, *TQ*

583 Good Fortune

584 Bells

585 The Chief, *LBC*

571 572 573

574 575 576

577 578 579

580 581 582

583 584 585

5,500 QUILT BLOCK DESIGNS

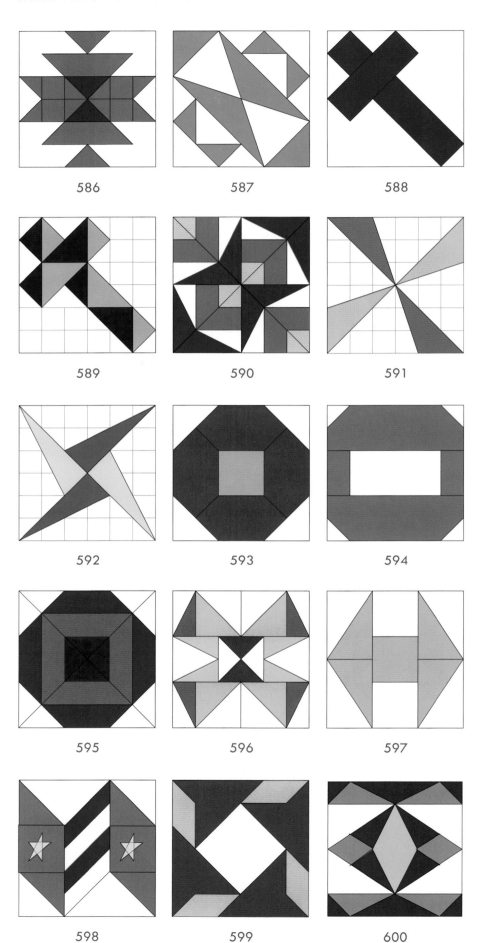

586   Squash Blossom, *QW*

587   Fair Play, *HH*

588   The Cross

589   Cross

590   Flutterbye

591   Twisted Ribbons

592   Wheel of Destiny, *FJ*

593   Wishing Ring, *KCS*

594   American Chain, *OJF*

595   The Kitchen Woodbox

596   Bow

597   The Bobbin, *QN*

598   Stars and Stripes, *NC*

599   Turkish Puzzle

600   Shooting Star

586   587   588

589   590   591

592   593   594

595   596   597

598   599   600

571

572

573

574

575

576

577

578

579

580

581

582

583

584

585

5,500 QUILT BLOCK DESIGNS

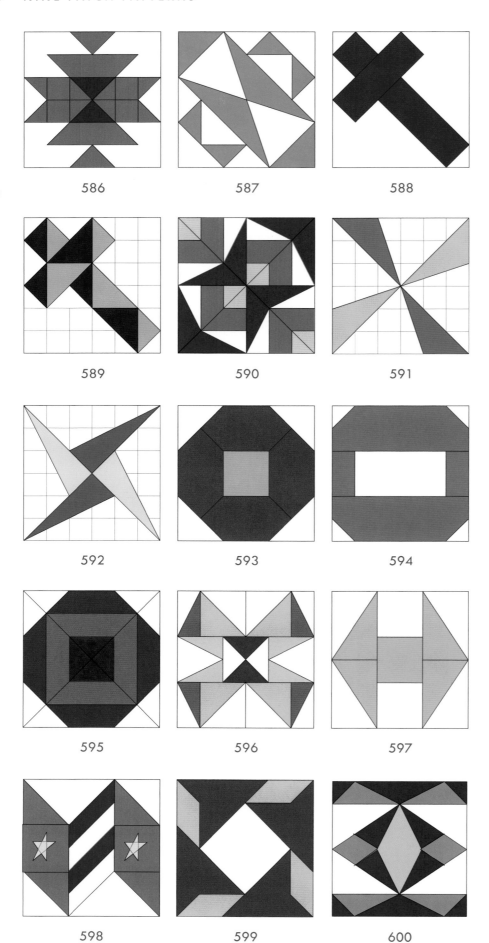

586 Squash Blossom, *QW*

587 Fair Play, *HH*

588 The Cross

589 Cross

590 Flutterbye

591 Twisted Ribbons

592 Wheel of Destiny, *FJ*

593 Wishing Ring, *KCS*

594 American Chain, *OJF*

595 The Kitchen Woodbox

596 Bow

597 The Bobbin, *QN*

598 Stars and Stripes, *NC*

599 Turkish Puzzle

600 Shooting Star

586

587

588

589

590

591

592

593

594

595

596

597

598

599

600

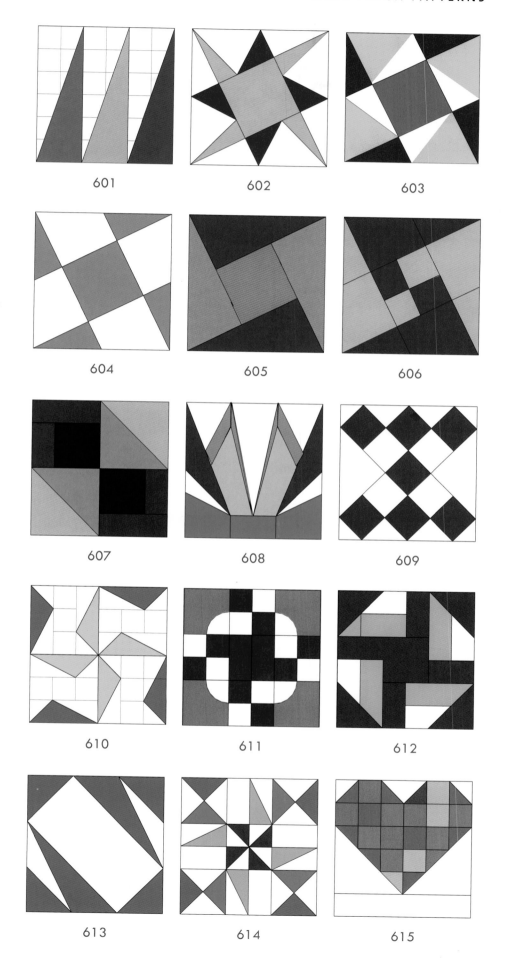

601

602

603

604

605

606

607

608

609

610

611

612

613

614

615

616

617

618

619

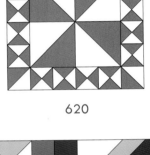

620

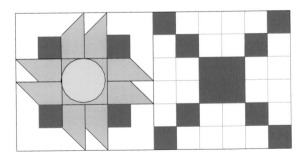

621

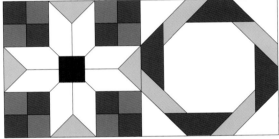

622

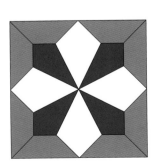

623

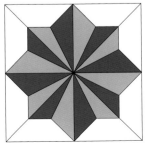

624

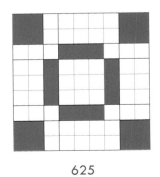

625

616 Voiliers, *LCPQ*

617 Emerald & Topaz, *QN*

618 Spider Web

619 Dutchman's Puzzle Variation

620 Triangles, *WD, 1943*

621 State Fair Block

622 Star & Web, *SSQ, 1986*

623 Home Again, *FJ*

624 The Whirling Star, *KCS* Patriotic Star

625 Hand Weave, *LAC*

626 Double Necktie

627 New Four Pointer, *KCS*

628 Puss in the Corner
    Double Nine Patch
    Fundamental Nine
        Patch, *QN*
    Golden Steps, *OCS*
    New Nine Patch
    Single Irish Chain

629 Double Nine Patch
    Dutch Nine Patch

630 Hen and Her Chicks

631 Swastika Patch, *LAC*
    Swastika
    Battle Ax of Thor
    Catch Me If You Can
    Chinese 10,000
        Perfections
    Favorite of the
        Peruvians
    Heart's Seal
    Mound Builders
    Pure Symbol of Right
        Doctrine
    Wind Power of the
        Osages

632 City Streets, *NC*
    Hand Weave

633 Farmer's Puzzle

634 Hand Weave, *NP*
    Handcraft, *NC*
    Handwoven, *NP*
    Interwoven, *NP*
    Over and Under, *NP*
    Strips and Squares, *NP*

635 Bradford Nine Patch

636 Broken Paths

637 Nonsuch, *LAC*

638 Flag In, Flag Out, *KCS*

639 Wedge and Circle

640 Aunt Tryphosa's
    Favorite

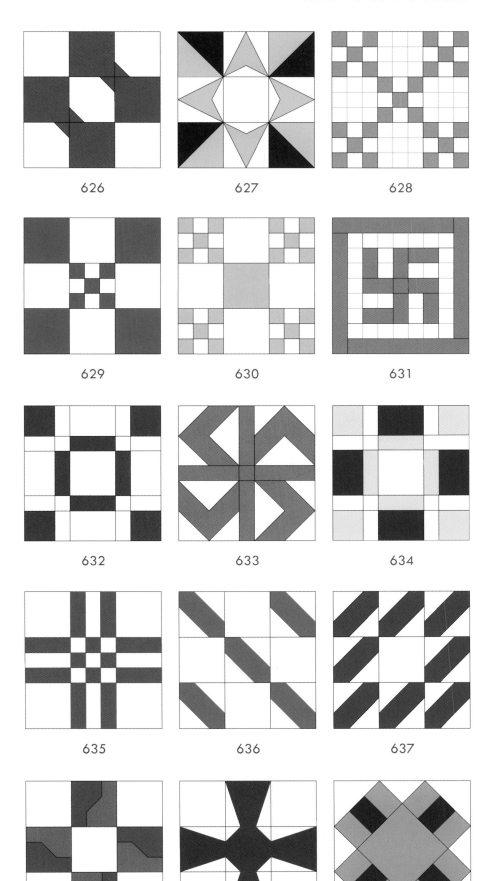

626

627

628

629

630

631

632

633

634

635

636

637

638

639

640

5,500 QUILT BLOCK DESIGNS

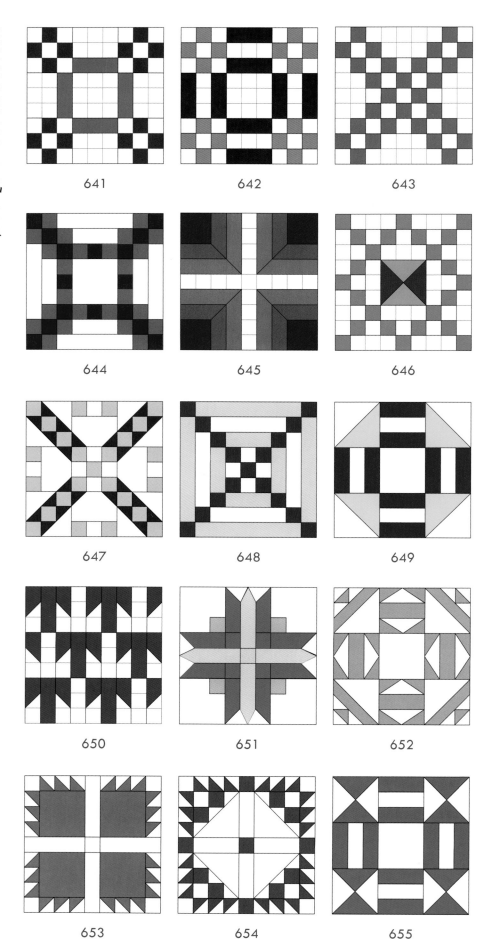

641   642   643

644   645   646

647   648   649

650   651   652

653   654   655

641   Puss in the Corner
       Five Patch, *LAC*
       Glorified Nine Patch

642   Building Blocks

643   Garden Path

644   Name Unknown

645   City Streets

646   Crosspatch

647   Dublin Chain
       New Irish Chain
       On the Square, *HH*

648   Alabama, *HH*

649   Golden Gate

650   Mixed T

651   Patchwork Posy

652   Mollie's Choice
       Joseph's Coat

653   Premium Star

654   Bear's Den

655   London Roads
       Arrow, *AMS*
       At the Square, *NP*
       Betty's Choice
       Colorado's Arrowhead
       Fireside Visitor, *CS*
       Rope and Anchor, *KCS*

656 London Roads

657 Dolly Madison Star
    President's Block

658 Pigeon Toes
    Resolutions, *NP*
    Turkey Tracks

659 Montana

660 Continental

661 Golda, Gem Star

662 Tile Puzzle

663 Voter's Choice

664 Double Pyramid

665 Independence Square

666 Four Clowns, *NC*

667 Chain & Hourglass

668 Bishop Hill, *NC*

669 Cross Patch, *AK, 1966*

670 Beggar Block, *LAC*
    Over and Under Quilt
    Design, *NP*

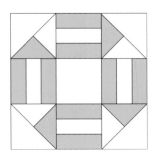
656

657

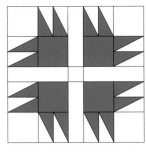
658

659

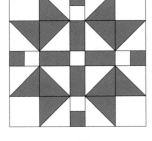
660

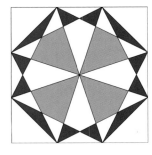
661

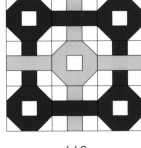
662

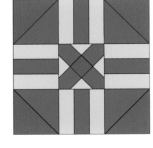
663

664

665

666

667

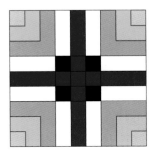
668

669

670

671 · 672 · 673

674 · 675 · 676

677 · 678 · 679

680 · 681 · 682

683 · 684 · 685

671 Beggar's Blocks
Cats and Mice
Spool and Bobbin, *NC,*
1936

672 Beggar's Blocks, *NP*

673 Homespun, *NP*

674 Santa Fe

675 Arkansas

676 Goose Tracks

677 Wedding March, *CoM*

678 Emma C

679 All Points

680 Sunburst

681 Crossroads, *NP*

682 Tangled Garters, *LAC*
Crossroads, *NP*
Garden Maze, *NC*
Queen of May, *HH*
Sun Dial, *NC*

683 Mrs. Dewey's Choice,
HH

684 Chicago Star, *LAC*

685 Dallas Star

686 Columbian Star, *LAC*

687 Prosperity Block, *NC, 1933*

688 Mona's Choice, *KCS*

689 Windmills All Around

690 Main Street

691 Housewife's Dream

692 Ribbon Star

693 Santa Fe Trail, *NC, 1934*

694 Meeting House Square, *NC*

695 Flying X

696 Nine Patch Variation

697 Winged Nine Patch

698 Love in a Tangle

699 Diamond Plaid Block, *NC*

700 Valley Falls Square, *Arlene Gier, SSQ*

686

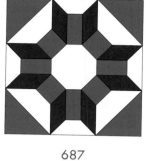
687

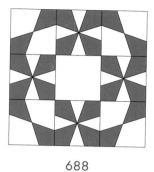
688

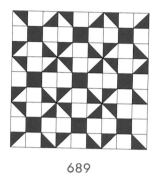
689

690

691

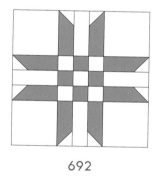
692

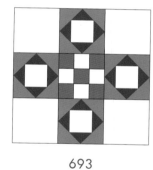
693

694

695

696

697

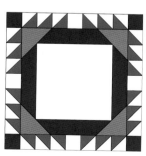
698

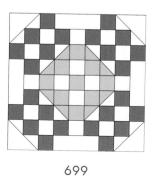
699

700

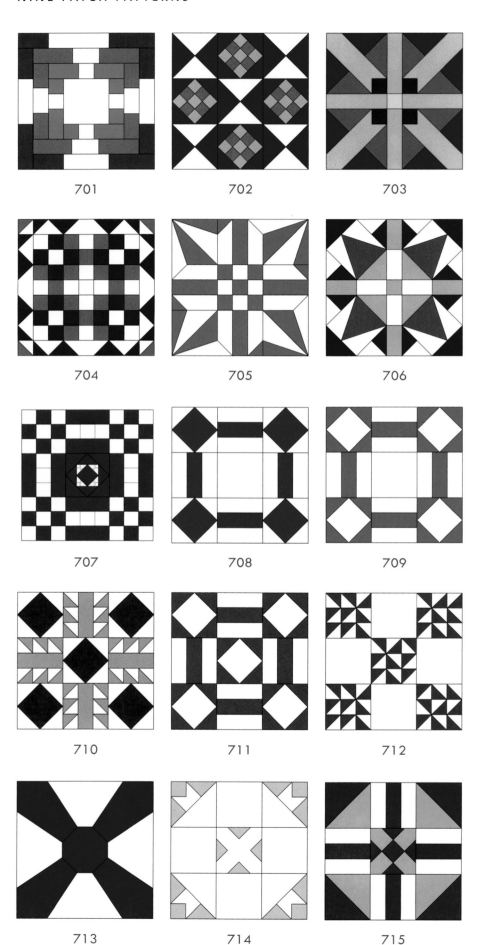

701
702
703

704
705
706

707
708
709

710
711
712

713
714
715

701 White House Steps, *LW*

702 Kentucky Patch

703 Far West, *NC*

704 Scotch Heather, *NC*

705 Sunburst, *LW*

706 Ladies' Delight, *NC*

707 The Cheesebox Quilt, *CG*

708 Puss in the Corner
Kitty Corner
Tic Tac Toe

709 Blockhouse, *NC*
Kitty Corner

710 Mother's Dream, *NP*
Grandmother's Dream
Turkey in the Straw, *FJ*

711 Peekaboo, *WW*

712 Windmill

713 Adam's Refuge, *SSQ, 1993*
New Cross and Crown, *CS*

714 Name Unknown

715 Everybody's Favorite, *HH*

716 Burnham Square, *LAC*
      Hole in the Barn Door,
      QN, 1977
      Star in the Window,
      QN, 1977

717 Beggar's Blocks
      Cats and Mice
      The Roman Square

718 Flagstones, *LAC*
      New Snowball, *HH*

719 Dewey Quilt Block

720 Skip to My Lou, *QM,
      1992*

721 Glory Be, *QM, 1992*

722 Starburst

723 Jackson Quilt Block
      Miss Jackson

724 Path and Stiles, *NC*
      Far West, *NC*
      Shoo Fly, *LAC*
      Stiles and Paths

725 Duck's Foot in the Mud

726 Missouri Puzzle, *CS*

727 Rolling Stones

728 Royal Star

729 Crow's Nest

730 Water Mill

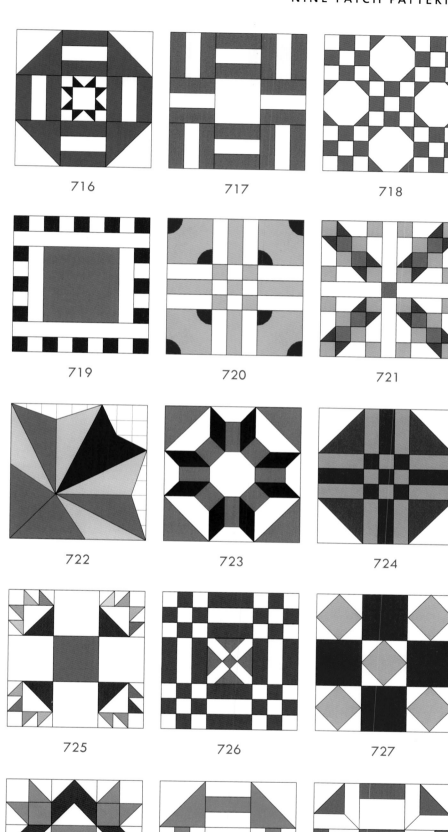

716

717

718

719

720

721

722

723

724

725

726

727

728

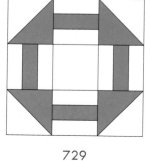

729

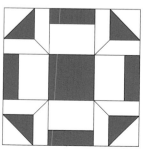

730

5,500 QUILT BLOCK DESIGNS

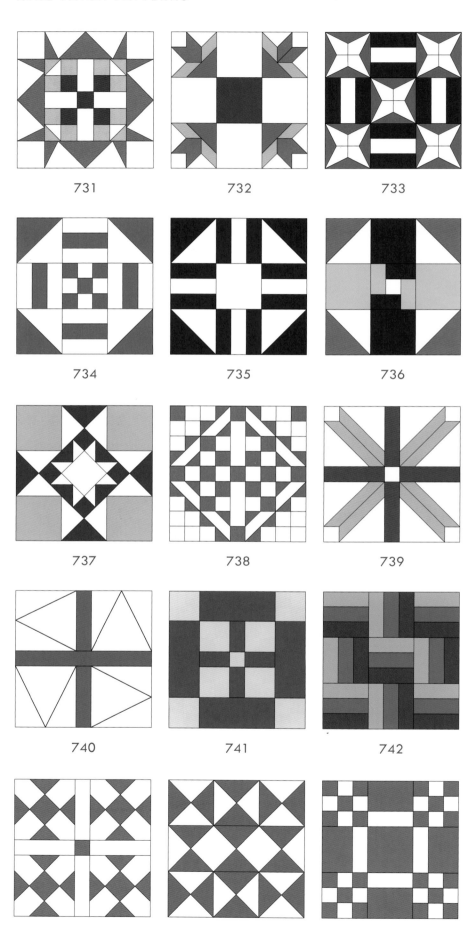

731 Trucker's Dream,
   Sandra Copeland,
   1988

732 Sage Bud, *KCS*
   Mexican Star

733 Star Spangled Banner

734 New Waterwheel

735 Friendship Quilt

736 Squared Chain

737 Rhode Island, *HH*

738 Medieval Walls, *NC*
   Medieval Mosaic, *NC*

739 Flyaway Feathers

740 Bowknot

741 The Comfort Quilt, *KCS*

742 The Roman Stripe

743 Bachelor's Puzzle, *CS*

744 Aunt Malvina's Quilt,
   CS

745 Five Patch, *LAC*
   Building Blocks, *1929*

746 Tin Man
   Oklahoma Boomer,
   LAC

747 Indian Hatchet

748 Bells

749 Joseph's Coat
   Scrapbag

750 Amethyst Chain, *NC*

751 Heather Square

752 Star and Cross

753 Indian Tomahawk

754 Quadrille, *NC*

755 Chain of Diamonds

756 Star of Wonder

757 Postage Stamp Block

758 Dutch Puzzle, *AMS*

759 Lehigh Maze, *NC*

760 No Name

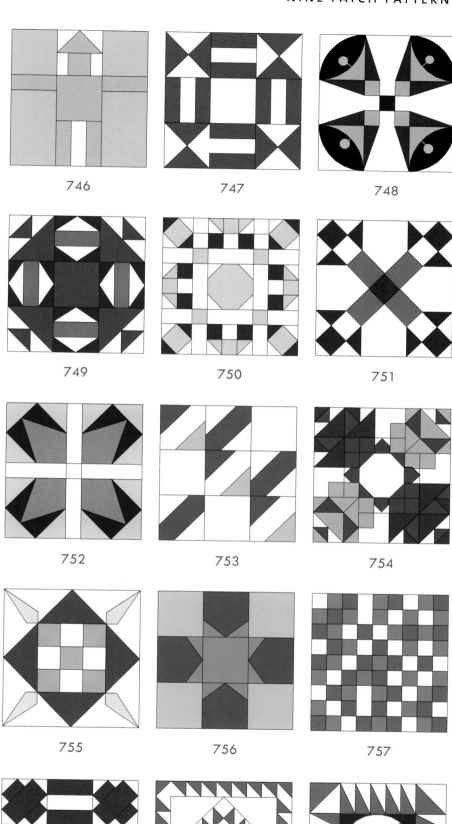

746

747

748

749

750

751

752

753

754

755

756

757

758

759

760

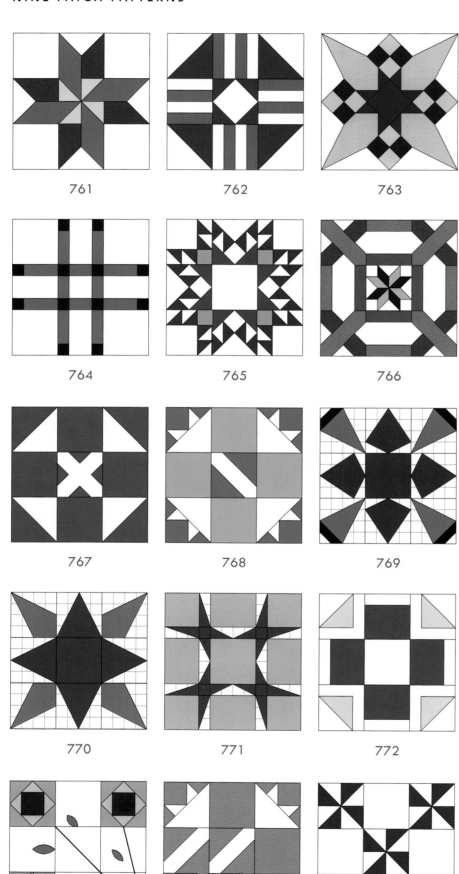

761   761   762   763

764   765   766

767   768   769

770   771   772

773   774   775

761   Two Colors, *CoM*

762   Crossroads, *NC*

763   Indianapolis

764   Tic Tac Toe

765   Doreen's Dutch Tiles
      (tulips appliquéd in
      corners), in memory
      of Doreen
      Speckmann,
      Nancy Rink, QN, 2000

766   The Compass and
      Chain

767   Flying Cross, *HH*
      Double Cross, *HH*

768   Montgomery

769   California Snowflake,
      QN

770   Starburst

771   Acrobats

772   Water Mill, *GC*

773   Triple Rose, *AMS*

774   Tassel Plant, *LAC*

775   Flutter Wheel, *LAC*
      Clover Leaf
      Pin Wheels
      Windmill

NINE PATCH PATTERNS **63**

5,500 QUILT BLOCK DESIGNS

776 Cluster of Stars, *LAC*

777 Star Chain, *QN, 1973*

778 Nevada (9)

779 Nine Patch T, *MD*

780 W.C.T.U., *LAC*

781 Stars and Stripes

782 Old Indian Trail, *KCS*

783 Klondike Star, *HH*

784 Star A, *LAC*
     An A Star, *NC*

785 Little Rock

786 Women's Choice, *QN*

787 Honolulu, *HH*

788 Journey Home
     (appliqués of things
     significant to the
     quilter in the blank
     spaces)

789 Aunt Em's Pattern

790 Spring Is Sprung, *SSQ*

776

777

778

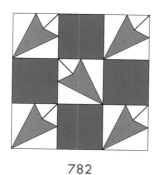 779

 780

 781

782

783

784

785

786

787

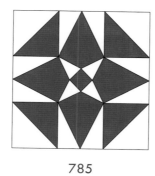  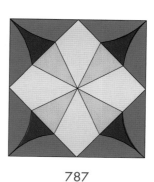

788

 789

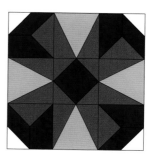 790

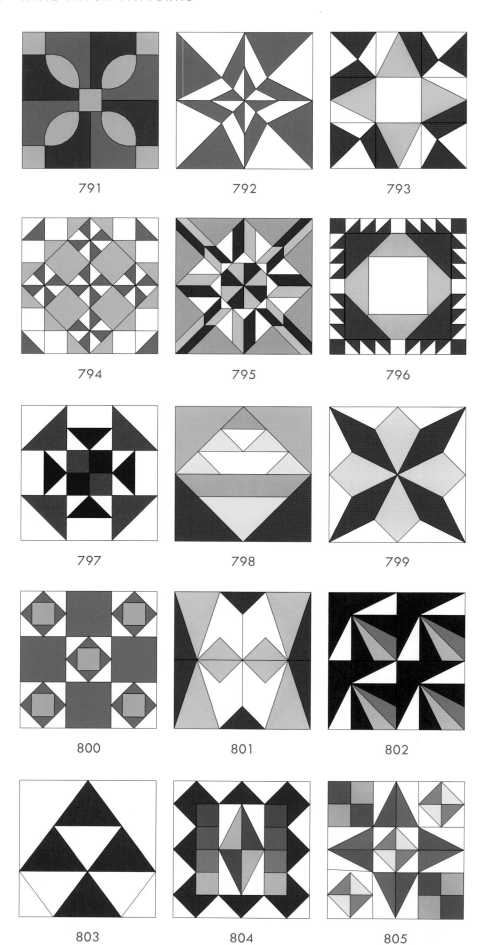

791 State of Idaho

792 Night and Day

793 Carnival, *NC*

794 South Dakota, *HH*

795 Prisms, *RD, LCPQ*

796 Love Entangled, *SSQ*

797 Monkey Wrench Variation

798 Ship Block

799 Guiding Star Cowboy's Star

800 Nine Patch Square Within a Square

801 King's Crown, *LR, QW, 1983*

802 Building the Stars

803 Charm, *LAC*

804 Hoosier Wonder, *QN*

805 Spring Star, *QN, 1994*

806 Holland Magic, *QN*

807 Amish Whirl, *QN*

808 Fort Knox, *QN*

809 Finnigan's Wake, *QN*

810 Star in Space, *QN*

811 Twin Darts

812 Cobra, *QN, 1994*

813 Alice's Favorite

814 The Kite

815 Honolulu Quilt Block,
   HH

816 Greek Cross, *LAC*

817 Dutch Mill, *LAC*

818 Magic Circle, *LAC*

819 Garden Maze, *NC*

820 County Fair

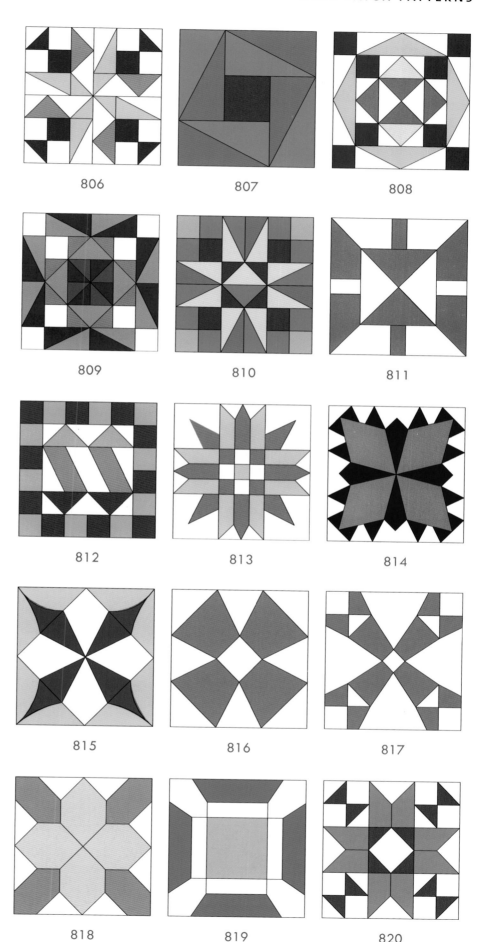

806

807

808

809

810

811

812

813

814

815

816

817

818

819

820

5,500 QUILT BLOCK DESIGNS

821

822

823

824

825

826

827

828

829

830

831

832

833

834

835

821 Star of Erin, *NC*

822 English Ivy, *KCS*
     Autumn Leaves, *NC*
     The Clover Blossom

823 Lone Tree
     English Thistle

824 Tree of Life

825 Amish Shoofly

826 Rolling Squares, *NC*

827 The Bat, *AMS*
     The Bat's Block, *NC*

828 Victorian Maze, *NC*

829 Mrs. Cleveland's
       Choice
     Mrs. Cleveland's
       Favorite

830 Happy New Year

831 Loop the Loop

832 Pieced Pinwheels

833 Texas Fireside

834 Nell's Swinging Star

835 Lost and Found

836

837

838

839

840

841

842

843

844

845

846

847

848

849

850

5,500 QUILT BLOCK DESIGNS

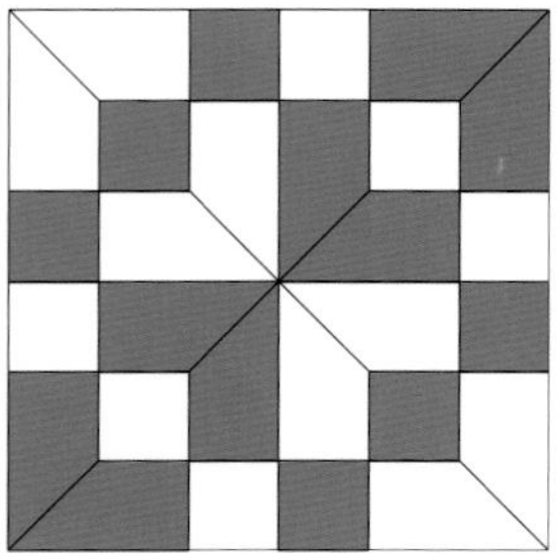

851

852

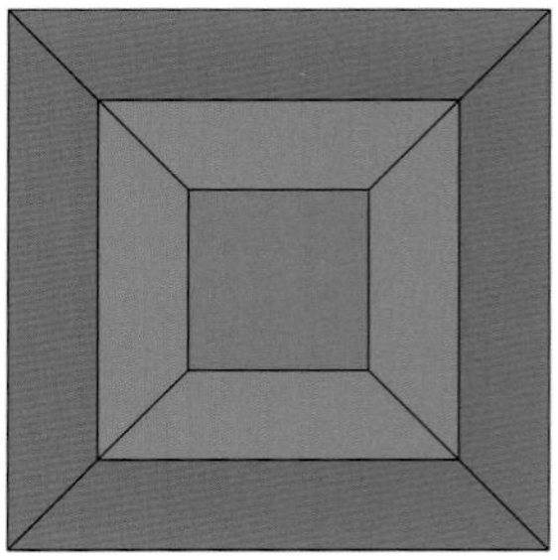

853

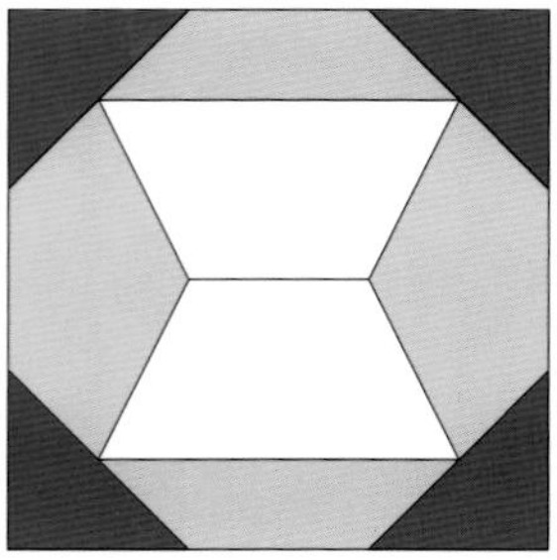

854

855

856

857

858

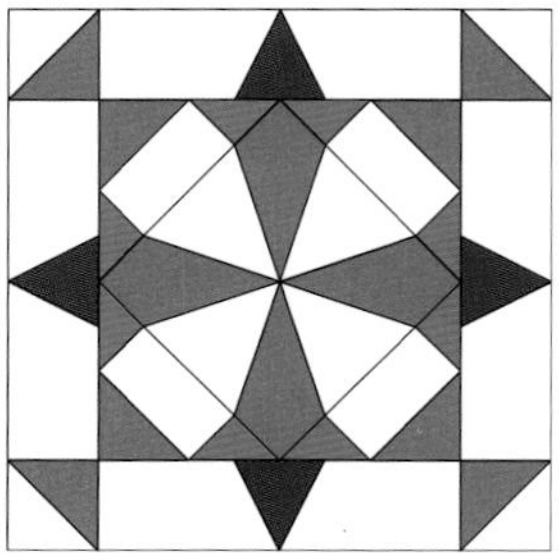

859

860

861

862

863

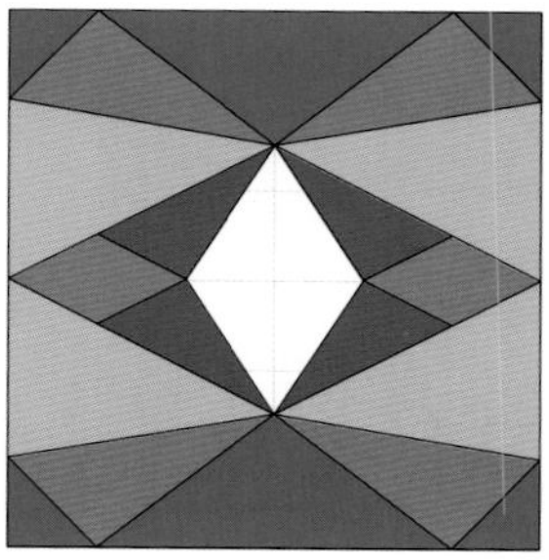

864

865

851 No Name

852 Alphabet Block L

853 Kitchen Woodbox, *KCS*

854 Hour Glass, *NC*

855 St. Paul

856 Tree Top Twist, *RMS, SSQ*

857 New York

858 St. Gregory's Cross

859 Star Flower, *GD*

860 Heavenly Bodies

861 Housewife

862 Whirling Star, *NC*

863 Tee

864 Shooting Star, *AG*

865 Arrowhead Star Variation

5,500 QUILT BLOCK DESIGNS

866 Orion's Wheel

867 Night Vision, *QN*

868 Lone Star, *AB, OCS*

869 Magnolia, *LW, OCS*
    Sawtooth

870 Confetti Block, *TQ*

871 Jet Stream, *SSQ*

872 King's Crown

873 Four Triangles, *FJ*

874 V-Block, *QN*

875 Cross and Diamond
    Star

876 Double Irish Chain, *LW*

877 Fred's Spool

878 Shadows
    Sunlight and Shadows
    Rainbow Block
    Roman Stripe

879 Windblown Lily

880 All Those Fish

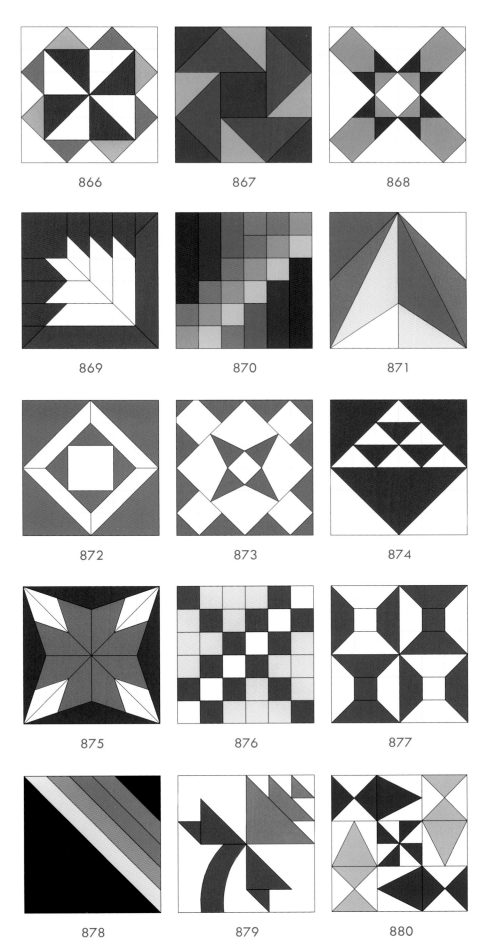

866

867

868

869

870

871

872

873

874

875

876

877

878

879

880

881 Amelia Earhart

882 Lock and Chain, *LAC*

883 Antique Red and White Quilt, *TQ*

884 Double Attic Windows

885 Lover's Locket, *GB, 1990*

886 Strawberry Patch

887 Massachusetts

888 Star Pattern

889 Treasure Box

890 Repeat X, *FJ*

891 Darts and Squares, *FJ*

892 Joseph's Necktie, *LAC*

893 Block of Many Triangles

894 The Crab

895 Night Sky, *MM*

896 Double Cross, *HH*
    Flying Cross, *HH*

897 State of New Jersey,
    HH

898 Starshadow, *QN*

899 Crossroads Star, *QN*

900 Paradox, *QN*

901 Modern Flame

902 Missouri Corn Field,
    QW

903 Idaho Star, *AK*

904 Cross and Crown

905 Stylized Eagle, *AK*

906 Love Entangled

907 Smith Autograph Quilt,
    CAM

908 Swastika Patch, *LAC*

909 Double Star Flower, *AK*

910 Bandstand

896 897 898
899 900 901
902 903 904
905 906 907
908 909 910

5,500 QUILT BLOCK DESIGNS

911

912

913

914

915

916

917

918

919

920

921

922

923

924

925

911 Honeybee

912 Four Star Block, *NC*

913 Lover's Knot

914 Lady of the White House

915 White House, *NC* Lady in the White House

916 Unnamed

917 Quiet Love, *SSQ, 1987*

918 Bridle Path, *KCS*

919 Mother's Fancy Star, *IS* Evening Star Mother's Fancy, *LAC*

920 Entertaining Motions

921 Triangle Puzzle, *LAC* Triangle Trails, *NC*

922 Eccentric Star

923 Nine Patch Star Grandmother's Choice

924 North Carolina Star

925 Afternoon Shadows, *SSQ, 1987*

926 Annapolis Patch

927 Sugar Loaf, *KCS*
    Arrowheads
    Flat Iron, *NC*

928 Winged Square, *OCS*

929 Arkansas Traveler

930 Radiant Star

931 London Square

932 Pine Burr, *NP*

933 Stars and Stripes

934 House That Jack Built,
    LAC
    Triple Stripe, *GD*

935 Arizona Star

936 Virginia Reel, *QWB*

937 Chuck-A-Luck, *NC*,
    1937

938 The H Square Quilt,
    KCS
    "4H" Club Quilt, *KCS*

939 Star Mosaic

940 Kankakee Checkers, *NC*

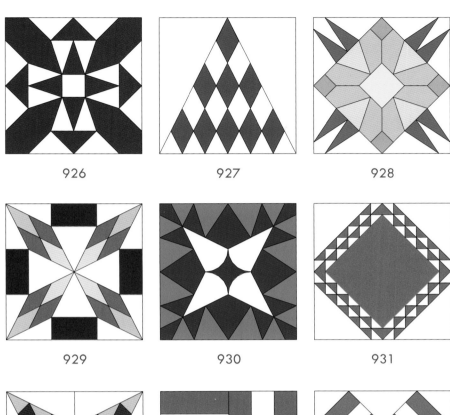

926   927   928

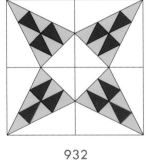 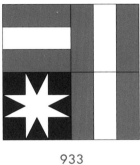 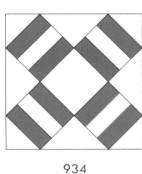

929   930   931

  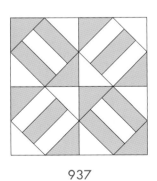

932   933   934

935   936   937

938   939   940

941
942
943

944
945
946

947
948
949

950
951
952

953
954
955

941 Dog Tooth Violet, *NC*

942 Sky Rocket
Starlight, *NP*
Jewel Boxes, *NP*

943 Autumn Night

944 Four Squares, *NC*

945 Chinese Holidays, *NC*

946 Sailboat

947 Thorny Thicket

948 Chuck-A-Luck, *NC*

949 Harlequin Star
Forgotten Star

950 Flying Geese

951 Water Wiggle

952 July's Summer Sky

953 Love's Dream

954 Children of Israel

955 Unnamed, *AMS*

956 Blue Skies

957 Happy Hunting
    Grounds

958 New Mexico

959 Ocean Wave, *KCS*

960 The Sapphire Quilt
    Block, *KCS*

961 Danish Star

962 Medallion Square

963 Cross and Crown

964 Holiday Crossing, *RMS,*
    SSQ, 1983

965 Hopes and Wishes

966 Snowbound, *RMS, SSQ,*
    1983

967 Crossroads

968 Exea's Star, *CS*
    Ella's Star, *HH*

969 State of South Dakota

970 Peach Blow

956

957

958

959

960

961

962

963

964

965

966

967

968

969

970

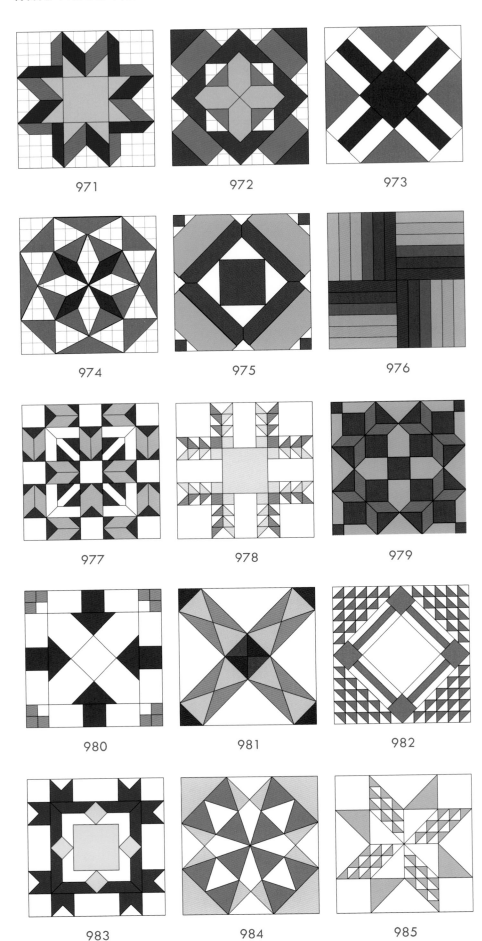

971   972   973

974   975   976

977   978   979

980   981   982

983   984   985

971   Christmas Star
      Bright Star

972   Three Cheers

973   At the Depot

974   Harrisburg Quilt Block

975   Magic Squares, *NC*

976   Paddle Wheel

977   Sailing Darts, *AK, 1965*

978   Texas Treasure, *NP*

979   Diamond Cross

980   Indian Arrow

981   America's Pride

982   State of Iowa, *HH*

983   Easy Ways

984   Vermont

985   The Twinkling Star

986 The Twinkling Star, *NC*

987 Aunt Rachel's Star, *1942*

988 Star Trek, *QN, 1974*

989 Quilt Without a Name

990 Crossed Arrows, *Ruby Hinson Duncan*

991 Danger Signals, *NP*

992 Augusta

993 Grandmother's Dream, *LAC*

994 Snowball, *AMS*

995 Illinois Road, *NC*

996 Tangled Arrows

997 Rising Star

998 King's Highway

999 Lone Star

1000 Pharlemina's Favorite, *HH*
　　　Charleston Quilt Block, *HH*
　　　Circle Four, *HH*

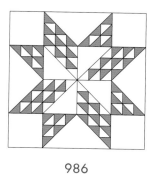
986

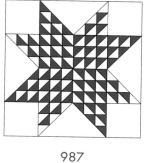
987

988

989

990

991

992

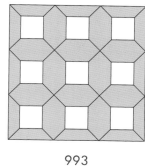
993

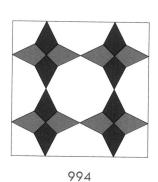
994

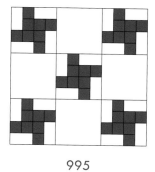
995

996

997

998

999

1000

5,500 QUILT BLOCK DESIGNS

1001   1002   1003

1004   1005   1006

1007   1008   1009

1010   1011   1012

1013   1014   1015

1001   A Scrap Patch

1002   Economy

1003   Yuletide, *HaM, SSQ, 1983*

1004   Flower and Fern, *RMS, QW, 1983*

1005   Ancient Castle, *Ruby Hinson Duncan, QW, 1982*

1006   Stony Point Quilt Block, *HH*
       State of Massachusetts, *HH*

1007   New Hour Glass

1008   Santa Fe Quilt Block
       President's Block

1009   St. Louis Star

1010   Prairie Belle Quilt Block

1011   Baltimore Belle
       Wild Goose Chase

1012   Morning Glory, *MM*

1013   Lost Children

1014   Eva's Delight
       Old Fashioned Pieced Block, *NC*

1015   Flora's Favorite

1016 Philippine Islands Quilt Block, *HH*

1017 Birds on the Tracks

1018 A Walk in the Garden

1019 Bats in the Belfry

1020 Pinwheel

1021 West Virginia

1022 Best Wishes

1023 Kiowa Cross, *SSQ*

1024 Double Square, *GD*

1025 Bright Side

1026 Kaleidoscope

1027 McDougall String Quilt, *SSQ*

1028 Star in the Window, *Betty McMillion, QW, 1984*

1029 Saturn Block

1030 This Way 'n That, *RMS, SSQ, 1986*

1016

1017

1018

1019

1020

1021

1022

1023

1024

1025

1026

1027

1028

1029

1030

1031    1032    1033

1034 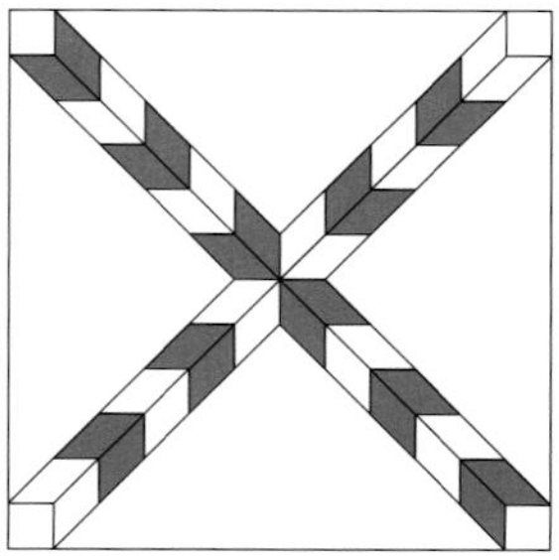   1035 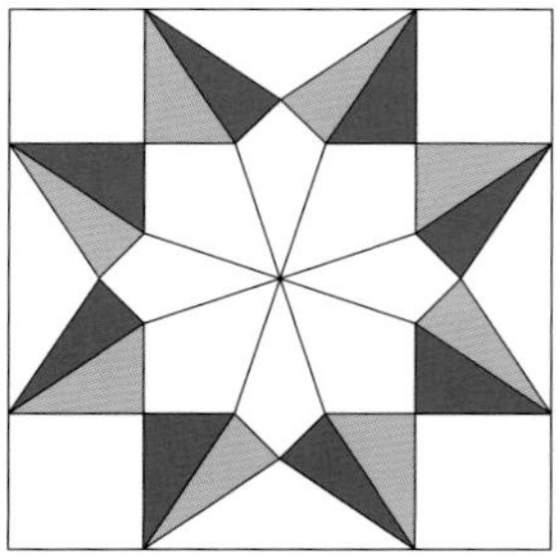   1036

1037 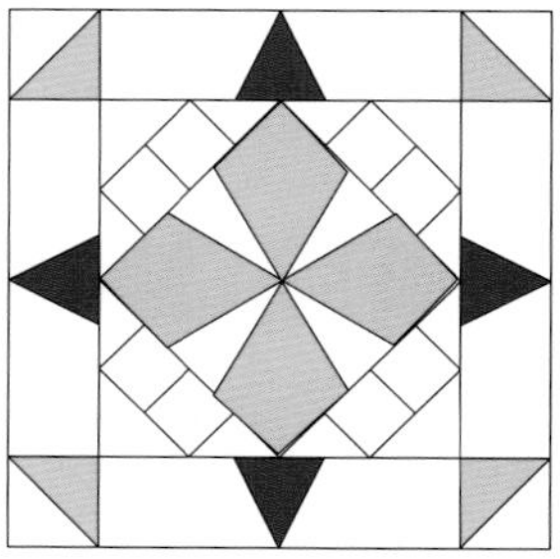   1038 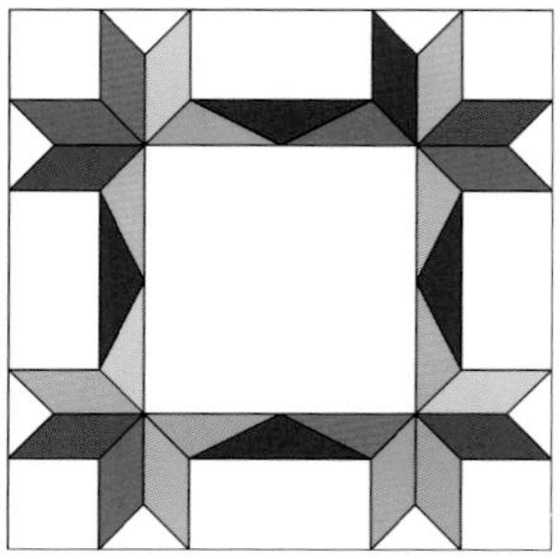   1039

1040    1041    1042

1043 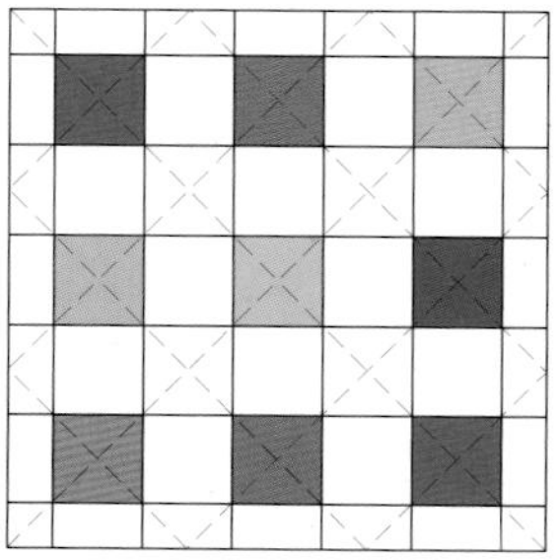   1044    1045

1031 Texas Tears
1032 Windowpane, *PQ*
1033 Economy Star
1034 Fantasy Flower, *MM*
1035 Goose Chase
1036 Custer's Last Stand
1037 Mexican Cross
1038 Strawflower
1039 Chicken Foot
1040 Golgotha
1041 Lost Ship
1042 Cabin Windows
1043 Pathfinder
1044 Church Windows
1045 Starry Sky

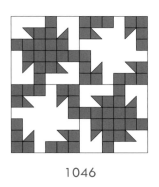
1046

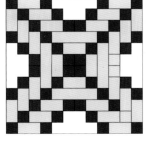
1047

1048

1049

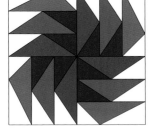
1050

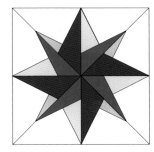
1051

1052

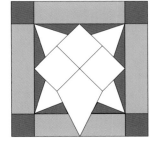
1053

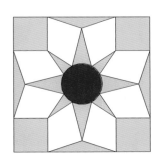
1054

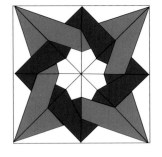
1055

1056

1057

1058

1059

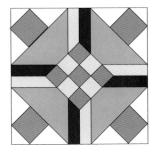
1060

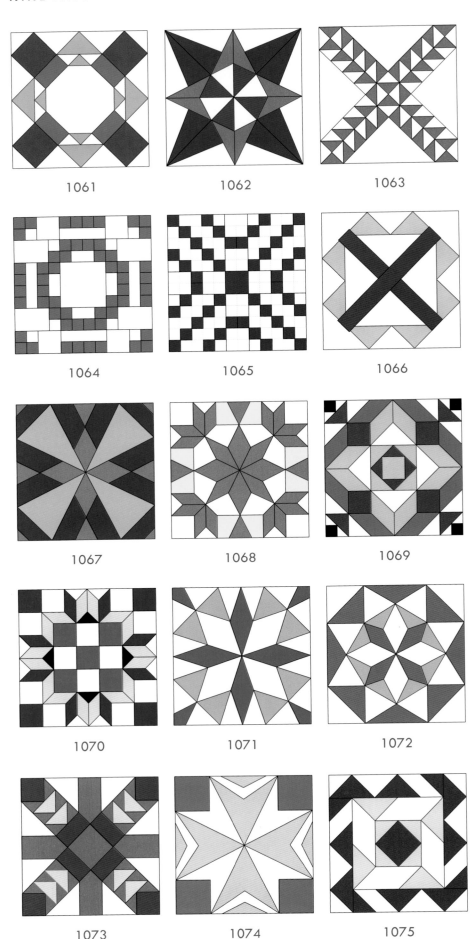

1061 All Kinds, *LAC*
   Beggar's Block
   Cats and Mice
   Turnstile, *NP*

1062 Sarah's Direction

1063 Flock of Birds, *NP*

1064 Summer Garden, *NC*

1065 Steps to the Garden,
   NC

1066 Texas Tears, *LAC*
   Cross and Crown
   Crowned Cross
   Double T, *NC*

1067 Diamond
   Kaleidoscope, *MM*

1068 Pinwheel Star

1069 Mosaic Squares, *NC*

1070 Friendship Star, *LW*

1071 Leo's Lion,
   Sandra Hatch, QW

1072 Harrisburg

1073 Spokane, *NP*

1074 Columbia, *HH*

1075 Spinning Jenny, *NC*

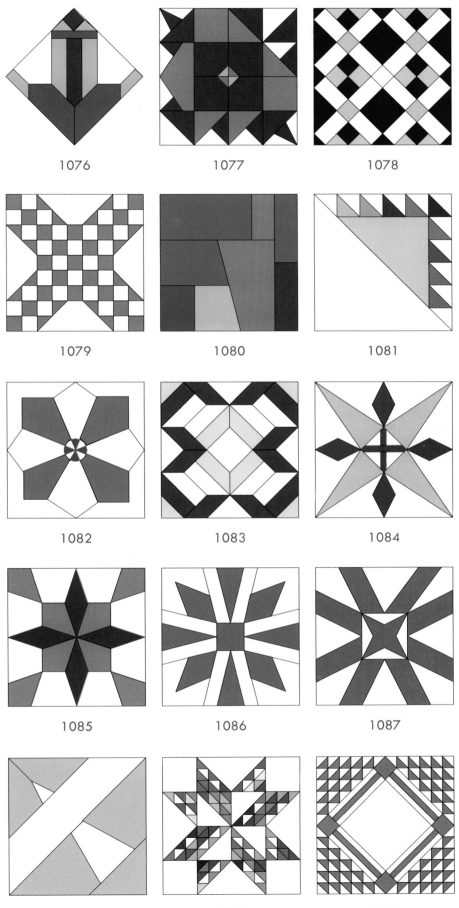

1076   1077   1078

1079   1080   1081

1082   1083   1084

1085   1086   1087

1088   1089   1090

1091   1092   1093

1094   1095   1096

1097   1098   1099

1100   1101   1102

1103   1104   1105

1091 Pretty Kettle of Fish, *QN, 1985*

1092 Railroad Crossing

1093 The String Quilt, *KCS*

1094 Virginia Reel, *CS*
Tangled Lines, *LAC*

1095 Celtic Plaid, *MM*

1096 Thousand Islands, *NC*

1097 Washington, *HH*

1098 Sundance

1099 Autograph Quilt, *KCS*

1100 Endless Squares, *NC*

1101 Autograph Patch

1102 Kentucky Crossroads, *NC*

1103 Picture Frames, *KCS*

1104 Silver Maple, *PP*

1105 Rough Diamond, *SSQ*

1106 Night and Day, *QWO*

1107 Railroad Crossing, *KCS*

1108 Jacob's Ladder, *KCS*

1109 Diamonds in the
Corners, *KCS*

1110 The Red, the White
and the Blue
Red Cross

1111 Timberline, *CR, QN,
1990*

1112 Cut Diamond, *VJ, SSQ,
1984*

1113 Friendship Chain, *KCS*

1114 Flowering Nine Patch,
KCS

1115 Southside Star, *KCS*

1116 Whirling Star

1117 Sunbeam Block, *KCS*
Squared Star, *HAS*
Whippoorwill, *NC*

1118 No Name

1119 Heather Square, *NC*

1120 A Beauty Block, *CS*

1106

1107

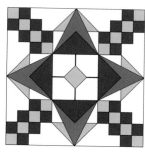

1108

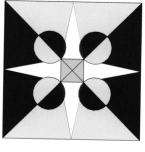

1109

1110

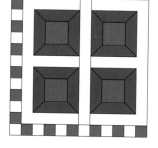

1111

1112

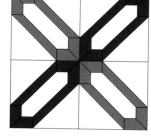

1113

1114

1115

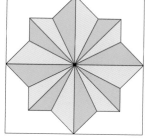

1116

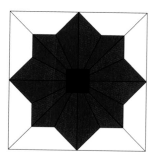

1117

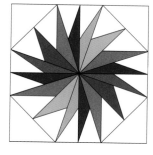

1118

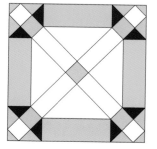

1119

1120

1121

1122

1123

1124

1125

1126

1127

1128

1129

1130

1131

1132

1133

1134

1135

1121 Spider's Den

1122 Maryland Beauty

1123 The Double Arrow, *KCS*

1124 Heart's Desire

1125 Grandmother's Choice

1126 Massachusetts

1127 Avian Waves, *TQr, 1990*

1128 In Narcissus Motif, *KCS*

1129 Sentry's Pastime, *NC*

1130 Star Above the Stable, *HMD, SSQ, 1984*

1131 Shepherd's Watch, *HMD, SSQ, 1984*

1132 Sunshine Over the Rockies, *Mary Lou Endres, QN, 1990*

1133 Courtenay Crown

1134 Flying Geese

1135 Blue Heaven, *NC*

1136 Michigan Favorite, *FJ*

1137 Candy Canes, *HaM, SSQ, 1983*

1138 Stars in Flight, *SSQ, 1985*

1139 Ribbons

1140 Star Explosion

1141 Heavenly Bodies

1142 Moorish Mosaic

1143 Ribbon Square

1144 Pink Dogwood, *QN*

1145 Spring Fancy, *Doris Sprecher, TQr*

1146 Calico Mosaic, *NC*

1147 Spring Tulips

1148 Four Patch Chain

1149 Chaos Theory, *QN*

1150 Sweet Buds, *RMS, SSQ, 1987*

1136 1137 1138

1139 1140 1141

1142 1143 1144

1145 1146 1147

1148 1149 1150

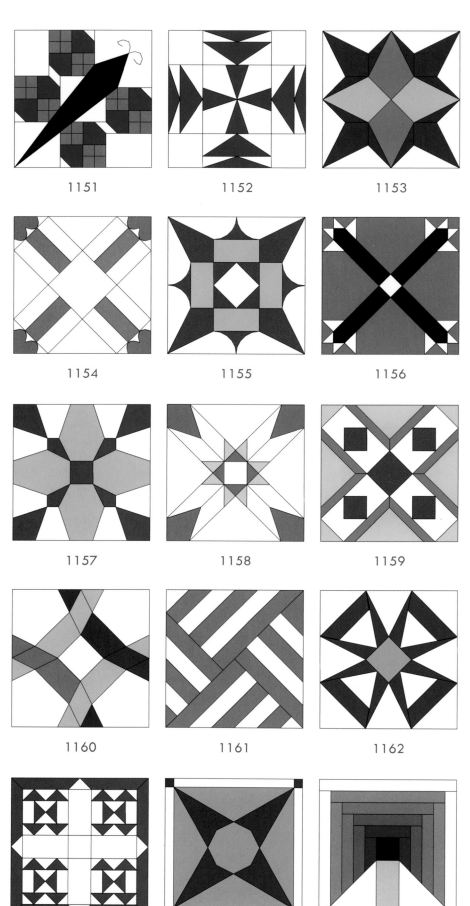

1151 Dragonfly, *Ruby Hinson Duncan, SSQ, 1988*

1152 Falling Leaves

1153 Tulip Bouquet

1154 Cupid's Arrows, *Judy St. John, QW, 1989*

1155 Dawn, *QW, 1986*

1156 Rosemary, *HH*

1157 Sapphire Net, *NC*

1158 Lone Star, *LW, OCS*

1159 Waterwheel

1160 Saracen Chain

1161 Chevrons

1162 Lover's Knot, *AB*

1163 Framed Cross, *QW, 1981*

1164 The Evening Star, *KCS*

1165 Tennessee Mine Shaft

1151 1152 1153

1154 1155 1156

1157 1158 1159

1160 1161 1162

1163 1164 1165

1166 Mexican Siesta, *NC*
Sombrero Appliqué, *NC*

1167 Victory, *CS*

1168 Star Explosion

1169 Walled City, *MM*

1170 Mother's Fancy, *LAC*

1171 Green Cross, *NC*

1172 Shooting Star

1173 The World's Fair

1174 Columbia Quilt Block

1175 Marigold Garden
(diagonal set), *QN*,
1982

1176 Indian Paint Brush, *QN*

1177 Chain Links

1178 Pleasant Paths, *FJ*

1179 Spinning Stars, *QN*

1180 Sailboats Variation

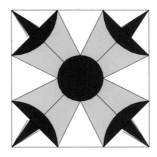

1166

1167

1168

1169

1170

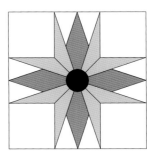

1171

1172

1173

1174

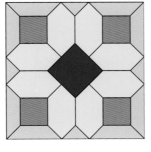

1175

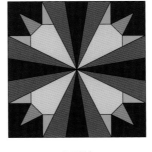

1176

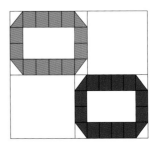

1177

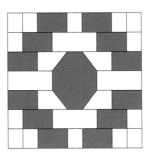

1178

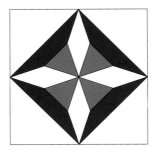

1179

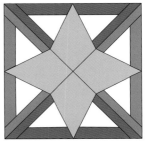

1180

1181

1182

1181 String Quilt
Broken Spider Web, *NC*
Ruby's Star

1182 Old Maid's Ramble,
WD

FOUR
PATCH
PATTERNS

4 X 4 GRID

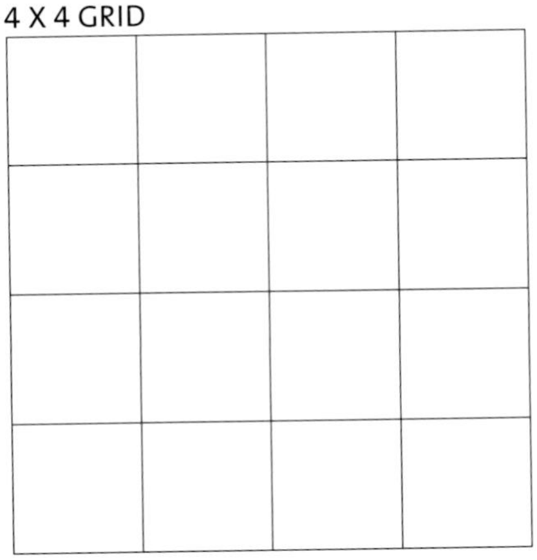

8 X 8 GRID

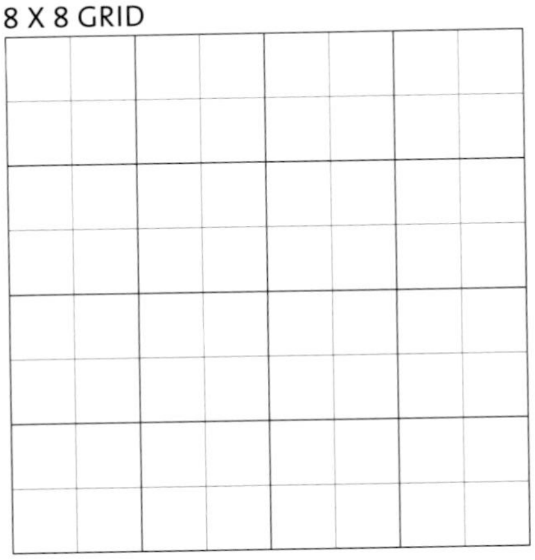

FOUR PATCH PATTERNS ARE MADE ON A GRID OF 4 x 4 SQUARES
THESE PATTERNS ARE EASILY DRAFTED TO ANY BLOCK SIZE DIVISIBLE BY 4

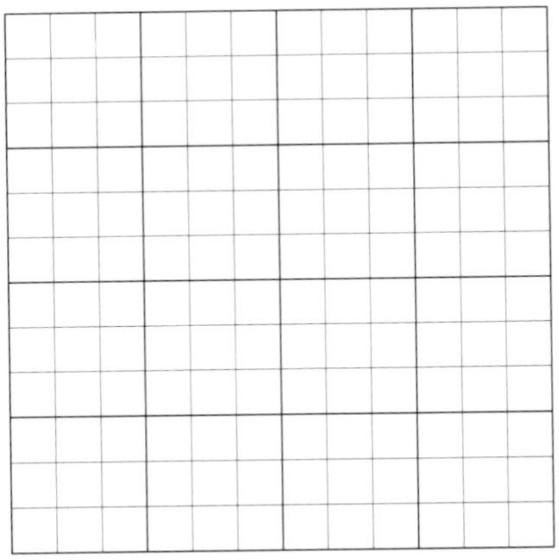

12 X 12 GRID

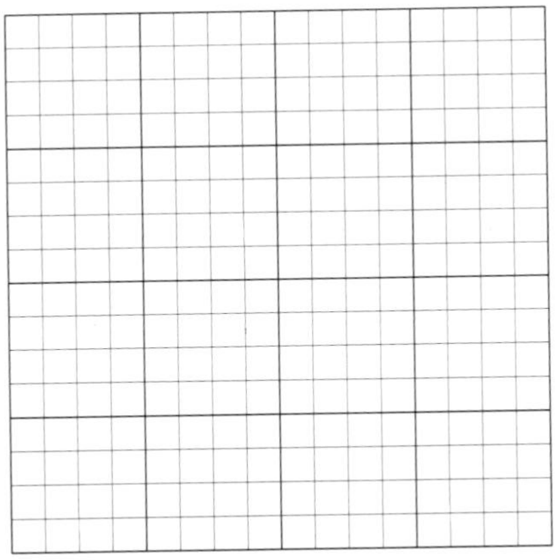

16 X 16 GRID

1183 Four Patch

1184 Mosaic #20, *LAC*
      Check
      Checkerboard
      Four Patch

1185 World's Fair Block, *LAC*

1186 Squares Within
      Squares, *NC*

1187 Carmen's Block, *NP*

1188 Autumn Tints

1189 Squares upon Squares,
      FJ
      Rocky Road

1190 Tam's Patch

1191 Cog Wheels, *KCS*

1192 London Stairs, *KCS*
      Endless Stairs, *HH*
      Endless Stair, *NC*
      Winding Stairway

1193 Hit or Miss
      Hairpin Catcher

1194 Sheep Fold Quilt, *KCS*
      Nine Patch, *LAC*
      A Plain Block, *LHJ, 1896*
      Irish Chain

1195 Arrowhead Puzzle

1196 Salute to Loyalty, *KCS*

1197 Scot's Plaid
      Bonnie Scotsman
      Scotch Quilt

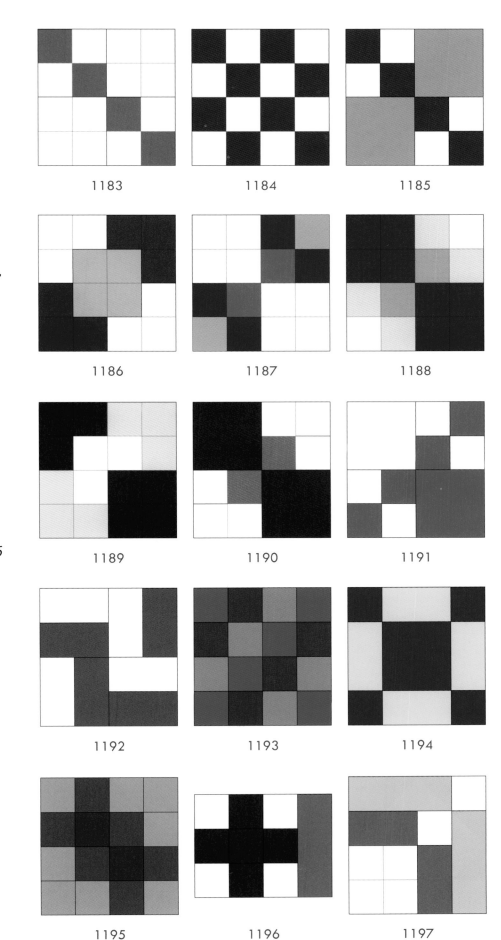

1183   1184   1185

1186   1187   1188

1189   1190   1191

1192   1193   1194

1195   1196   1197

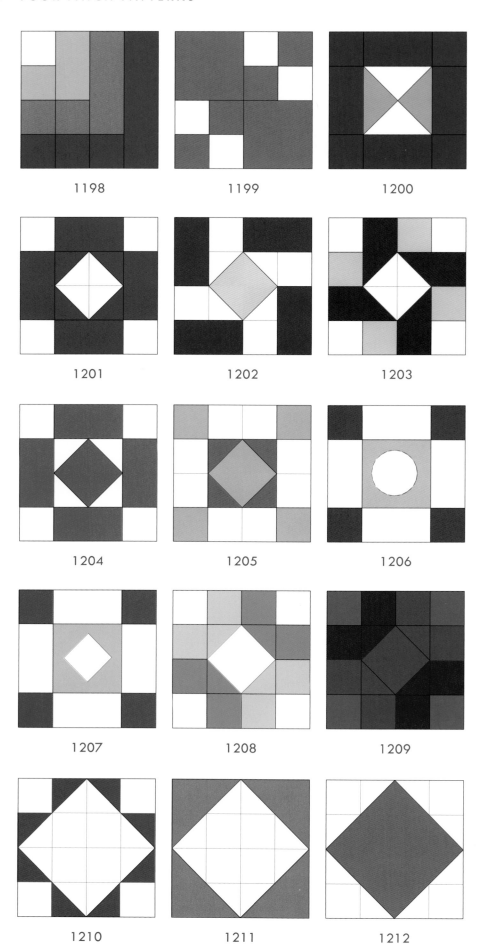

1198 Rainbow Flower

1199 Four Patch

1200 Windows

1201 Oh, Susannah
      Mr. Roosevelt's Necktie
      Susannah, *LAC*

1202 Susannah

1203 Susannah

1204 New Album, *LAC*
      Geometric, *QW*

1205 Fair and Square, *KCS*

1206 Circle in a Frame, *KCS*

1207 The Yellow Square, *KCS*

1208 Mr. Roosevelt's Necktie

1209 Y-Bridge
      Mr. Roosevelt's Necktie

1210 Art Square, *LAC*
      Village Square, *NC*
      Dottie's Choice, *FJ*

1211 Shoofly

1212 Broken Sash, *NC*
      Dutch Tile, *NC*
      Diamond in the Square
      Friendship Album
       Quilt
      Triangle Design

1213 Right and Left, *LAC*

1214 Sugar Bowl Quilt, *NC*

1215 Southern Belle

1216 Electric Fan, *HH*

1217 Shooting Squares, *NP*

1218 Letter L

1219 Windmill

1220 Four Knaves

1221 Economy
Hour Glass, *LAC*
This and That, *KCS*
Thrift Block, *NC*

1222 Twelve Triangles, *KCS*
Shadow Boxes

1223 Album

1224 King's Crown, *KCS*

1225 Square and Points, *KCS*
Eight Point Star

1226 Evening Star
Two Patch Quilt, *OCS*

1227 Evening Star, *LAC*
Cluster of Stars

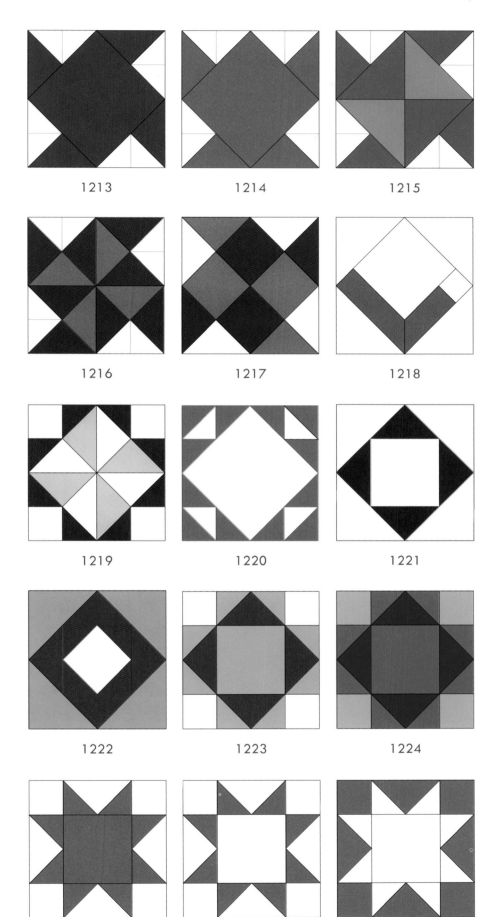

1213　　　　1214　　　　1215

1216　　　　1217　　　　1218

1219　　　　1220　　　　1221

1222　　　　1223　　　　1224

1225　　　　1226　　　　1227

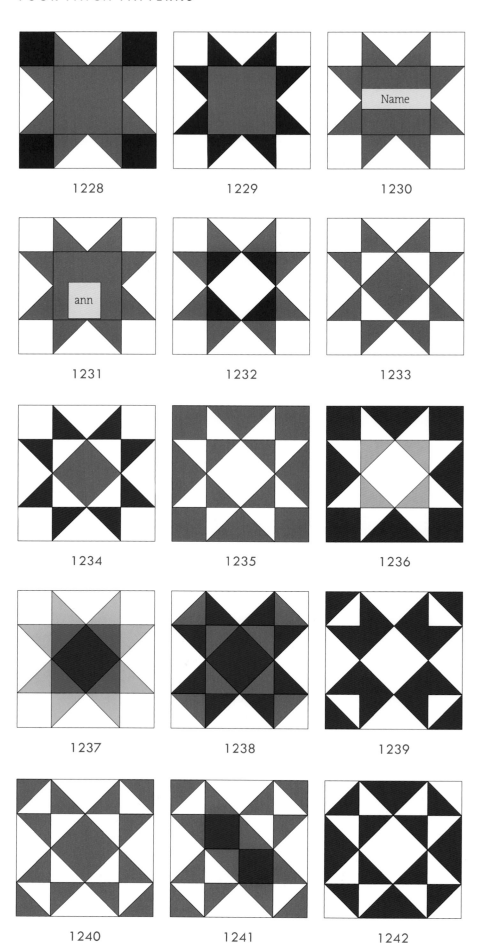

1228

1229

1230

1231

1232

1233

1234

1235

1236

1237

1238

1239

1240

1241

1242

1228 Austin, *HH*
Optical Sawtooth

1229 Sawtooth, *FF, 1884*
Nameless Star, *NC*
Sawtooth

1230 Album Quilt

1231 Coral Court Friendship
Star

1232 Variable Star

1233 Crystal Star, *KCS*

1234 Crystal Star
Joining Star, *NP*
Lone Star
Peaceful Hours
Star of Virginia
Texas Star

1235 Ohio Star
Mosaic #10, *LAC*

1236 The Cog Block, *KCS*

1237 Eight Pointed Star, *FJ*

1238 Tippecanoe and Tyler,
Too

1239 Star

1240 An Envelope Motif, *KCS*

1241 Chisholm Trail, *KCS*

1242 Mosaic #19, *LAC*
Mosaic #7, *NC*

1243 Wheel of Time, *CS*

1244 Four Patch Fox and
Goose, *KCS*

1245 Old Grey Goose, *NP*

1246 Margaret's Choice
Quilt Block

1247 Blazing Arrow Point
Blazing Arrows

1248 Moon and Star

1249 Sarah's Choice, *CS*

1250 Barbara Frietchie Star
Pieced Star
Pierced Star
Star Puzzle, *LAC*
Wind Mill Quilt

1251 Annie's Choice
Anna's Choice

1252 Solitaire

1253 Pigs in a Blanket

1254 Magic Cross Design,
1931

1255 Martha Washington
Star
Flying Cloud, *CS*
Solomon's Star, *NC*

1256 Dewey's Victory, *CS*
Annie's Choice, *CS*
Martha Washington
Star, *1926*
Octagonal Star, *1928*
Queen Victoria

1257 Star & Pinwheels, *NC*

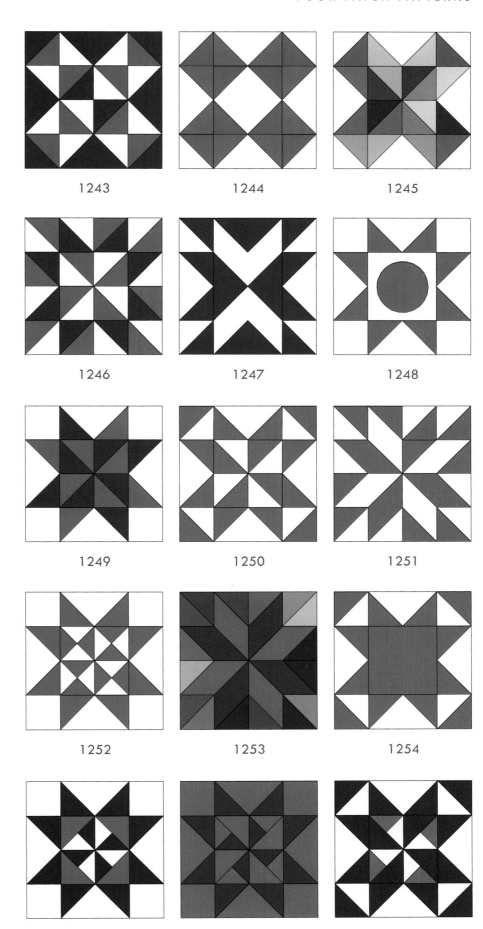

1243 1244 1245
1246 1247 1248
1249 1250 1251
1252 1253 1254
1255 1256 1257

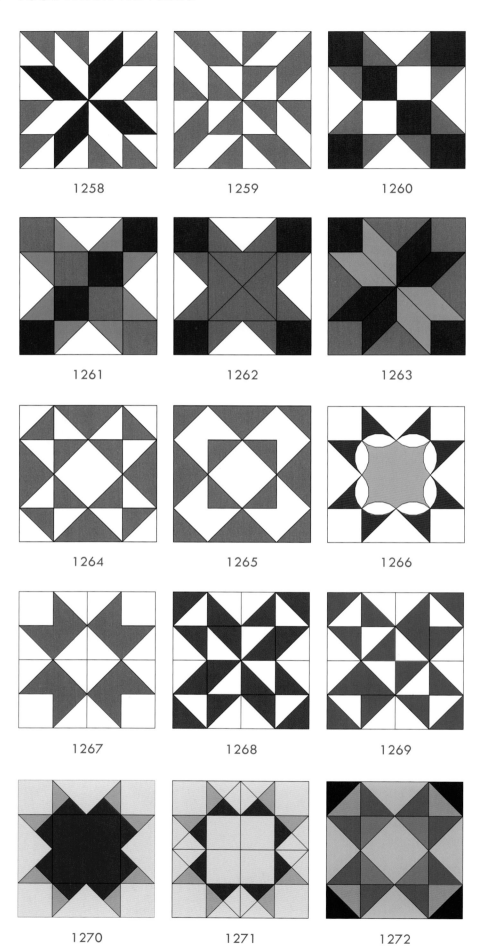

1258   1259   1260

1261   1262   1263

1264   1265   1266

1267   1268   1269

1270   1271   1272

1258   Star of the Milky Way

1259   Squire Smith's Choice

1260   Indian Star, *KCS*

1261   Winged Four Patch, *KCS*

1262   Arrow Star

1263   Sunlight and Shadows, *KCS*

1264   Star

1265   Star

1266   French Star
        Flaming Sun, *NC*
        Gleaming Sun

1267   Ribbon Star, *LAC*

1268   Mosaic #13, *LAC*

1269   Mosaic #11, *LAC*

1270   Centennial

1271   Aunt Addie's Album, *HH*

1272   Rolling Star Quilt

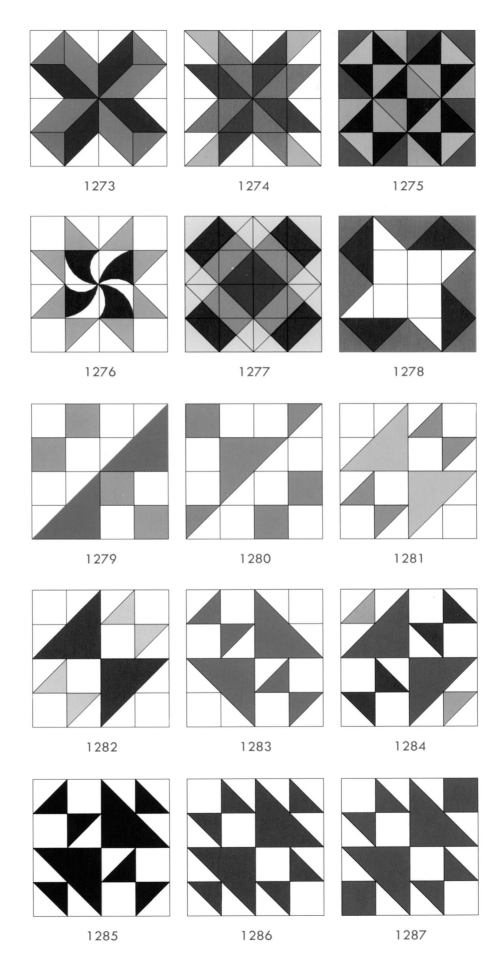

1273   1274   1275

1276   1277   1278

1279   1280   1281

1282   1283   1284

1285   1286   1287

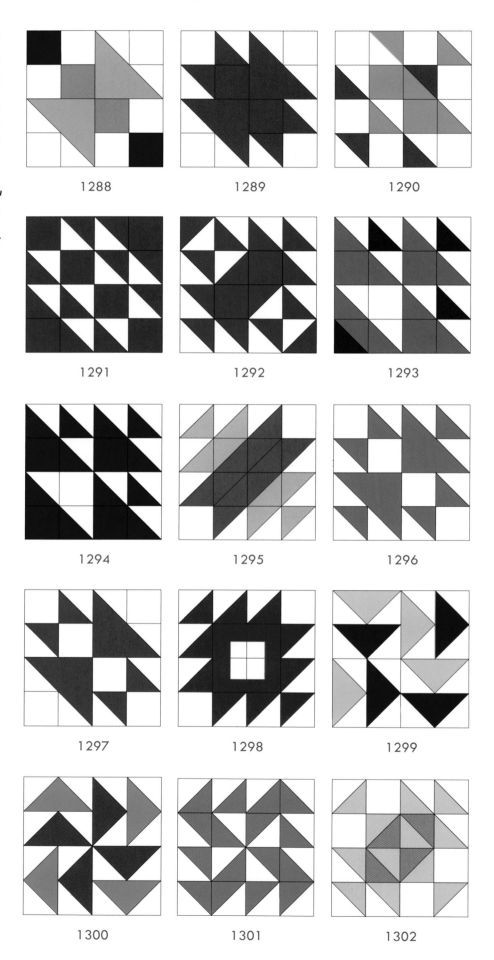

1288   1289   1290

1291   1292   1293

1294   1295   1296

1297   1298   1299

1300   1301   1302

1288   Buckeye Beauty, *KCS*
Double Four Patch
Gay Scrap Quilt, *LW*
Going to Chicago, *NP, 1933*
Jacob's Ladder
New Four Patch, *1884*
Railroad, *NC, 1934*
Railroad Crossing
World's Fair, *1933*

1289   The Anvil

1290   Wild Duck

1291   Hovering Hawks
Hovering Birds
Triple X

1292   Double Cross, *HH*

1293   Airplane

1294   Aircraft, *NC*
Dutchman's Puzzle

1295   Mrs. Taft's Choice

1296   Double X

1297   Double X

1298   Rocky Mountain Puzzle

1299   Return of the Swallows

1300   Dutchman's Puzzle, *LAC*
Dutchman's Wheel, *OF, 1898*
Wheel, *OF, 1894*
Wild Goose Chase

1301   Yankee Puzzle

1302   Flying Dutchman

1303   Bachelor's Puzzle
Building Blocks, *GD*
Kansas Whirligig, *QW, 1989*
The Pinwheel, *KCS*
Road to Jerusalem, *NC*

1304   Swastika, *KCS*
Battle Ax of Thor
Catch Me If You Can
Chinese 10,000 Perfections
Devil's Dark Horse

Devil's Puzzle
Favorite of the Peruvians
Flyfoot
Heart's Seal
Indian Emblem, *KCS*
Mound Builders
Pure Symbol of Right
  Doctrine
Spider
Virginia Reel
Wind Power of the Osages
Winding Blades, *KCS*
Whirligig, *HHJ*
Zig Zag, *CoM*

1305 Little Lost Sailboat

1306 Ladies Wreath, *LAC*

1307 Ship
  The Mayflower, *KCS*
  Tad Lincoln's Sailboat
  Little Ship of Dreams

1308 Flying Fish

1309 Cotton Reel

1310 Big Dipper
  Bow Ties, *NC*
  Envelope Quilt, *KCS*
  Hour Glass, *KCS*
  Pork and Beans
  The Whirling Blade, *KCS*
  Yankee Puzzle

1311 Broken Dishes
  Double Square, *KCS*

1312 Double Square

1313 Triangle Combination

1314 Small Triangles, *KCS*

1315 Triangles and Squares,
    KCS

1316 Trails
  Bright Futures

1317 The Cypress, *KCS*

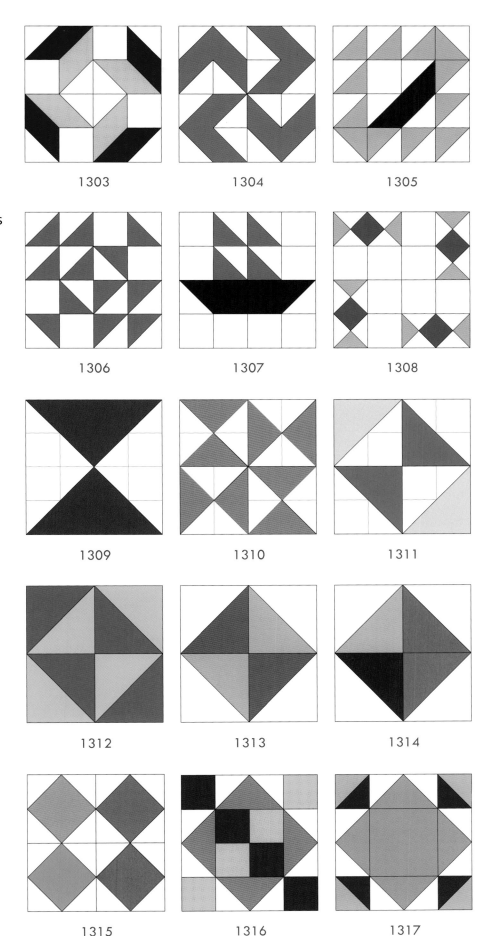

1303   1304   1305

1306   1307   1308

1309   1310   1311

1312   1313   1314

1315   1316   1317

1318   1319   1320

1321   1322   1323

1324   1325   1326

1327   1328   1329

1330   1331   1332

1318 The Cypress

1319 Signature

1320 Mosaic #16, *LAC*
Connecticut, *NP*

1321 Mosaic #12, *NC*
Hour Glass, *NP*

1322 Checkerboard Quilt

1323 Canadian Gardens, *NP*

1324 Linking Blocks

1325 Anvil

1326 Peace and Plenty

1327 Broken Path

1328 End of the Road, *KCS*

1329 Blockade, *KCS*

1330 Friendship

1331 Friday the 13th, *KCS*

1332 Rail Fence

1333

1334

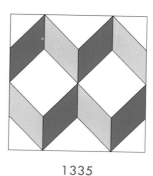
1335

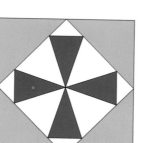
1336

1337

1338

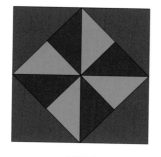
1339

1340

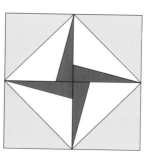
1341

1342

1343

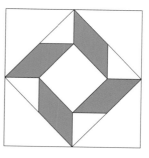
1344

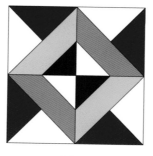
1345

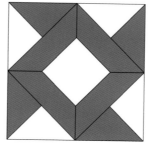
1346

1347

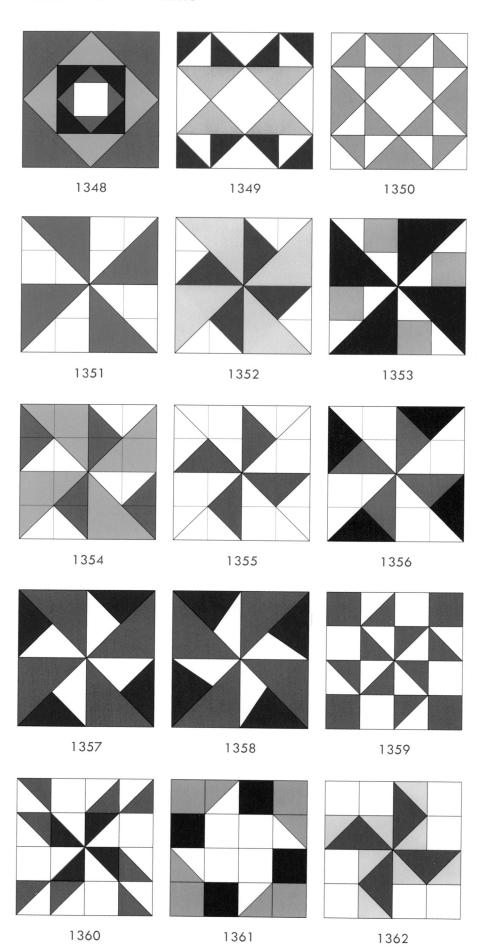

1348

1349

1350

1351

1352

1353

1354

1355

1356

1357

1358

1359

1360

1361

1362

1348 Square on Square, *NP*

1349 Mosaic #15, *LAC*

1350 Mosaic #19, *LAC*

1351 Pinwheel
Broken Wheel
Corn Design
Crow's Foot
Fan Mill
Four Leaf Clover
Fly
Kathy's Ramble
Millwheel
Mosaic #9, *LAC*
Old Crow
Sugarbowl
Watermill
Water Wheel
Windmill, *OF, 1898*

1352 Double Pinwheel
Old Windmill, *NC*
Windmill

1353 Brave World, *FJ, 1944*
Brown World, *NC*

1354 Broken Pinwheel

1355 Turnstile, *LAC*

1356 Whirlwind

1357 Whirligig

1358 Double Pinwheel

1359 Flying X, *KCS*
Double Quartet
X Quartet, *WW*

1360 Year's Favorite

1361 Pinwheel
Paper Pinwheels, *NP*

1362 Louisiana, *HH*

1363 Whirlwind
Modern Envelope, *KCS*
Pinwheel
Twin Sisters, *LAC*
Water Wheel
Windmill, *GD*

1364 Windmill, *GC*
Whirligig, *KCS*

1365 Arkansas Crossroads,
KCS

1366 Streak of Lightning

1367 Shadow Box

1368 Jewel

1369 Birds in the Air

1370 Birds in the Air

1371 Flock
Flock of Geese

1372 Sawtooth

1373 Northern Lights

1374 Double X

1375 Nelson's Victory

1376 Window

1377 Broken Dish

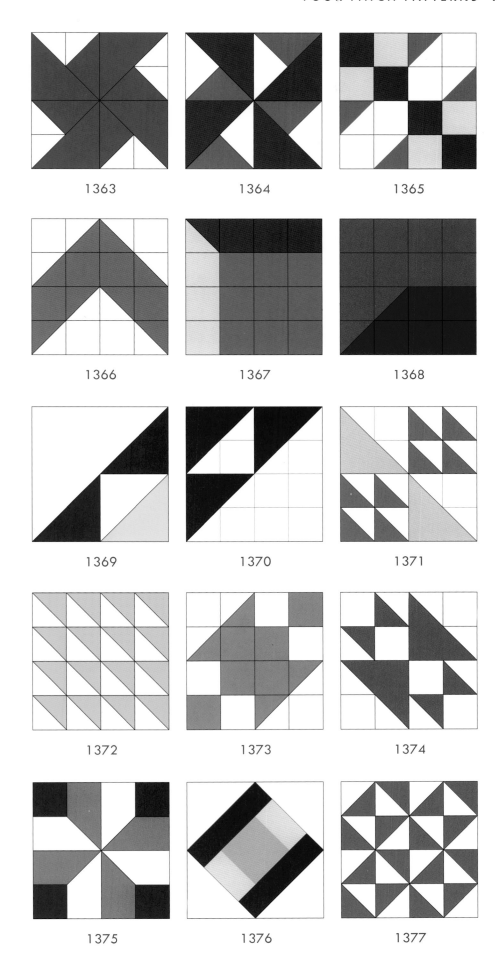

1363

1364

1365

1366

1367

1368

1369

1370

1371

1372

1373

1374

1375

1376

1377

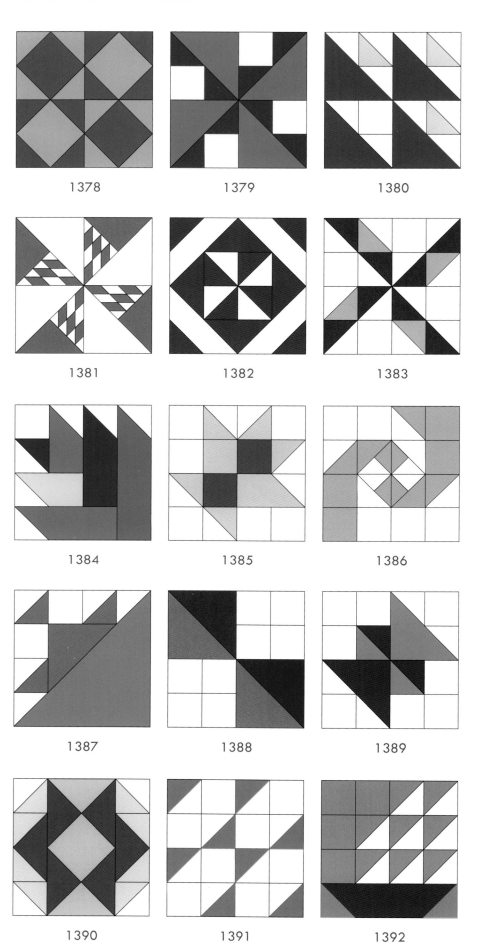

1378   Small Triangle Quilt

1379   Spinner

1380   Aircraft

1381   Dutch Windmill

1382   Mosaic #8, *NC*

1383   Windmill

1384   Pineapple Plant

1385   Baby Bunting

1386   Snail's Trail, *KCS*

1387   Ships at Sea

1388   Cotton Reels

1389   Picket Fence

1390   Butterfly

1391   The X-Quisite, *LAC*

1392   Sailboat

1393 Box, *LAC*

1394 Contrary Husband, *KCS*
Box, *LAC*
Box Car Patch, *NC*
Eccentric Star, *GC*
Open Book
The Open Box, *AG*
Roads to Berlin

1395 Roads to Berlin, *KCS*

1396 Flying Bats, *KCS*
Around the Chimney
Diamond Point
Slashed Album, *LAC*

1397 Mosaic #1
Hither and Yon
Spool

1398 Windmill

1399 Churn Dash, *NC*

1400 Cheyenne, *KCS*

1401 Little Cedar Tree

1402 A Signature Quilt, *KCS*

1403 Red Cross

1404 Heart

1405 The Anvil

1406 Connecticut, *HH*
Shoemaker's Puzzle,
HH

1407 Block Island Puzzle

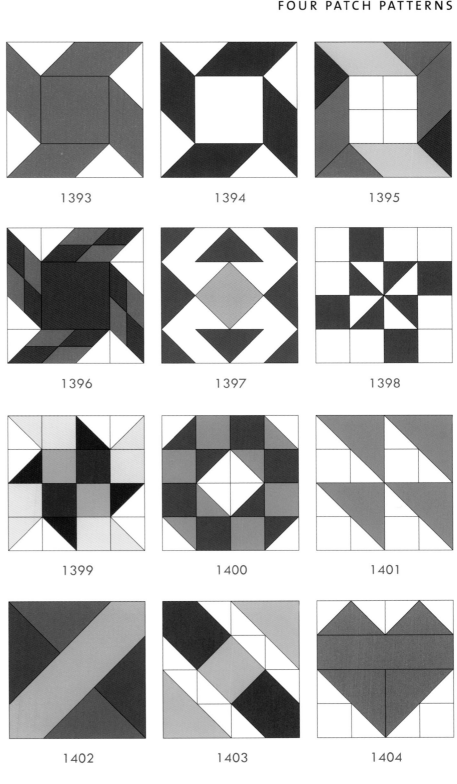

1393   1394   1395

1396   1397   1398

1399   1400   1401

1402   1403   1404

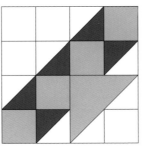 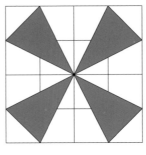 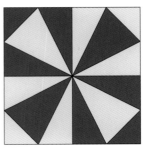

1405   1406   1407

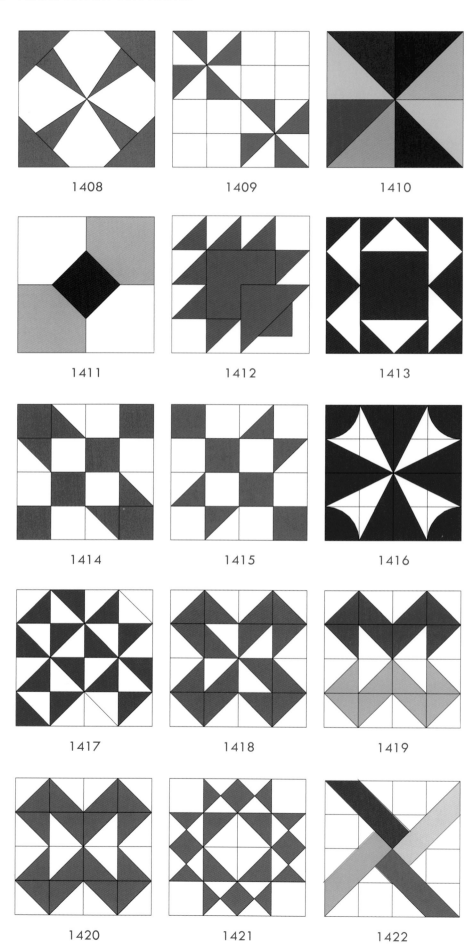

1408   Plain Sailing, *CoM*

1409   Flashing Windmills, *NC*
        Pinwheels

1410   The Gay Pinwheel

1411   Bowtie
        Colonial Bow Tie, *GC*
        Necktie, *LAC*
        Peekhole, *WW, 1931*

1412   Swallow

1413   Buzzard's Roost

1414   Road to Oklahoma, *KCS*

1415   Road to Oklahoma
        Crockett Cabin Quilt

1416   Spider Web

1417   Broken Dishes
        Old Tippecanoe, *LAC*
        Broken Promises, *QN*

1418   Colorado Block
        Colorado Beauty

1419   Double Z

1420   Hourglass
        Double Z

1421   Square & Star

1422   Windmill

1423 Ribbon Block, *KCS*
      Beach and Boots, *NC*
      Ribbon Border, *LAC*
      Watered Ribbon &
         Border, *LAC*

1424 Pinwheel

1425 Old Windmill

1426 Puss in the Corner, *LAC*

1427 Sunshiny Day

1428 Tea Leaf

1429 Crazy Quilt

1430 Crazy Quilt Flower

1431 Tulip

1432 Beacon Lights

1433 Noon & Light

1434 Royal Star

1435 The Seasons, *KCS*
      Maud's Album Block,
        NP
      Pointed Tile

1436 Mother's Choice, *KCS*
      Cotton Boll, *KCS*
      Formal Garden
      Mother's Choice, *KCS*
      A Cross Is Mother's
        Choice, *KCS*

1437 Pointed Tile

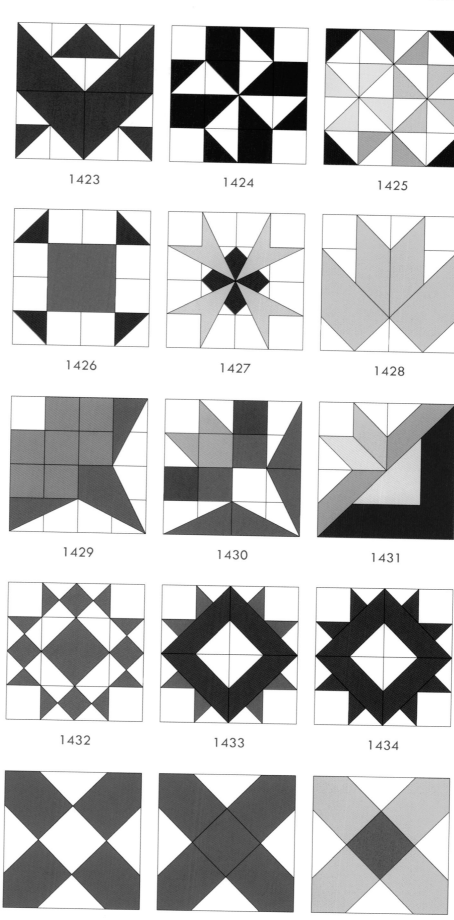

1423   1424   1425

1426   1427   1428

1429   1430   1431

1432   1433   1434

1435   1436   1437

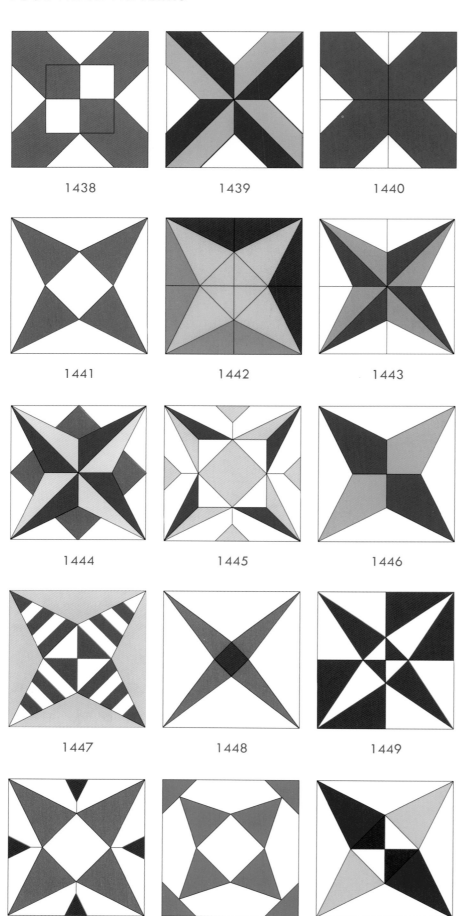

1438

1439

1440

1441

1442

1443

1444

1445

1446

1447

1448

1449

1450

1451

1452

1438 Indian Star, *KCS*

1439 King's X, *FJ*
Hide and Seek, *AK*

1440 Lattice, *NP*
A Quilt of Variety, *KCS*
Cotton Boll, *KCS*
Five Cross, *CS*
Five Crosses, *NC*
Lovely Patchwork, *NC*
The Quint Five Quilt,
KCS

1441 World Without End
Amethyst
Diamond Star
Golden Wedding Quilt,
NP
The Priscilla, *LAC*
Star and Diamond
Rocky Road to Kansas
(strip pieced scraps),
LAC

1442 Kaleidoscope

1443 Job's Troubles

1444 Star

1445 World's Fair, *LW*

1446 World Without End
Black and White, *OCS*
Bamboo Quilt, *OCS*
Diamonds Galore, *OCS*

1447 Kite, *CS*

1448 Massachusetts Priscilla

1449 Crossed Canoes, *LAC*
The Dragon Fly, *KCS*
Indian Canoes, *KCS*
Santa Fe Quilt, *CoM*
Twinkling Star

1450 Forgotten Star

1451 Milkmaid's Star, *KCS*

1452 Sugar Cone

1453 Duck Tracks

1454 Pinwheel

1455 Poinsettia

1456 Arrowhead

1457 Winged Square

1458 Meteor

1459 Pale Star

1460 Trailing Star
    Mosaic, *LAC*
    Mosaic #1, *NC*
    Old Poinsettia, *NC*
    Spinning Stars, *NP*

1461 Clay's Choice
    Beauty Patch
    Clay's Favorite
    Clay's Star
    Harry's Star
    Henry of the West
    Star of the West

1462 Pinwheel Askew

1463 Mosaic #12, *NC*

1464 Mosaic #9, *LAC*

1465 The North Star, *KCS*
    Whirling Star

1466 Shooting Star, *LAC*
    Meteor Quilt, *NP*
    Stardust, *KCS Quilt
        Contest*

1467 Pineapple Quilt, *1862*

1453   1454   1455

1456   1457   1458

1459   1460   1461

1462   1463   1464

1465   1466   1467

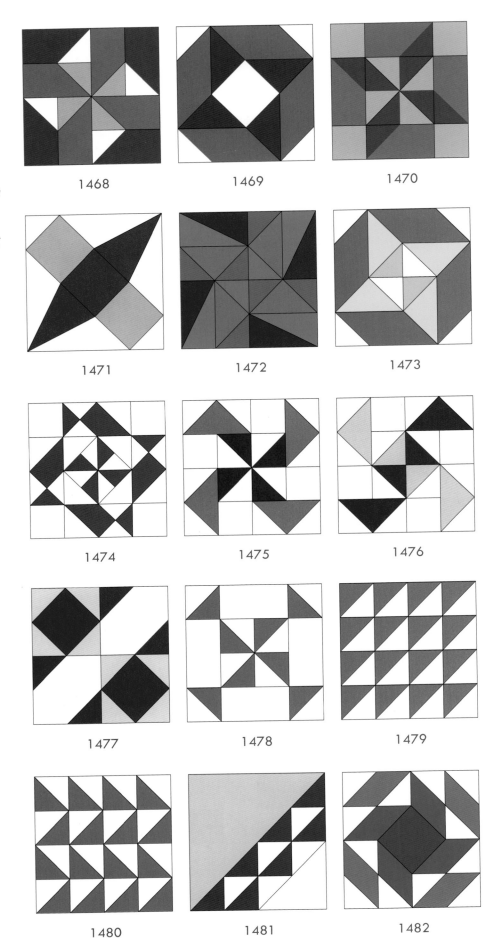

1468   1469   1470

1471   1472   1473

1474   1475   1476

1477   1478   1479

1480   1481   1482

1468 Petronella, *QM, 1992*

1469 Rose Trellis, *NC*

1470 Shooting Star

1471 Blue Heaven

1472 Popcorn

1473 Next Door Neighbor Square Up, *HH*

1474 Catch as You Can

1475 Seesaw

1476 Next Door Neighbor

1477 Monastery Windows, *NC*

1478 Windmill, *OCS*

1479 Mosaic #10, *NC*
Mosaic #17, *LAC*
Ann and Andy
Triangle Tiles

1480 Hopscotch, *NC*

1481 Path Through the Woods, *CaS*

1482 Mosaic #6

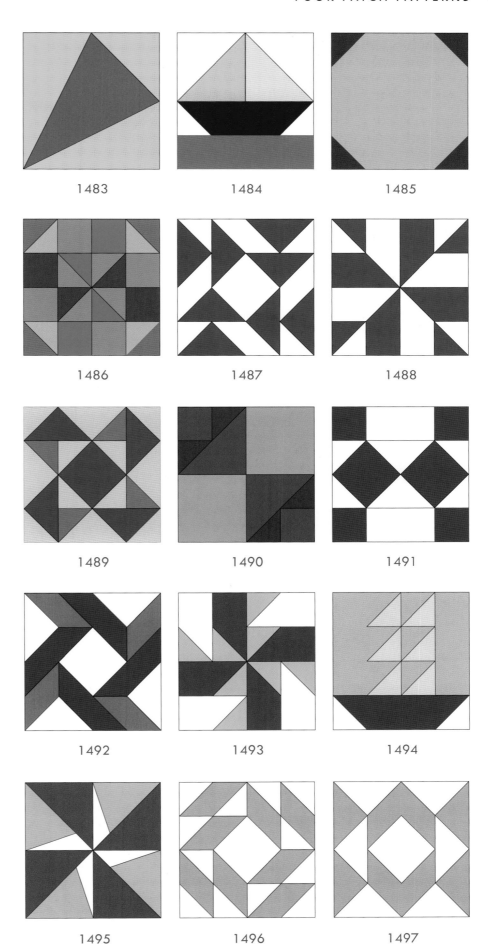

1483

1484

1485

1486

1487

1488

1489

1490

1491

1492

1493

1494

1495

1496

1497

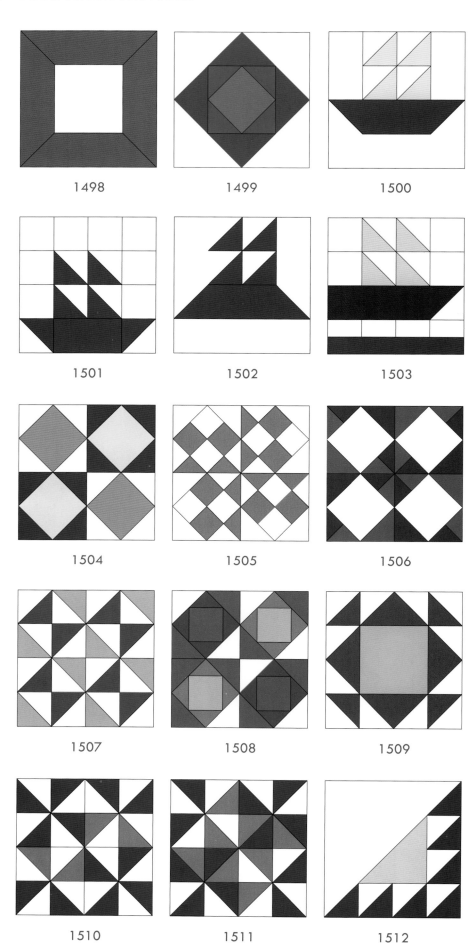

1498

1499

1500

1501

1502

1503

1504

1505

1506

1507

1508

1509

1510

1511

1512

1498 The Diversion Quilt, *KCS*

1499 Economy, *KCS*

1500 The Ship, *MD*

1501 Fishing Boats, *NC*

1502 Sailboat Oklahoma, *KCS*

1503 Sailboat Quilt, *NP*

1504 Alamanizer, *NC*
      Eight Point All Over, *QN*
      Pavement Pattern
      Shoo Fly
      Triangles and Squares, *KCS*
      Triangle Beauty, *OCS*

1505 Yokohama Banner, *NC*
      Whirling Squares, *NP*

1506 Arrowhead Puzzle, *AMS*

1507 Port and Starboard, *NC*

1508 This and That, *KCS*

1509 Magic Triangles, *OCS*

1510 Simplicity, *HH*

1511 Milly's Favorite, *1911*

1512 Lend and Borrow, *KCS*
      Geometric
      Indian Meadow, *WW*
      Little Saw Tooth, *WW*
      Rocky Glen, *WW*
      Saw Tooth, *WW*

1513 Oklahoma Square
    Dance, *KCS*
    Square Dance, *OCS*
    Starry Night
    All Around the Star, *NC*

1514 Airplane

1515 Signature

1516 Seesaw

1517 Migration

1518 Quilt in Light and Dark

1519 Idle Moments

1520 Counterpane, *NC*

1521 Country Village

1522 Light and Shadows, *NC*

1523 Gold Nuggets, *AK*

1524 Diversion Quilt, *KCS*

1525 Islam, *NC*

1526 Granny's Choice

1527 Our Editor

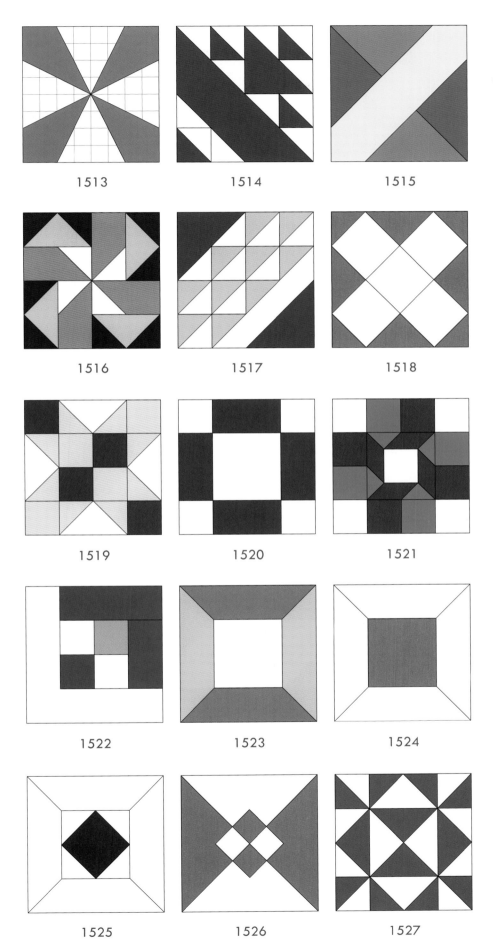

1513　1514　1515

1516　1517　1518

1519　1520　1521

1522　1523　1524

1525　1526　1527

5,500 QUILT BLOCK DESIGNS

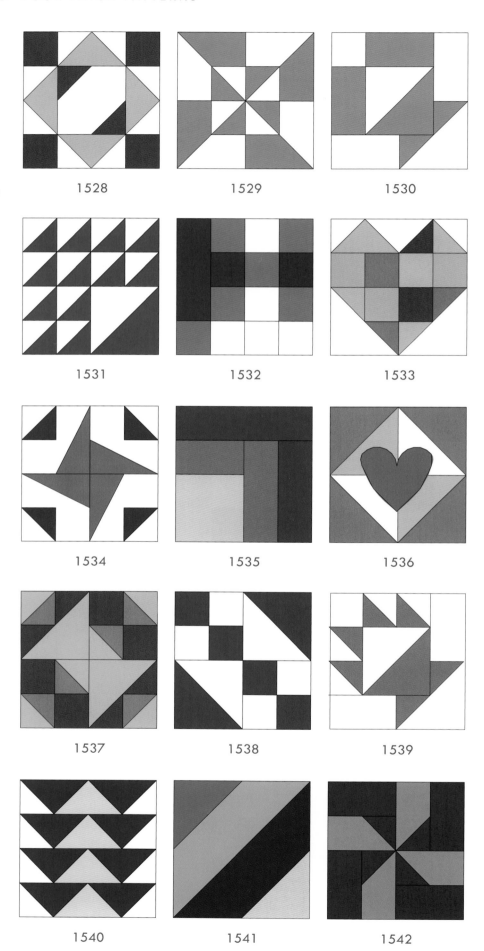

1528
1529
1530
1531
1532
1533
1534
1535
1536
1537
1538
1539
1540
1541
1542

1528 Signature Friendship Quilt, *KCS*

1529 Double Windmill

1530 Fish Basket Block

1531 Friendship Quilt

1532 Diagonal Square, *OCS*

1533 Romance, *TQr, 1992*

1534 Liberty Star, *QW, 1988*

1535 Garden Shadows, *QM, 1994*

1536 Heart Spangled Star

1537 Grandma's Spool

1538 Jewel Box

1539 Cactus Pot Block

1540 Tit for Tat

1541 Lightning, *LS, 1990*

1542 Maypole Dance, *QM*

1543 Bonny Scotland, *JM*

1544 The Sail Boat, *KCS*

1545 A Victory Quilt, *KCS*
Arrowhead

1546 A Scrap Zigzag, *KCS*

1547 The Maple Leaf, *KCS*

1548 Posy Patch

1549 Simple Block
Flower Bed

1550 Ship of Dreams

1551 Picture Window

1552 Fox Chase
Biloxi

1553 Light and Dark, *KCS*

1554 Electric Fan, *CS*

1555 Star of the East, *FJ*
Midnight Stars, *NC*

1556 Pinwheel, *AG*

1557 Sunshiny Day, *FJ*

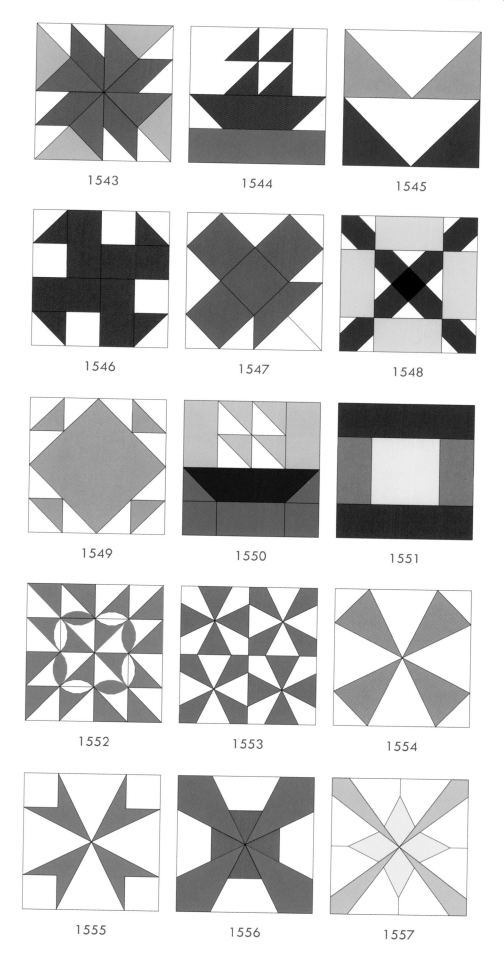

1543

1544

1545

1546

1547

1548

1549

1550

1551

1552

1553

1554

1555

1556

1557

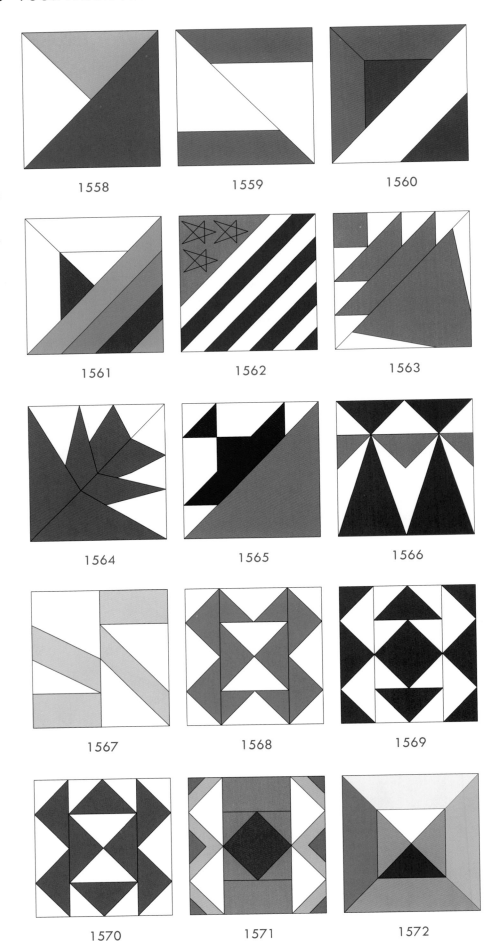

1558
1559
1560
1561
1562
1563
1564
1565
1566
1567
1568
1569
1570
1571
1572

1558 Pigeons in the Coop, *QN*
Rocky Mountain
Shadow Box
Waste Not, Want Not

1559 Good Luck, *FJ*

1560 No Name

1561 Peter's Quilt, *Nancy Crow*

1562 Red, White and Blue, *FJ*

1563 Winter Cactus, *MJ*

1564 Winter Cactus, *MJ*

1565 Ship at Sea, *Dakota Farmer, 1927*

1566 Lilies, *QW, 1980*

1567 College Chain, *1902*

1568 Brown Goose
Devil's Claws
Double Z
Framed X, *FJ*
Gray Goose
Old Gray Goose, *NC*
Old Maid's Puzzle
Mosaic #22, *LAC*

1569 Empire Star, *HH*
Star of the West

1570 Fool's Puzzle, *CoM*

1571 Diamond Stripe

1572 Terrace Floor, *Helen White, QN, 1999*

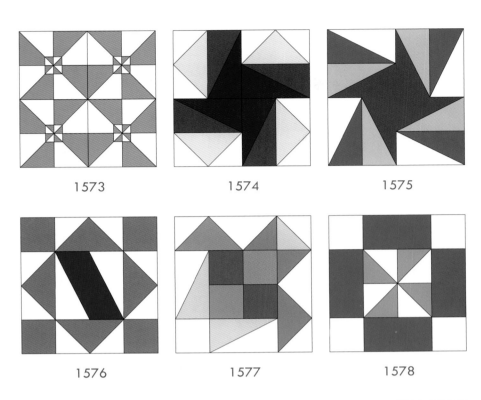

1573   1574   1575

1576   1577   1578

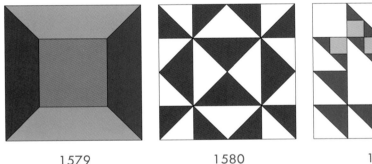

1579   1580   1581

1582   1583   1584

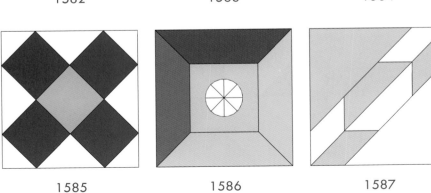

1585   1586   1587

1588

1589

1590

1591

1592

1593

1594

1595

1596

1597

1598

1599

1600

1601

1602

1588 Old Maid's Rambler

1589 All That Jazz, *JM*
Kitty Corner, *JM*

1590 Four Leaf Clover, *NM*

1591 Flower Bed, *NC*
A Simple Design, *NC*

1592 Saddlebag

1593 Nine Patch Star

1594 Judy's Star, *JM*

1595 Star Shine

1596 Buck 'n Wing

1597 Merry-Go-Round, *RMS,
SSQ, 1986*

1598 Jim Dandy, *NC*

1599 Prudence's Star, *OCS*

1600 Fish Tales

1601 Land of Lincoln, *JM*

1602 Spools
Dog Bone

1603 White House Steps

1604 Frame

1605 Swastika

1606 Odds and Ends

1607 Tea Rose

1608 Going Home

1609 Paddle Wheel

1610 Necktie, *KCS*

1611 Bow Tie Wreath
     Magic Circle
     Morning Patch, *LAC*

1612 Irish Chain

1613 Flying Clouds

1614 Steps to Glory

1615 Interlocking O's,
     Doris Dace

1616 Fanny's Favorite
     Diamond Ring, *CS*
     Grandma's Choice,
       1938
     My Favorite, *NC, 1933*
     Old Favorite, *NC*

1617 No Name, *LCPQ*

1603   1604   1605

1606   1607   1608

1609   1610   1611

1612   1613   1614

1615   1616   1617

1618   1619   1620

1621   1622   1623

1624   1625   1626

1627   1628   1629

1630   1631   1632

1618   Sunny Lanes, *NP*

1619   Flying Clouds

1620   Buckeye Beautiful

1621   Jewel Box

1622   The White Cross

1623   The Rosebud

1624   Century of Progress

1625   Patio Garden, *MM*

1626   Carrie Nation Quilt, *KCS*

1627   Four Patch

1628   Aunt Em's Pattern

1629   Postage Stamp

1630   The Red Cross Quilt, *KCS*

1631   Geese in Flight, *NC*

1632   Autumn Star, *NC*

1633 Scroll Work, *AMS*

1634 Iowa Star, *LAC*
Texas Ranger

1635 Signal Light, *NP*

1636 Lucky Star, *LW*

1637 Star of Four Points, *KCS*
Twinkling Stars, *CoM*
Time and Tide

1638 Star and Dot, *1910*

1639 Periwinkle
Snowball, *Carrie Hall*

1640 Flaming Star, *NP*
Northern Lights, *NP*
Eight Pointed Star, *LAC*
Mariner's Compass,
HAS
Mother's Delight

1641 Blazing Star
Four Pointed Star
Mother's Delight, *CaS*
St. Louis, *CaS*

1642 Blazing Star, *NC*

1643 Blazing Star

1644 Rainbow Star, *MM*

1645 Star Bound, *QN, 1990*

1646 Sparkling Crystals

1647 Rolling Star
Kaleidoscope

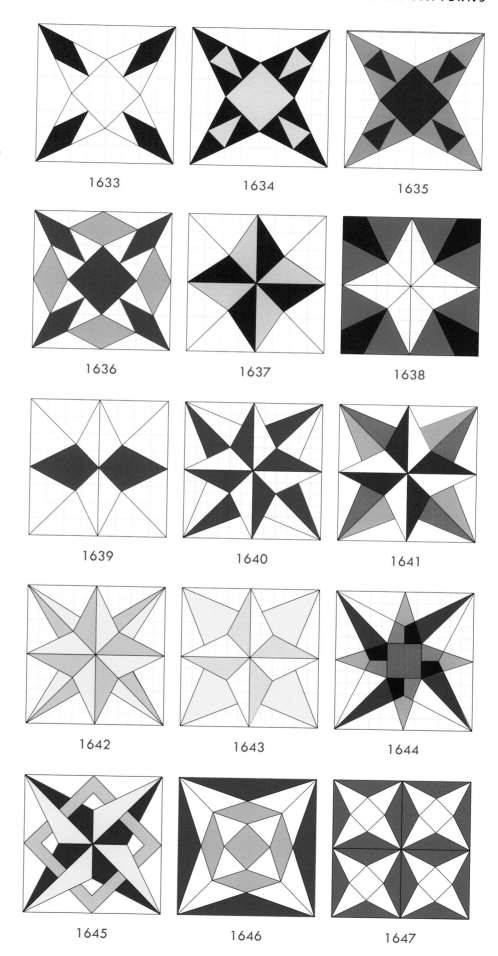

1633   1634   1635

1636   1637   1638

1639   1640   1641

1642   1643   1644

1645   1646   1647

5,500 QUILT BLOCK DESIGNS

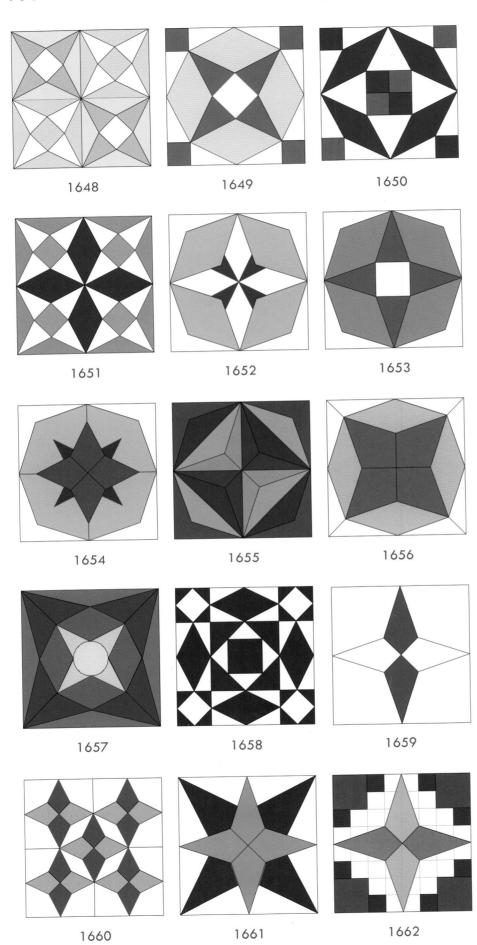

1648

1649

1650

1651

1652

1653

1654

1655

1656

1657

1658

1659

1660

1661

1662

1648 Golden Wedding

1649 Her Sparkling Jewels,
      KCS
      Arrowhead, *WBM*
      The Gem Block, *WBM*
      Idaho, *WBM*
      Sparkling Jewel, *NC*

1650 Jewel, *KCS*

1651 Amethyst
      Crazy Quilt Star, *NC*
      Diamond Star
      North Dakota, *HH*
      The Priscilla, *LAC*
      Quilt Star, *NC*
      Rocky Road to Kansas,
      LAC
      Star and Diamond
      The Windmill
      Windmill Star, *GC*
      World Without End

1652 Unnamed,
      GLB, 1858

1653 Windmill Star, *KCS*

1654 No Name

1655 Diamond Ring

1656 Marathon

1657 Autumn Moon, *RMS,*
      SSQ, 1987

1658 Storm at Sea, *KCS*

1659 The Kite Quilt, *KCS*
      Arkansas Snowflake,
      KCS
      Arkansas Star, *KCS*
      Star Kites, *NC*

1660 Pontiac Star, *CS*

1661 Double Star, *HH*

1662 Steps to the Stars

1663 Indian Hatchets, *LAC*

1664 Robbing Peter to Pay Paul
Triangle of Squares, *NC*

1665 Signatures for Golden Memories, *KCS*
Friendship
Golden Memories
Paths to Piece, *HM*

1666 Kansas Dugout

1667 Robbing Peter to Pay Paul

1668 Friendship Quilt, *KCS*

1669 A Striped Plain Quilt, *KCS*

1670 Road to Tennessee

1671 Thirteen Squares

1672 Pennsylvania Crossroads

1673 Kentucky Chain

1674 Interwoven Puzzle, *1933*

1675 Star and Cross

1676 Night and Day, *NC*
Geometric Illusion
Mosaic #4, *LAC*
White Cross

1677 Pillar to Post

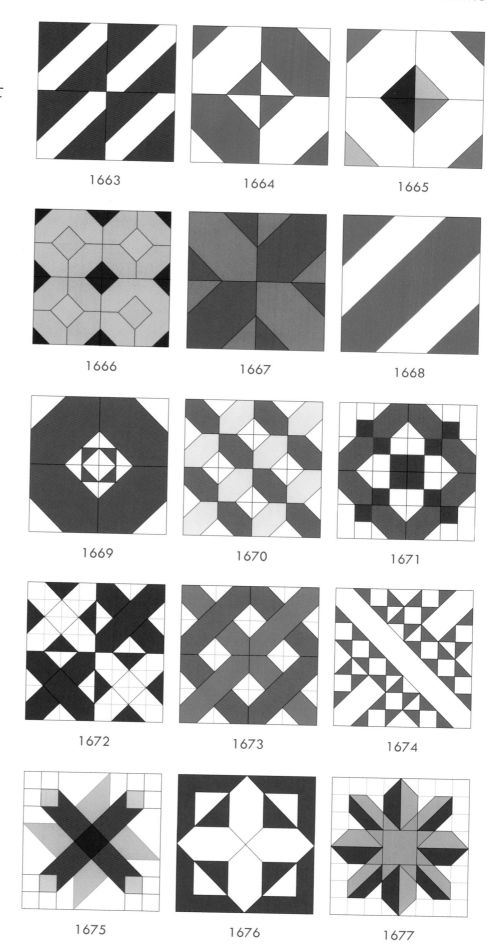

1663   1664   1665

1666   1667   1668

1669   1670   1671

1672   1673   1674

1675   1676   1677

1678

1679

1680

1681

1682

1683

1684

1685

1686

1687

1688

1689

1690

1691

1692

1678 Snowy Morning, *HaM*, *SSQ, 1983*

1679 Devil's Puzzle

1680 Flyfoot

1681 Good Fortune, *CS*
Cross Bars, *NP*

1682 Three Crosses

1683 Gem Block, *WW*
The Road to Paris

1684 Broken Dishes, *NM*, *1918*
The Dewey, *NP*
Double Squares, *LAC*
Jack in the Pulpit, *CS*

1685 Mother's Favorite

1686 The Friendship Quilt

1687 Mosaic #1, *LAC*
Mosaic #3, *NC*

1688 Jericho

1689 Jaywalker, *NC*

1690 Columbia Pinwheel

1691 Name Unknown

1692 Name Unknown

1693 Diadem

1694 Fort Sumter, *NC*

1695 Mosaic #2, *NC*
Mosaic #5, *LAC*
Jack in the Pulpit
Toad in the Puddle

1696 Scotch Plaid, *CaS*
Scotch Squares, *NC*

1697 Four Corner Puzzle, *KCS*

1698 Ella's Star, *QWO,*
1987

1699 Ring Around the Posy

1700 Four Points, *LAC*
Four Point, *HHJ*
Lattice and Square, *NC*

1701 Star and Arrows

1702 Aztec Jewel,
Virginia Outerbacker,
QN

1703 Rock of Ages

1704 Mountain Peak, *KCS*
Cross Stitch, *NC*
Maud's Album Quilt,
NP
Old Italian Design, *FJ*
Snow Block, *NC*
Snowflake, *LAC*

1705 Diamond Ring
My Favorite, *NC*
Old Favorite, *NC*

1706 Home Treasure
Flying X, *NC*

1707 Around the Corner, *NC*

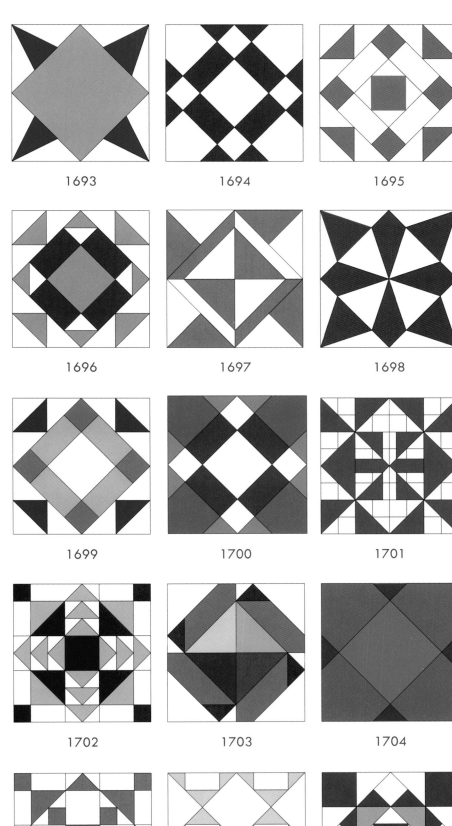

1693 1694 1695

1696 1697 1698

1699 1700 1701

1702 1703 1704

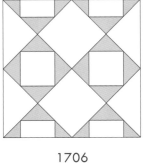

1705 1706 1707

5,500 QUILT BLOCK DESIGNS

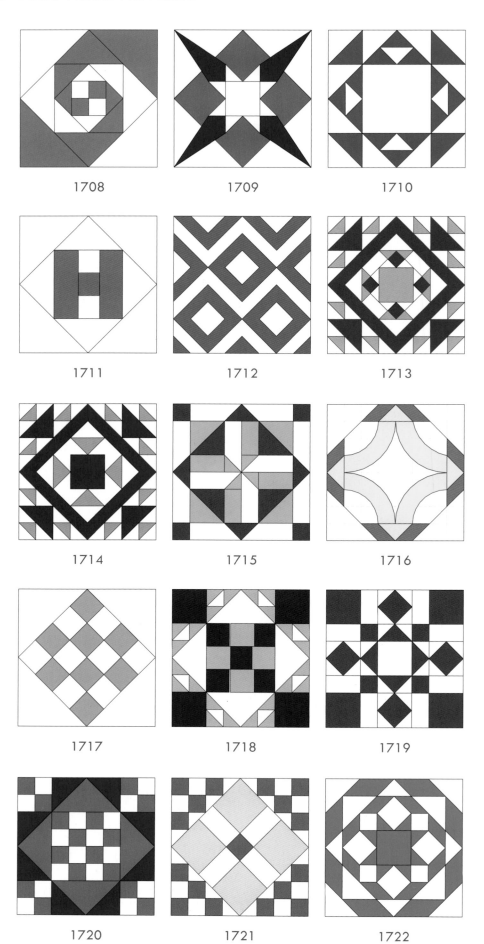

1708   1709   1710

1711   1712   1713

1714   1715   1716

1717   1718   1719

1720   1721   1722

1708   Journey to California, *KCS*

1709   The Album, *KCS*

1710   Grandmother's Favorite, *KCS*

1711   The Gate or H Quilt, *KCS*

1712   Depression, *KCS*

1713   Arrant Redbirds Variation

1714   Arrant Red Birds

1715   Framed Star

1716   Friendship Knot

1717   Coffin Star

1718   Summer's Dream

1719   Temple Court Hull's Victory

1720   Road to California

1721   Pride of Ohio

1722   Star and Chains, *LAC* Rolling Star Ring Around the Star

1723 Coxcomb, *NC*

1724 Country Path

1725 Twisted Ribbons, *QN, 1993*

1726 Crazy Anne Pinwheel, *FJ*

1727 Wings of Eagles

1728 Pennsylvania

1729 Interlocking Squares, *KCS*

1730 Crazy Loons

1731 Navajo

1732 Banded Triangle, *MLM, SSQ, 1983*

1733 Bows and Paper, *HaM, SSQ, 1983*

1734 Spring Has Come

1735 Expanding Universe, *MM*

1736 Porto Rico

1737 Star Premo

1723

1724

1725

1726

1727

1728

1729

1730

1731

1732

1733

1734

1735

1736

1737

5,500 QUILT BLOCK DESIGNS

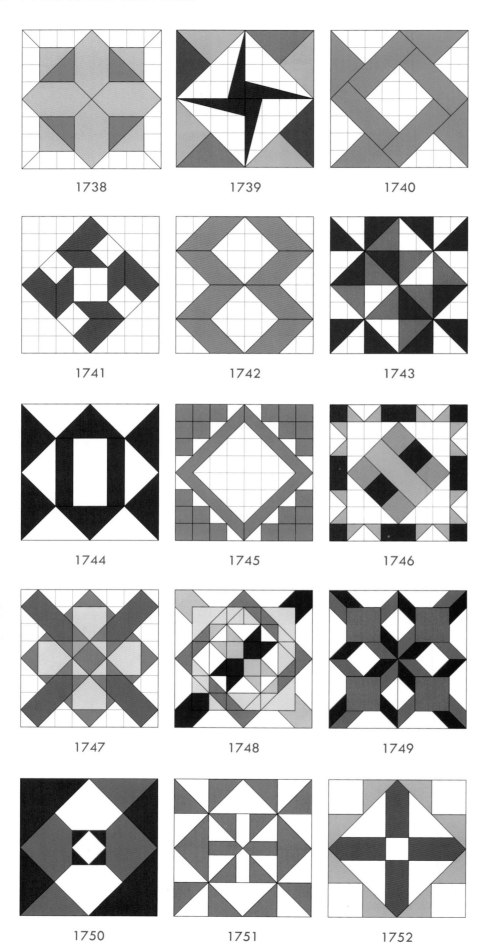

1738   1739   1740

1741   1742   1743

1744   1745   1746

1747   1748   1749

1750   1751   1752

1738   Empire Cross

1739   Waste Not Variation

1740   Water Wheel

1741   Kansas Beauty, *CS*

1742   John's Original Quilt Block

1743   Milly's Favorite

1744   Broken Path

1745   Memory Block, *LAC*
Album, *MD*

1746   Lily

1747   Shaded Crossroad

1748   Nancy's Fancy

1749   West Virginia, *HH*

1750   Square Block, *QW, 1982*

1751   Belle of West Virginia, *HH*
Frankfort, *HH*

1752   Cross Within Cross, *NP*
Grandmother's Choice
French Patchwork

1753 Grandmother's Cross

1754 Far Horizons

1755 Good Enough, *HH*

1756 Cats and Mice

1757 Crazy Loons

1758 Our Next President
 Quilt
 President's Choice

1759 Twist Patchwork

1760 Five Patch Star, *OCS*

1761 Star Points, *FJ*

1762 Duck and Ducklings

1763 Garden Patch

1764 Court House Lawn, *NC*

1765 Light and Shadows,
 KCS

1766 Casement Window,
 KCS

1767 The Red Cross Quilt,
 KCS
 Washington Sidewalk

1753 1754 1755
1756 1757 1758
1759 1760 1761
1762 1763 1764
1765 1766 1767

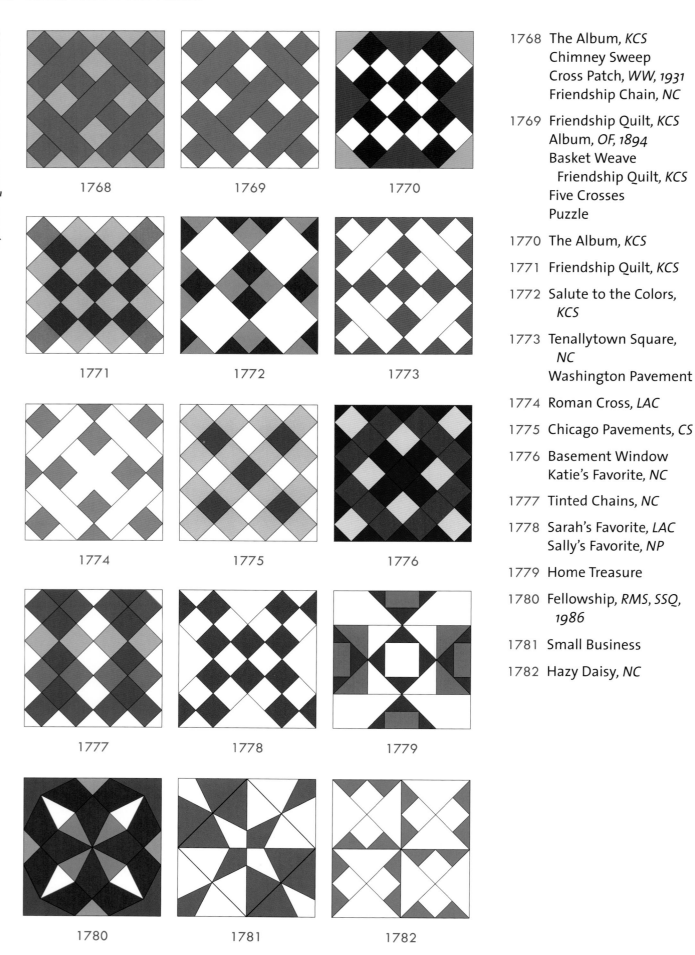

1768 | 1769 | 1770

1771 | 1772 | 1773

1774 | 1775 | 1776

1777 | 1778 | 1779

1780 | 1781 | 1782

1768 The Album, *KCS*
  Chimney Sweep
  Cross Patch, *WW, 1931*
  Friendship Chain, *NC*

1769 Friendship Quilt, *KCS*
  Album, *OF, 1894*
  Basket Weave
    Friendship Quilt, *KCS*
  Five Crosses
  Puzzle

1770 The Album, *KCS*

1771 Friendship Quilt, *KCS*

1772 Salute to the Colors, *KCS*

1773 Tenallytown Square, *NC*
  Washington Pavement

1774 Roman Cross, *LAC*

1775 Chicago Pavements, *CS*

1776 Basement Window
  Katie's Favorite, *NC*

1777 Tinted Chains, *NC*

1778 Sarah's Favorite, *LAC*
  Sally's Favorite, *NP*

1779 Home Treasure

1780 Fellowship, *RMS, SSQ, 1986*

1781 Small Business

1782 Hazy Daisy, *NC*

1783 Spindles and Stripes, *KCS*

1784 Beautiful Star, *LAC*
Arrow Star

1785 Oriental Star, *NC*
Dervish Star, *GD*
Star of the Orient, *NC*

1786 Exploding Star

1787 Home Again, *FJ*

1788 Concord

1789 Wandering Flower, *KCS*

1790 Shooting Star, *MM*

1791 Compass Kaleidoscope

1792 Mill and Stars, *NC*

1793 Star, *OCS*
Star of the East, *OCS*

1794 Four Seasons, *RMS, SSQ*

1795 Seminole Star

1796 Winding Walk

1797 Fox Chase
Biloxi
Winding Walk

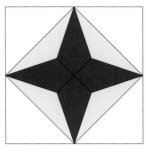
1783

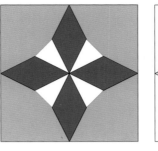
1784

1785

1786

1787

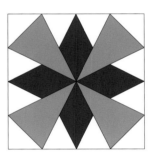
1788

1789

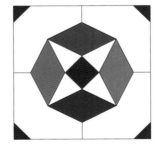
1790

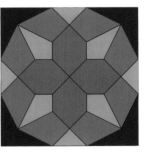
1791

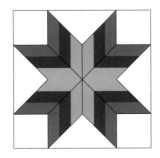
1792

1793

1794

1795

1796

1797

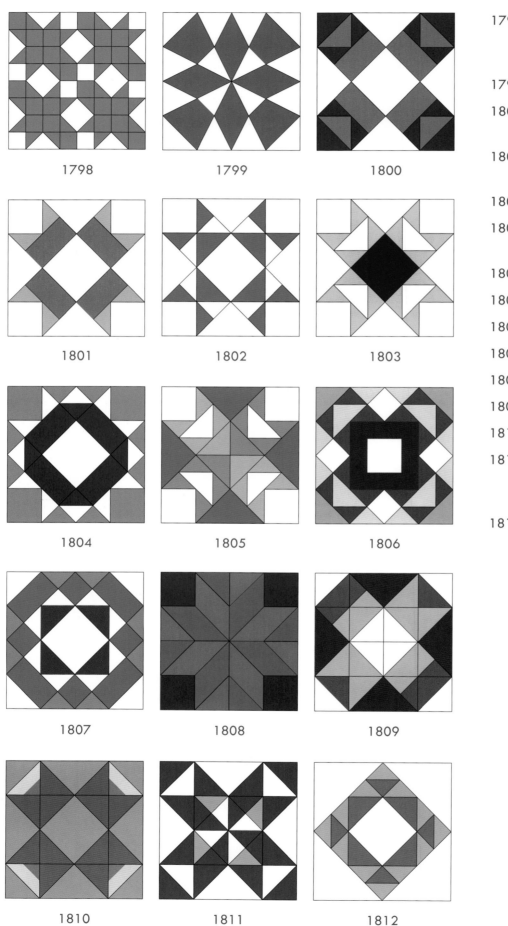

1798 Cubes and Tile, *NC*
Cube Lattice, *LAC*
Idle Moments, *NC*

1799 Concord

1800 Aunt Nancy's Favorite, *CS*

1801 Autograph Quilt Block, *CS*

1802 Missouri Star, *NC*

1803 Northumberland Star
Eight Pointed Star, *NC*

1804 Memory Blocks, *NC*

1805 Wild Geese

1806 Colonial Garden, *PF*

1807 Tombstone Quilt, *NC*

1808 Pinwheel, *1899*

1809 Open Window

1810 Diamond Stripe

1811 Stars and Pinwheels
Stars and Squares, *LAC*
Rising Star

1812 Memory Wreath
The Wedding Ring

1813 Virginia Reel
Monkey Wrench
Indiana Puzzle
Snail's Trail

1814 Wheel of Fortune

1815 Jig Jog Puzzle

1816 Broken Band, *1920*

1817 Pineapple Variation

1818 Star Light
Perpetual Motion, *NC,*
1936

1819 Old Poinsettia Block
Mosaic #18, *LAC*
Spinning Stars

1820 Pinwheel Star

1821 Eight Hands Around,
LAC

1822 Stockyard's Star for
Nebraska

1823 Free Trade Block
Coronation, *NP*
Free Trade Patch

1824 Odd Fellows Chain, *LAC*
Odd Fellow's March,
1918
Old Maid's Ramble
San Diego, *NP*

1825 White Hemstitch, *GD*

1826 Cross and Square, *NC*
Home Treasure, *OCS*

1827 Crown of Thorns, *NP*

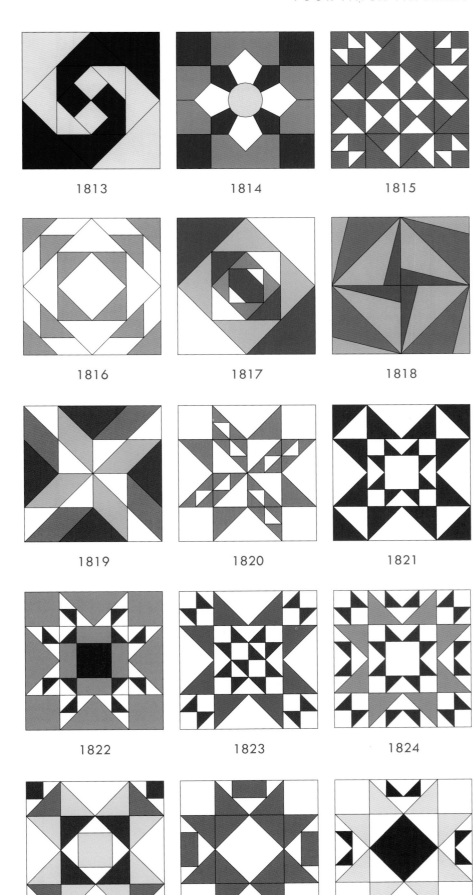

1813   1814   1815

1816   1817   1818

1819   1820   1821

1822   1823   1824

1825   1826   1827

1828
1829
1830

1831
1832
1833

1834
1835
1836

1837
1838
1839

1840
1841
1842

1828 Susannah, *NP*

1829 Star of Bethlehem

1830 No Name, *LCPQ*

1831 Illinois Corn & Beans,
    SSQ, 1986

1832 Cross on Cross

1833 Checkerboard Star, *MM*

1834 Diamond Star

1835 King's Star

1836 White Mountain Star,
    Gloria Cosgrove,
    SSQ

1837 Lucky Pieces, *NP*

1838 Blueberry Patch

1839 Rambler, *KCS*
    Blossom Time
    Spring Beauty, *KCS*
    I Excel
    IXL, *KCS*
    Old Maid's Ramble
     (2 colors), *LAC*

1840 Railroad Crossing

1841 Friendship Quilt

1842 Pyramids, *NC*

1843 Indian Trails, *KCS*
    Bear's Paw, *LAC*
    Forest
    Irish Puzzle
    North Wind
    Rambling Road
    Winding Walk

1844 Kansas Troubles, *LAC*
    Delectable Mountains
    Grand Right and Left, *FJ*

1845 Barrister's Block, *LAC*
 Lawyer's Puzzle
 The Saw, *PP*

1846 The Lost Ship
 Delectable
  Appalachians, *QT*
 Rocky Glen

1847 New Barrister's Block,
 NC

1848 World's Fair Puzzle, *LAC*

1849 Wild Goose Chase

1850 Square Deal, *KCS*

1851 Sunshine, *LAC*

1852 Roll on Columbia

1853 Old Maid's Puzzle, *FJ*

1854 Merry-Go-Round, *KCS*
 Eternal Triangle

1855 An Ocean Wave of
  Many Prints, *KCS*
 Ocean Wave
 Octagon, *CoM*
 Odd Fellows Quilt
 Odds and Ends, *CoM*
 Waves of the Ocean,
  HH

1856 Bright Stars, *NC*

1857 Devil's Claws, *LAC*
 Bright Stars, *NC*
 Corner Star
 Cross Plains, *CS*
 The Crowfoot, *MD*
 Des Moines, *HH*
 Idaho Beauty, *HH*

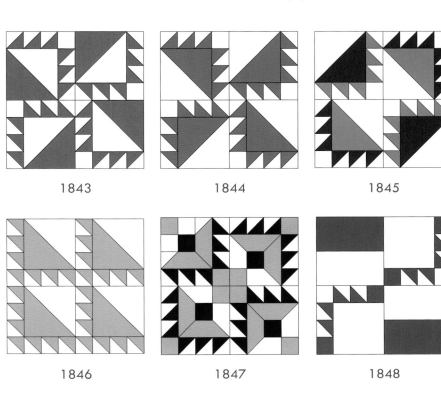

1843 1844 1845

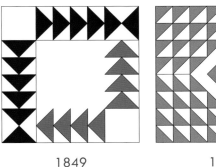
1846

1847 1848

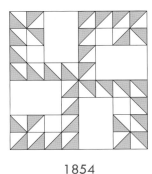
1849 1850 1851

1852 1853 1854

1855 1856 1857

1858

1859

1860

1861

1862

1863

1864

1865

1866

1867

1868

1869

1870

1871

1872

1858 Cinderella, *TQr, 1991*

1859 Windmill

1860 Jagged Edge

1861 Indian Hatchet

1862 Century Grandmother's Pinwheel

1863 Blindman's Fancy, *LAC*

1864 Indian Hatchet

1865 Delectable Mountains

1866 Sawtooth Puzzle

1867 Mineral Wells, *NP*

1868 Sugar Bowl Block

1869 Lily Quilt Pattern, *LAC* Des Moines, *HH* Botch Handle

1870 Parasol

1871 Name Unknown

1872 Name Unknown

1873 The Bride's Bouquet

1874 Nosegay

1875 Shooting Star

1876 Single Lily

1877 Four Buds, *PF*

1878 Indian Patch, *FJ*

1879 Starry Path

1880 Utah Star

1881 Breeches Quilt, *WBM, 1939*
   Britches Quilt, *AMS*
   Dutchman's Breeches
   Dutchman's Puzzle, *NC*
   Mississippi
   Mississippi Daisy, *HH*

1882 Little Boy's Breeches, *KCS*
   Little Boy's Britches, *KCS*

1883 Roman Stripe
   Rainbow Block
   Shadow Quilt
   Shadows

1884 Fun Patch
   Houndstooth
   Houndstooth Scrap Patch
   Scrap Bag
   Scrap Patch

1885 Tallahassee Block

1886 Indian Chief

1887 Cowboy Star, *KCS*
   Arkansas Traveler
   Teddy's Choice, *LAC*
   Travel Star

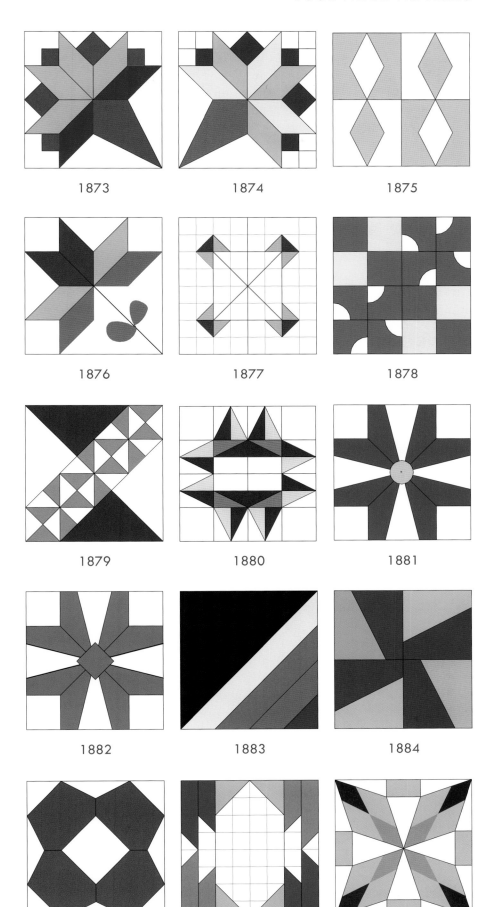

1873   1874   1875

1876   1877   1878

1879   1880   1881

1882   1883   1884

1885   1886   1887

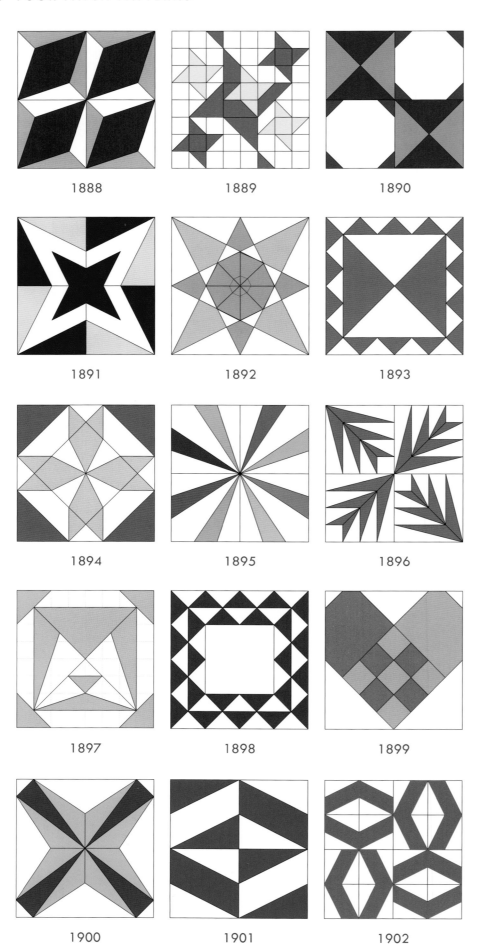

1888   1889   1890

1891   1892   1893

1894   1895   1896

1897   1898   1899

1900   1901   1902

1888 Blue Boutonnieres

1889 Stars Galore, *Clara Buschschulte, QN*

1890 Buttons and Bows

1891 Stars and Stripes

1892 Southern Star

1893 Aunt Mary's Double Irish Chain, *CS*

1894 Aimee's Choice

1895 Endless Chain, *LW* Crazy Star, *GD*

1896 Palm Leaf Hosannah

1897 Mystic Emblem

1898 Our Village Green, *1935*

1899 Woven Heart

1900 Wandering Path

1901 Left and Right, *NC, 1935* Chevron

1902 Beg and Borrow, *NC*

1903 Ocean Wave, *OF*

1904 Hummingbird
Dramatic Patch, *OCS*
Rock Garden

1905 Fairy Star, *NC*

1906 Double Z, *NC*

1907 Calypso, *Vickie Loh*

1908 Arrowhead
Laurel Wreath
Michigan Beauty
Star of Many Points

1909 Kansas Star

1910 Maltese Cross, *NP*

1911 Black Beauty, *NC*
Blackford's Beauty, *LAC*
The Hunt, *FJ*
Mrs. Smith's Favorite,
NCS, 1930
Star and Stripe, *NC*
Stepping Stones, *KCS*

1912 Ruby Roads, *NC*

1913 Evening Star

1914 Jupiter Star

1915 The Spider Web, *KCS*

1916 Morning Star
Kaleidoscope Quilt

1917 A Spider Web Gone
Awry
North Carolina Star

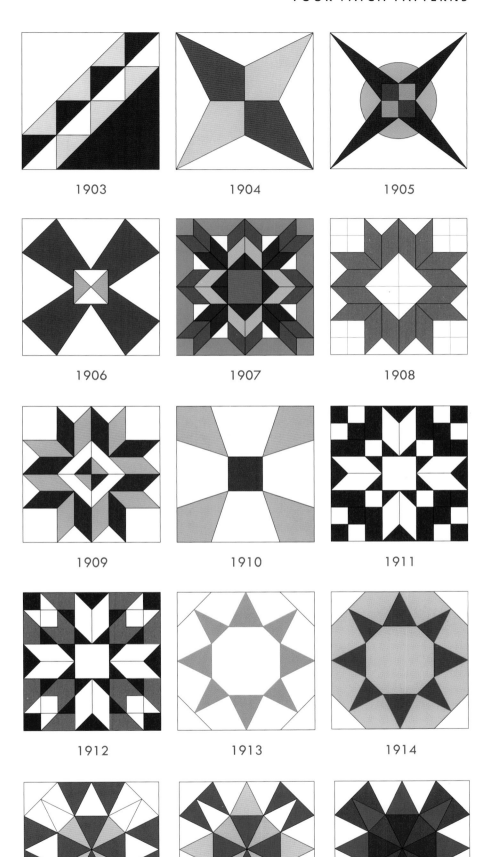

1903   1904   1905

1906   1907   1908

1909   1910   1911

1912   1913   1914

1915   1916   1917

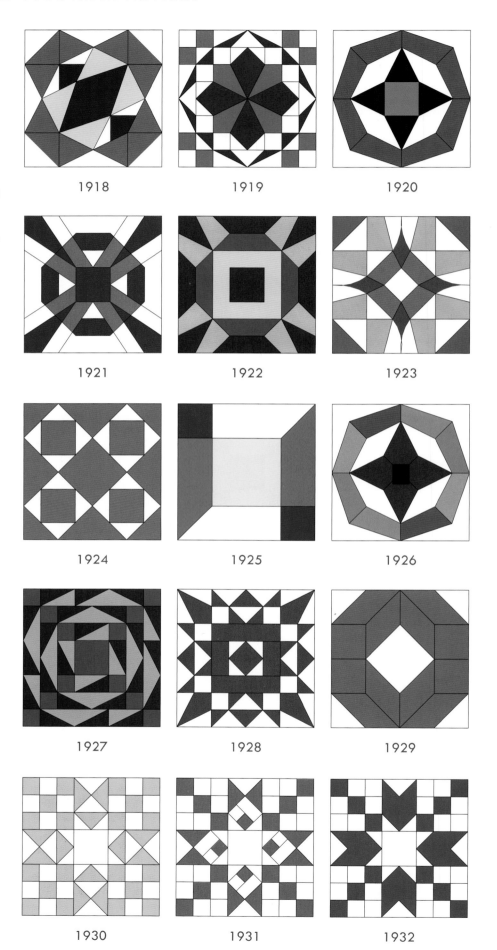

1918   Dove in the Window

1919   Little Giant

1920   A Coverlet in Jewel Tones, *KCS*

1921   True Lover's Knot

1922   Satellite

1923   Dogwood, *LW*

1924   Pride of Holland, *FJ*

1925   Unnamed, *OCS*

1926   Star & Crown

1927   Windy City, *QN*

1928   Constellation

1929   Optical Illusion

1930   Winged Nine Patch, *KCS*

1931   Arrowhead

1932   Good Cheer Stepping Stones

1933 Mountain Meadows

1934 Albany

1935 Black Diamond Quilt Block

1936 Baton Rouge Quilt Block
Good Friends

1937 Summer Star, *KCS*

1938 Arrow Points, *NP*

1939 Arrowhead, *KCS*
The Arrowhead Quilt, *HAS*

1940 Arrowheads

1941 Friendship Star, *OCS*

1942 West Virginia

1943 Sunburst

1944 Springfield, *HH*
Springfield Patch, *LAC*

1945 No Name Star

1946 Peaceful Hours

1947 Diamond Star
Eight Diamonds and a Star, *AMS*
Oriental Star, *NC*

1933   1934   1935

1936   1937   1938

1939   1940   1941

1942   1943   1944

1945   1946   1947

1948 1949 1950

1951 1952 1953

1954 1955 1956

1957 1958 1959

1960 1961 1962

1948 The Name Is Hesper, *KCS*

1949 Album Flower

1950 Goshen Star, *CS*

1951 Watermill

1952 Gem Star, *QM, 1993*

1953 Reminiscences, *HaM, SSQ, 1983*

1954 Texas Star

1955 Double Star

1956 State of South Carolina Cross and Square

1957 Sister Mary's Star

1958 World's Pride Quilt Block

1959 Jane's Favorite

1960 Olympia

1961 Dervish Star

1962 1904 Star

1963 Jacob's Ladder
New Double Four
Patch

1964 State House, *NC*
Double Four Patch, *HHJ*
New Four Patch, *1914*

1965 Missouri Windmills,
QN

1966 Hither and Yon
Spool

1967 Grandmother's Prize
Puzzle
Housewife

1968 Acorns

1969 Specialty Square, *RMS*,
SSQ, 1987

1970 Memory Chain, *FJ*

1971 Chain Links Quilt, *NC*

1972 Flying Checkers

1973 Good Luck Token

1974 Tulip Twirl, *QM, 1992*

1975 Salt Lake City

1976 No Name

1977 Old Maid's Ramble,
LAC
Double Triangle

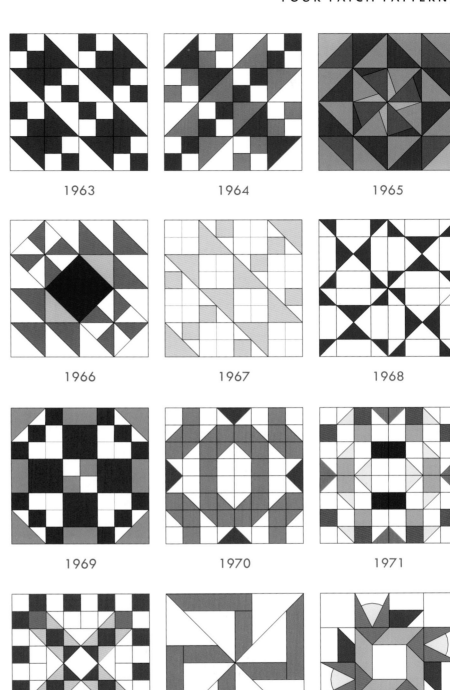

1963   1964   1965

1966   1967   1968

1969   1970   1971

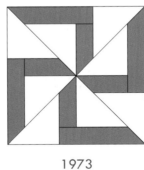

1972   1973   1974

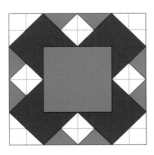
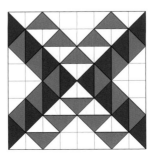

1975   1976   1977

5,500 QUILT BLOCK DESIGNS

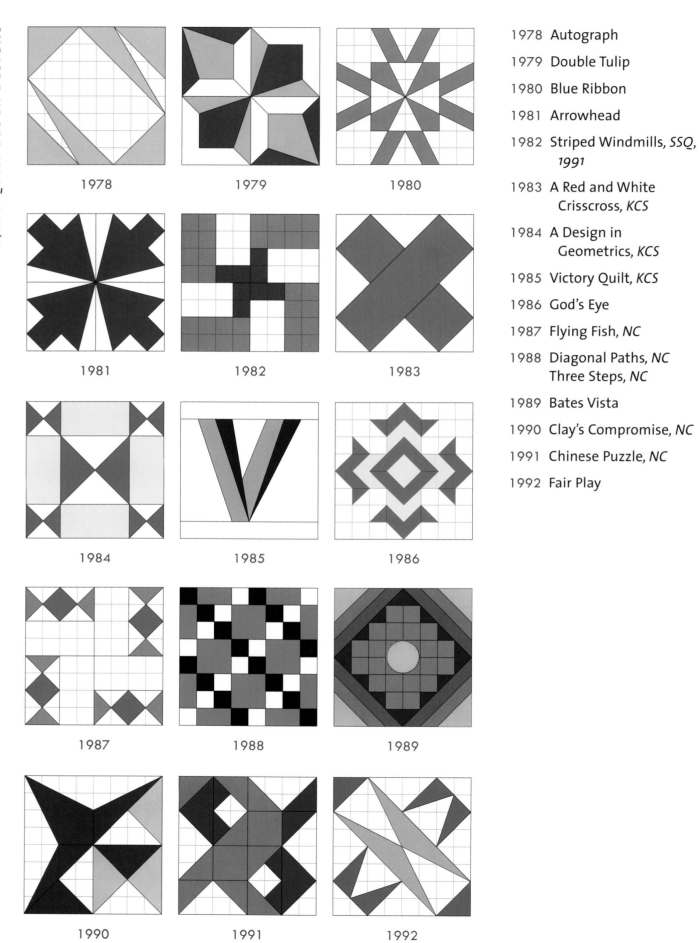

1978 Autograph

1979 Double Tulip

1980 Blue Ribbon

1981 Arrowhead

1982 Striped Windmills, *SSQ, 1991*

1983 A Red and White Crisscross, *KCS*

1984 A Design in Geometrics, *KCS*

1985 Victory Quilt, *KCS*

1986 God's Eye

1987 Flying Fish, *NC*

1988 Diagonal Paths, *NC* Three Steps, *NC*

1989 Bates Vista

1990 Clay's Compromise, *NC*

1991 Chinese Puzzle, *NC*

1992 Fair Play

1993 Whirligig
     Farmers' Wife
     Double Pinwheel, *NC*

1994 Whirligig

1995 Morning Star

1996 King's Cross
     Kaleidoscope
     Octagons, *NP*
     Semi-Octagon, *HHJ*
     Will o the Wisp, *FJ*
     Windmill, *KCS*

1997 Double Pinwheel

1998 Starburst, *Arleen Boyd*

1999 Cupid's Arrowpoint

2000 Mary's Squares

2001 Electric Fan

2002 Sister Nan's Cross

2003 Wandering Jew

2004 Spool and Bobbin, *NC,*
     1936

2005 Reverse X, *GC*

2006 Missouri Windmills

2007 Harvest Home

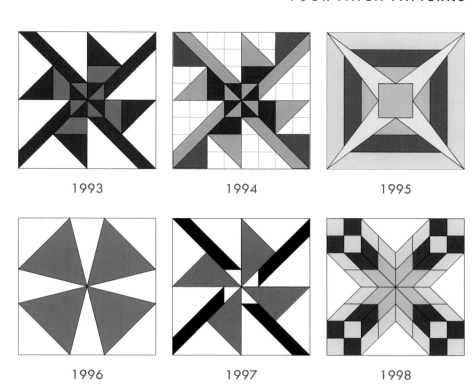

1993   1994   1995

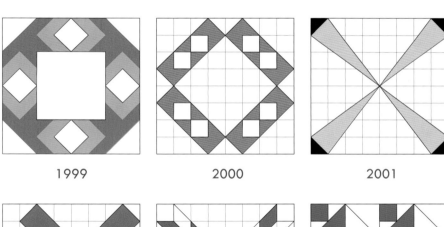

1996   1997   1998

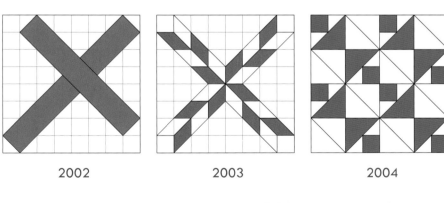

1999   2000   2001

2002   2003   2004

2005   2006   2007

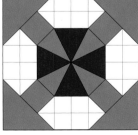

5,500 QUILT BLOCK DESIGNS

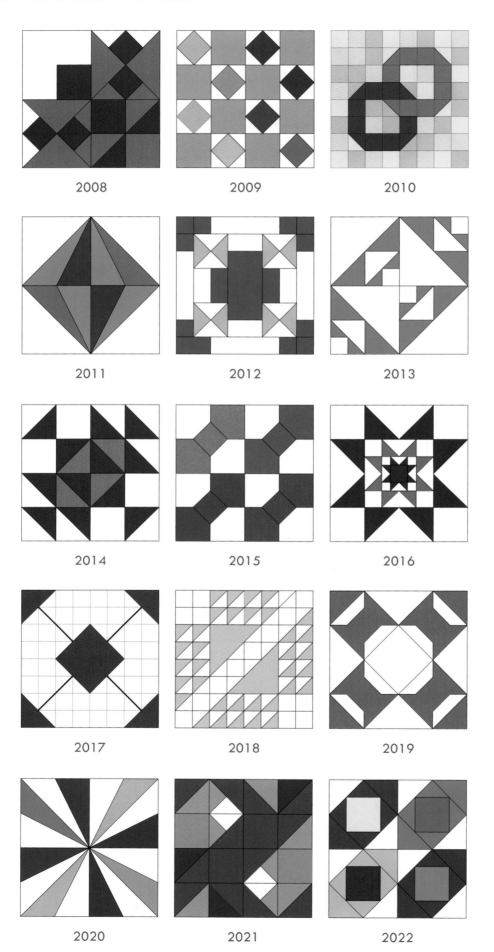

2008 2009 2010

2011 2012 2013

2014 2015 2016

2017 2018 2019

2020 2021 2022

2008 Floral Centerpiece

2009 Four Patch Scrap

2010 Wedding Rings

2011 Chinese Lanterns, *NC*

2012 Scottish Cross, *KCS*

2013 Blacks and Whites, *NC*

2014 Flying Dutchman, *NC*

2015 Necktie, *NC*

2016 Stars in a Star

2017 Spider Web

2018 Bismarck
Primrose Path, *NP*

2019 The Secret Drawer, *KCS*
Arkansas Traveler
Spools

2020 Thrifty Wife, *KCS*

2021 Block of Many
Triangles, *KCS*

2022 This and That, *KCS*

2023

2024

2025

2026

2027

2028

2029

2030

2031

2032

2033

2034

2035

2036

2037

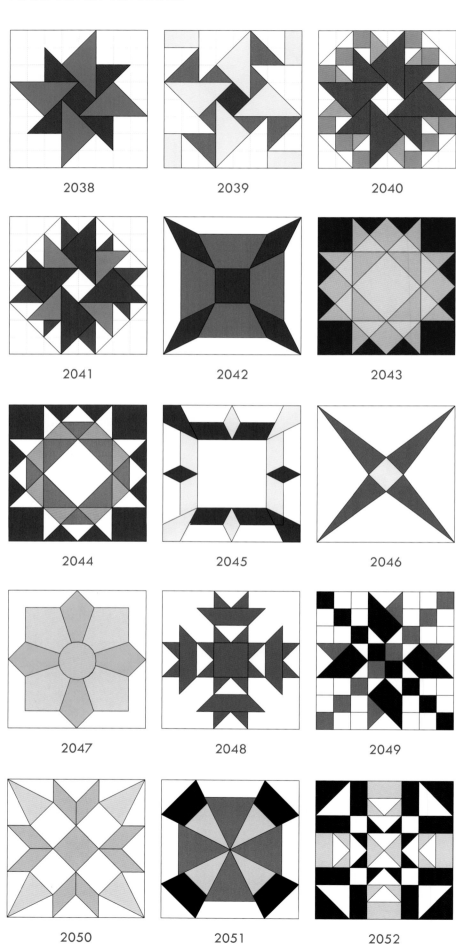

2038

2039

2040

2041

2042

2043

2044

2045

2046

2047

2048

2049

2050

2051

2052

2038 Double Windmill, *NC*

2039 Whirligig, *NC*

2040 Peony and Forget Me Nots, *NC*

2041 Double Aster, *NC*

2042 Square and Diamonds, *KCS*

2043 Square and Triangles, *KCS*

2044 Georgetown Puzzle, *NC*
Memory Fruit, *NC*

2045 A Frame with Diamonds, *KCS*

2046 Hobby Nook, *KCS*

2047 Eight Point Snowflake, *KCS*

2048 Cross and Star

2049 Arrowheads

2050 Prairie Queen

2051 Denver, *HH*
Amazing Windmill, *NC*
Autumn Leaves
Boston Pavement
Farmer's Wife
Merry-Go-Round, *NC*
Mystic Maze, *NC*
Spider Web

2052 Tracks in the Snow, *HaM, SSQ, 1983*

2053 Northern Lights, *NC*

2054 End of Day

2055 Bowtie in Pink and White, *KCS*

2056 Midget Necktie, *KCS*

2057 The World Fair Quilt, *KCS*

2058 A Friendship Block in Diamonds, *KCS*

2059 Thousand Stars Quilt, *KCS*

2060 Parquetry for a Quilt Block, *KCS*

2061 The Windmill

2062 Flying Kite, *KCS* Pinwheel, *GC*

2063 Kaleidoscope, *NP*

2064 Plaited Block, *NC*

2065 Autumn Stars, *PF* Golden Chains, *NC*

2066 John's Pinwheel

2067 Path Through the Woods, *CaS* Linton Pathway

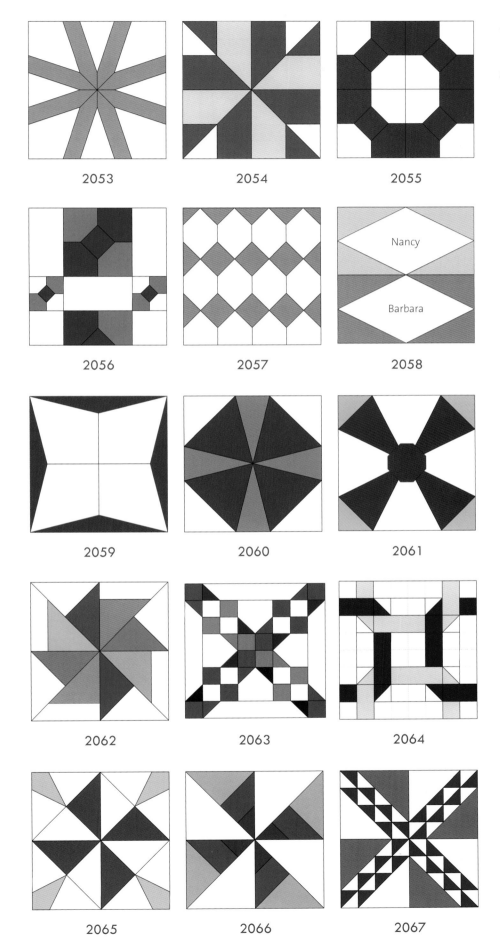

2053   2054   2055

2056   2057   2058

2059   2060   2061

2062   2063   2064

2065   2066   2067

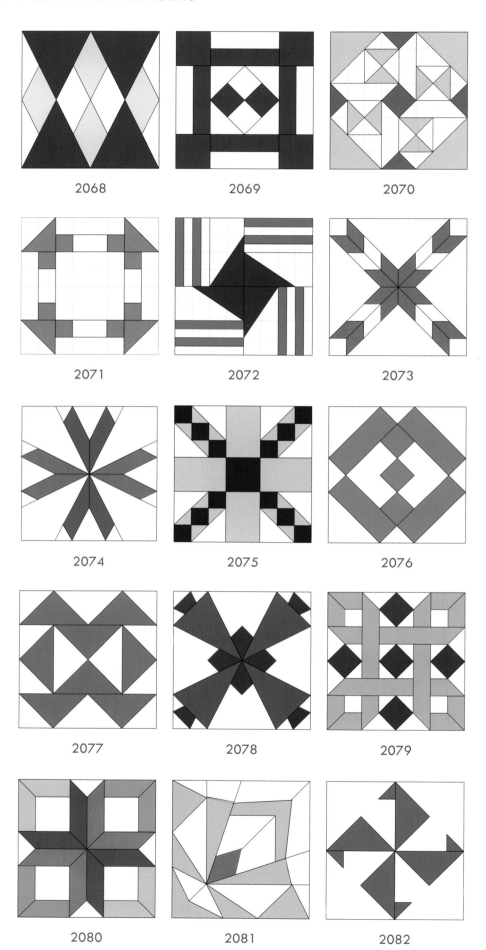

2068

2069

2070

2071

2072

2073

2074

2075

2076

2077

2078

2079

2080

2081

2082

2068 Four Diamonds

2069 Coxey's Camp, *LAC*
Coxey's Army, *NC*

2070 Spinning Hour Glass,
NC

2071 Ruins of Jericho, *NC*

2072 The Old Stars and
Stripes, *1991*

2073 The Winding Blade

2074 The V Block

2075 Buffalo Ridge, *NC*
Country Roads, *QW*,
1979
Grandmother's Fancy,
CoM

2076 Board Meeting

2077 No Name Available

2078 Pennsylvania Tree, *HH*

2079 Diamond Knot, *NC*

2080 Box Quilt, *NP*

2081 Queen's Treasure, *OCS*

2082 Lindy's Plane

2083 Stuffed Stockings, *HaM, SSQ, 1983*

2084 Jet Stream

2085 Flying Kites, *MLM, SSQ, 1982*

2086 Tilted Triangles

2087 Nosegay, *NC*
Stepping Stones, *KCS*

2088 Spider Web, *KCS*

2089 Vermont, *NP*

2090 Choices, *MM*

2091 Brickwork

2092 Pineapples

2093 Stepping Stones, *NP*
Road to California, *LAC*
Crossroads, *NCS, 1938*

2094 Odd Fellow's Cross

2095 Railroad

2096 Garden Mosaic

2097 Bowbells, *NC*

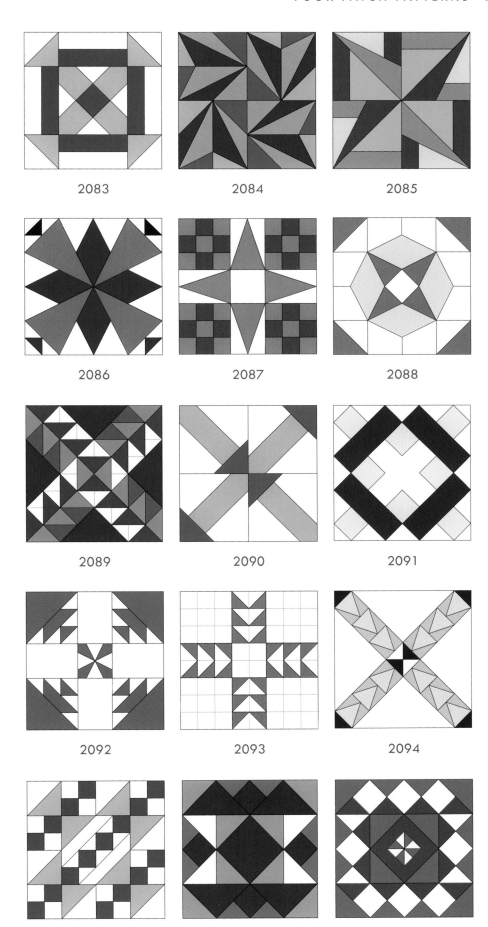

2083   2084   2085

2086   2087   2088

2089   2090   2091

2092   2093   2094

2095   2096   2097

2098

2099

2100

2101

2102

2103

2104

2105

2106

2107

2108

2109

2110

2111

2112

2098 Pine Burr Block

2099 Tulips, *AMS*

2100 Missouri Star

2101 Mississippi Star, *AK*

2102 Blowing in the Wind

2103 Wheel of Fortune

2104 Unnamed, *1880*

2105 Shady Pine

2106 World's Fair

2107 Flyfoot

2108 King's Cross

2109 Arrow Crown

2110 Flowering Cross

2111 Divided Cross

2112 Gothic Pattern

2113 Lena's Choice

2114 Fields and Fences, *QM, 1993*

2115 Flower Bed

2116 Glitter, Glitter

2117 Monterey

2118 Green Mountain Star
Aunt Mary's Star

2119 Crossword Puzzle

2120 Fluffy Patches, *SSQ, 1986*

2121 Fantasy World,
MLM, SSQ, 1986

2122 Starry Cross

2123 Alpha

2124 Table for Four, *NP*

2125 Watermill, *GC*

2126 Colombian Puzzle

2127 Double Square

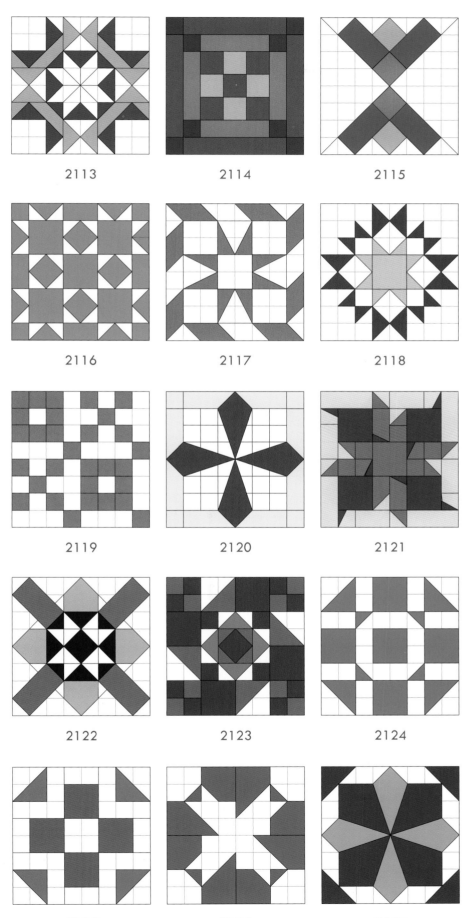

2113

2114

2115

2116

2117

2118

2119

2120

2121

2122

2123

2124

2125

2126

2127

2128	2129	2130
2131	2132	2133
2134	2135	2136
2137	2138	2139
2140	2141	2142

2128 Farmer's Fields

2129 Harbor View

2130 Alaska, *HH*

2131 Crow's Foot, *LAC*
　　　Arrowheads, *NP*

2132 Signs of Spring, *FJ*

2133 Triple Link Chain, *NC*

2134 Depression, *KCS*

2135 Name Unknown

2136 Mosaic #2, *LAC*

2137 Square on Square, *NP*
　　　Scrap, *CS*

2138 Broken Crystals

2139 Triangles and Squares

2140 Design for Pariotism,
　　　KCS

2141 Square Diamond

2142 Fox and Geese

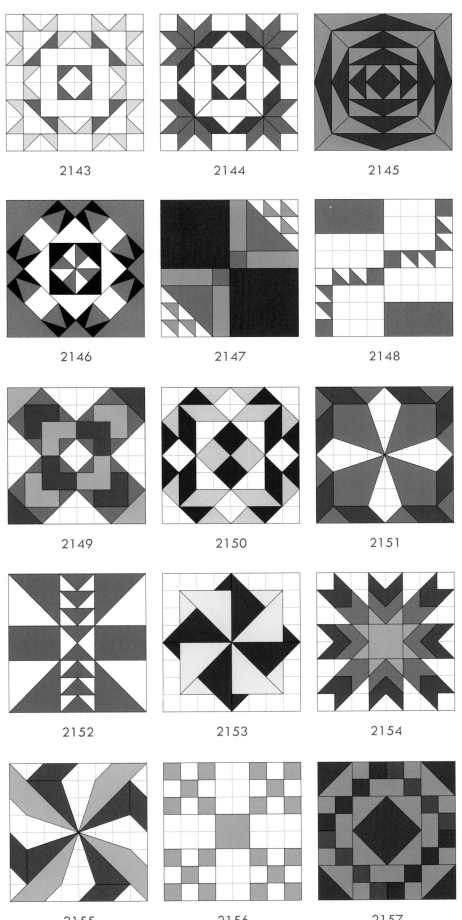

2143

2144

2145

2146

2147

2148

2149

2150

2151

2152

2153

2154

2155

2156

2157

5,500 QUILT BLOCK DESIGNS

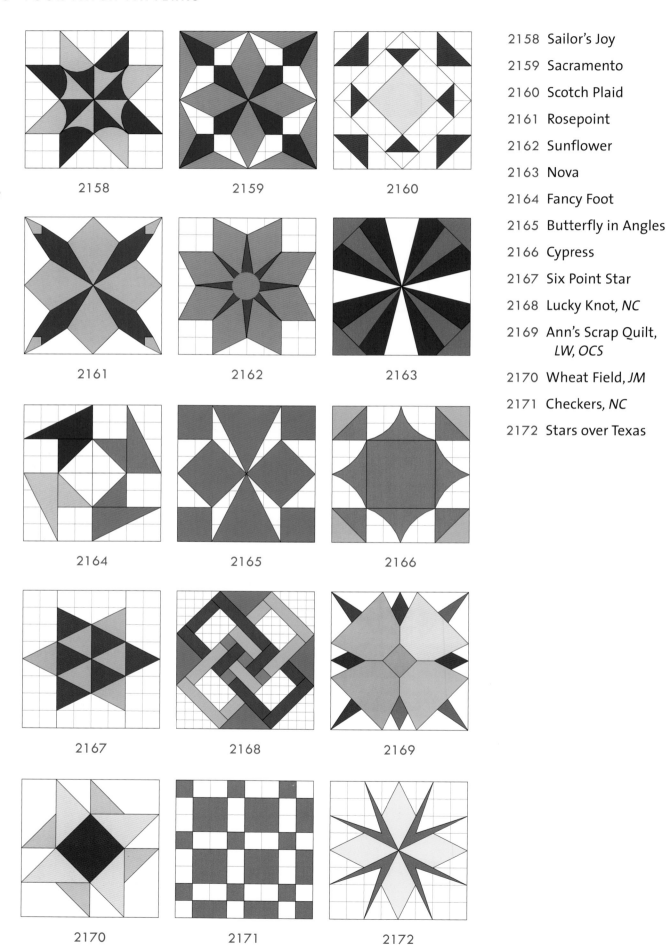

2158   2159   2160

2161   2162   2163

2164   2165   2166

2167   2168   2169

2170   2171   2172

2158   Sailor's Joy

2159   Sacramento

2160   Scotch Plaid

2161   Rosepoint

2162   Sunflower

2163   Nova

2164   Fancy Foot

2165   Butterfly in Angles

2166   Cypress

2167   Six Point Star

2168   Lucky Knot, *NC*

2169   Ann's Scrap Quilt, *LW, OCS*

2170   Wheat Field, *JM*

2171   Checkers, *NC*

2172   Stars over Texas

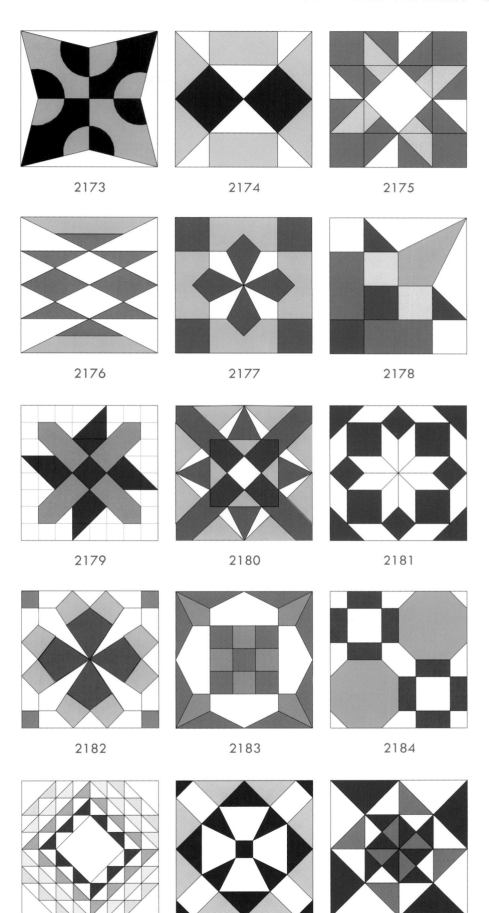

2173

2174

2175

2176

2177

2178

2179

2180

2181

2182

2183

2184

2185

2186

2187

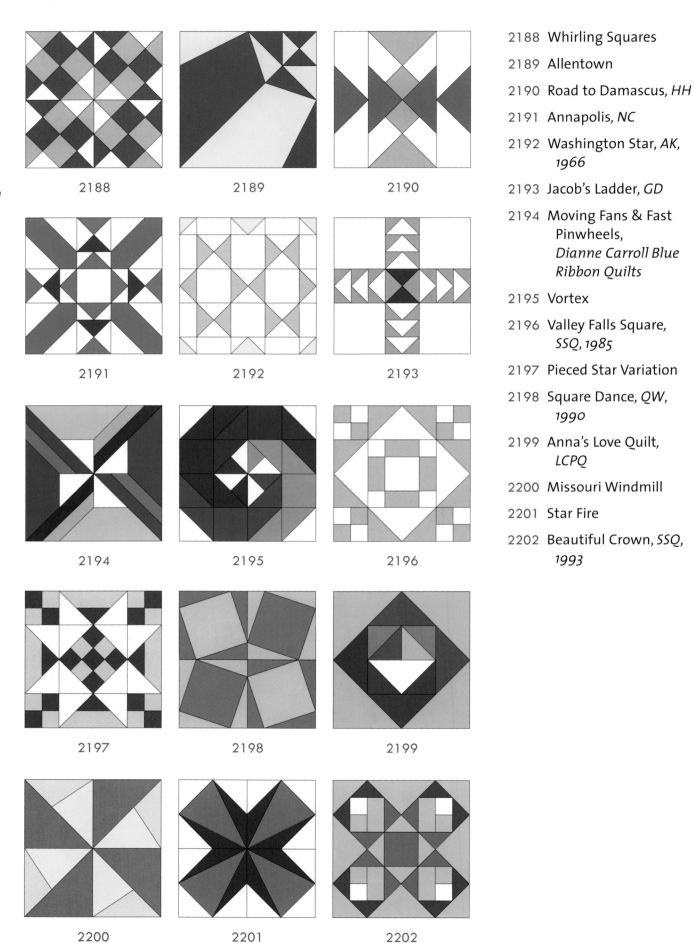

2188 Whirling Squares

2189 Allentown

2190 Road to Damascus, *HH*

2191 Annapolis, *NC*

2192 Washington Star, *AK*, *1966*

2193 Jacob's Ladder, *GD*

2194 Moving Fans & Fast Pinwheels, *Dianne Carroll Blue Ribbon Quilts*

2195 Vortex

2196 Valley Falls Square, *SSQ, 1985*

2197 Pieced Star Variation

2198 Square Dance, *QW, 1990*

2199 Anna's Love Quilt, *LCPQ*

2200 Missouri Windmill

2201 Star Fire

2202 Beautiful Crown, *SSQ, 1993*

2188   2189   2190

2191   2192   2193

2194   2195   2196

2197   2198   2199

2200   2201   2202

2203 Cat's Eye, *QW, 1988*

2204 Stars and Squares, *KCS*
　　 Rising Star

2205 Rising Star Block

2206 Eight Hands Around,
　　 LAC

2207 Lone Star

2208 Primrose Path

2209 Calico Bouquet

2210 Mayflower

2211 Wild Waves

2212 Turkey Giblets, *NC*

2213 Blue Fields Variation,
　　 LCPQ

2214 V-Block, *LAC*
　　 Victory Quilt
　　 Churchill Block

2215 Grandmother's Own

2216 Inspiration

2217 Columbia Puzzle

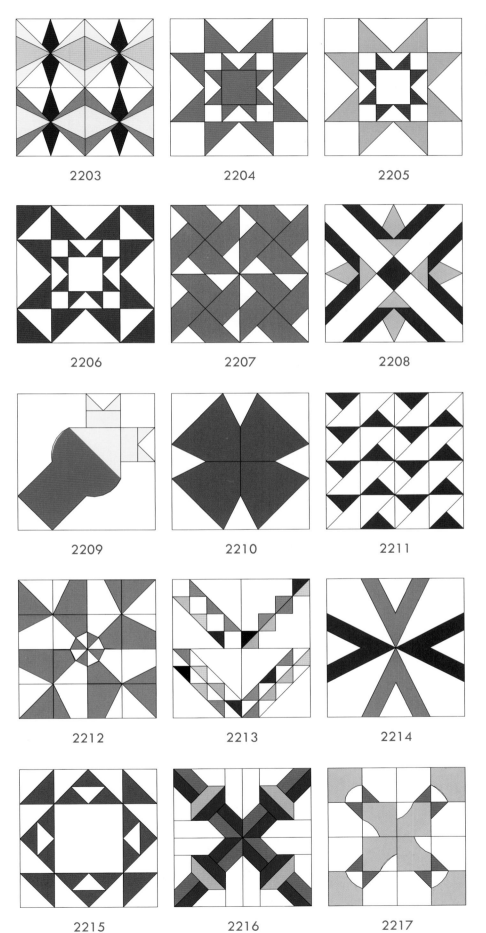

2203　　　2204　　　2205

2206　　　2207　　　2208

2209　　　2210　　　2211

2212　　　2213　　　2214

2215　　　2216　　　2217

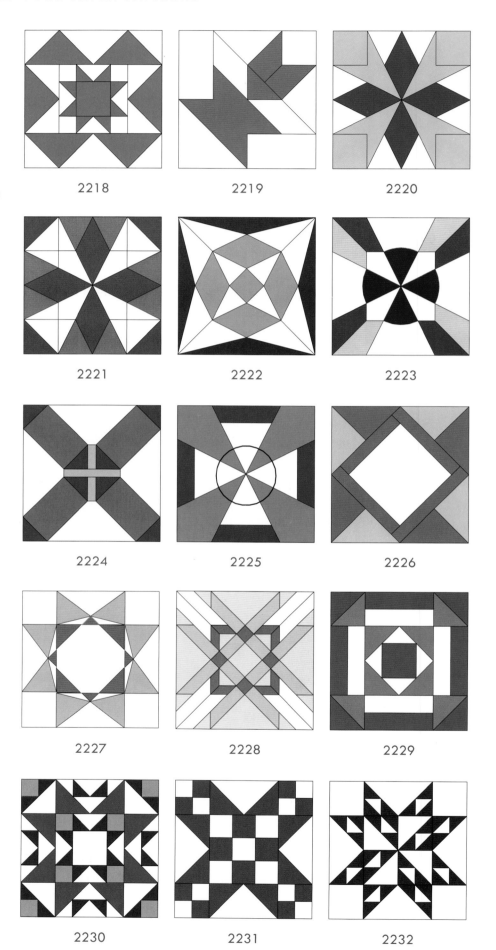

2218 Eight Hands Around

2219 The Disk
  Basket of Diamonds,
    KCS
  Flower Basket, *KCS*
  Flower Pot, *HH*
  Jersey Tulip
  Rainbow Cactus

2220 Key West

2221 Key West Beauty

2222 Night Before
    Christmas, *OCS*

2223 Holiday Bells, *OCS*

2224 Double Cross

2225 State of Nevada

2226 Economy Quilt Block

2227 Charm Star, *AMS*

2228 Holiday Crossroads,
    HaM, 1983

2229 Triangles and Stripes,
    LAC

2230 Castle Garden, *NC*

2231 Mrs. Lloyd's Favorite,
    CS

2232 Sparkling Star

2233 Lemon Star

2234 Criss-Cross, *GC*

2235 Locked Star

2236 Pieced Tulips

2237 Sugar Bowl Block

2238 Moynihan's Crusade,
     QW, 1985

2239 Green Cross

2240 Sun and Stars Quilt

2241 Tulips

2242 Squares and Diamonds

2243 Jewel, *GC*

2244 Beacon Lights, *NP*

2245 Colonial Pavement,
     OCS

2246 Shooting Star

2247 Duck Creek Puzzle

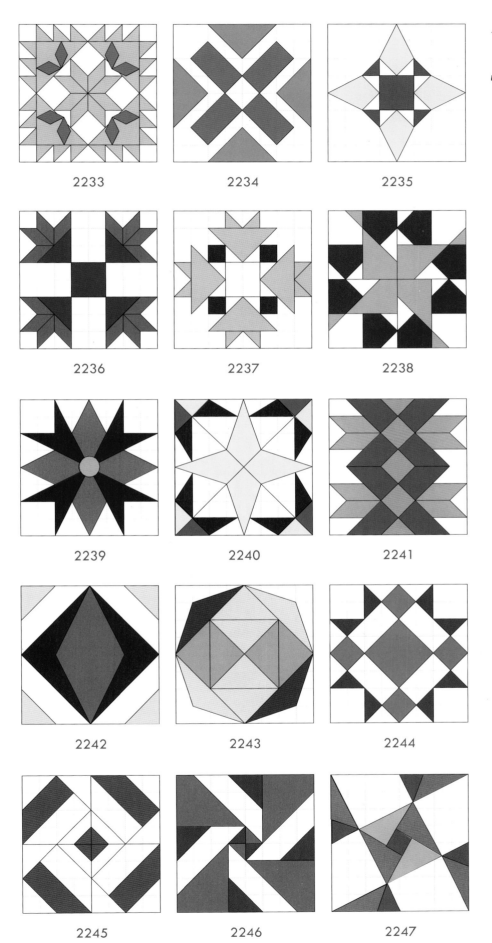

2233 2234 2235

2236 2237 2238

2239 2240 2241

2242 2243 2244

2245 2246 2247

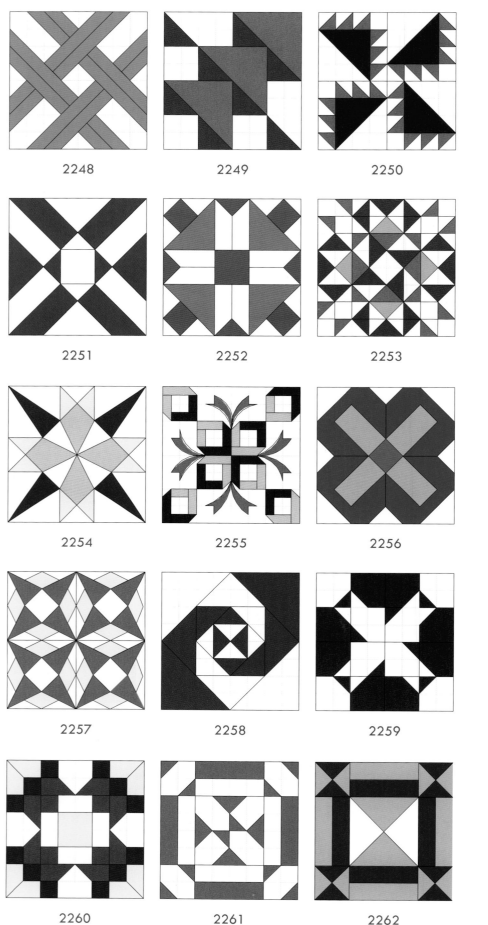

2248

2249

2250

2251

2252

2253

2254

2255

2256

2257

2258

2259

2260

2261

2262

2248 Irish Plaid, *NC*

2249 Totem

2250 Irish Puzzle, *LAC*
  Climbing Rose
  Flying Dutchman
  Forest Path
  Indian Trail
  Kansas Troubles
  North Wind
  Old Maid's Ramble
  Prickly Pear
  Rambling Road
  Rambling Rose
  Storm at Sea
  Tangled Tares
  Weather Vane

2251 Land's End, *QN*

2252 Neighborhoods, *MM*

2253 Indian Maize, *NC*

2254 Star of Mystery

2255 Surprise Package, *QEQ, 1991*

2256 Cross of Geneva, *NC*

2257 Geometrical Star Quilt Block

2258 Nautilus

2259 Colombian Puzzle, *CS*

2260 April Tulips, *QN*

2261 Girl's Joy, *LAC*
  Maiden's Delight, *NC*

2262 Hobson's Kiss, *NC*

2263 Flower Pot, *GC*

2264 Jewel Star, *AK, 1963*

2265 John F. Kennedy Star,
   AK, 1964

2266 Windmill and Outline

2267 Criss Cross, *FJ*

2268 Full Blown Tulip, *OCS*

2269 Arkansas Diamond, *NC*

2270 Crazy Pieces, *MoM*

2271 Snail's Trail, *LAC*
   Journey to California,
   KCS
   Ocean Wave
   Whirligig Quilt

2272 Four-Four Time, *FJ*

2273 Four Squares, *NC*

2274 Star and Square, *OF,
   1894*
   Courtyard Square, *AK*

2275 Double Windmill, *NC*

2276 Bacon Patch, *NC*

2277 Manila Quilt Design,
   1899

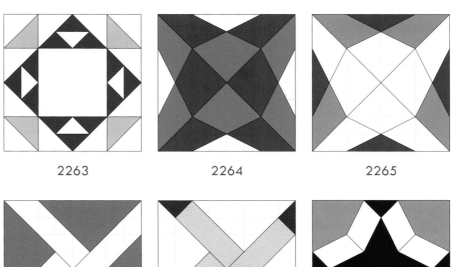

2263 2264 2265

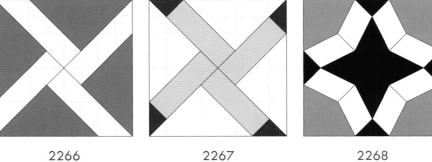

2266 2267 2268

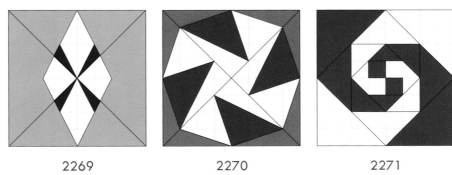

2269 2270 2271

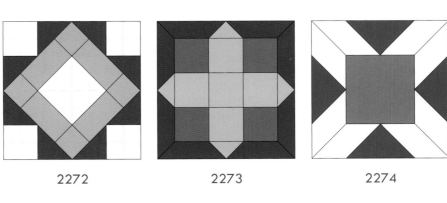

2272 2273 2274

2275 2276 2277

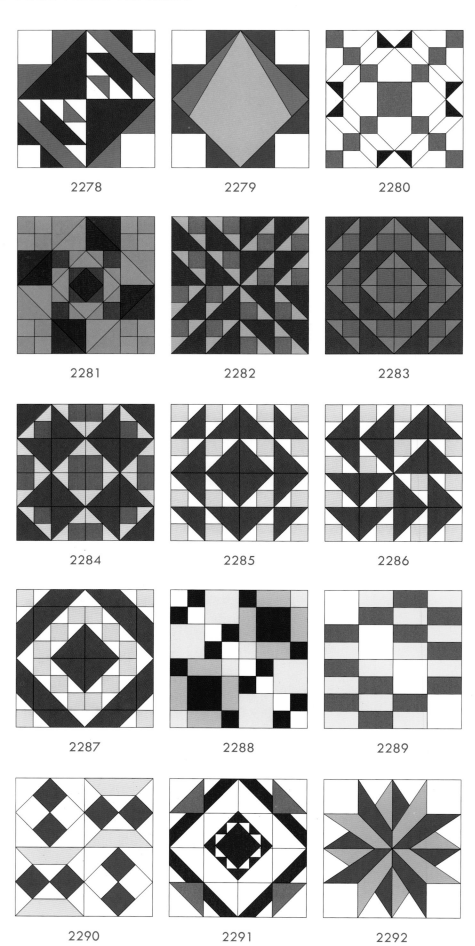

2278

2279

2280

2281

2282

2283

2284

2285

2286

2287

2288

2289

2290

2291

2292

2278 Path to Bethlehem, *HMD, SSQ, 1984*

2279 A Child Is Born, *HMD, SSQ, 1984*

2280 Diamond Cross, *Michelle Clary, SSQ, 1982*

2281 Alpha, *Crea Guarino, SSQ, 1982*

2282 Six Windows of Sunshine, Window #1, *QN*

2283 Six Windows of Sunshine, Window #2, *QN*

2284 Six Windows of Sunshine, Window #3, *QN*

2285 Six Windows of Sunshine, Window #4, *QN*

2286 Six Windows of Sunshine, Window #5, *QN*

2287 Six Windows of Sunshine, Window #6, *QN*

2288 Four Squares, *NC*

2289 Ohio Trail, *NC*

2290 Conventional

2291 Golden Stairs, *LW, OCS*

2292 North Star, *LW, OCS*

2293 Wheels, *PF*

2294 Taking Wing, *QN*

2295 Whirling Star, *LW, OCS*

2296 Star and Crescent, *KCS*
Alaska Chinook, *NC*
Compass
Four Winds, *NP*
Friendship Medley
  Quilt
King's Crown
Lucky Star
Star Crescent
Star of the Four Winds
Star of the West

2297 Four Leaf Clover, *NC*

2298 Florentine Diamond,
  CS

2299 Diamond Solitaire, *WB*

2300 Arkansas Traveler
Travel Star

2301 Diamond Chain, *NC*
Linked Diamonds

2302 A Rosette of Points,
  KCS

2303 Riviera, *NC*

2304 Mountain Star, *QN*
Stars and Stripes, *LCPQ*

2305 New Star, *AK*

2306 Shooting Stars, *NC*

2307 Ohio, *HH*
Ohio Star
State of Ohio, *HM*

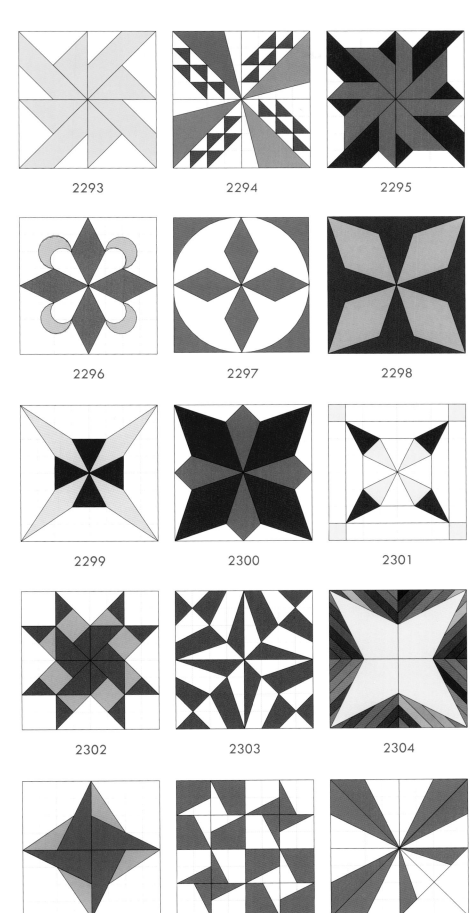

2293 2294 2295

2296 2297 2298

2299 2300 2301

2302 2303 2304

2305 2306 2307

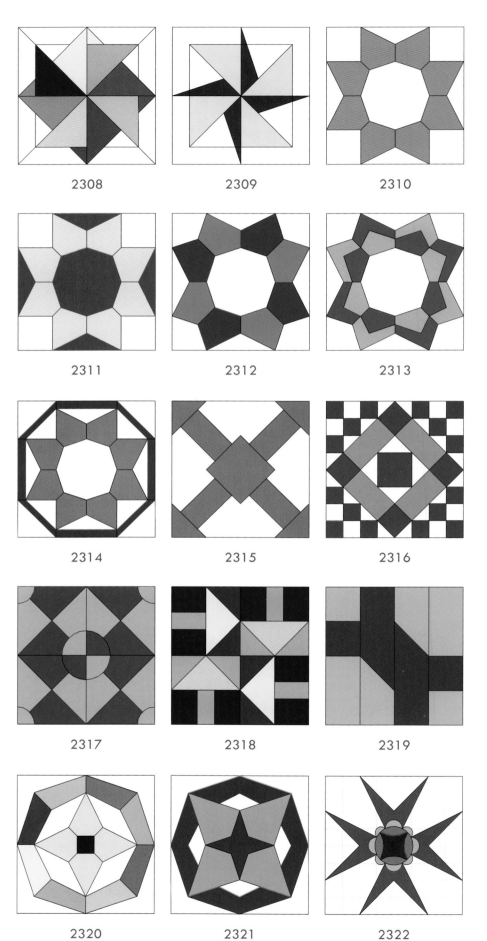

2308

2309

2310

2311

2312

2313

2314

2315

2316

2317

2318

2319

2320

2321

2322

2308 Spinning Color Wheel, *QN*

2309 Pinwheel Parade, *AK, 1966*

2310 Friendship Star, *KCS, 1933*
 Alma's Choice, *NC*

2311 Missouri Daisy, *KCS*

2312 Ring Around the Rosy, *HH*

2313 Ring Around the Rosy, *HH*
 Mother's Choice, *KCS*

2314 Sunflower Quilt, *1900*

2315 I Do

2316 Unnamed, *GLB, 1858*

2317 Lansing

2318 Campaign Trail, *QN*

2319 Millie's Quilt

2320 Star and Crown

2321 Drucilla's Delight

2322 North Star

2323 3D Nine Patch

2324 Buried Treasure

2325 St. Valentine

2326 Topaz Trail (8x10), *NC*

2327 Hide and Seek

2328 Wild Goose Chase

2329 Rolling Stone

2330 Satellite

2331 Diamonds, *AB, OCS*

2332 MacKenzie's Square,
        NC

2333 Alabama Rambler, *NC*

2334 Pieced Flower, *QW*

2335 Colombian Puzzle

2336 Roads to Oklahoma
        Crossed Roads to
        Oklahoma

2337 Cul-de-Sac
        Neighborhood
        Our Neighborhood

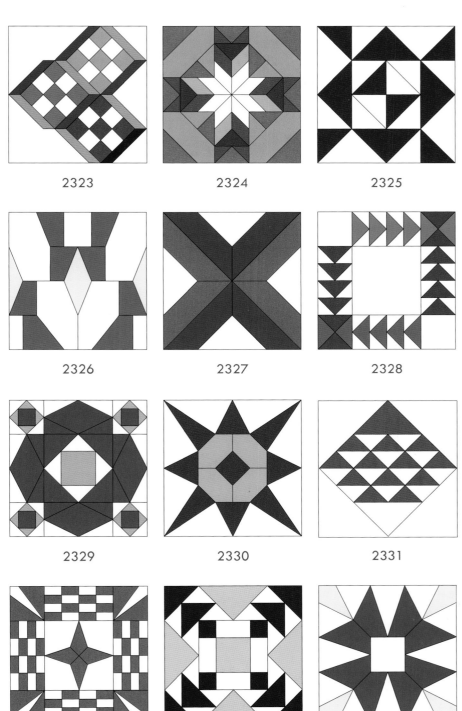

2323   2324   2325

2326   2327   2328

2329   2330   2331

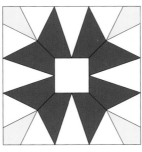

2332   2333   2334

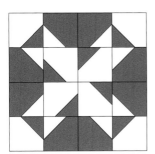

2335   2336   2337

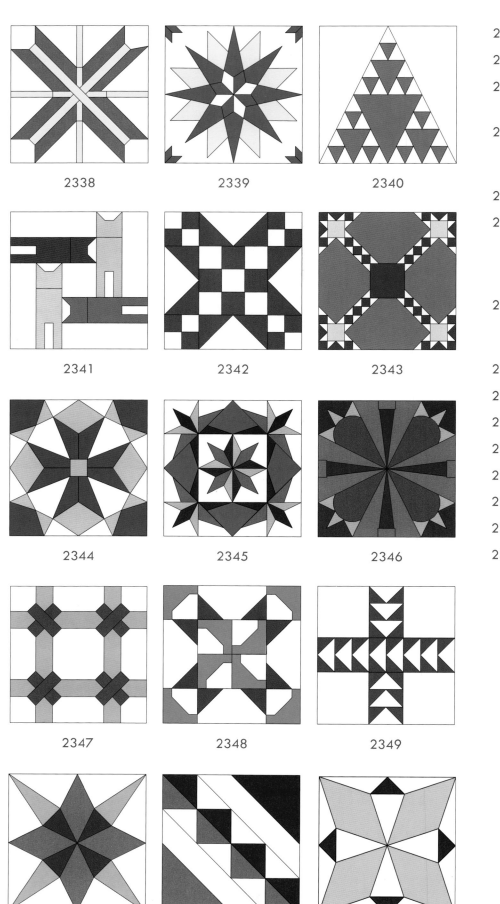

2338   2339   2340

2341   2342   2343

2344   2345   2346

2347   2348   2349

2350   2351   2352

2338 Glove Design, *AMS*

2339 Blazing Star, *GD*

2340 Triangular Triangle, *LAC*

2341 Calico Cat, *Nanette Moore, QN, 1991*

2342 Mrs. Lloyd's Favorite

2343 Beautiful Flower Garden, *Zelma DePriest, QW, 1983*

2344 Medieval Castle, *Sandra Hatch, SSQ, 1985*

2345 Wild Iris

2346 Indian Paint Brush

2347 Nauvoo Lattice, *NC*

2348 Columbia Puzzle, *LAC*

2349 Railroad Crossing

2350 A Diamond Field, *OCS*

2351 No Name

2352 Diamond

2353 Ozark Trail

2354 Annamae's Star

2355 Star and Cone

2356 Laced Star

2357 Shoemaker's Puzzle

2358 Butterfly

2359 Star of the West

2360 Love Doves (reverse second block to face first), *SSQ, 1993*

2361 Flags and Ships (8x6 grid)

2362 Ancient Nine Patch

2363 Arkansas Traveller

2364 Windy City, *JM*

2365 Stars in a Star Variation

2366 Four Patch Chain

2367 Lori's Star, *Wanda Sturrock*

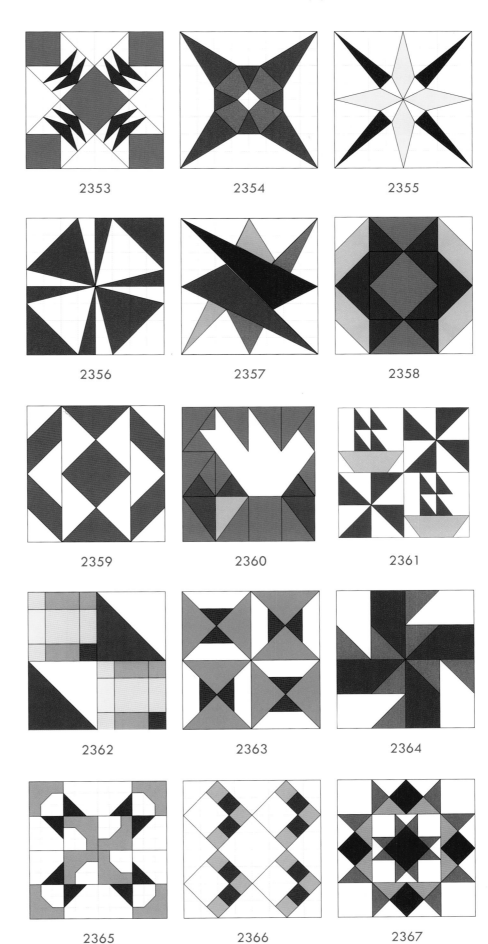

2353   2354   2355

2356   2357   2358

2359   2360   2361

2362   2363   2364

2365   2366   2367

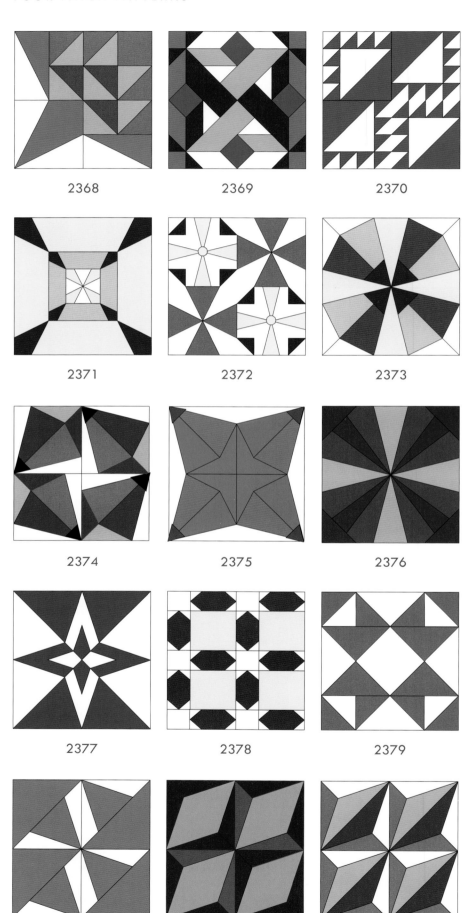

2368

2369

2370

2371

2372

2373

2374

2375

2376

2377

2378

2379

2380

2381

2382

2368 Nosegay, *SSQ, 1987*

2369 Razzle Dazzle, *Judy Rehme, QW, 1986*

2370 Flamingo's Flight, *SSQ*

2371 Prisms, *Caldelina Schumann, QW, 1989*

2372 Pink Dogwood, *Ruby Hinson Duncan, QW, 1987*

2373 Parasol, *MLM, QW*

2374 Parasol Variation, *MLM, QW*

2375 Parasol Variation 2, *MLM, QW*

2376 Nova, *SSQ, 1987*

2377 Natchez Star

2378 Mother's Morning Star, *QW*

2379 Mosaic, *LAC*

2380 Dilemma, *QWO*

2381 Cosmic Cube, *MM*

2382 Art Deco Tulip, *MM*

2383 Helping Hands, *RMS, SSQ, 1987*

2384 Boardwalk, *QN, 1985*

2385 Beacon

2386 Beyond the Stars

2387 Latticework
Kentucky Chain

2388 High Noon

2389 Heavenly Stars, *QN, 1988*

2390 Stars and Arrows

2391 Name Unknown

2392 Garden Square Block

2393 Grandfather's Choice

2394 Vestibule

2395 Cross and Square

2396 Love's Dream (heart
appliqué in center
square), *SSQ, 1987*

2397 Duck Wheel,
Carol Bruce

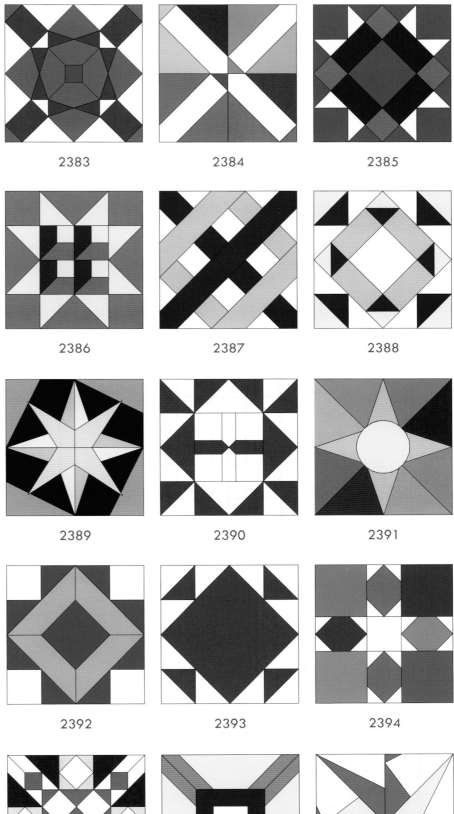

2383   2384   2385

2386   2387   2388

2389   2390   2391

2392   2393   2394

2395   2396   2397

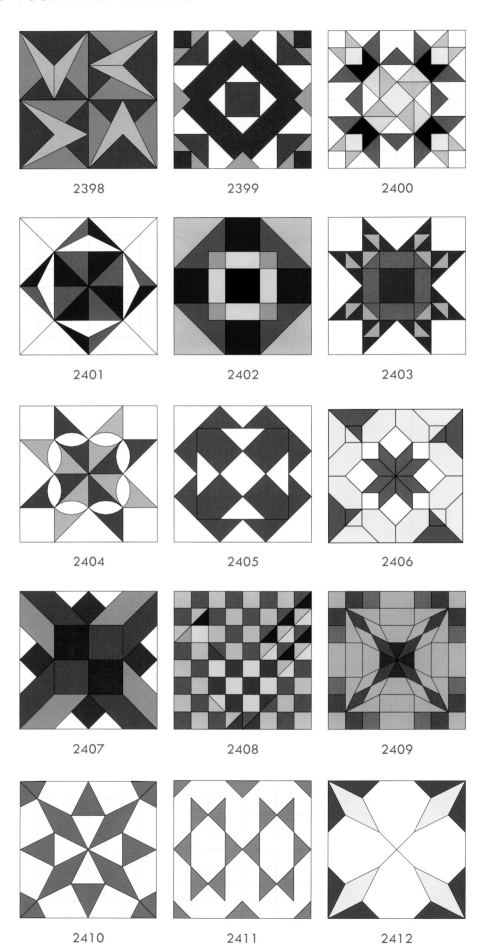

2398
2399
2400

2401
2402
2403

2404
2405
2406

2407
2408
2409

2410
2411
2412

2398 Mother's Dilemma, *RMS, SSQ*

2399 Magic Squares

2400 Indian Maize

2401 Rising Star, *QW Star Quilts*

2402 Community Center, *MM*

2403 Stockyard's Star

2404 Star Burst Quilt

2405 Four T's

2406 Godey Design

2407 Jamestown Square, *NC*

2408 Rhode Island Red, *NM, 1928*

2409 Raspberry Parfait, *QM, 1992*

2410 Your Lucky Star, *OCS*

2411 Washington Star

2412 May Time Quilt, *WB*

2413 Double Twist Star
Block

2414 Cornhusker's Star,
Jan Stehlik, LCPQ

2415 Space Station, *Mr.
Leslie Robson, SSQ*

2416 Diamond Solitaire,
AMS

2417 Tulip Garden,
*Mrs. Eldon Bauer,
QN, 1970*

2418 Whirligig

2419 Castles in Spain, *NP*

2420 Texas Two Step

2421 Patience Corners, *LAC*

2422 Twist Patchwork

2423 Geometric

2424 T-Square

2425 Improved Nine Patch

2426 Aunt Abbie's Own

2427 Geometric Album

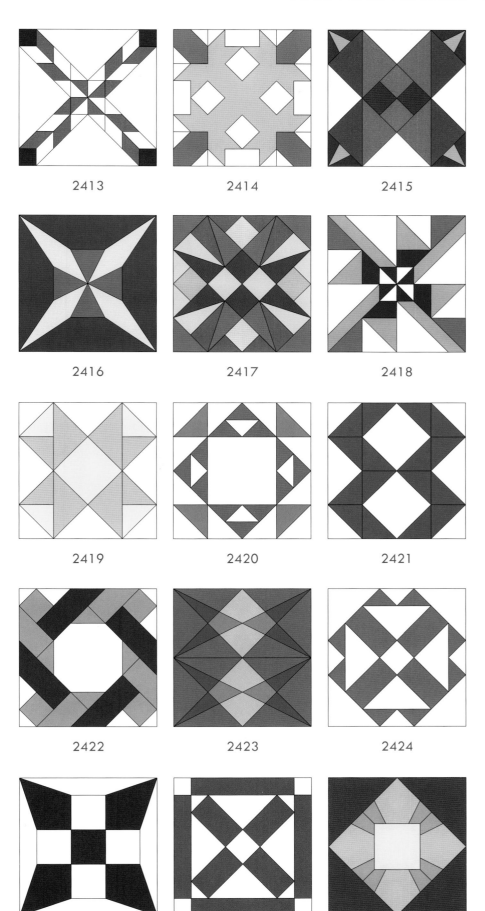

2413 2414 2415

2416 2417 2418

2419 2420 2421

2422 2423 2424

2425 2426 2427

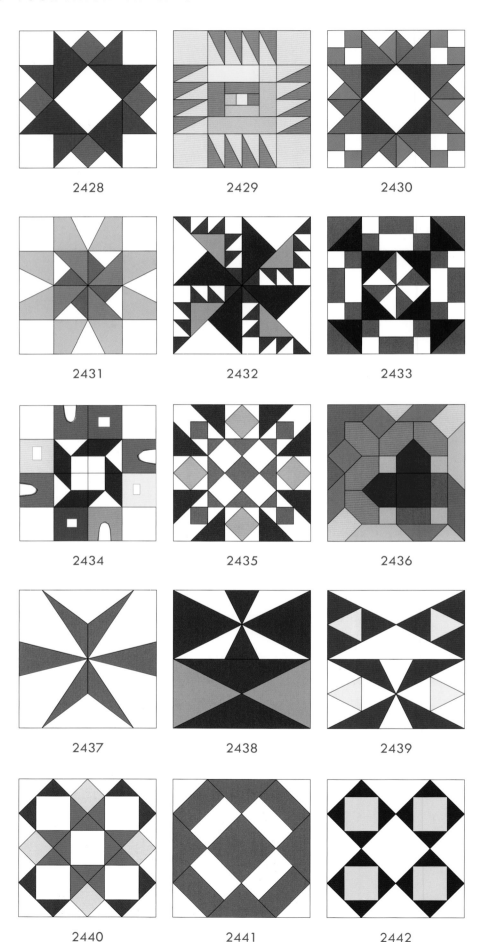

5,500 QUILT BLOCK DESIGNS

2428 Home Grown

2429 Friends & Family, *RMS*

2430 Use It All

2431 Telluride Puzzle, *QN*

2432 Kansas Troubles Variation

2433 Secret Passage

2434 Country Village, *QW*

2435 Cross and Square

2436 Crusader's Heart

2437 The Star Fish (6x8), *NC*

2438 Whirlwind, *WW*

2439 42nd Street

2440 Federal Square, *NC*

2441 Grecian Square

2442 The Star and Block, *LCPQ, 1979*

2443 Godey Design

2444 Saw Toothed Star, *GH*
Single Star, *GH*

2445 Free Trade, *KCS*

2446 Galaxy

2447 Lisa's Choice

2448 Charm Quilt
Dog Bone

2449 Scrap Bag Squares, *QN*

2450 The North Star, *KCS*

2451 The Four Corners, *NC*

2452 Rose Garden, *NC*

2453 Zig-Zag, *WW*

2454 Shepherd's Crossing,
KCS
Four Square, *NC*
Grandmother's Own,
LAC

2455 Morning Patch, *LAC*

2456 Ray, *NC*

2457 Tete-A-Tete, *NC*

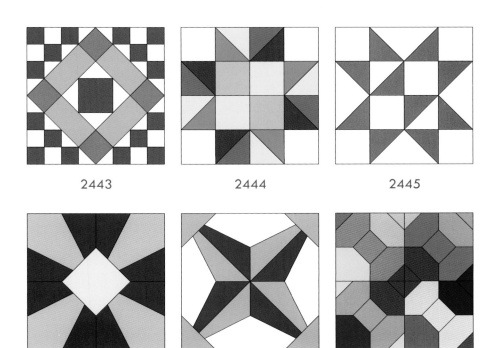

2443   2444   2445

 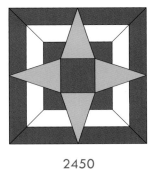 

2446   2447   2448

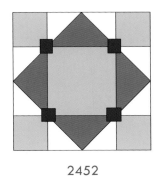  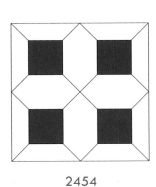

2449   2450   2451

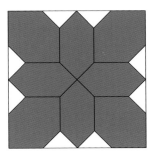 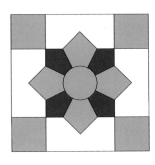 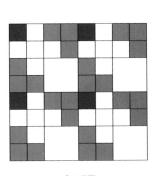

2452   2453   2454

2455   2456   2457

5,500 QUILT BLOCK DESIGNS

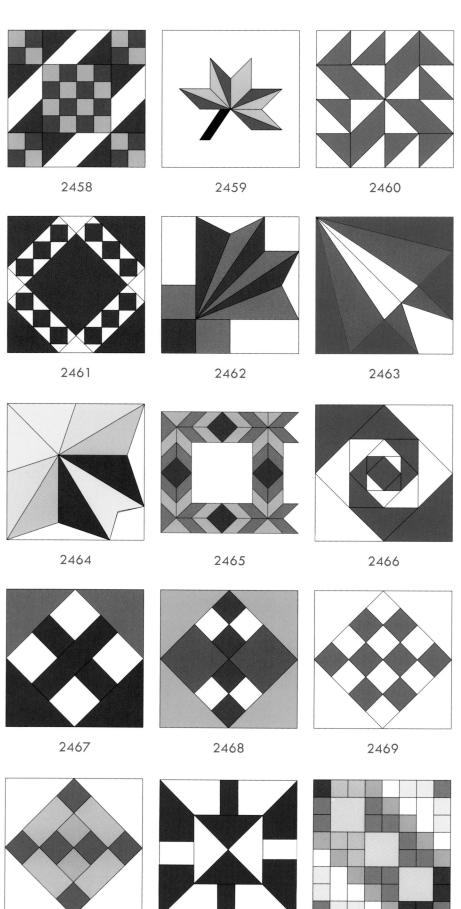

2458

2459

2460

2461

2462

2463

2464

2465

2466

2467

2468

2469

2470

2471

2472

2458 Sunny Lanes, *NP*

2459 Autumn Leaves, *QWB,
1976*

2460 Rosie's Purina
Whirligig

2461 Blue Fields

2462 Victorian Fan, *SSQ,
1982*

2463 First Morning Rays,
SSQ, 1982

2464 Starburst, *SSQ, 1982*

2465 Cupid's Arrow Point

2466 Virginia Reel, *MoM*
Pig's Tail, *MoM*

2467 Pattern Without a
Name, *NC*

2468 Improved Four Patch

2469 Kansas Dugout

2470 Lola, *AK*

2471 Twin Darts, *FJ*

2472 Attic Stairs, *NC*

2473 Brickwork, *MM*

2474 Arrowhead Puzzle
 (continuous design)

2475 Pieced Heart

2476 Irish Spring

2477 Stacked Stars

2478 Banner Quilt, *OCS*

2479 Hedgework

2480 Ozark Mountains, *NC*

2481 Flying Geese, *NC*

2482 Cross and Crown

2483 Spinning L

2484 Birds and Kites, *NC*

2485 The Chieftain, *NC*

2486 Windmill, *AMS*

2487 Day and Night, *OCS*

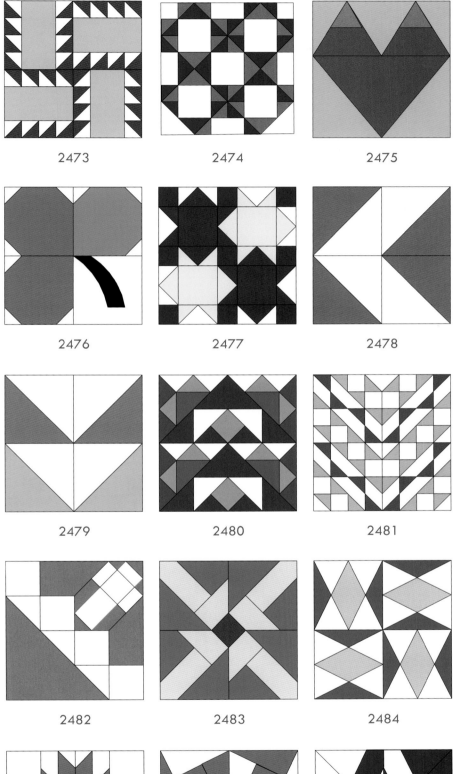

2473   2474   2475

2476   2477   2478

2479   2480   2481

2482   2483   2484

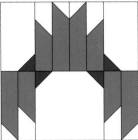
2485

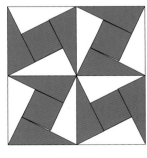
2486

2487

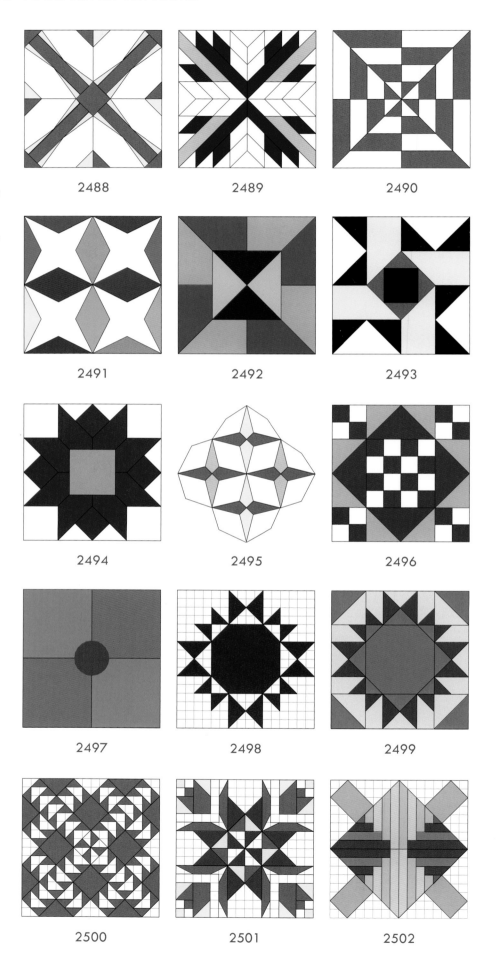

2488

2489

2490

2491

2492

2493

2494

2495

2496

2497

2498

2499

2500

2501

2502

2488 Michael's Joke

2489 Little Penguins, *NC*

2490 Market Square, *NC*

2491 Diamond Chain

2492 Geometry

2493 Waterwheel

2494 Diamond Star

2495 Rock Garden

2496 Road to California

2497 Necktie Variation

2498 Wheel of Fortune, *LAC*
Rising Sun
Wheel of Luck, *NC*

2499 Wheel of Fortune
Buttons and Bows

2500 Railroad Crossing

2501 Dutch Dreams, *QM*,
1992

2502 Calico Grove, *QM, 1992*

2503 Plum Island Compass

2504 Season's Joy, *HaM,
       SSQ, 1983*

2505 Reindeer on the Roof,
       HaM, SSQ, 1983

2506 Starry Path, *AB, OCS*

2507 Morning Star

2508 Bossburg Wonder

2509 Sitka Quilt Block

2510 Star of the Night

2511 Sixteen Patch

2512 Aunt Lucinda's Double
       Irish Chain
       Aunt Lucinda's Quilt
       Block

2513 Sue's Delight

2514 Footbridge

2515 Candles

2516 Sunburst

2517 World's Fair

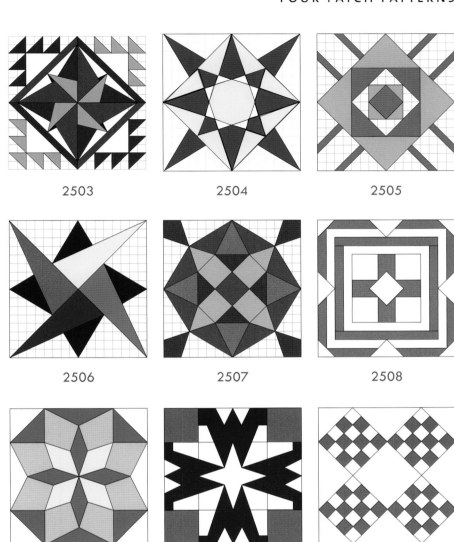

2503   2504   2505

2506   2507   2508

2509   2510   2511

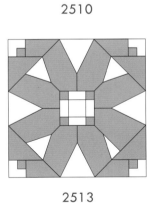
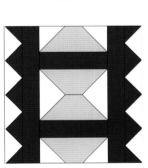
2512   2513   2514

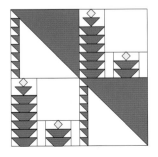
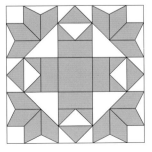

2515   2516   2517

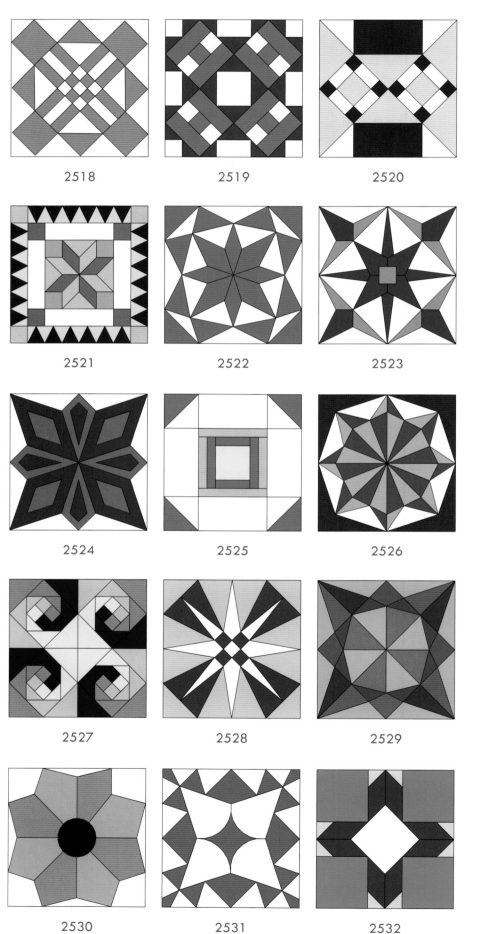

2518

2519

2520

2521

2522

2523

2524

2525

2526

2527

2528

2529

2530

2531

2532

2518 Sonnie's Playhouse

2519 Five Square

2520 Peace and Plenty

2521 Old Spanish Tile

2522 Western Spy

2523 West Virginia

2524 Star of Empire

2525 Yankee Charm

2526 Parasol

2527 Galaxy

2528 Santa's Guiding Star, *AMS, 1931*

2529 Fitz's Phenomena, *Karen Fitzgerald, QW, 1982*

2530 Eight Points in a Square, *KCS*

2531 Radiant Star

2532 Leaves and Flowers, *KCS*

2533 Wild Goose Chase

2534 Chrysanthemum Block

2535 Spinning Star

2536 Mayflower, *QN, 1988*

2537 Broken Crystals

2538 Spider Web

2539 North Star, *HMD* and
       SSQ, 1984

2540 South Carolina, *HH*

2541 Railroad Crossing, *QN*

2542 Stellar Reflections, *QW,
       1991*

2543 Glory Vine, *NC*

2544 Wild Iris, *QN, 1992*

2545 Stripes & Stars, *QM,
       1994*

2546 Missouri's Gateway
       Star, *AK*

2547 Enigma, *NC*

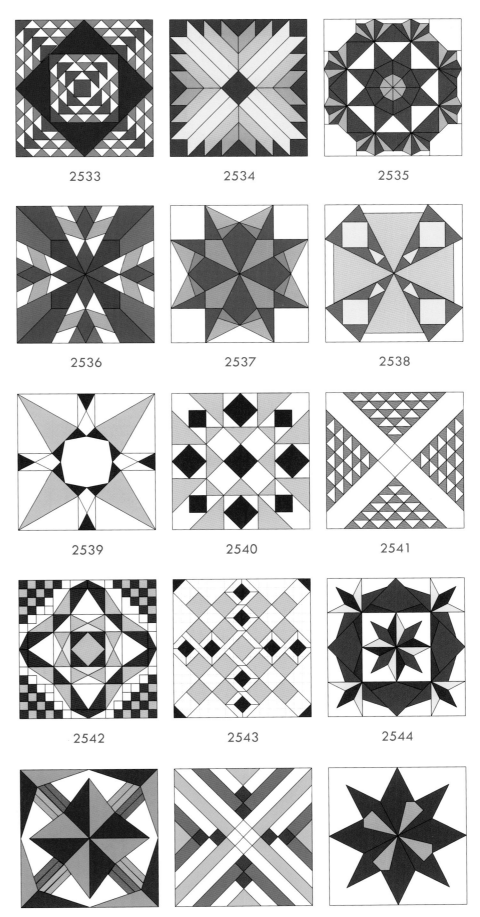

2533   2534   2535

2536   2537   2538

2539   2540   2541

2542   2543   2544

2545   2546   2547

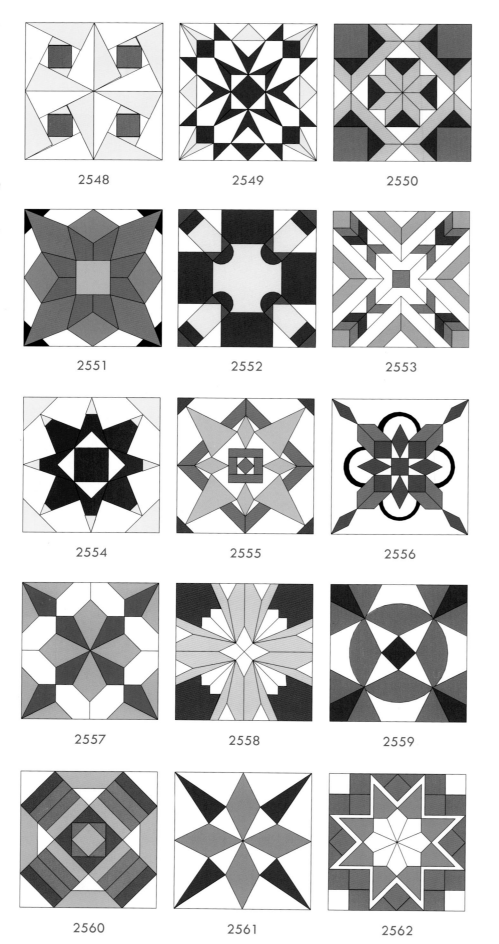

2548

2549

2550

2551

2552

2553

2554

2555

2556

2557

2558

2559

2560

2561

2562

2548 Kaleidoscope, *FJ*

2549 Constellation, *NC*

2550 Magic Carpet

2551 Sea & Shadows

2552 Starry Pavement, *OCS*

2553 Persian Star

2554 Space Ships, *QN*

2555 Stars and Triangles

2556 Bachelor's Puzzle, *GD*

2557 Print and Plain, *FJ*

2558 Star of the Night, *HH*

2559 Rose in Summer, *OCS*

2560 Garden Gazebo,
      Rhoda Goldberg

2561 Star and Cone, *PF*

2562 Plaid Star

2563 Twinkling Star, *NC*

2564 Morning Star, *LW, OCS*

2565 Rising Star, *LW, OCS*

2566 Enigma Star

2567 Connecticut Yankee

2568 Dutch Mill

2569 Kitchen Woodbox

2570 Lattice Square
      Interwoven Puzzle
      Lattice Strips

2571 Twisted Thread Box
      Twisted Spool Box
      Twisted Spools
      Twisting Spool

2572 Rock Garden, *AMS*

2573 Scottish Cross

2574 Shooting Star

2575 State Fair Block

2576 Tulip and Star

2577 Desert Rose, *NC*

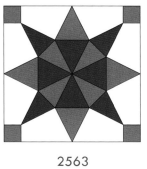
2563

2564

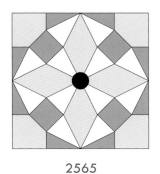
2565

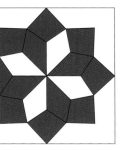
2566

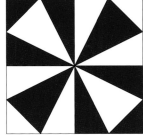
2567

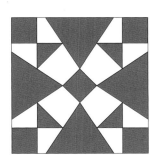
2568

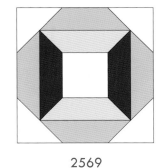
2569

2570

2571

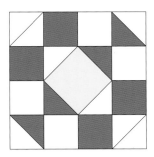
2572

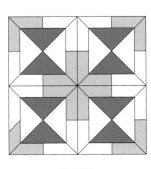
2573

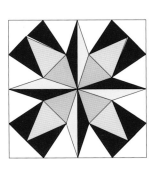
2574

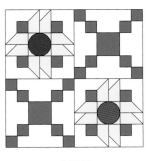
2575

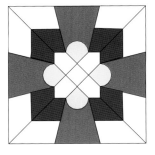
2576

2577

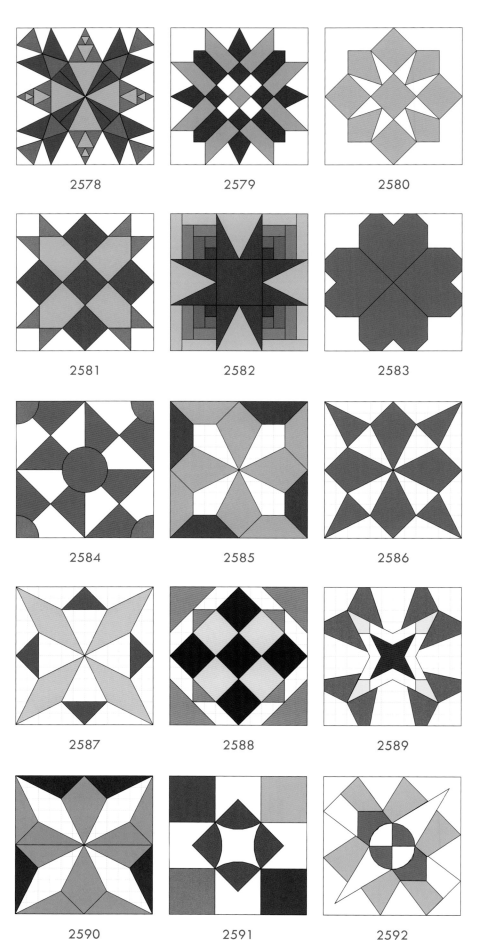

2578

2579

2580

2581

2582

2583

2584

2585

2586

2587

2588

2589

2590

2591

2592

2578 Arrow of Peace

2579 Alice's Favorite

2580 Nine Patch Star, *LW, OCS*

2581 Wild Irish Rose, *JM*

2582 Black Magic (diagonal set), *Elizabeth Stevens, Blue Ribbon Quilts*

2583 Four Leaf Clover

2584 Grecian Square Greek Square

2585 Unnamed

2586 Whirling Star, *GD*

2587 Diamond

2588 Block & Tackle, *JM, Ultimate Book of Quilt Block Patterns*

2589 Shooting Star, *PP*

2590 Century of Progress, *FJ* Counter Charm, *HH*

2591 Window Squares, *GC*

2592 Victory, *CS*

2593 Faceted Crystals

2594 Lady of the Lake, *HH*

2595 Goblet Four

2596 Scrap Quilt Bouquet

2597 South Dakota

2598 Star Chain
Yankee Star
Yankee Star Chain

2599 Star Ray
Sun Ray

2600 Blazed Trail, *NC*

2601 Large Star, *LHJ*, *1896*
Crow's Foot, *NP*

2602 Maltese Cross Block,
NC

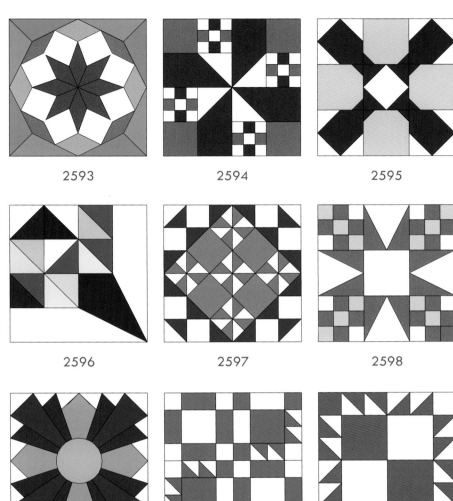

2593

2594

2595

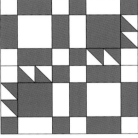

2596

2597

2598

2599

2600

2601

2602

FIVE PATCH PATTERNS

5 X 5 GRID

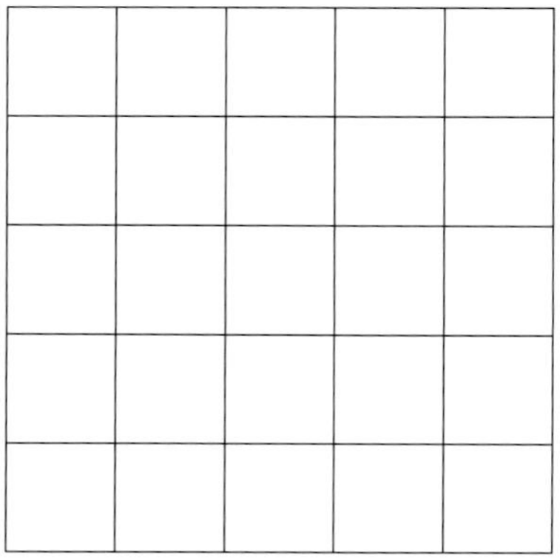

10 X 10 GRID

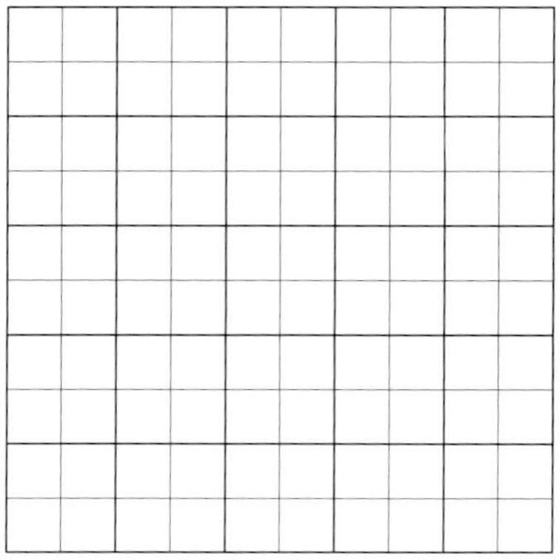

THESE PATTERNS ARE DRAFTED ON A GRID 5 x 5 SQUARES
DRAFT THESE PATTERNS TO ANY BLOCK SIZE DIVISIBLE BY 5

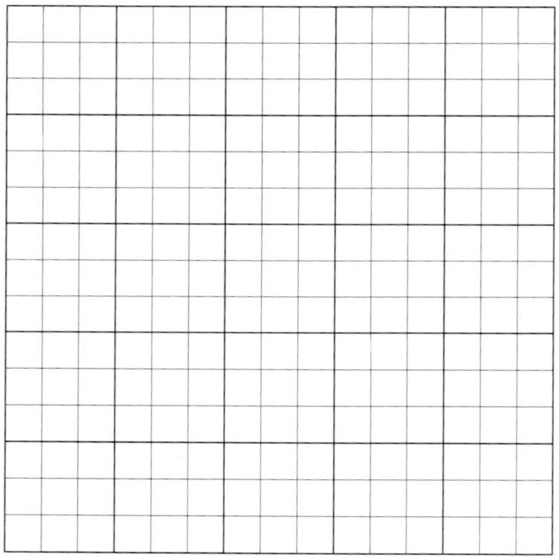

15 X 15 GRID

2603 Sunshine and Shadow

2604 Double V, *KCS*

2605 Brock House

2606 Children's Delight, *LAC*

2607 Five Patch

2608 Plaid

2609 Flying Square, *LAC*

2610 Star & Cross

2611 Blocks in a Box

2612 Multiple Square

2613 Unnamed, *QN*

2614 Missouri River Valley

2615 Alaska Homestead

2616 Fool's Square, *KCS*

2617 Butterfly at the
    Crossroads, *KCS*
    Algonquin Charm, *NC*
    Simple Sue

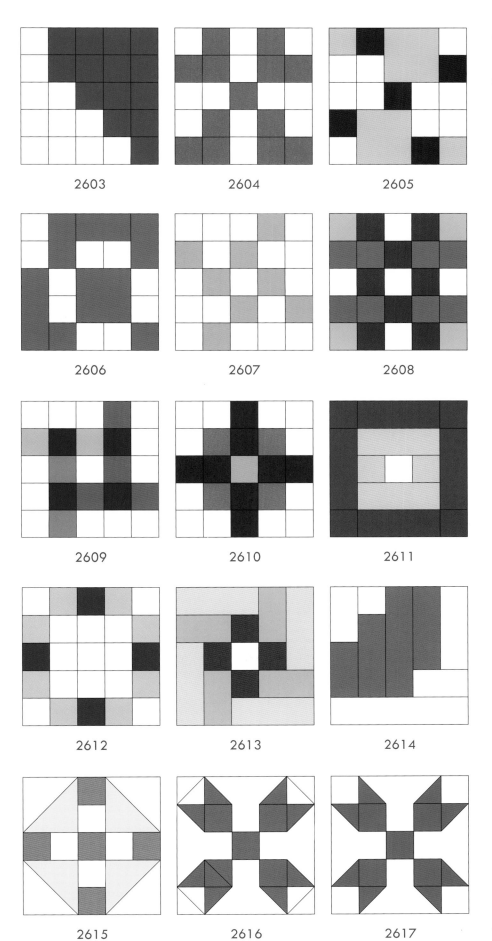

2603 2604 2605

2606 2607 2608

2609 2610 2611

2612 2613 2614

2615 2616 2617

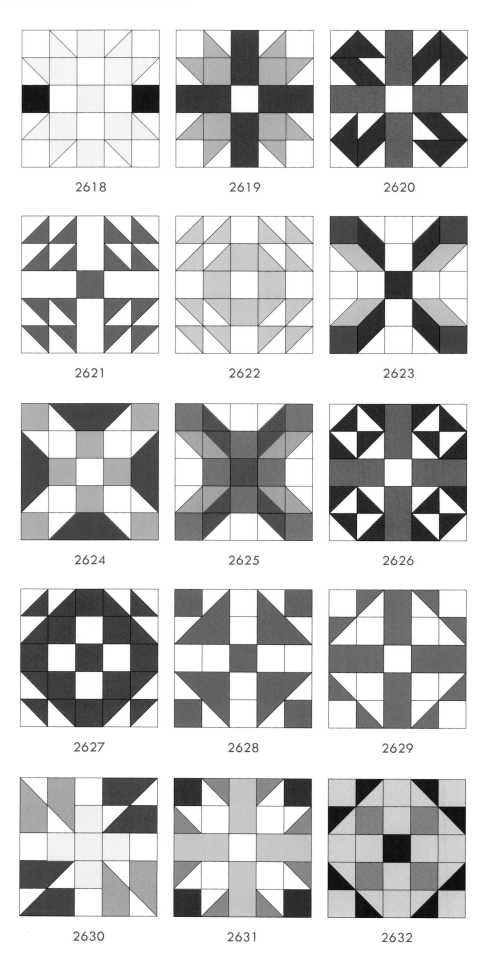

2618   2619   2620

2621   2622   2623

2624   2625   2626

2627   2628   2629

2630   2631   2632

2618 Sister's Choice, *LAC*
       Churn Dasher, *HH*
       Five Patch Star
       Four & Star
       4X Star, *LAC*
       Star and Cross

2619 E-Z Quilt, *KCS*

2620 Jack in the Box, *KCS*
       Whirligig
       Wheel of Fortune, *NC*

2621 Flying Geese
       Handy Andy
       Wheel of Chance, *NC*

2622 Single Wedding Ring,
           KCS
       Georgetown Circle
       Memory Wreath
       Nest and Fledgling,
           KCS
       Odd Scraps Patchwork,
           LAC
       Rolling Stone, *TFW,*
           1920
       Wedding Ring, *LAC*

2623 Wild Rose and Square

2624 Rolling Star

2625 Jack's Blocks

2626 Red Cross, *LAC*

2627 Duck and Ducklings

2628 Grandmother's Choice,
           LAC
       Duck and Ducklings

2629 Grandmother's Choice
       Cross Within a Cross
       French Patchwork

2630 Z-Cross
       Crazy House, *LAC*

2631 Bright Jewel

2632 Marion's Choice

2633 Rocky Mountain Chain, *HH*
Tumbling Blocks, *CoM*

2634 Georgia, *HH*
State of Georgia, *WB,*
1935

2635 Bat Wing

2636 Broken Arrows

2637 Domino

2638 Follow the Leader
Crazy Ann
Twist and Turn

2639 Captain's Wheel

2640 Farmer's Daughter, *LAC*
Two Crosses, *NC*

2641 Crazy Ann

2642 Honey's Choice
Grandma's Choice, *NC*
Grandma's Favorite, *CS*

2643 Clown, *LAC*

2644 Providence Block, *NC*

2645 Double Sawtooth

2646 Lady of the Lake

2647 Square & Half Square

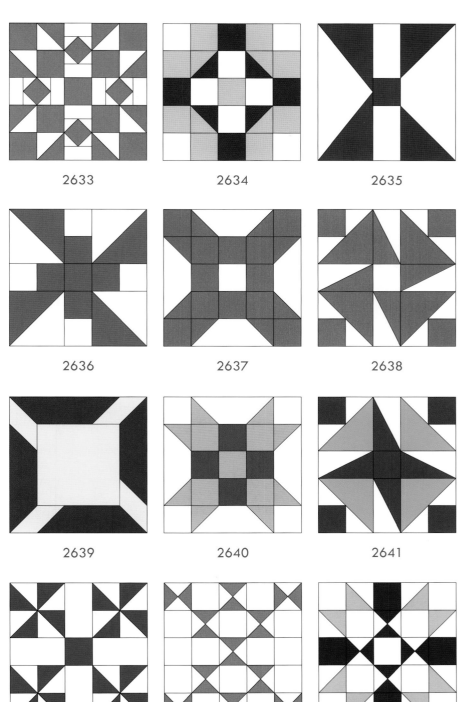

2633   2634   2635

2636   2637   2638

2639   2640   2641

2642   2643   2644

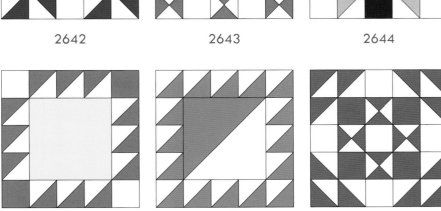

2645   2646   2647

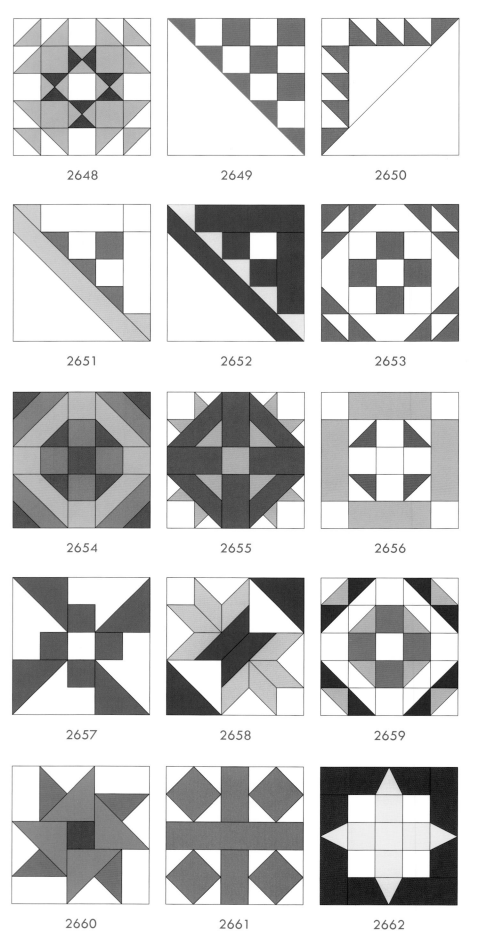

2648 Handy Andy

2649 Steps to the Altar

2650 Star of Hope

2651 King's Crown
     John's Favorite

2652 Greek Cross

2653 Mrs. Keller's Nine
     Patch

2654 Ombre

2655 David & Goliath
     Bull's Eye
     Doe and Darts
     Flying Darts
     Four Darts

2656 Philadelphia Pavement
     Philadelphia Block, *NC*

2657 Propeller, *LAC*
     Broken Arrows, *QW*,
       1979

2658 Queen Charlotte's
       Crown, *NC*
     Queen's Crown, *NC*
     Basket Design, *NC*
     Indian Meadow

2659 Wedding Rings

2660 Hope of Hartford

2661 Garden of Eden

2662 Grandmother's Cross

2663 Eagle

2664 Kicks

2665 Crazy House, *LAC*

2666 Churn Dash

2667 Double Wrench, *FF,*
   1884
   Aeroplane, *WW, 1931*
   Airplane, *HHJ*
   Alaska Homestead
   Bear Paw Design, *CoM*
   Bride's Knot, *1913*
   The Broad Axe, *1928*
   Churn Dash
   The Crow's Nest, *KCS*
   Dragon's Head, *WW*
   French 4's, *NP*
   Hens and Chickens
   Hole in the Barn Door
   Honey Dish
   Maltese Cross, *1913*
   Monkey Wrench, *OF,*
   1898
   Pioneer Patch
   Square Triangles
   T Design
   T Quartette
   True Lover's Knot
   Wrench, *OF, 1896*

2668 Pinwheel Square, *LAC*

2669 Wishing Ring, *MD*

2670 Tents of Armageddon
   Ocean Waves, *LAC*
   Thousands of Triangles

2671 Square Dance

2672 Souvenir

2673 Hills of Vermont

2674 Pinwheel

2675 Spinning Star

2676 Grandmother Percy's
   Puzzle, *HH*

2677 Home Circle
   Mrs. Anderson's Quilt,
   MD
   Rolling Square, *MD*
   Garden of Eden, *MD*

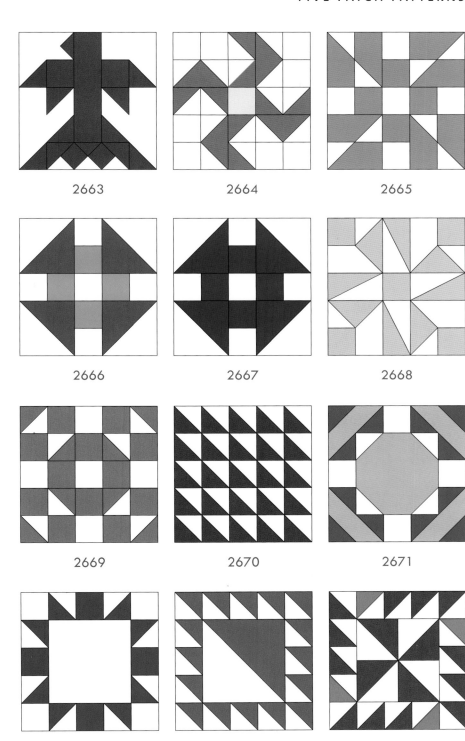

2663

2664

2665

2666

2667

2668

2669

2670

2671

2672

2673

2674

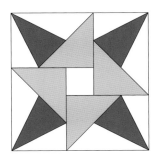

2675

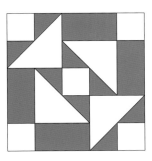

2676

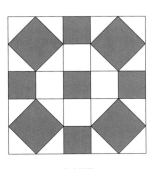

2677

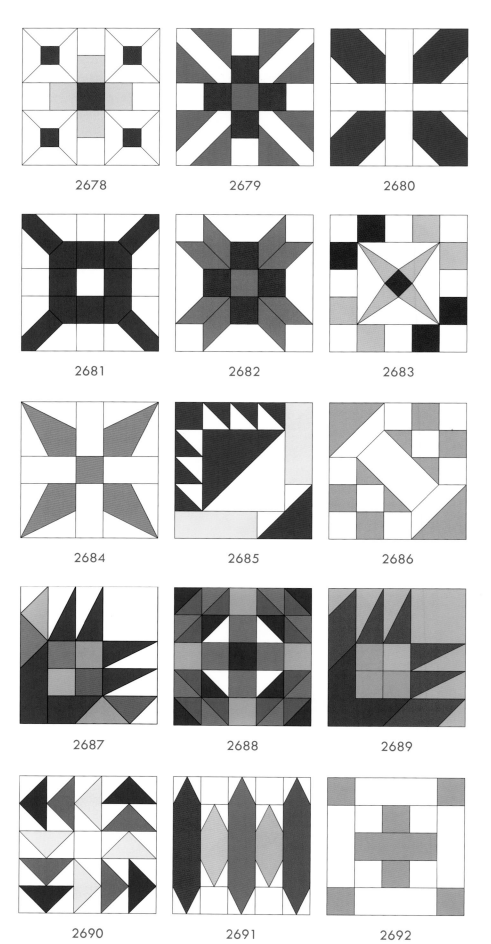

2678
2679
2680

2681
2682
2683

2684
2685
2686

2687
2688
2689

2690
2691
2692

2678 Tete A Tete, *NC, 1937*
Tote a Tote

2679 No Name, *OCS*

2680 Spool Block, *NC*

2681 Sunbeam, *WW*

2682 Miller's Daughter, *NC, 1937*

2683 Young Man's Fancy, *LW*

2684 King David's Crown

2685 Altar Candle

2686 Spool

2687 Fish

2688 Odd Scraps Patchwork

2689 Southern Pine

2690 Flying Geese

2691 Picket and Posts, *AK, 1966*

2692 Red Cross, *NP*

2693 Candle in the Window, *Mrs. Elmer Wicklund, SSQ*

2694 Clown's Choice

2695 Crown of Thorns
Georgetown Circle
Memory Wreath

2696 Star and Octagon, *1930s*

2697 English Wedding Ring, *NP*
Mill Wheel, *NP*
Odd Scraps Patchwork, *LAC*
Old-Fashioned
Wedding Ring
Vice President's Block, *NC*

2698 Wedding Ring, *KCS*
Old English Wedding
Ring, *KCS*

2699 Dewey Dream Quilt, *1899*

2700 Round the Corner, *NP*
Johnny Round the
Corner, *NP*

2701 New England Block, *1930*
Greek Cross, *KCS*

2702 Father's Choice

2703 Christmas Star
Red Cross, *HH*

2704 Baton Rouge Block, *NC*

2705 King's Crown

2706 Strength in Union

2707 Strength in Union, *NC*

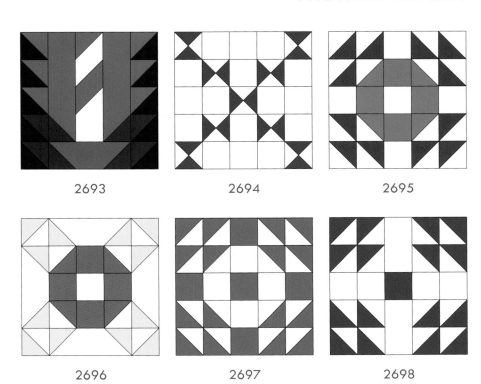

2693　　　2694　　　2695

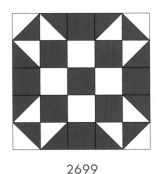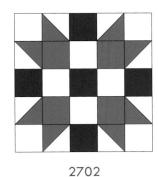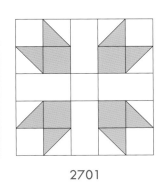

2696　　　2697　　　2698

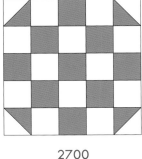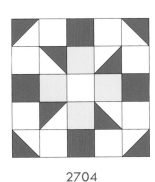

2699　　　2700　　　2701

2702　　　2703　　　2704

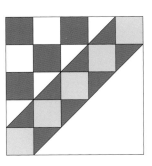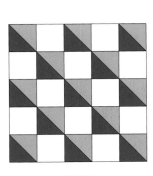

2705　　　2706　　　2707

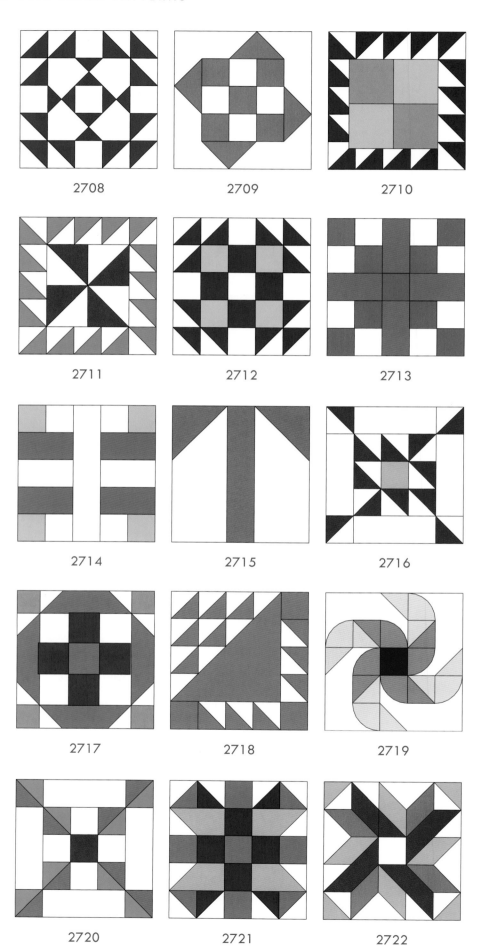

2708 Handy Andy, *LAC*
Foot Stool, *NC*
Mrs. Jones Favorite

2709 Rolling Nine Patch, *AK*

2710 Gay Two Patch Quilt, *OCS*

2711 Beginner's Delight, *OCS*

2712 English Wedding Ring

2713 Country Roads

2714 Double R

2715 Skinny T Quilt

2716 Twister

2717 Santa Fe Trail, *JM*

2718 Lady of the Lake

2719 Amish Pin Wheel

2720 Whirling Square, *NC*

2721 Sister's Choice

2722 Flying Stars

2723 Times Remembered, *LCPQ, 1865*

2724 Star and Cross Block for Hearth & Home Quilt

2725 Duck's Foot

2726 Churn Dasher, *HH*

2727 Guam Quilt Block, *HH*

2728 Banded Cross Block, *HH*

2729 Sacramento Quilt Block, *HH* Sacramento City, *NC*

2730 Nine Patch Star, *HH*

2731 Souvenir of Friendship

2732 Tumbling Ties, *QN*

2733 Indian Design

2734 Bricks and Blocks, *SSQ, 1985*

2735 Pieced Heart Block

2736 Red Cross, *1887*

2737 Job's Tears

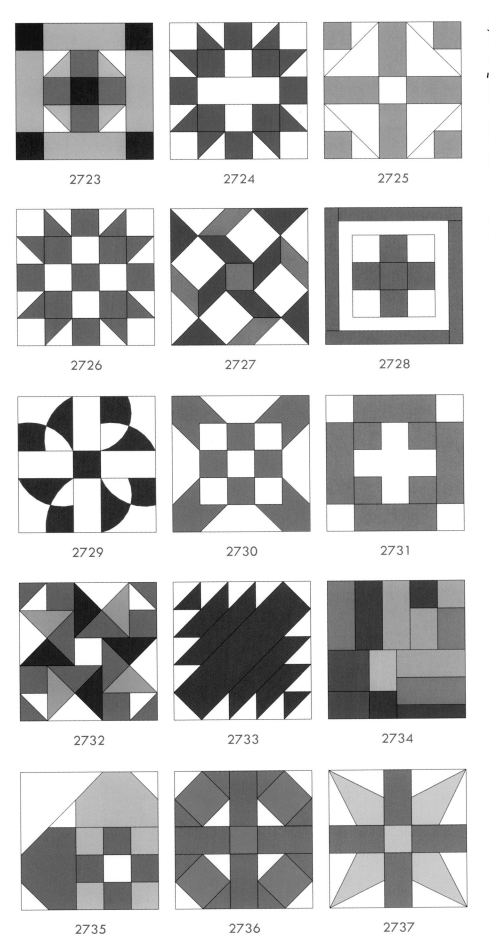

2723

2724

2725

2726

2727

2728

2729

2730

2731

2732

2733

2734

2735

2736

2737

2738

2739

2740

2741

2742

2743

2744

2745

2746

2747

2748

2749

2750

2751

2752

2738 Snowflake

2739 Formal Garden

2740 Cross Patch

2741 Friendly Pleasures

2742 Prairie Sunrise, *HH*

2743 Grandmother's Puzzle

2744 Double Basket, *HHJ*

2745 Wheels, *QW, 1988*

2746 Corner Star

2747 Memory Block

2748 Diamond Panes, *NC*

2749 Texas Puzzle, *AK, 1965*

2750 Duck's Foot, *HH*

2751 Spinning Tops, *NC*

2752 Duck and Ducklings
      Corn and Beans
      Ducklings
      Fox and Geese, *NC*
      Hen and Chickens
      Handy Andy
      Shoo Fly
      Wild Goose Chase, *CaS*

2753 Wild Goose Chase, *LW*

2754 Whirling Five Patch, *KCS*

2755 Duck and Ducklings, *LAC*
   Aunt Kate's Choice

2756 Monkey Wrench, *NC*

2757 Red Cross, *CS*

2758 Wedding Ring

2759 Jack in the Box

2760 Alpine Cross, *NC*

2761 Building Blocks, *NC*

2762 Japanese Friendship Block, *SSQ, 1990*

2763 Does Double Duty, *NC*

2764 Lily Pond, *NC*

2765 Pattern Without a Name, *NC*

2766 Autumn Leaf

2767 Old Indian Trail

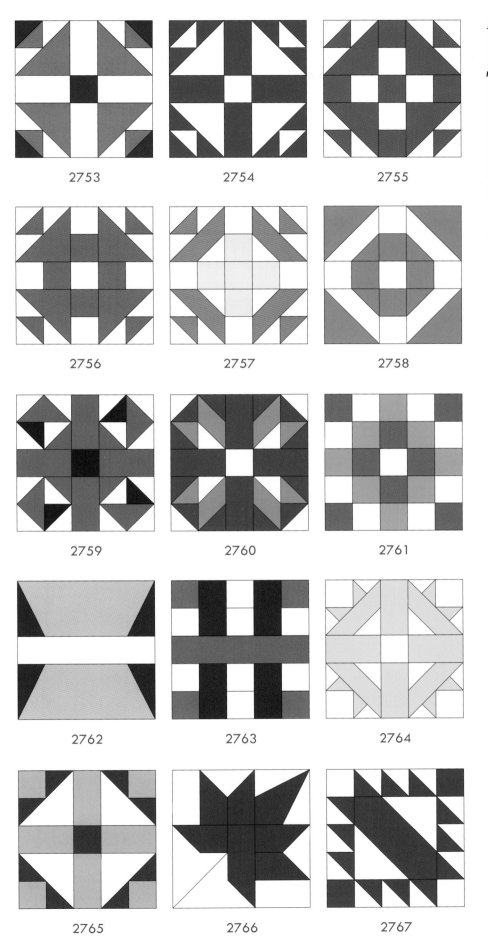

2753

2754

2755

2756

2757

2758

2759

2760

2761

2762

2763

2764

2765

2766

2767

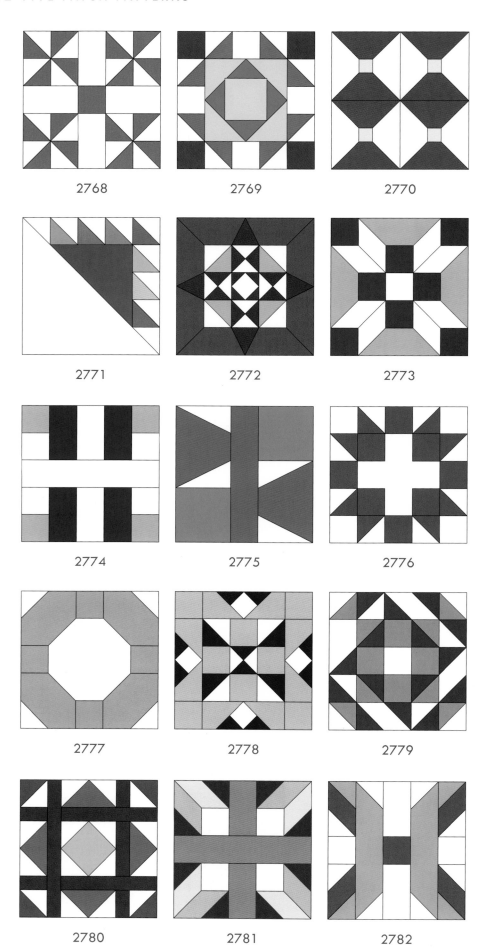

2768

2769

2770

2771

2772

2773

2774

2775

2776

2777

2778

2779

2780

2781

2782

2768 Grandma's Choice
Simple Design, *LAC*

2769 Tea Party

2770 Grandmother's Own

2771 Sawtooth

2772 Prairie Sunrise

2773 Farmer's Daughter, *CS*
Corner Posts, *KCS*
Flying Birds, *NC*
Jack's Blocks, *GC*
Rolling Stone

2774 Does Double Duty, *NC*

2775 Twist Around, *MM*

2776 Friendship Block
A Name on Each
Friendship Block
Hearth & Home Quilt,
HH
Star and Cross, OCS

2777 Wedding Ring

2778 Alaska Territory

2779 Comet
Halley's Comet

2780 Crossroads
Crossed Roads

2781 Dakota Gold
Gold Brick

2782 Domino

2783 Double Irish Chain
Grandmother's Irish
Chain, *CS*
Irish Chain
Cube Lattice
Mary Moore's Double
Irish Chain (with
four-leaf clover
appliqué in plain
blocks)
Double Irish Cross
(with four-leaf clover
appliqué in plain
blocks)
Double Irish Chain
(with four hearts
appliqué in plain
blocks)
Tiger Lily (with tiger
lily appliqué in plain
blocks)

2784 Triple Irish Chain
Single Irish Chain
Three Irish Chains,
MoM

2785 Nine Patch Irish Chain

2786 Forty Niner Quilt

2787 Irish Chain

2788 Single Irish Chain

2789 Double Irish Chain

2790 Steps to the Light
House, *NP*
Steps to the White
House, *NC*

2791 Irish Chain, *CoM*

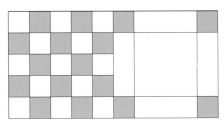

2783

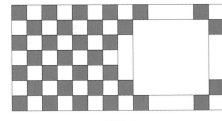

2784

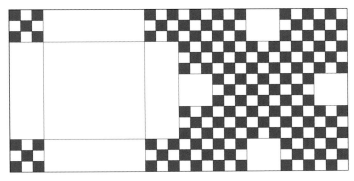

2785

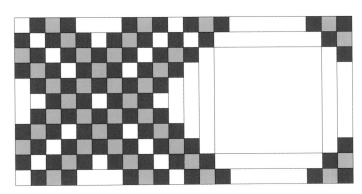

2786

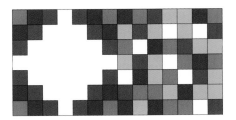

2787

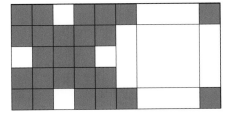

2788

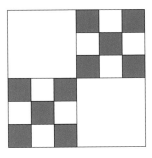

2789

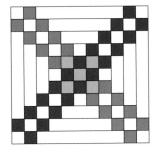

2790

2791

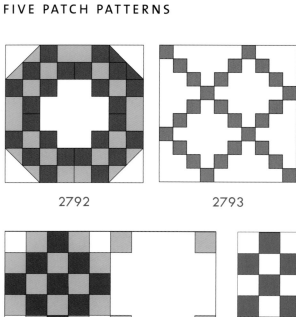

2792

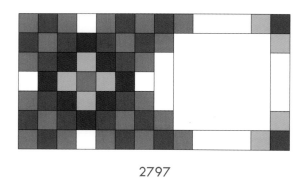

2793

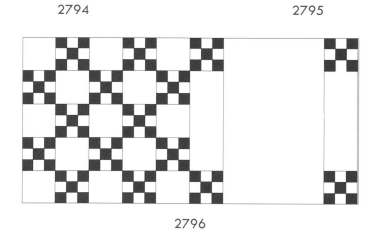

2794   2795

2796

2797   2798

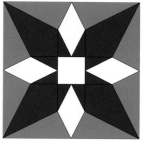

2799   2800   2801

2792   An Irish Chain Hint

2793   Chained Five Patch
       Double Irish Chain
       Mrs. Hoover's Colonial
          Quilt
       Nellie's Choice

2794   Domino Chain

2795   Dogwood Blossoms

2796   Double Irish Chain

2797   Jewel Box

2798   Double Irish Chain

2799   Blue Heaven, *NC*

2800   Lasting Blossom, *RMS*,
       SSQ,

2801   Joseph's Coat, *LAC*
       Polly's Favorite

2802 Odd Fellows, *LAC*
Baltimore Belle, *CS*
An Effective Square,
HH
Flying Geese
Odd Fellows Cross, *NC*
Odd Fellows Patch

2803 Windmill, *1930*

2804 New Jersey, *NP*

2805 Linton, *LAC*
Sun and Shade, *NP*

2806 Darting Minnows

2807 Sewing Circle, *HH*,
1900

2808 Cathedral Window, *NC*,
1933

2809 Woodland Path, *NC*,
1934

2810 Pigeon Toes

2811 Mare's Nest

2812 Ladies' Delight, *LAC*

2813 Century of Progress

2814 Dutch Mill, *LAC*
Holland Mill, *NC*

2815 Easy Do

2816 Handy Andy

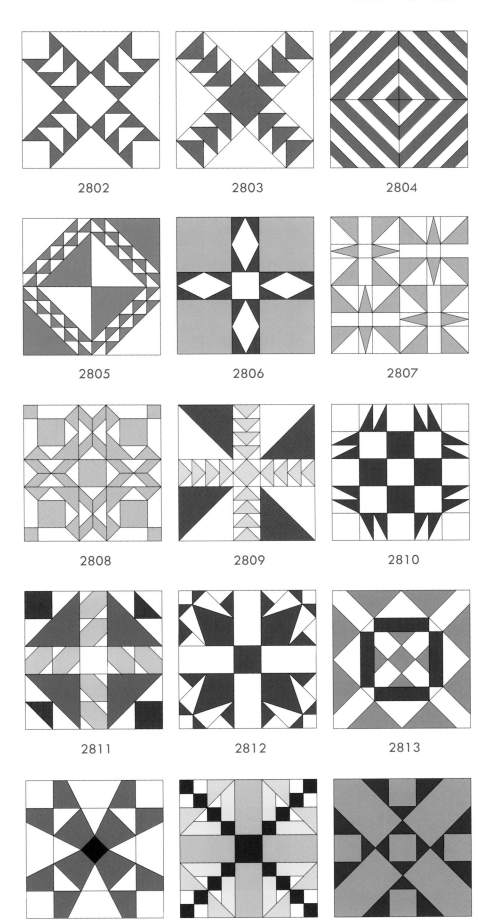

2802

2803

2804

2805

2806

2807

2808

2809

2810

2811

2812

2813

2814

2815

2816

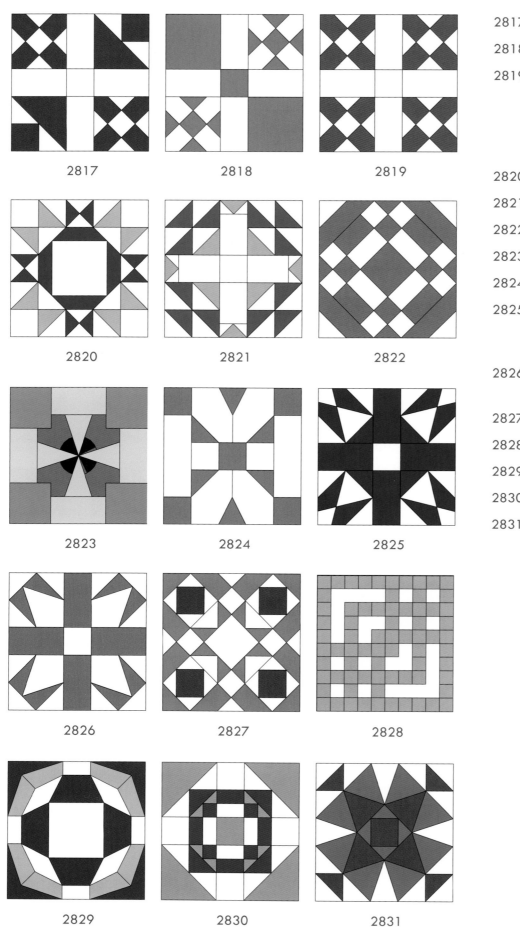

2817 Leap Frog, *LAC*

2818 Widower's Choice

2819 Bachelor's Puzzle, *LAC*
   The Seasons, *NC*
   Joy's Delight, *NCS*
   Mrs. Anderson's
      Favorite, *NCS*

2820 King David's Crown

2821 Album

2822 Domino Square

2823 Four Leaf Clover

2824 Oregon

2825 New Star, *LAC*
   Heavenly Problem, *NP*
   Heavenly Puzzle, *NC*

2826 Cross and Star, *LAC*
   Star and Cross, *NC*

2827 Devil's Claws

2828 Carpenter's Square

2829 Rustic Wheel

2830 Harmony Square, *NC*

2831 Wisconsin

5,500 QUILT BLOCK DESIGNS

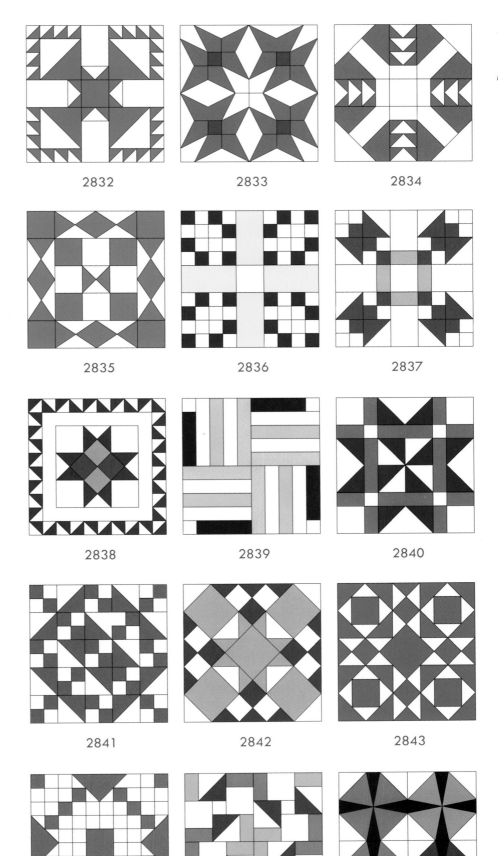

2832

2833

2834

2835

2836

2837

2838

2839

2840

2841

2842

2843

2844

2845

2846

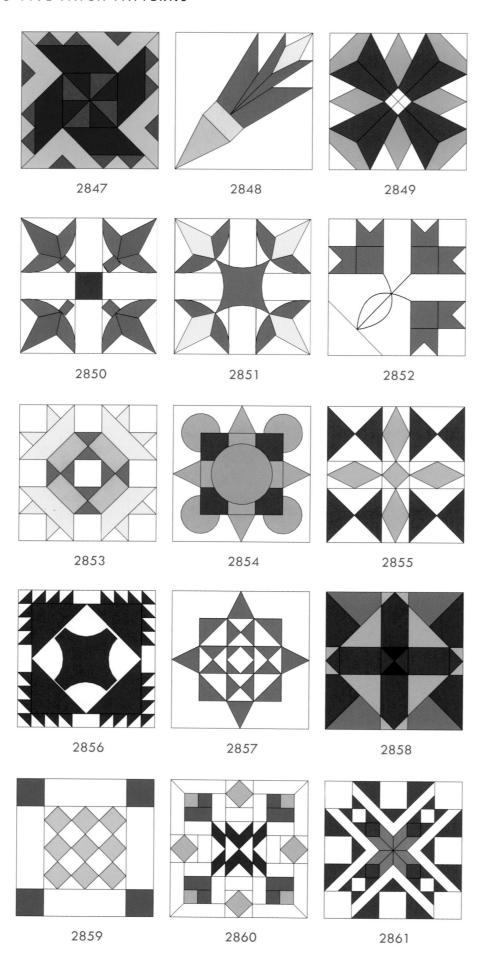

5,500 QUILT BLOCK DESIGNS

2847
2848
2849
2850
2851
2852
2853
2854
2855
2856
2857
2858
2859
2860
2861

2862 Fish in the Dish

2863 Pine Burr

2864 Granny's Favorite

2865 Broken Branch

2866 Jericho Walls

2867 Fair and Square

2868 Album

2869 Friendship

2870 Domino and Square,
    LAC
    Domino and Squares,
    NC

2871 Triangle Puzzle, *GD*

2872 Airplane

2873 Carrie's Choice

2874 Japanese Gardens

2875 Maine Woods

2876 Cross and Crown
    Goose Tracks
    Signal

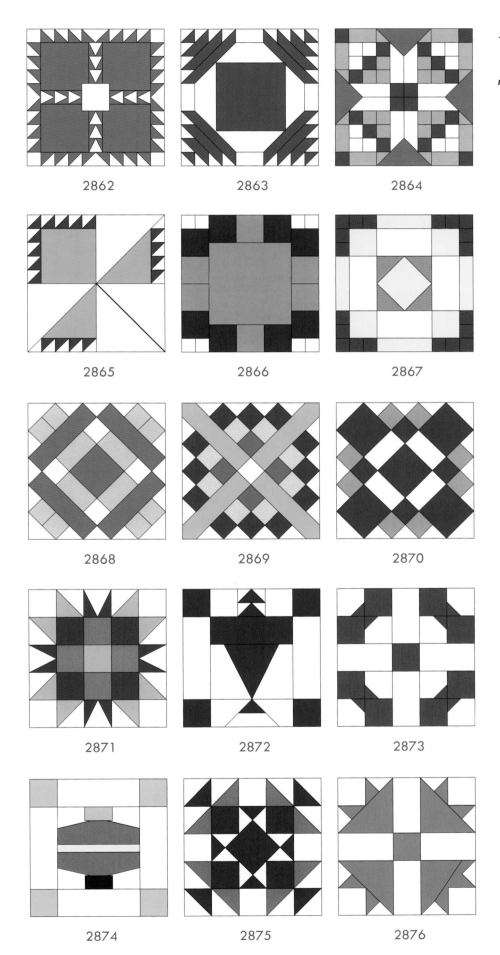

2862   2863   2864

2865   2866   2867

2868   2869   2870

2871   2872   2873

2874   2875   2876

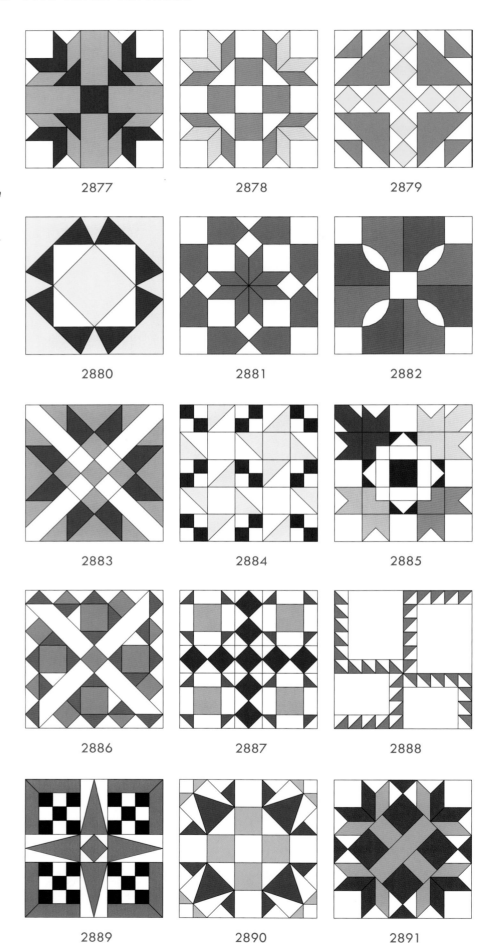

2877

2878

2879

2880

2881

2882

2883

2884

2885

2886

2887

2888

2889

2890

2891

2877 Doe and Darts

2878 Bull's Eye

2879 Bird's Nest

2880 Cousteau's Calypso

2881 St. Louis Block
St. Louis Star, *LAC*
Star of St. Louis, *NC*
Variable Star, *NC*

2882 Idaho

2883 Mexican Cross

2884 Milky Way

2885 Autumn Leaves

2886 Grape Vine

2887 Indian Squares, *NC*
Through the Years, *NC*

2888 Grandmother's
Pinwheel

2889 Waverly Star (strip
pieced center points)

2890 Quilter's Delight, *NC*

2891 Washington Quilt
Block

2892 The Wind Wheel Quilt Block

2893 Hartford Quilt Block, *HH*

2894 Church Windows, *NC*

2895 Evening Quiet, *RMS, SSQ, 1983*

2896 Expectations, *HaM, SSQ, 1983*

2897 French Garden, *QM, 1992*

2898 Mystic Maze

2899 No Name

2900 Solomon's Temple, *KCS*
    King Solomon's
    Temple, *CS*

2901 Zig-Zag

2902 Aunt Mary's Squares, *GC*

2903 Double Star, *HH*

2904 Mexican Rose,
    Marguerite Ickis
    Mexican Star
    North Star
    Panama Block, *NC*
    Shining Hour, *FJ*
    Star and Cross, *LAC*

2905 Rain or Shine, *NC*

2906 Sunbeam Crossroad, *NC*

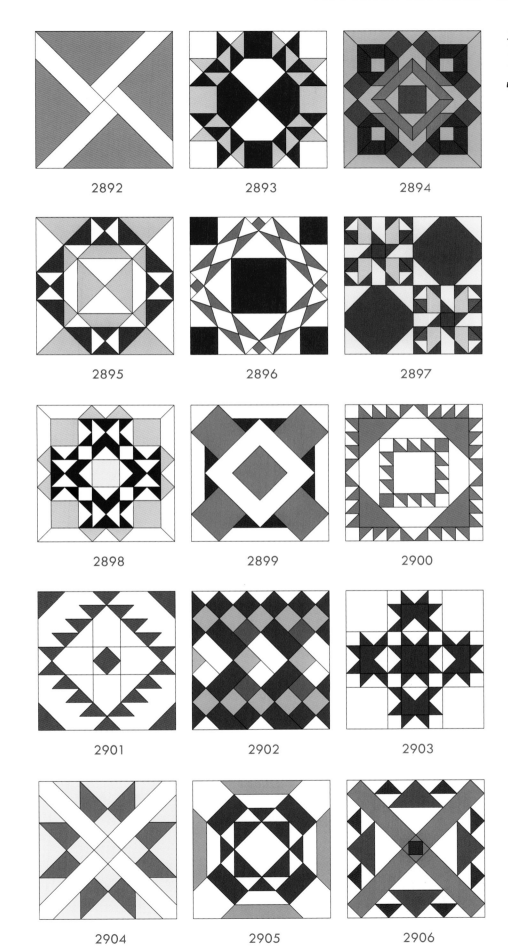

2892   2893   2894

2895   2896   2897

2898   2899   2900

2901   2902   2903

2904   2905   2906

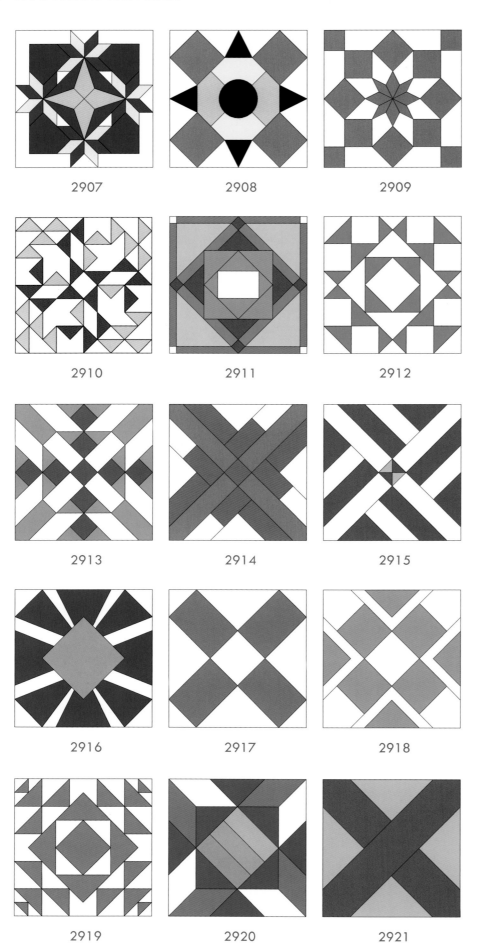

2907

2908

2909

2910

2911

2912

2913

2914

2915

2916

2917

2918

2919

2920

2921

2907 Victorian Star,
   Alice Vail, SSQ

2908 Chained Star, LW

2909 Starlight, LAC

2910 Yellow Clover, NC

2911 Aunt Anna's Album
   Block, CS

2912 Hill and Crag, NC

2913 Garden Paths, NC

2914 Whirling L, QN

2915 Mary Tenny Gray Travel
   Club Patch

2916 Drive a Crooked Mile,
   MM

2917 Crossroads

2918 Crisscross, GC

2919 Lighthouse, NC

2920 No Name, OCS

2921 Old Italian Block, NC

2922 Broken Irish Chain, *NC*

2923 Prairie Sunrise

2924 Star and Corona, *NC*

2925 Scrapbag, *NC*

2926 Hartford

2927 Prized Possession

2928 Blue Bell Block, *NC*

2929 Polly's Favorite

2930 The Texas Star Quilt Block

2931 Ice Cream Cone

2932 Single Chain and Knot, *NC*

2933 Cross and Crown, *LAC*
    Bouquet's Quilt, *NP*
    Tulip Wreath

2934 Cross and Crown

2935 Flying Geese, *LW*

2936 Square and a Half, *LAC*

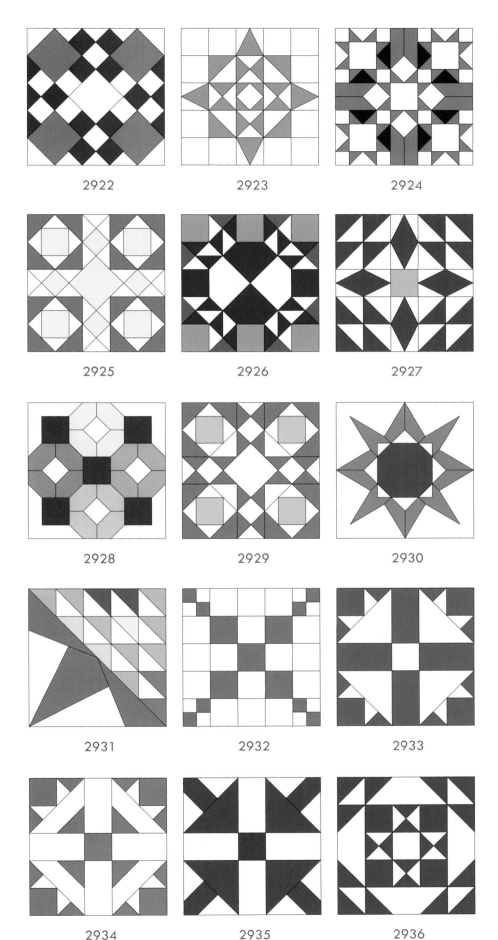

2922 2923 2924

2925 2926 2927

2928 2929 2930

2931 2932 2933

2934 2935 2936

5,500 QUILT BLOCK DESIGNS

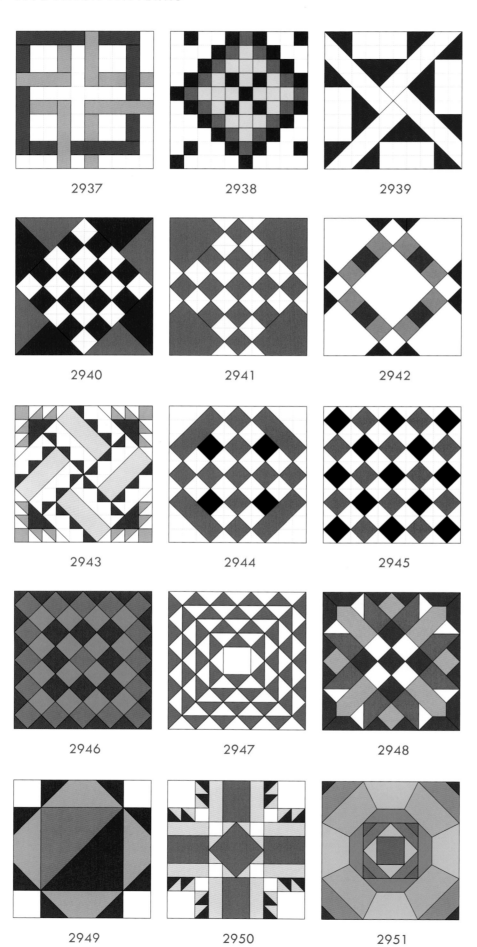

2937

2938

2939

2940

2941

2942

2943

2944

2945

2946

2947

2948

2949

2950

2951

2937 Crosswords, *FJ*

2938 Bold Squares, *OCS*

2939 Pathfinder, *NC*
Pioneer Block, *NC*

2940 Country Checkers

2941 New Double Irish
Chain

2942 Yreka Square, *NC*

2943 Labyrinth, *MM*

2944 Doors and Windows,
NC
Windows and Doors,
NC
New Double Irish
Chain, *NC*

2945 Blue Heather, *NC*
Checkerboard Squares
Cobblestones, *NC*

2946 Trip Around the World

2947 Minnesota, *NP*
Depression, *NP*

2948 Ragged Robin, *AB*
Alice's Favorite, *MD*

2949 The Animals Stood By,
HMD, SSQ, 1984

2950 Rejoice, *HMD, SSQ,
1984*

2951 Confederate Rose, *NC*

2952 Roman Roads, *NC*
  Odd Star, *NC*

2953 Puritan Maiden, *NC*

2954 Federal Chain

2955 Atlanta, *HH*
  Love Chain

2956 Patch Quilt Design, *NC*

2957 Rosemary

2958 State of Oregon, *HH*

2959 Railroad Crossing

2960 Diamonds in the
  Corners, *KCS*

2961 Butterfly Wings, *QM,*
  1992

2962 Memory Block

2963 Heart

2964 Star and Cross
  Mexican Cross
  Mexican Rose
  Mexican Star

2965 Going Home, *Nancy*
  Johnson-Srebro,
  TQ #26

2966 Diamonds Are Forever,
  MM

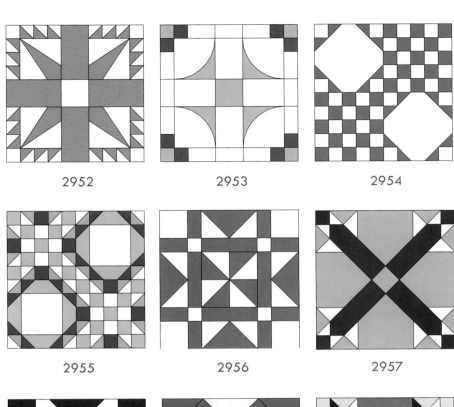

2952

2953

2954

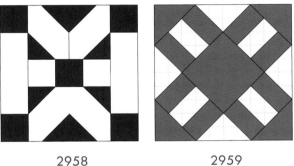

2955

2956

2957

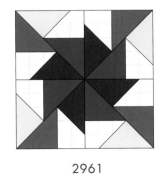

2958

2959

2960

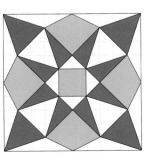

2961

2962

2963

2964

2965

2966

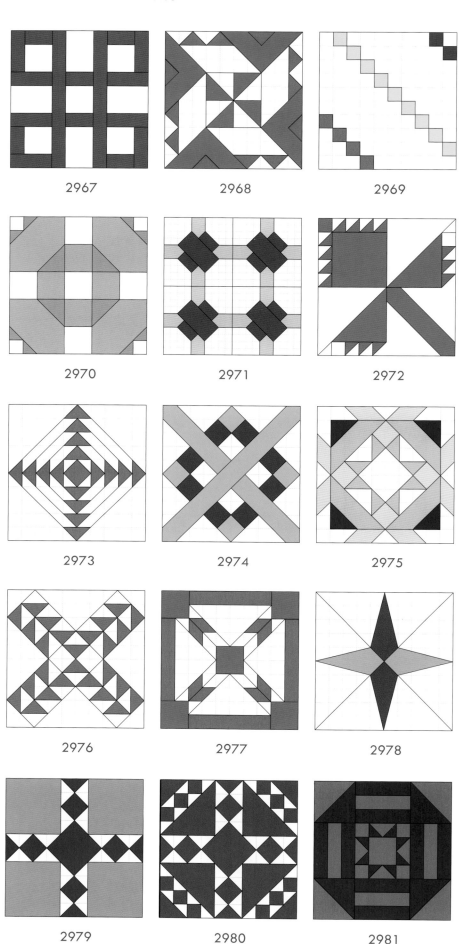

2967 Stripes and Squares

2968 Dutch Waterways

2969 Kite's Tail

2970 Whirling Snow, *RMS, 1982*

2971 Nauvoo Lattice

2972 Lily of the Field

2973 Church Steps

2974 Across the Square, *RMS*

2975 Diamonds of Hope, *Joyce Mueller, QN 2000*

2976 Old Maid's Puzzle

2977 The Air Port, *KCS*

2978 Danish Stars, *KCS*

2979 A Four Square Block with Diamonds

2980 Coronation Block

2981 Star in the Window

2982 Pieced Heart Block

2983 Gentleman's Fancy

2984 Double Link, *AMS*
Friendship Links, *NC*
Friendship Quilt

2985 Hit or Miss

2986 Viola's Scrap Quilt

2987 Modern Blocks, *OCS*

2988 Country Charm, *OCS*

2989 Hill and Hollow, *NC*

2990 Grandmother's Choice

2991 Lincoln Quilt Block, *HH*

2992 California Snowflake

2993 Morning Star, *SSQ*

2994 Stars and Squares, *SSQ*,
1986

2995 Joshua's Turn, *SSQ*,
1987

2996 Rainbow Square, *AG*

2982   2983   2984

2985   2986   2987

2988   2989   2990

2991   2992   2993

2994   2995   2996

2997

2998

2999

3000

3001

3002

3003

3004

3005

3006

3007

3008

3009

3010

3011

2997 Flying Geese

2998 Starry Nine Patch

2999 Tumbling Star, *SSQ*

3000 Star for Lahoma, *SSQ*

3001 Kaleidoscope,
       Quilts and Co.

3002 Bell's Star

3003 Sunbeam, *WW, 1928*

3004 Constellation, *QM,
       1992*

3005 The Farmer's Wife

3006 Pine Burr

3007 A Simple Design, *LAC*

3008 Broken Heart, *1931*

3009 Criss Cross, *HH*

3010 Railroad Crossing

3011 Idle Hours, *FJ*

3012 Confederate Rose, *NC*
Conventional Rose, *FJ*

3013 The Flashing Star, *AK,*
1965

3014 Farmer's Wife

3015 Starflower Wreath,
LW, OCS

3016 Marigold Garden, *QN*

3017 Marigold Garden, *QN*

3018 Nine Patch Nose Gay,
MoM

3019 Rays of Sunlight

3020 Road to Home, *RMS,*
SSQ, 1985

3021 Cowboy's Star

3022 The Rainbow Square,
Gammell

3023 Magnolia Block, *NC*

3024 Star of Manhattan, *AK*

3025 Star and Corona, *NC*

3026 Flying Star, *NC*

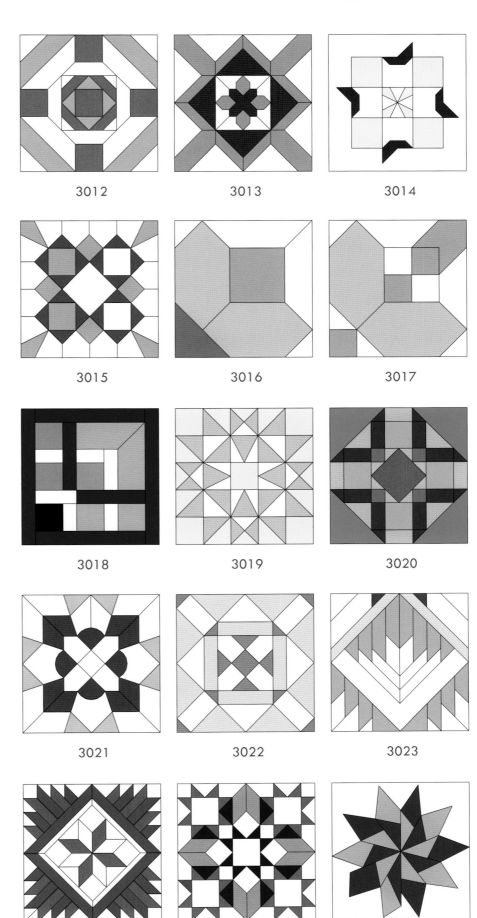

3012   3013   3014

3015   3016   3017

3018   3019   3020

3021   3022   3023

3024   3025   3026

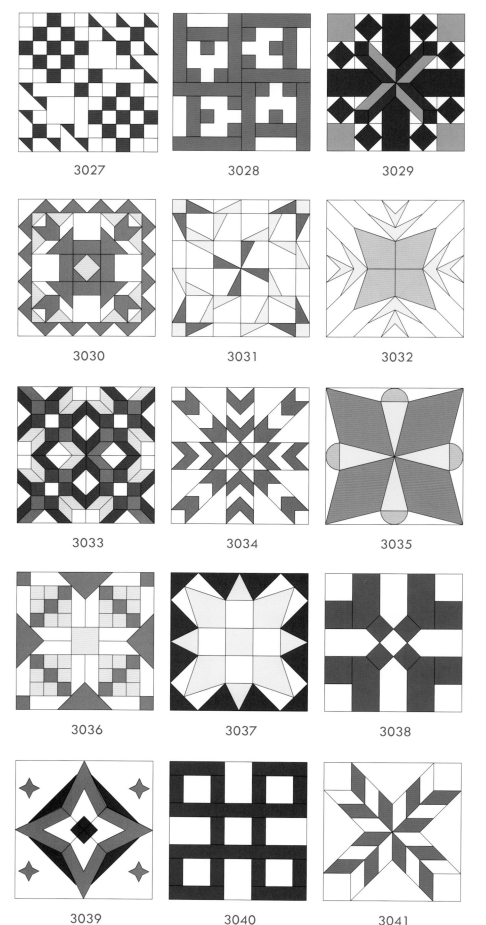

3027

3028

3029

3030

3031

3032

3033

3034

3035

3036

3037

3038

3039

3040

3041

3027 Spanish Squares, *NC*

3028 Four E Block, *LAC*

3029 City Blocks, *QN*

3030 Constellation

3031 Star and Mill Block, *NC*

3032 Double Star, *OCS*

3033 Climbing Roses, *NC*

3034 Indian Patch

3035 Star of the West
       Compass
       Four Birds
       Four Winds
       King's Star

3036 Granny's Favorite, *NC*

3037 New Star of North
       Carolina, *NC*

3038 Mother's Own, *CS*
       Forks

3039 Nativity Star, *QN*

3040 Strip Squares, *LAC*
       Stripes and Squares,
       NC

3041 Crossroads, *OF, 1898*

3042 Baker's Dozen, *JM*

3043 Ellis Island Block, *JM*

3044 Mrs. Keller's Nine
     Patch

3045 Hero's Welcome, *JM*

3046 November Nights, *JM*

3047 China Doll, *JM*

3048 Sunday Best, *JM*

3049 The Commons, *MM*

3050 Triple Square and
     Double Circle,
     Kei Kobayashi

3051 Pinwheel Skew

3052 White House Rose

3053 Old Star, *LAC*
     Roman Roads, *NC*
     Cross and Star, *CS*

3054 Premium Star, *LAC*

3055 Squares and Square,
     NP

3056 Squares and Oblongs
     Geometric Block

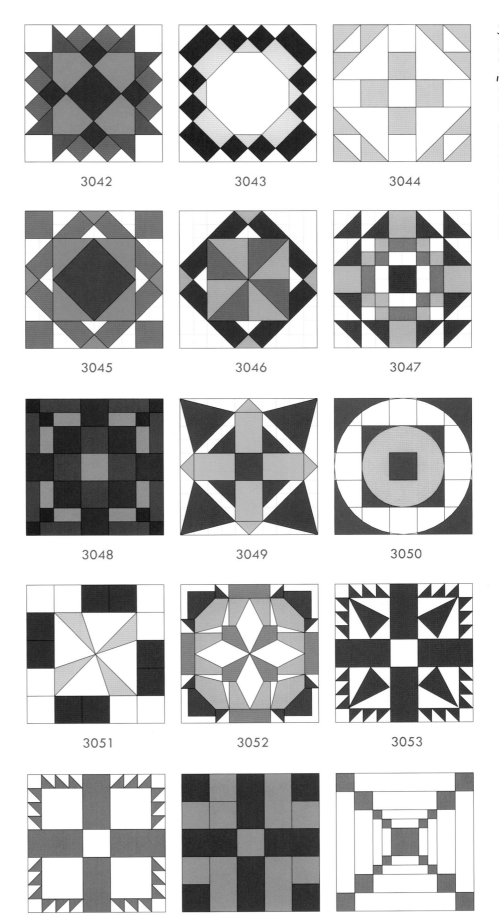

3042   3043   3044

3045   3046   3047

3048   3049   3050

3051   3052   3053

3054   3055   3056

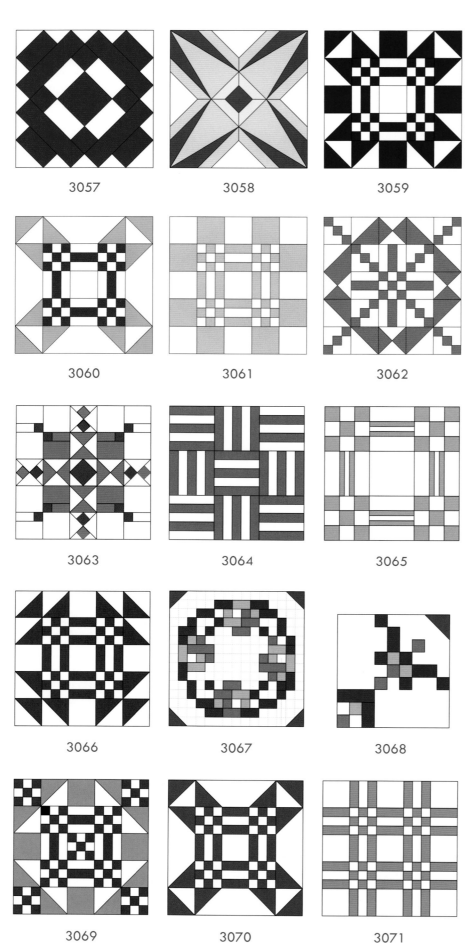

3057   3058   3059

3060   3061   3062

3063   3064   3065

3066   3067   3068

3069   3070   3071

3057 Lincoln, *HH*
      Album, *LAC*

3058 Framed Star

3059 New Mexico
      Mexican Block
      Missouri Puzzle

3060 The New Mexican Star

3061 Album Quilt, *LAC*
      Album Patch

3062 Walled City, *MM*,
      2001

3063 Maryland, *HH*

3064 Five Stripes, *LAC*
      Colt's Corral, *PP*

3065 Mountain Homespun,
      NC

3066 Goose in the Pond, *LAC*
      Gentleman's Fancy,
         Modern Priscilla
      Geometric Garden, *MD*
      Mrs. Wolf's Red
         Beauty, *MD*
      Patchwork Fantasy,
         HM
      Scrap Bag, *KCS*
      Spider's Den
      Unique Nine Patch
      Young Man's Fancy

3067 Early American Wreath,
         Ann Orr

3068 Early American Wreath
      (corner block)

3069 Missouri Puzzle
      Queen's Crown, *NC*
      Young Man's Fancy

3070 New Mexico, *HH*

3071 Squares and Stripes
      Album Quilt
      South Carolina Album
         Block

3072 Father's Fancy, *JM*, *QN*

3073 An Odd Patchwork

3074 Burgoyne Surrounded
 Beauregard's
  Surroundings
 Burgoyne's Puzzle, *HAS*
 Homespun, *MoM*
 An Odd Patchwork, *LAC*
 Road to California
 Wheel of Fortune

3075 Balance

3076 Checkered Square

3077 Bachelor's Puzzle

3078 Unnamed, *CoM*, *1923*

3079 All My Family, *RMS*,
 SSQ, *1987*

3080 Railroad Crossing, *NC*

3081 State of West Virginia

3082 Old Blue
 Tulip Variation

3083 Country Lanes

3084 The Kite

3085 Dragonfly, *Ruby
 Hinson Duncan*

3086 Blue Blades Flying

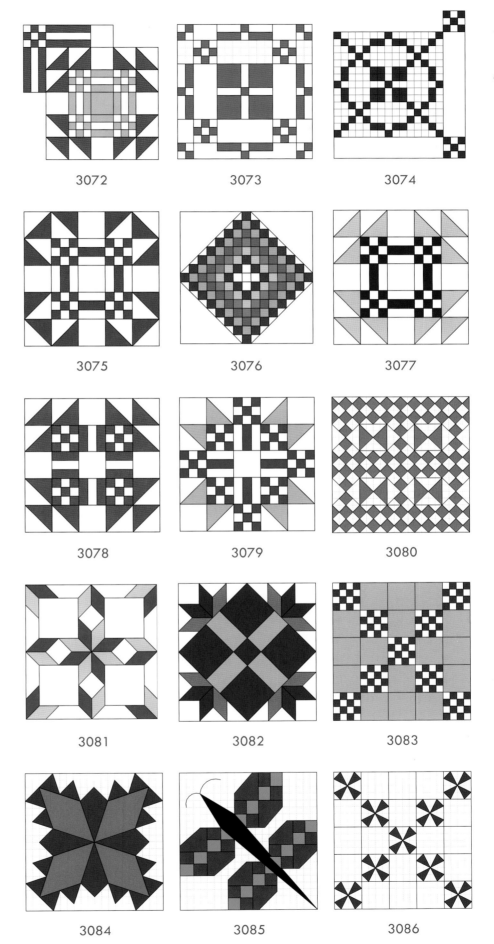

3072 3073 3074

3075 3076 3077

3078 3079 3080

3081 3082 3083

3084 3085 3086

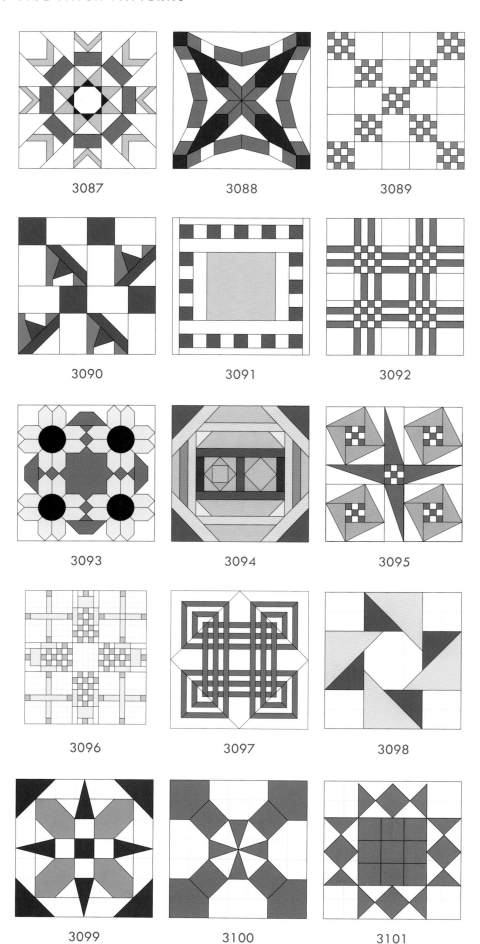

3087
3088
3089

3090
3091
3092

3093
3094
3095

3096
3097
3098

3099
3100
3101

3087 President Truman,
Zelma DePriest,
Aunt Kate's Quilting
Bee, 1973

3088 Peggy Anne's Special,
KCS

3089 Country Lanes,
MoM
Cross in the Square

3090 Over the Waves,
Zelma DePriest, QW,
1983

3091 Dewey Block, *CS*

3092 Unnamed Four Patch

3093 Modern Daisy, *NC*

3094 Amy's Inspiration
(22 grid)

3095 Blue for Julie (21 grid),
Jan Magee, QN

3096 Pineapple Squares
(23 grid), *NC*

3097 All Tangled Up
(26 grid)

3098 Broken Saw Blades, *NC*

3099 Name Unknown

3100 Housewife's Dream

3101 Uncle Sam's Hourglass

3102 Diamond Cross
Ratchet Wheel

3103 Walls of Jericho

3104 Red Cross

3105 Dove

3106 Rosebud, *AMS*
Tea Rose

3107 Country Roads

3108 Bear's Paw
Cat's Paw
Chinese Block Pattern
Duck's Foot in the
Mud, *NC*

3109 Bear's Tracks
Bear's Foot, *LAC*
Bear's Paw
The Best Friend
Cat's Paw, *NP*
Duck's Foot in the Mud
Hand of Friendship
Illinois Turkey Track,
MD
Tea Leaf Design

3110 Nine Patch

3111 Hemstitch

3112 Stonemason's Puzzle,
LAC
City Streets, *NP*

3113 Lincoln's Platform, *LAC*
Three in a Corner

3114 Prickly Pear, *KCS*

3115 Hens & Chickens, *LAC*

3116 Autumn Leaf

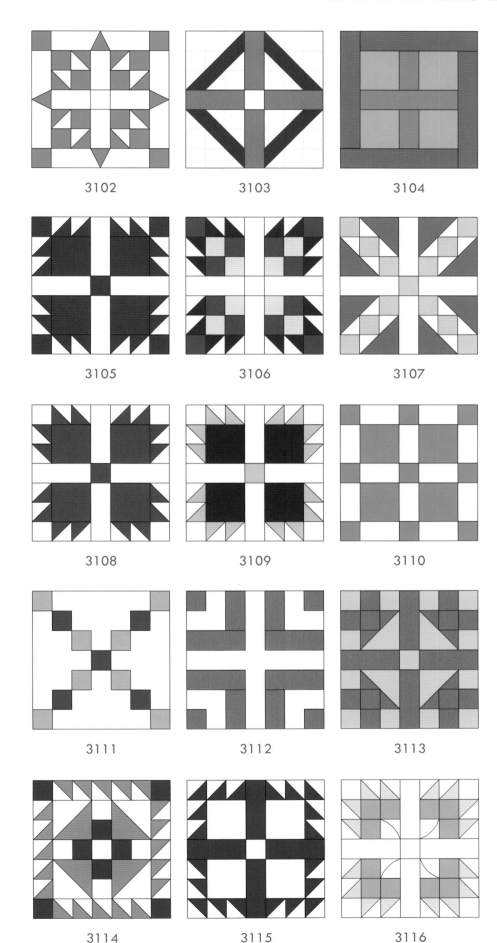

3102   3103   3104

3105   3106   3107

3108   3109   3110

3111   3112   3113

3114   3115   3116

5,500 QUILT BLOCK DESIGNS

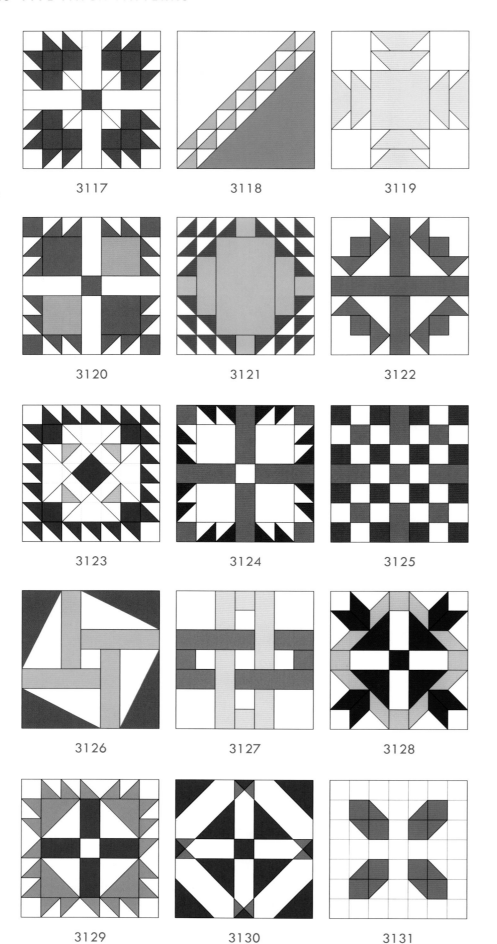

3117	3118	3119
3120	3121	3122
3123	3124	3125
3126	3127	3128
3129	3130	3131

3117 Peony

3118 City Square

3119 Easter Lily

3120 Doves in the Window, *NC*
       Four Birds, *NC, 1935*

3121 Old Maid's Puzzle

3122 Cross and Crown

3123 Queen Victoria's Crown

3124 Path of Thorns

3125 Shadow Cross

3126 Lacy Latticework

3127 Chain Link

3128 David & Goliath
       Four Darts
       Bull's Eye
       Flying Darts
       Doe and Darts

3129 No Name, *QW, 1979*

3130 My Country for Loyalty, *KCS*

3131 Lone X, *PP*

3132 Our Country, *KCS*

3133 Schoenrock Cross, *NC*

3134 Party Platform, *QN*

3135 Fancy Flowers

3136 Road to California

3137 Star of the Night, *NC*

3138 Seminole Square, *NC*

3139 The Stanley

3140 Four Queens

3141 Duck's Foot in the Mud

3142 Indian Design

3143 Courthouse Steps

3144 Whatchamacallit

3145 Log Cabin

3146 Four Queens

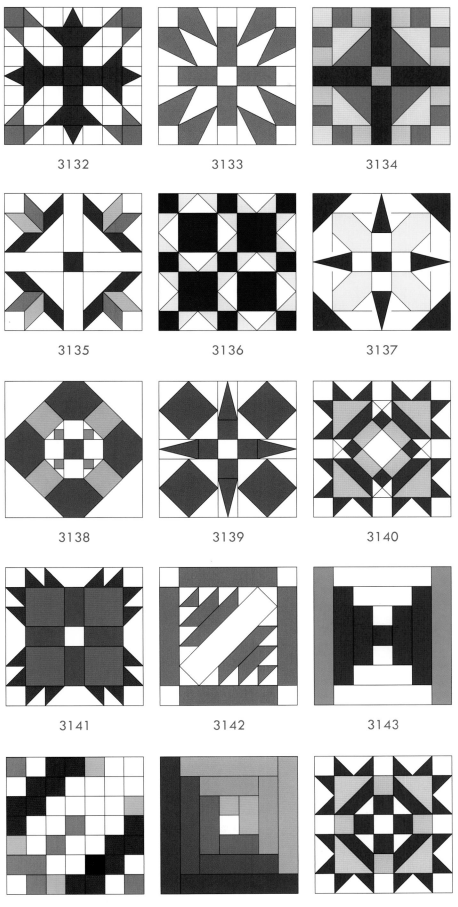

3132

3133

3134

3135

3136

3137

3138

3139

3140

3141

3142

3143

3144

3145

3146

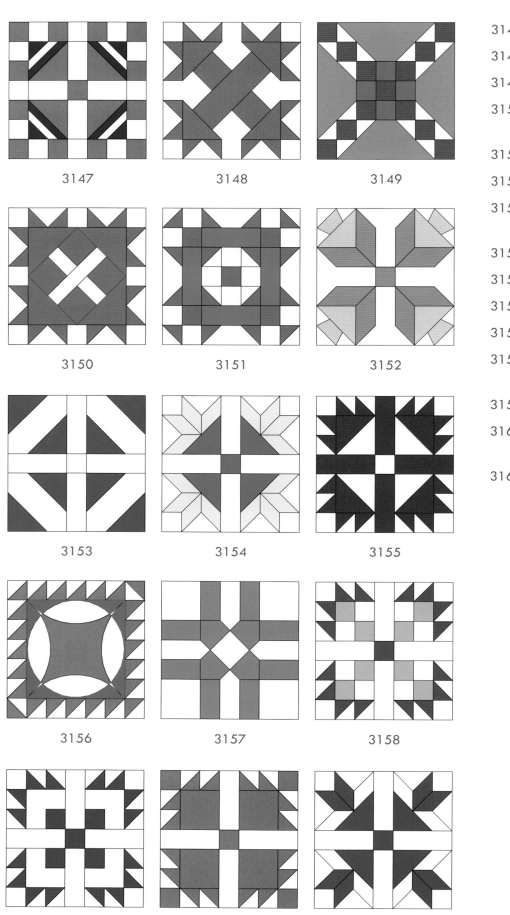

3147   3148   3149

3150   3151   3152

3153   3154   3155

3156   3157   3158

3159   3160   3161

3147 Abe Lincoln's Platform

3148 Corner Star

3149 Fox and Geese, *1898*

3150 Cluster of Lilies, *KCS*
Pond Lily

3151 Greek Cross, *KCS*

3152 Candleglow

3153 The White Square
Quilt, *KCS*

3154 Pieced Tulips

3155 Cross and Crown

3156 Christmas Spirit, *SSQ*

3157 Mother's Own

3158 Bear's Paw, *GC*
The Best Friend, *GC*

3159 Autumn Tints, *NC*

3160 Dove in the Window,
LAC

3161 Goose Tracks, *LAC*
Blue Birds Flying, *HM*
Italian Beauty
Pride of Italy

3162 Dove at the
  Crossroads, *CS*
  Lily Pond, *NC*
  Sage Bud

3163 Cross and Crown

3164 Fanny's Fan, *LAC*
  Modern Tulip, *GC*

3165 Old Fashioned Quilt

3166 Crossed Square,
  HHJ

3167 Old Maid's Puzzle, *CoM*

3168 Bouquet, *LW*

3169 Stars Over Tennessee,
  AK, 1966

3170 Boxed Squares, *MM*

3171 Scrap Basket, *MM*

3172 Lily Quilt Pattern, *LAC*
  Botch Handle
  Des Moines, *HH*

3173 Chimney Sweep,
  Coats and Clark
  Maltese Cross

3174 Queen Victoria's
  Crown, *PP*

3175 Acanthus, *NC*

3176 Mosaic Rose, *AK*

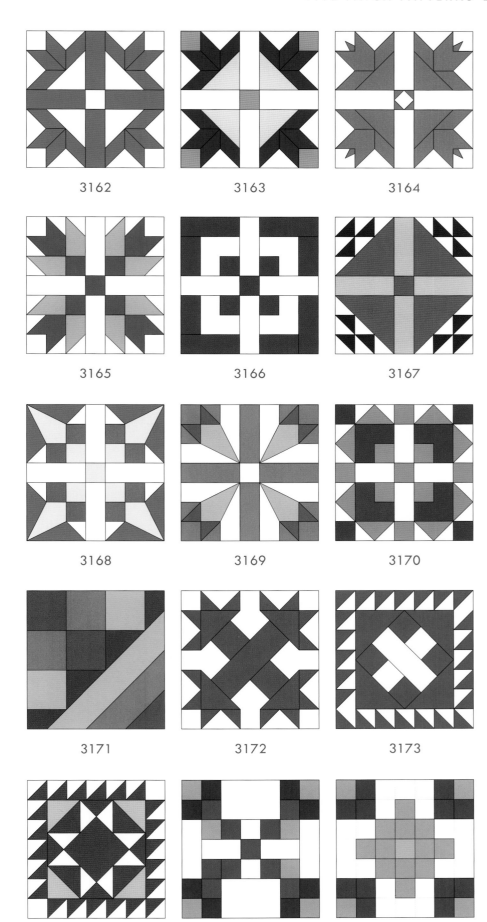

3162	3163	3164
3165	3166	3167
3168	3169	3170
3171	3172	3173
3174	3175	3176

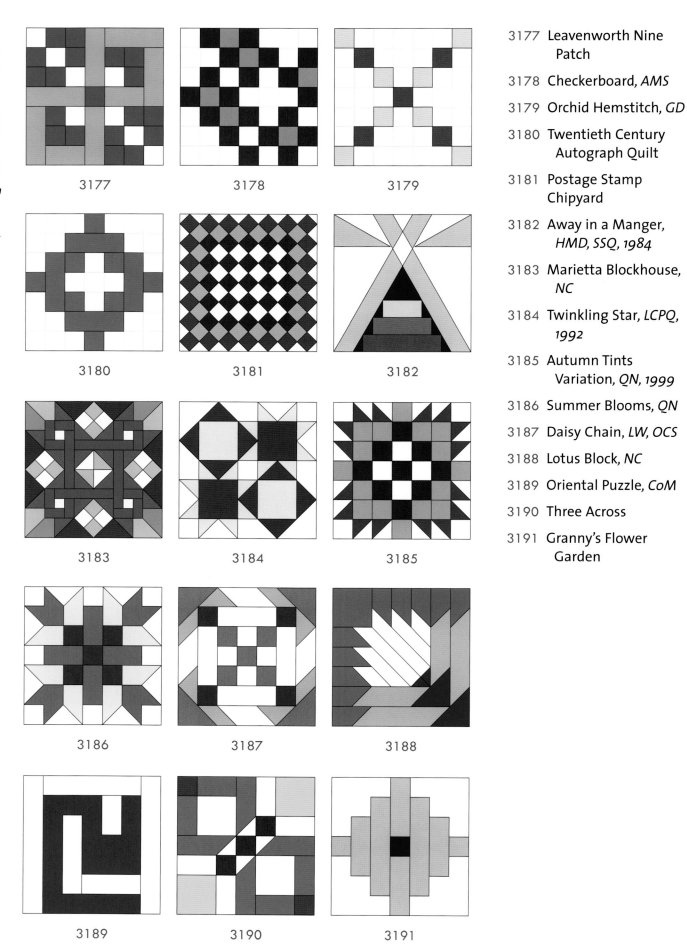

3177
3178
3179

3180
3181
3182

3183
3184
3185

3186
3187
3188

3189
3190
3191

3177 Leavenworth Nine Patch

3178 Checkerboard, *AMS*

3179 Orchid Hemstitch, *GD*

3180 Twentieth Century Autograph Quilt

3181 Postage Stamp Chipyard

3182 Away in a Manger, *HMD, SSQ, 1984*

3183 Marietta Blockhouse, *NC*

3184 Twinkling Star, *LCPQ, 1992*

3185 Autumn Tints Variation, *QN, 1999*

3186 Summer Blooms, *QN*

3187 Daisy Chain, *LW, OCS*

3188 Lotus Block, *NC*

3189 Oriental Puzzle, *CoM*

3190 Three Across

3191 Granny's Flower Garden

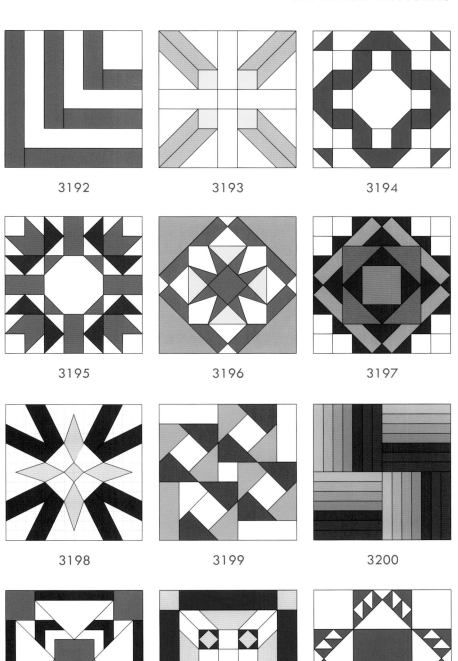

3192   3193   3194

3195   3196   3197

3198   3199   3200

3201   3202   3203

3204   3205   3206

5,500 QUILT BLOCK DESIGNS

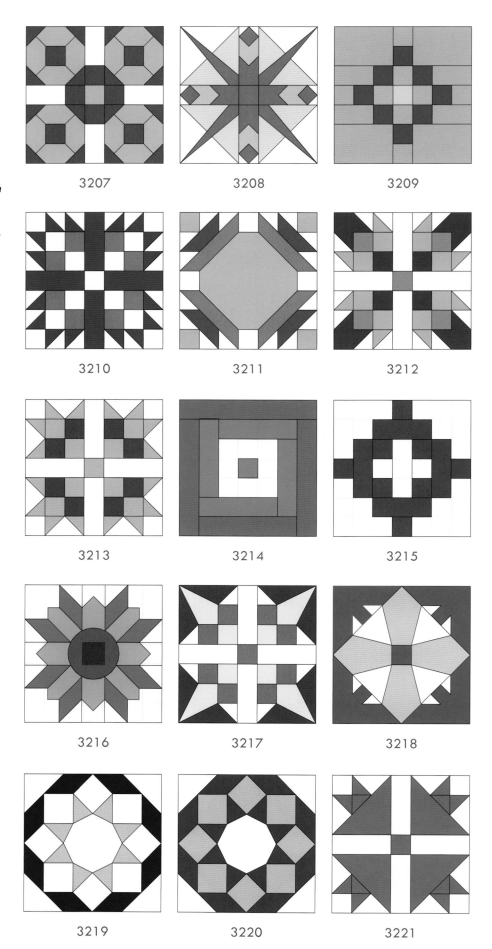

3207
3208
3209
3210
3211
3212
3213
3214
3215
3216
3217
3218
3219
3220
3221

3207 Mrs. Wilson's Favorite

3208 Horizon Star, *QWO*

3209 Southwest Cross

3210 Best Friends

3211 Altar Steps, *PP*

3212 Name Unknown

3213 Pink Magnolia

3214 Amish Squares

3215 Autograph Quilt

3216 The Gardener's Prize, *AMS*

3217 Saint Nicholas' Adventures, *OCS*

3218 Swords and Plowshares, *KCS*

3219 The Kansas Dust Storm, *KCS*

3220 Grandma's Brooch, *KCS*

3221 Goose Tracks
The Crossroads, *TFW*
Crow's Foot
Dove in the Window, *KCS*
Duck Paddle, *HHJ*
Fancy Flowers, *GC*
Lily Corners

3222 Circling Swallows

3223 Crystal Star

3224 St. Louis Star

3225 St. Louis Star Variation

3226 Swirls

3227 Pineapple

3228 No Name, *QW, 1984*

3229 Spring Tulips,
  Big Block Quilts, 1994

3230 Bluebirds Flying, *QN,
  1985*

3231 Cross and Crown
  Variation

3232 Birds in the Air

3233 Bachelor's Puzzle

3234 No Name (hearts
  appliquéd in light
  squares), *SSQ, 1985*

3235 Petit Park, *QN*

3236 Montana Maze, *NC*
  Mountain Maze

3222

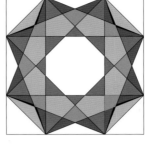

3223

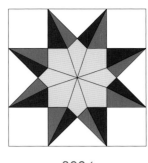

3224

3225

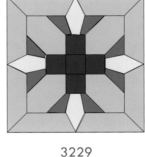

3226

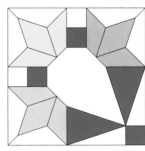

3227

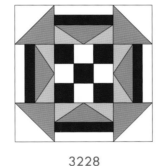

3228

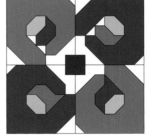

3229

3230

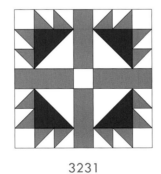

3231

3232

3233

3234

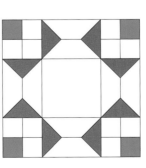

3235

3236

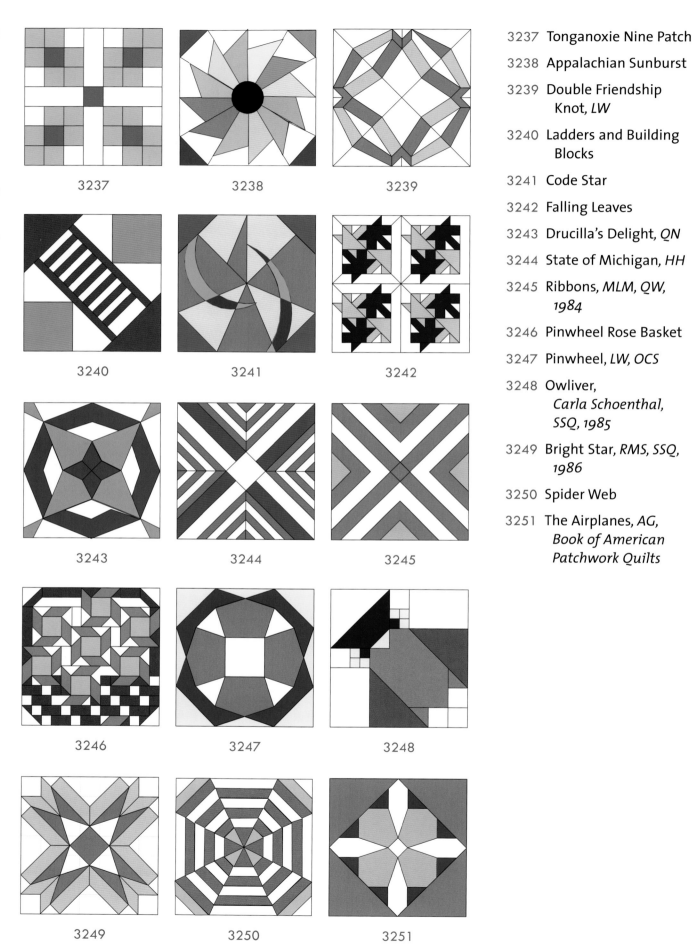

3237

3238

3239

3240

3241

3242

3243

3244

3245

3246

3247

3248

3249

3250

3251

3237 Tonganoxie Nine Patch

3238 Appalachian Sunburst

3239 Double Friendship Knot, *LW*

3240 Ladders and Building Blocks

3241 Code Star

3242 Falling Leaves

3243 Drucilla's Delight, *QN*

3244 State of Michigan, *HH*

3245 Ribbons, *MLM, QW, 1984*

3246 Pinwheel Rose Basket

3247 Pinwheel, *LW, OCS*

3248 Owliver, *Carla Schoenthal, SSQ, 1985*

3249 Bright Star, *RMS, SSQ, 1986*

3250 Spider Web

3251 The Airplanes, *AG, Book of American Patchwork Quilts*

3252 Pieced Pineapple, *OCS*

3253 Wishing Star

3254 Friendship Square

3255 Stained Glass Star,
    Jane LaRocca, SSQ

3256 Nebraskaland

3257 Persian, *LAC*

3258 Guthrie, *HH*

3259 Yellow Lilies, *NC*

3260 Dogwood, *PP*

3261 Migration South,
    Donna Meese, SSQ,
    1986

3262 Jan's Bicentennial Star,
    QW, 1987

3263 Tudor Rose, *NC*

3264 St. Paul, *HH*
    Lady of the Lake,
    Prairie Farmer

3265 Vice President's Quilt,
    LAC

3266 Star in Stripes

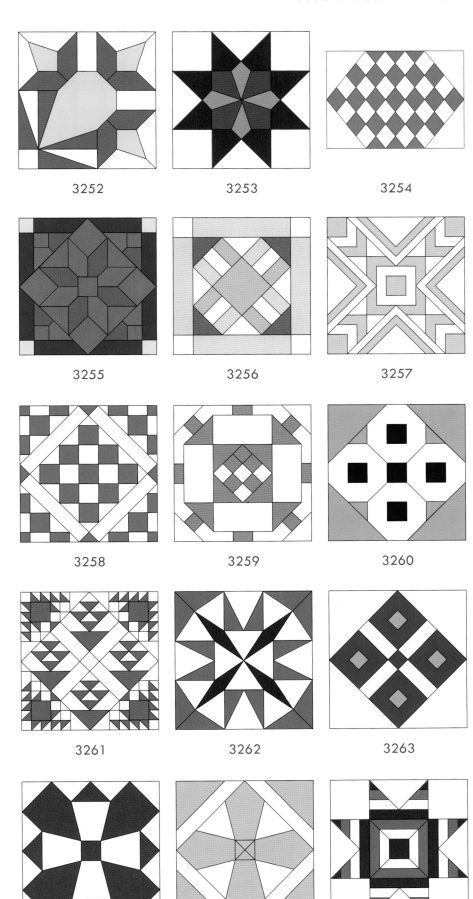

3252   3253   3254

3255   3256   3257

3258   3259   3260

3261   3262   3263

3264   3265   3266

3267	3268	3269
3270	3271	3272
3273	3274	3275
3276	3277	3278
3279	3280	3281

3267 Rhode Island Maple Leaf Star, *AK*

3268 Madame X

3269 True Lover's Knot
Hand
California Oakleaf
Sassafras Leaf

3270 State of Nebraska, *HH*

3271 Wild Iris, *PP*

3272 Ribbon Square, *LAC*

3273 Dove in the Window

3274 Cross

3275 Whirling Square, *NC*

3276 Texas Two Step, *JM*

3277 Log Cabin

3278 Chimneys and Cornerstones

3279 Log Cabin Sherbet

3280 Log Cabin Star

3281 Feathered Log Cabin, *JM, QN, 1993*

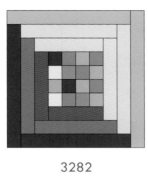
3282

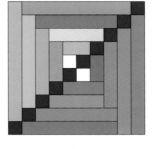
3283

3284

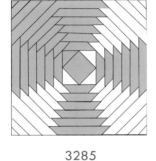
3285

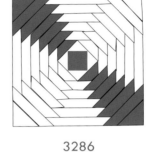
3286

3287

3288

3289

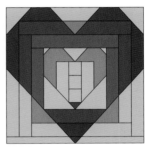
3290

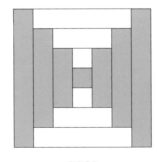
3291

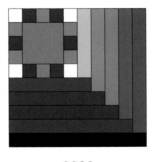
3292

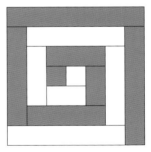
3293

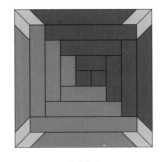
3294

3295

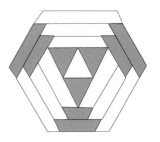
3296

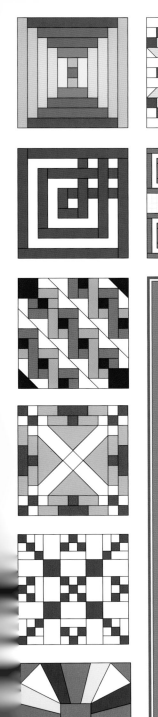

ELEVEN
PATCH
PATTERNS

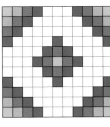
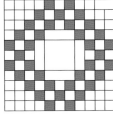
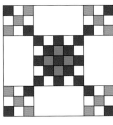
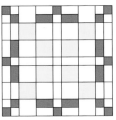
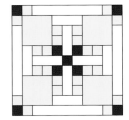
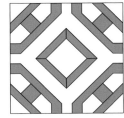
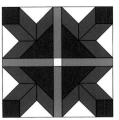

11 X 11 GRID

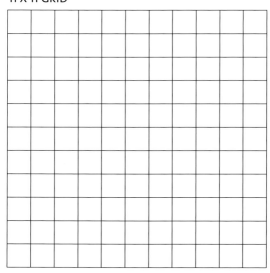

DRAFT TO AN 11" OR 22" BLOCK

3297 Fields and Fences, *NC*

3298 Easter Tide

3299 New Star

3300 Lily Pool

3301 Courthouse Steps

3302 Miss Jackson

3303 White House Steps

3304 Carpenter's Square,
     LAC

3305 Gordian Knot

3306 Interlaced Blocks, *LAC*
     True Lover's Knot

3307 Persian, *LAC*

3308 Mountain Paths, *QM,*
     1992

3309 Chinese Square, *FJ*

3310 Cross of Temperance
     Cross of Tennessee

3311 Broken Windmills, *NC*

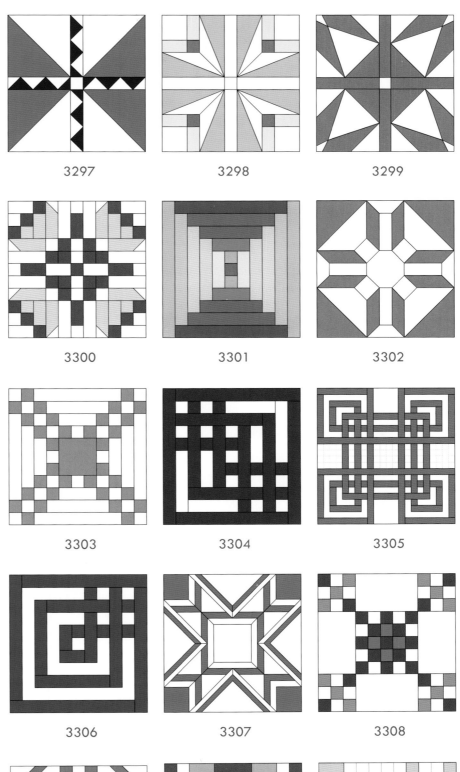

3297

3298

3299

3300

3301

3302

3303

3304

3305

3306

3307

3308

3309

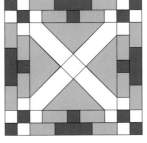

3310

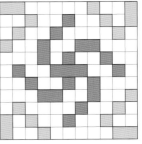

3311

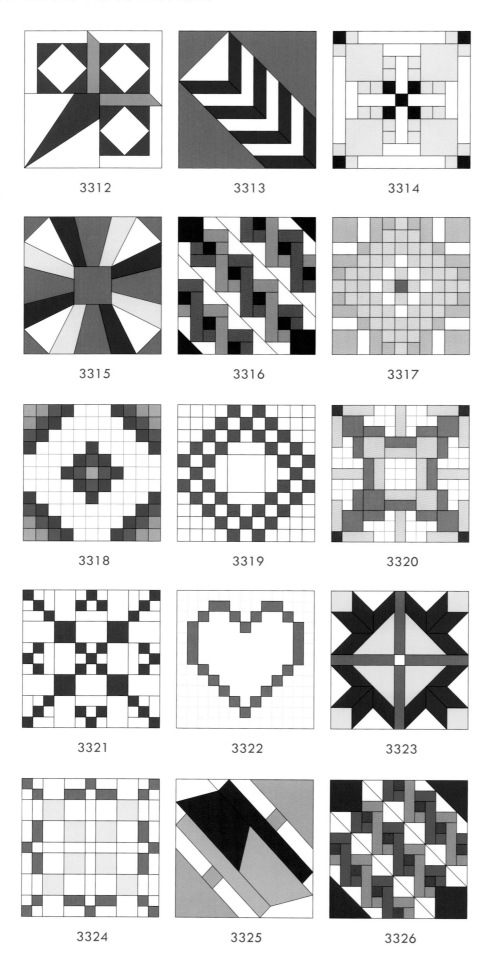

3312

3313

3314

3315

3316

3317

3318

3319

3320

3321

3322

3323

3324

3325

3326

3312 Friendship Bouquet, *AB, OCS*

3313 Sergeant's Chevron, *FJ*

3314 Tahitian Postage Stamp, *QW*

3315 Fanfare

3316 Weaving Paths, *NC*

3317 Golden Glow

3318 Hanging Diamond

3319 Irish Chain, *PP*

3320 Homespun Block, *NC*

3321 Beautiful Mosaic, *FJ*

3322 Pieced Heart

3323 Pieced Tulip Block

3324 Chariot Wheel, *NC*
    Quilter's Delight, *NC*

3325 Tree and Truth Block,
    Mary Walker, 1932

3326 Weaving Paths, *NC*

3327 Crossword Puzzle

3328 King's Highway

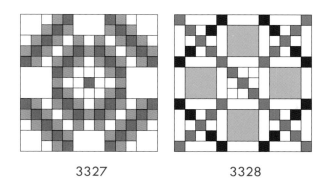

3327   3328

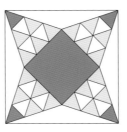

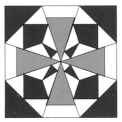

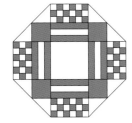
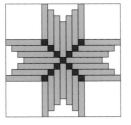
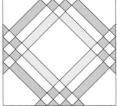
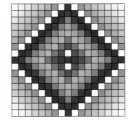

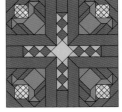

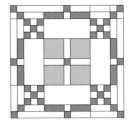

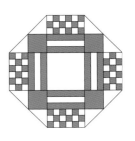

EIGHTEEN PATCH PATTERNS

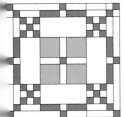

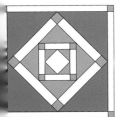
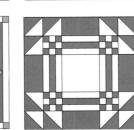
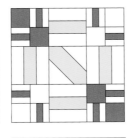
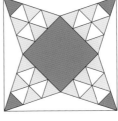

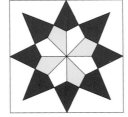

18 X 18 GRID

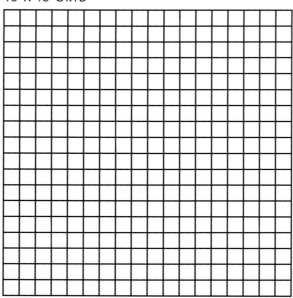

THESE PATTERNS ARE MADE ON A GRID 18 X 18 SQUARES

3329 Miss Nancy

3330 North Star

3331 In Red and White

3332 Bride's Puzzle

3333 Harlequin Star

3334 Enigma

3335 Patchwork Cushion
Top, *KCS*

3336 Lattice Weave, *AK*

3337 Carpenter's Star
(19 patch)

3338 Golden Gates, *LAC*

3339 Missouri Puzzle

3340 Odd Patchwork

3341 Road to California
(17 patch)

3342 Oriental Puzzle, *NC*

3343 Mosaic Block (17 grid)
Grandma's Square
Trip Around the World
(as a continuous
design):
A Trip Around the
World
Grandma's Dream
Postage Stamp
Squares Around the
World
Sun and Shadow
Sunshine and Shadow

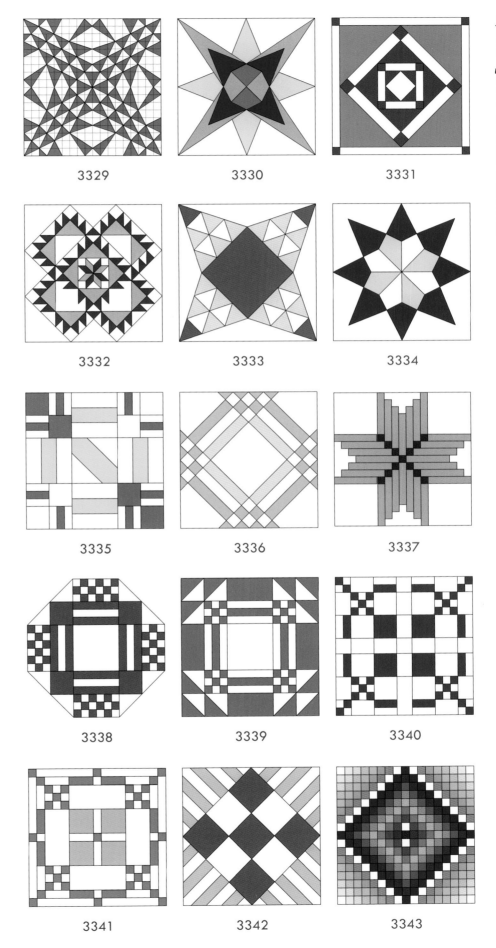

3329   3330   3331

3332   3333   3334

3335   3336   3337

3338   3339   3340

3341   3342   3343

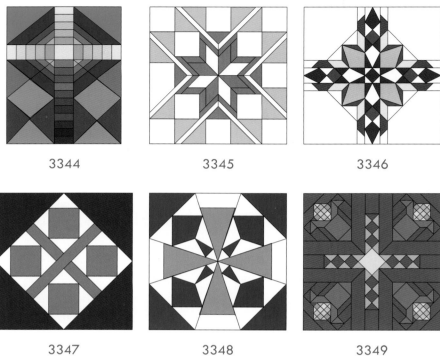

3344   3345   3346

3347   3348   3349

3350

3344 Cross

3345 New Star, *LAC*

3346 Old Rugged Cross

3347 The Savior's Cross

3348 Spider Web

3349 Indian Corn

3350 Summer Rose, *QM*

TWENTY-FOUR PATCH PATTERNS

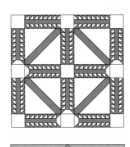
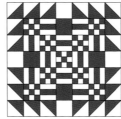

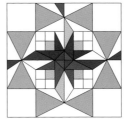
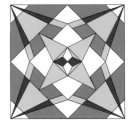
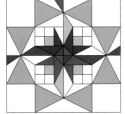
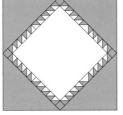

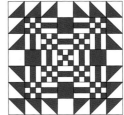
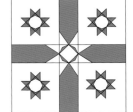
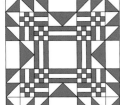
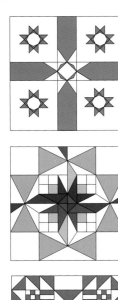

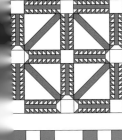
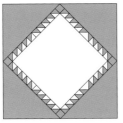

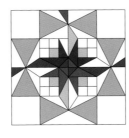

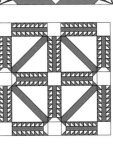
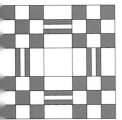

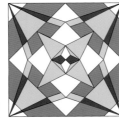
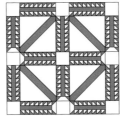

24 X 24 GRID

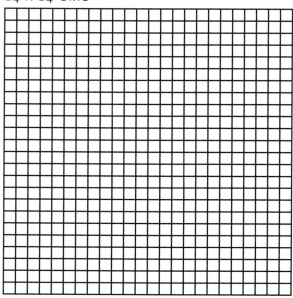

THESE PATTERNS ARE MADE ON A GRID 24 X 24 SQUARES
THEY ARE EASILY DRAFTED TO ANY BLOCK SIZE DIVISIBLE BY 4

3351 State of Nebraska, *HH*
Nebraska, *NC*
Iowa

3352 Shadow Star, *AMS*
Shepherd's Light

3353 Sawtooth Diamond

3354 Unnamed

3355 Kaleidoscope

3356 Nebraska, *HH*

3357 New York Beauty

3358 Bouquet Star
Galactica Star
Star Bouquet

3359 Mountain Homespun,
NC

3360 Cubes and Bars, *AMS*,
1933

3361 Nebraska, *NC*

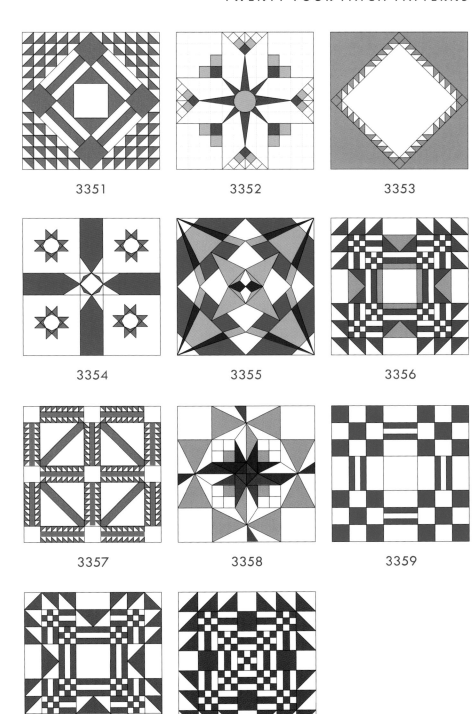

3351

3352

3353

3354

3355

3356

3357

3358

3359

3360

3361

TWELVE

---·---·---·---·---·---·---·---·---

PATCH

---·---·---·---·---·---·---·---·---

PATTERNS

12 X 12 GRID

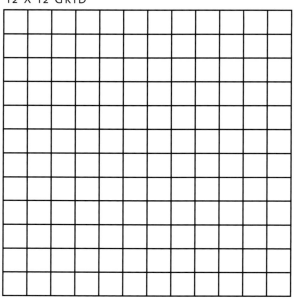

THESE PATTERNS ARE MADE ON A GRID 12 X 12 SQUARES
THEY ARE EASILY DRAFTED TO ANY BLOCK SIZE DIVISIBLE BY 4

3362 Cross and Crown

3363 Sage Bud of Wyoming

3364 The Presidential
Armchair

3365 Eastertide Quilt

3366 Wind Star for New
Hampshire

3367 Birds in a Square

3368 Rhode Island Maple
Leaf Star

3369 Golden Gate

3370 Autumn Leaf

3371 Arizona's Cactus
Flower

3372 Pennsylvania
Pineapple, *WB*

3373 Lincoln's Hat

3374 Quebec, *NC*

3375 Nebraska Windmill, *QN*

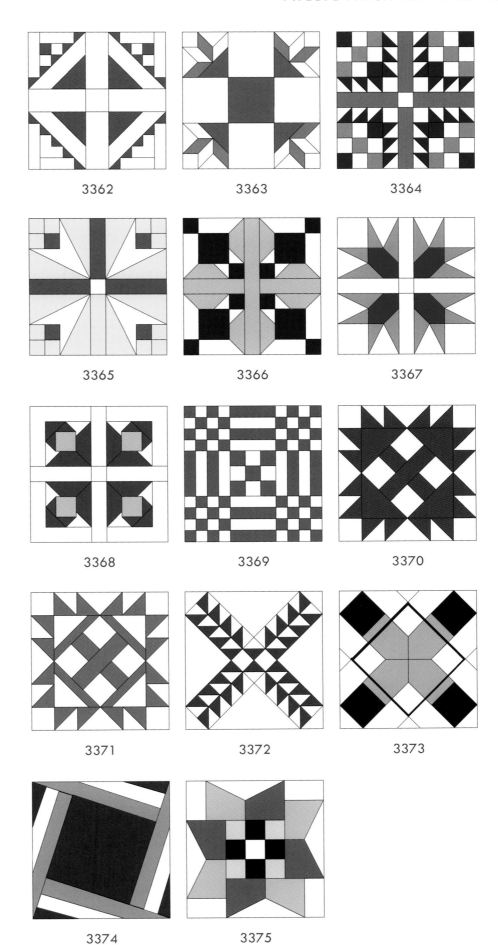

3362

3363

3364

3365

3366

3367

3368

3369

3370

3371

3372

3373

3374

3375

T E N
PATCH
PATTERNS

10 X 10 GRID

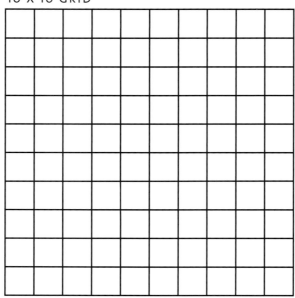

THESE PATTERNS ARE MADE ON A GRID 10 X 10 SQUARES
DRAFT THESE PATTERNS TO ANY BLOCK SIZE DIVISIBLE BY 5

3376 Christmas Cactus

3377 Crossed Squares, *NC*

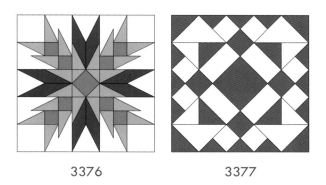

3376   3377

EIGHT PATCH PATTERNS

8 X 8 GRID

THESE PATTERNS ARE MADE ON A GRID 8 X 8 SQUARES
THEY ARE EASILY DRAFTED TO ANY BLOCK SIZE DIVISIBLE BY 4

3378 North Pole, *QM, 1997*

3379 Priscilla's Dream

3380 Tulip Tile, *AK*

3381 Tracy's Puzzle, *AK*

3382 Broken Star, *NC*

3383 Completed Square, *HH*
       Odd Fellow's Cross

3384 Illinois Star, *NC*

3385 Ships A-Sailing, *WB*

3386 Unnamed

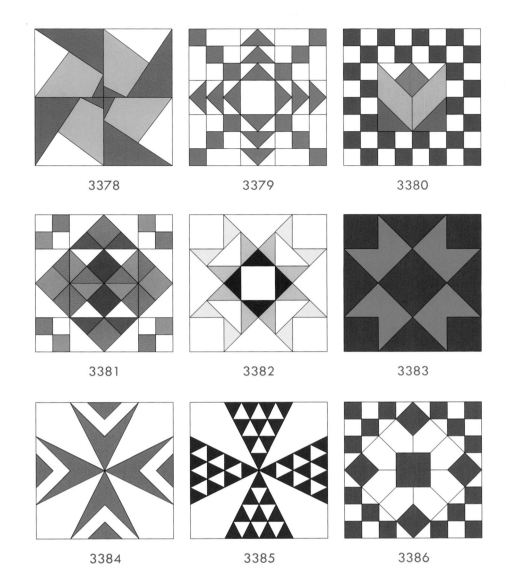

3378 3379 3380

3381 3382 3383

3384 3385 3386

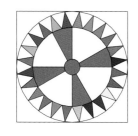
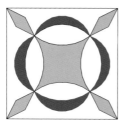
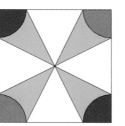
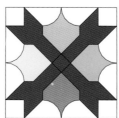
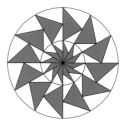

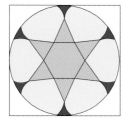

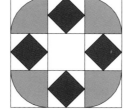
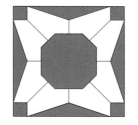
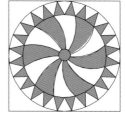

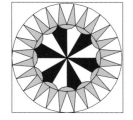
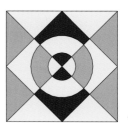

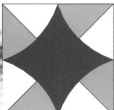
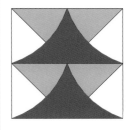

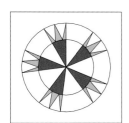

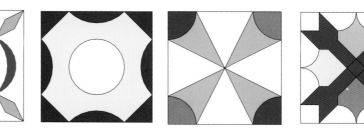

CIRCLES AND
CURVES
PATCH
PATTERNS

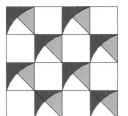

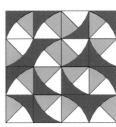
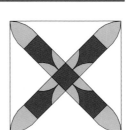

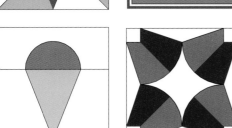

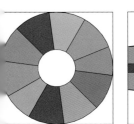
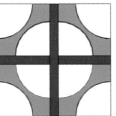
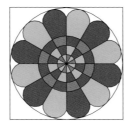
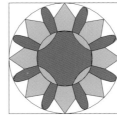
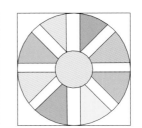
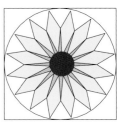

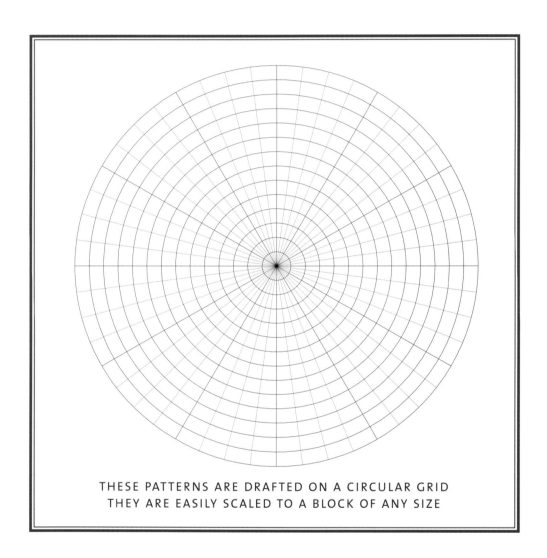

THESE PATTERNS ARE DRAFTED ON A CIRCULAR GRID
THEY ARE EASILY SCALED TO A BLOCK OF ANY SIZE

3387 Grecian Star

3388 Mohawk Trail
  Baby Bunting
  Chinese Fan
  Fan
  Path of Fans, *NC*

3389 Dresden Plate
  Chrysanthemum, *LAC*
  Aster
  Friendship Ring
  Friendship Wreath
  Grandmother's
    Sunbonnet
  Grandmother's
    Sunburst

3390 Baby Bunting, *LAC*
  Broken Saw, *CoM*
  Chinese Fan, *NC*
  The Wanderer, *CoM*

3391 Rainbow Block, *NC*
  Indian Raid
  Summer Fancy, *LW,
    OCS*

3392 Trenton

3393 Blue Blazes

3394 Pig Pen, *KCS*
  Fair Play, *LAC*
  Quarter Turn
  Wedding Ring

3395 Nocturne

3396 Josephine Knot

3397 Hidden Flower

3398 Queen's Crown

3399 Queen's Crown

3400 Pullman Puzzle
  Baseball
  Roman Pavements, *NC*
  Snowball

3401 Compass
  Robbing Peter to Pay
    Paul

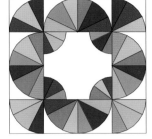

3387

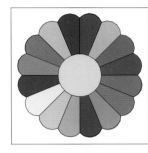

3388

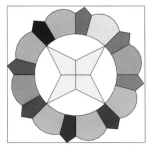

3389

3390

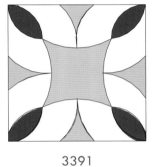

3391

3392

3393

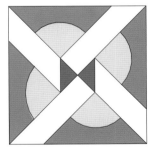

3394

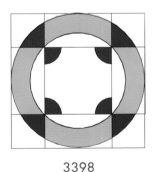

3395

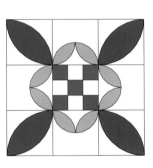

3396

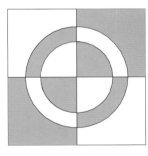

3397

3398

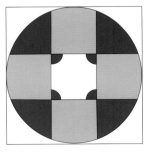

3399

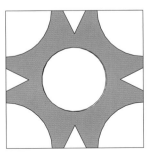

3400

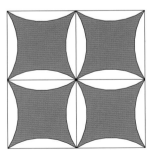

3401

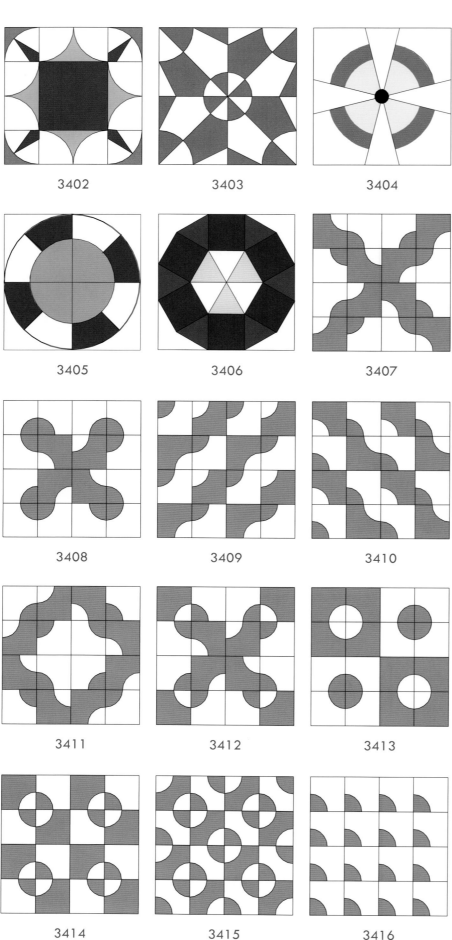

3402 — 3403 — 3404

3405 — 3406 — 3407

3408 — 3409 — 3410

3411 — 3412 — 3413

3414 — 3415 — 3416

3402 Queen's Pride

3403 Old Maid Combination

3404 Air Ship Propeller
Texas Tulip

3405 Circle Within Circle

3406 Four O'Clock

3407 Drunkard's Path
Boston Trail
Crazy Quilt
Crooked Path, *NP*
Country Cousin, *NC*
Drunkard's Trail
Endless Trail, *NP*
Old Maid's Puzzle
Pumpkin Vine
Robbing Peter to Pay Paul
Solomon's Puzzle
Wanderer's Path in the
Wilderness
Wandering Path of the
Wilderness
Wonder of the World, *LAC*
World's Wonder, *NC*
(with alternate plain
squares):
Oregon Trail, *CaS*
Solomon's Puzzle, *CaS*

3408 Wonder of the World
Wish U Well

3409 Falling Timbers

3410 Vine of Friendship
Diagonal Stripes
Dove
Falling Timbers
Snake Trail

3411 Dove, *KCS*

3412 Fool's Puzzle

3413 Polka Dots, *AMS*

3414 Snowball

3415 Steeplechase
Indiana Puzzle, *CaS*
Rob Peter to Pay Paul
Snowball

3416 Dirty Windows, *NC*
Snowy Windows, *QN*

3417 Around the World

3418 Drunkard's Path
Variation
Falling Timbers, *AMS*

3419 Drunkard's Trail, *GC*
Rocky Road to Dublin,
GC

3420 Country Husband
Oregon Trail, *CaS*
Road to California, *WB*
Rocky Road to Dublin

3421 Millwheel
Bow and Arrows
Maltese Cross
Marble, *KCS*
Pullman's Puzzle
The Silk Patch
Snowball, *NC*
Steeplechase

3422 Snowball, *LAC*

3423 Chain Quilt, *KCS*

3424 Ghost Walk, *NC*

3425 Old Maid's Puzzle
Sunshine and Shadow,
QN

3426 Cleopatra's Puzzle, *NC*
King Tut's Crown

3427 Fool's Puzzle
Canadian Puzzle
Happy Thought

3428 Fool's Puzzle, *LAC*
Arkansas Troubles

3429 Wonder of the World
I Wish You Well
Tumbleweed

3430 Turtle on a Quilt, *KCS*
The Terrapin, *KCS*

3431 Boston Puzzle
The Winding Blade,
KCS

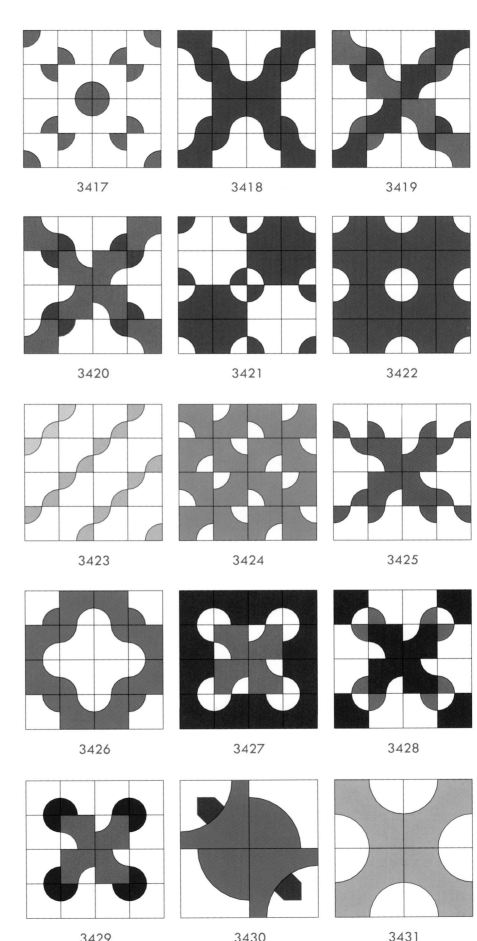

3417 3418 3419
3420 3421 3422
3423 3424 3425
3426 3427 3428
3429 3430 3431

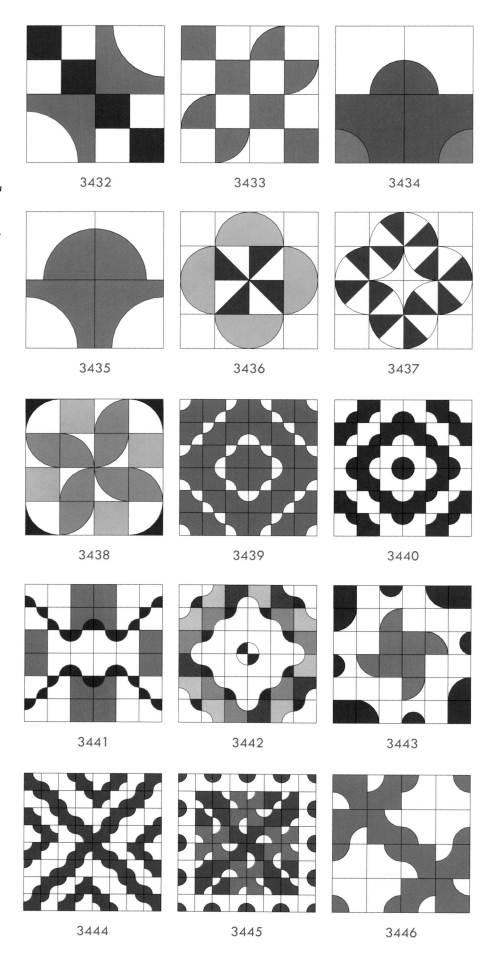

3432

3433

3434

3435

3436

3437

3438

3439

3440

3441

3442

3443

3444

3445

3446

3432 Pictures in the Stairwell

3433 Oklahoma Dogwood

3434 Mushrooms, *FJ*

3435 Seashells, *OCS*

3436 Time and Energy, *QN*

3437 The Winding Trail

3438 Windflower, *LW*

3439 Chain Links, *AMS, 1958*

3440 Nonesuch, *AMS*
Love Ring
Jigsaw Puzzle, *KCS*
Ozark Puzzle, *LCPG*

3441 The Road Home, *NC*

3442 Around the World

3443 Unnamed, *LW, OCS*

3444 Rob Peter to Pay Paul

3445 Quilter's Delight, *NC*

3446 Wonder of the World

3447 Indian Patch

3448 Twinkling Star
Star and Crescent

3449 Grecian Square
Greek Square

3450 Scrap Happy, *OCS*

3451 Electric Fan, *KCS*

3452 Alabama Beauty

3453 Homemaker

3454 Indiana

3455 Country Crossroads

3456 Crossroads
Crossroads to
Bachelor's Hall, *HH*
Crossed Roads to Texas

3457 Caesar's Crown

3458 Millwheel, *OCS*
Wagon Wheel

3459 Compass, *KCS*

3460 Utah

3461 Ohio Beauty

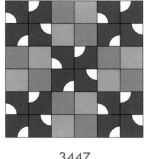
3447

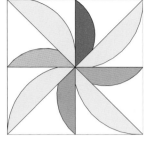
3448

3449

3450

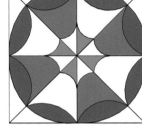
3451

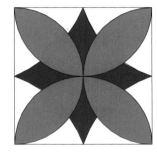
3452

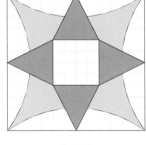
3453

3454

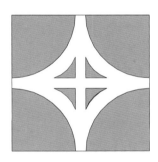
3455

3456

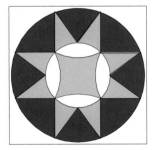
3457

3458

3459

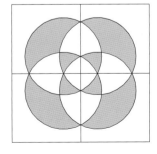
3460

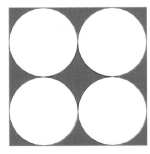
3461

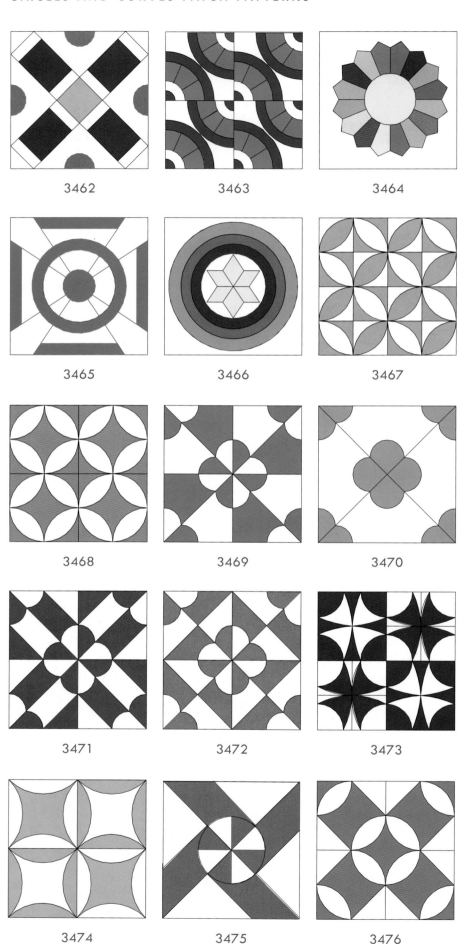

5,500 QUILT BLOCK DESIGNS

3462

3463

3464

3465

3466

3467

3468

3469

3470

3471

3472

3473

3474

3475

3476

3462 Old Missouri

3463 Snake in the Hollow

3464 Dresden Plate

3465 Nevada

3466 Rainbow Star

3467 Orange Peel
Flower Petals
Melon Patch

3468 Bay Leaf

3469 Hearts and Gizzards
Borrow and Return
Dutch Rose, *NC*
Dutch Windmill, *OCS*
Hearts and Flowers
Lazy Daisy
Lover's Knot, *NP*
Morning Glory, *AMS*
Petal Quilt
Pierrot's Pom Pom
Primrose, *TFW*
Snowball
Springtime Blossoms, *MD*
Tennessee Snowball, *WW*
Wheel of Fortune
Windmill, *OCS*

3470 Hearts and Gizzards, *LAC*
Friendship Quilt, *QN*
Hearts
Pierrot's Pom Pom
Aunt Jerusha, *NC*

3471 Martha's Choice, *NC*
Virginia's Choice, *NC*

3472 Springtime Blossoms

3473 Winding Ways, *LAC*
Four Leaf Clover, *NC*
Nashville, *HH*
Robbing Peter to Pay Paul
Wheel of Mystery, *KCS*

3474 Robbing Peter to Pay Paul
Dolly Madison's Workbox
Love Ring, *KCS*
Mary's Choice

Orange Peel
Sugar Bowl, *NP*
Turn About Quilt, *LW*

3475 Boston Puzzle

3476 Name Unknown

3477 Baseball, *LAC*
Circle Design, *GC*

3478 Odds and Ends

3479 Circle Cross

3480 Robbing Peter to Pay
Paul

3481 Baseball, *LAC*
Snowball (strip
piece assorted
fabrics to form
the segments, center
strips white),
QW, 1979
Fireball (strip pieced
with center strips
red), *QW, 1979*

3482 New Moon

3483 Yuletide, *AK*

3484 Tobacco Leaf

3485 Merry Go Round, *OCS*

3486 The Formal Flower
Bed, *KCS*

3487 Square and Compass
Fore and Aft

3488 Four Patch, *OCS*
Southern Moon, *OCS*

3489 Pride of the Prairie,
LW, OCS
Spinning Whirligigs

3490 Evelyne's Whirling
Dust Storm, *KCS*

3491 Sun, Moon & Stars

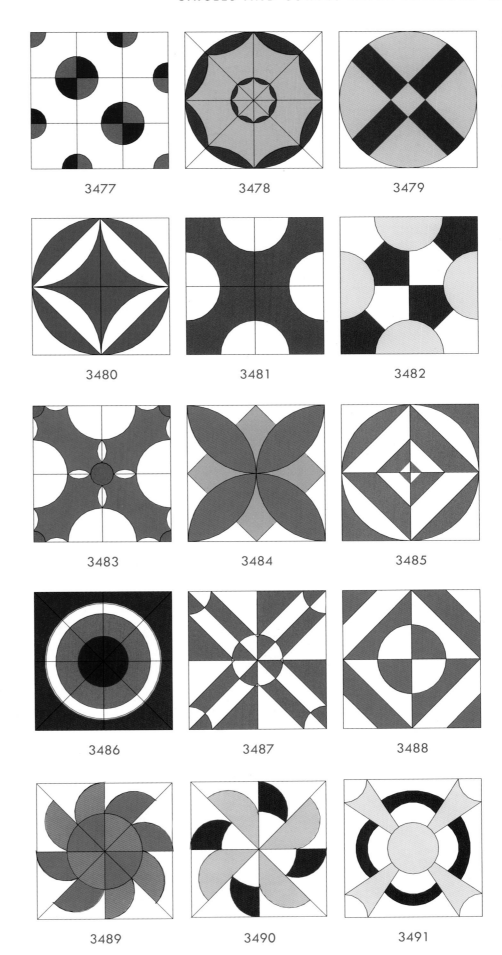

3477 3478 3479

3480 3481 3482

3483 3484 3485

3486 3487 3488

3489 3490 3491

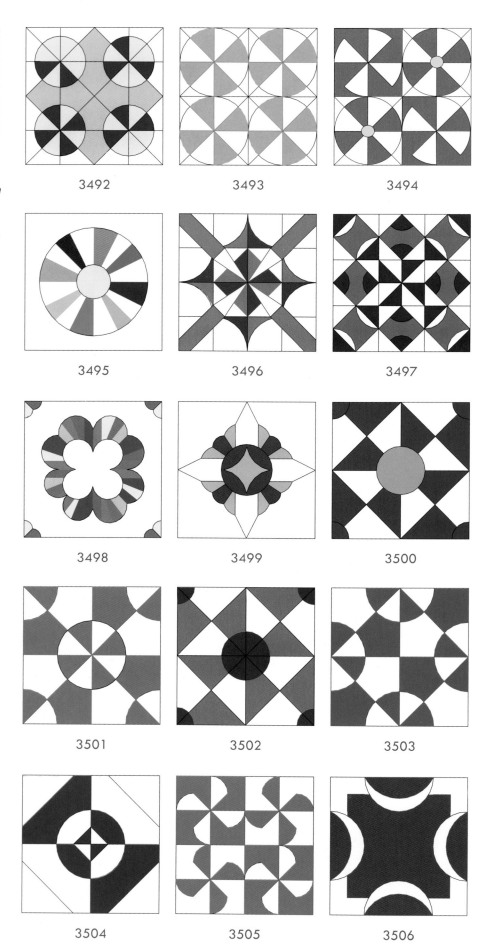

3492

3493

3494

3495

3496

3497

3498

3499

3500

3501

3502

3503

3504

3505

3506

3492 Moon and Stars

3493 Moon and Stars, *LAC*

3494 Grandma's Red and White Quilt

3495 Wheel of Life

3496 Grandmother's Choice

3497 Arkansas
State of Maine, *HH*

3498 Ferris Wheel

3499 Fancy Dresden Plate

3500 Greek Square, *LAC*

3501 Snowball
Windmill Design, *TFW*

3502 Lansing, *HH*

3503 Love in a Tangle, *KCS*
Pinwheel

3504 Sunshine and Stained Glass

3505 Electric Fans

3506 Bridle Path Star, *AK*

3507 Wheel of Fortune

3508 Savannah Star
Savannah Beautiful Star, *LAC*

3509 Snowball Wreath, *LW, OCS*

3510 Irish Chain, *GC*

3511 The Kansas Beauty

3512 Job's Tears
    Endless Chain
    Kansas Troubles
    Rocky Road to Kansas
    Slave Chain
    Texas Tears

3513 Friendship Ring, *KCS*

3514 Sunburst

3515 Lillian's Favorite, *CS*
    Monkey Puzzle, *AMS*

3516 Reminiscent of the
    Wedding Ring, *KCS*
    Remnant Ovals (curved
      segments strip pieced
      with scrap fabrics), *KCS*

3517 Four Leaf Clover, *KCS*

3518 Pin Cushion, *LAC*
    Cushion Design
    Orange Peel
    Rob Peter and Pay Paul
    Pincushion and Cucumbers

3519 Compass, *LAC*
    Corn and Beans, *NC*

3520 Dolly Madison's Workbox,
    CaS
    Butter and Eggs, *NC*
    Mutual Benefit, *CS*
    Peter and Paul
    Robbing Peter to Pay Paul
    Steeplechase

3521 Tea Leaf, *LAC*
    Bay Leaf, *GD*
    Circle upon Circle, *MD*
    Compass
    Lafayette Orange Peel, *HAS*
    Lover's Knot, *GC*
    Pincushion
    True Lover's Knot, *NC*

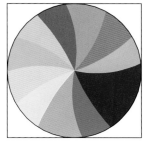 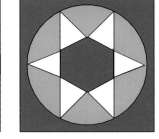 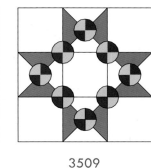

3507   3508   3509

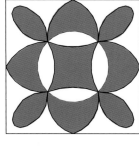 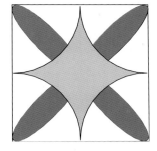 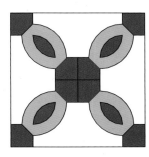

3510   3511   3512

3513   3514   3515

 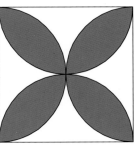 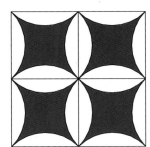

3516   3517   3518

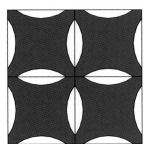  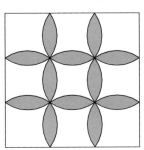

3519   3520   3521

3522 Winner's Circle

3523 Chinese Gongs, *NC*

3524 Estelle's Choice, *HH*
      Jockey Cap
      Millwheel

3525 Elsie's Favorite

3526 New State Quilt Block

3527 Rose Dream, *KCS*
      Broken Square, *KCS*
      Endless Chain, *NC*
      Lover's Bowtie
      Lover's Knot
      Martha
      True Lover's Knot, *HAS*

3528 Whale Block, *LAC*

3529 Light and Dark, *AK*

3530 London Bridge, *AK*

3531 Orange Peel, *LAC*
      Lafayette Orange Peel
      Save a Piece

3532 Melon Patch
      Flower Petals

3533 Joseph's Coat, *OCS*

3534 Melon Patch, *WW*
      Magic Circle

3535 Grist Mill, *NC*
      Melon Patch Quilt, *LW*

3536 Nine Patch

3537 Improved Nine Patch
Bailey Nine Patch, *MD*
Circle upon Circle, *KCS*
Dinner Plate
Four Leaf Clover, *KCS*
Nine Patch Variation
Bridge Quilt (with card
suits appliquéd), *KCS*

3538 Black Beauty, *CS*
Red Buds, *NC*

3539 Washington Snowball,
CS

3540 Virginia Snowball, *NC*
Washington Snowball,
HH

3541 Snowball, *LAC*
Baseball
Pullman Puzzle

3542 Jupiter's Moons

3543 Hearts and Diamonds,
HAS

3544 Ladies Beautiful Star

3545 The Star Sapphire, *KCS*

3546 Circle and Star, *HH*

3547 Compass Point

3548 Twist and Turn, *AB, OCS*
Summer and Winter,
OCS

3549 The Car Wheel Quilt,
KCS

3550 Carolina Favorite, *LW,*
OCS

3551 Ladies' Fancy, *LAC*

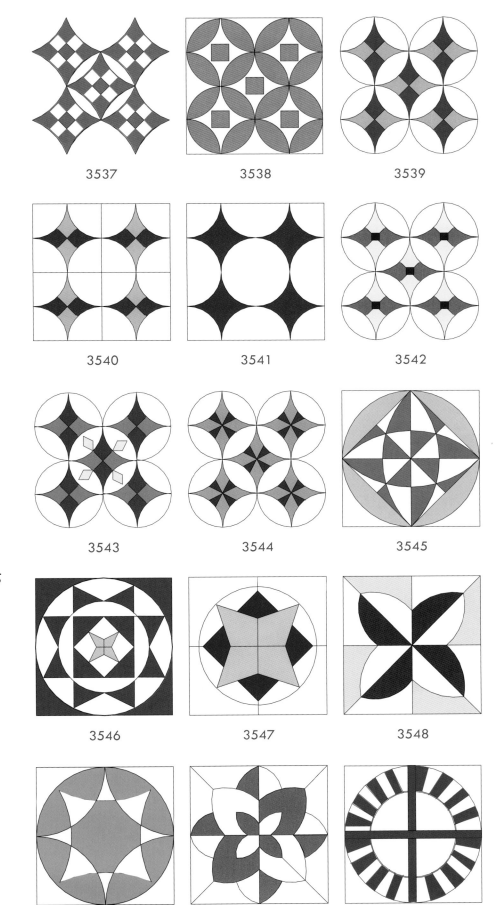

3537   3538   3539

3540   3541   3542

3543   3544   3545

3546   3547   3548

3549   3550   3551

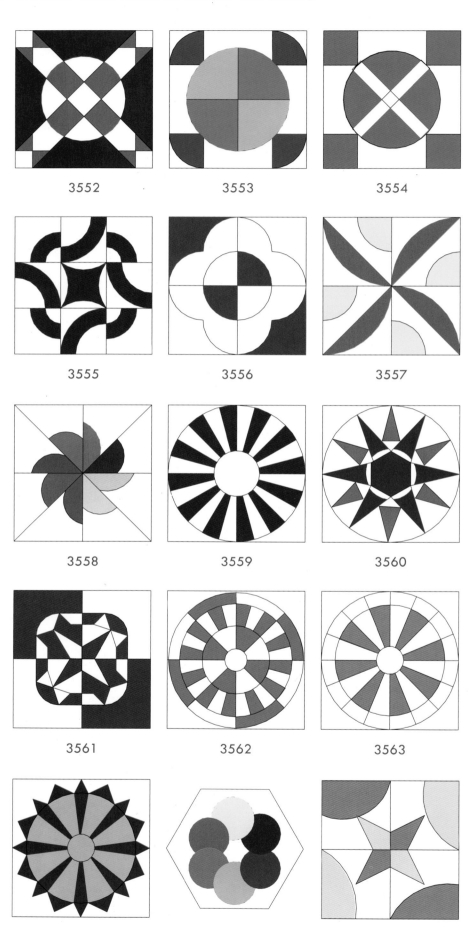

3552   Hazel Valley Crossroads, *KCS*

3553   Pilot Wheel, *GC*

3554   Cart Wheel, *GC*

3555   Broken Circle, *KCS*

3556   Snowball Flower, *OCS*

3557   Waving Plumes, *LW, OCS*

3558   The Pinwheel

3559   True Lovers' Buggy Wheel, *KCS* Wheel of Chance

3560   Rolling Pin Wheel

3561   Oklahoma, *HH*

3562   Wheel of Fortune

3563   Wheel of Fortune

3564   Oriental Star

3565   Roses of Picardy

3566   Twist and Turn, *LW, OCS*

3567 The Lover's Chain
Lover's Links

3568 Springtime, *QW, 1983*

3569 Mississippi Oakleaf
Cactus Blossom Patch,
LAC
Cactus Bloom, *NC*

3570 The Royal, *LAC*
Grecian Cross
Royal Cross

3571 Snail's Trail

3572 Wings, *LAC*

3573 Bird's Eye View

3574 Boston

3575 East and West
The Broken Stone, *KCS*
Lover's Quarrel, *AMS*
New Wedding Ring

3576 Give and Take

3577 Illinois Snowball

3578 Tangled Trails, *PF, 1854*

3579 Bush's Points of Light,
SSQ, 1992

3580 Sun Over
Transmountain,
*Sheila Rodriguez,
PQ, 1986*

3581 Moon Over the
Mountain

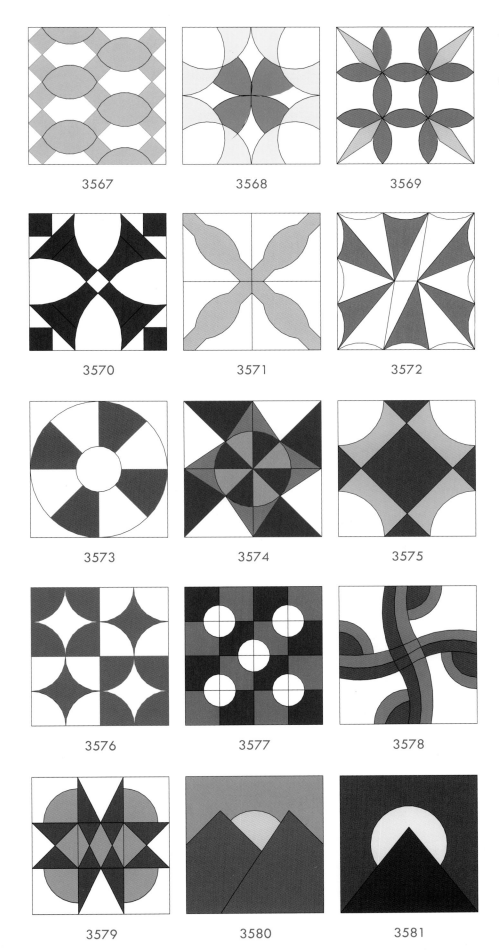

3567   3568   3569

3570   3571   3572

3573   3574   3575

3576   3577   3578

3579   3580   3581

5,500 QUILT BLOCK DESIGNS

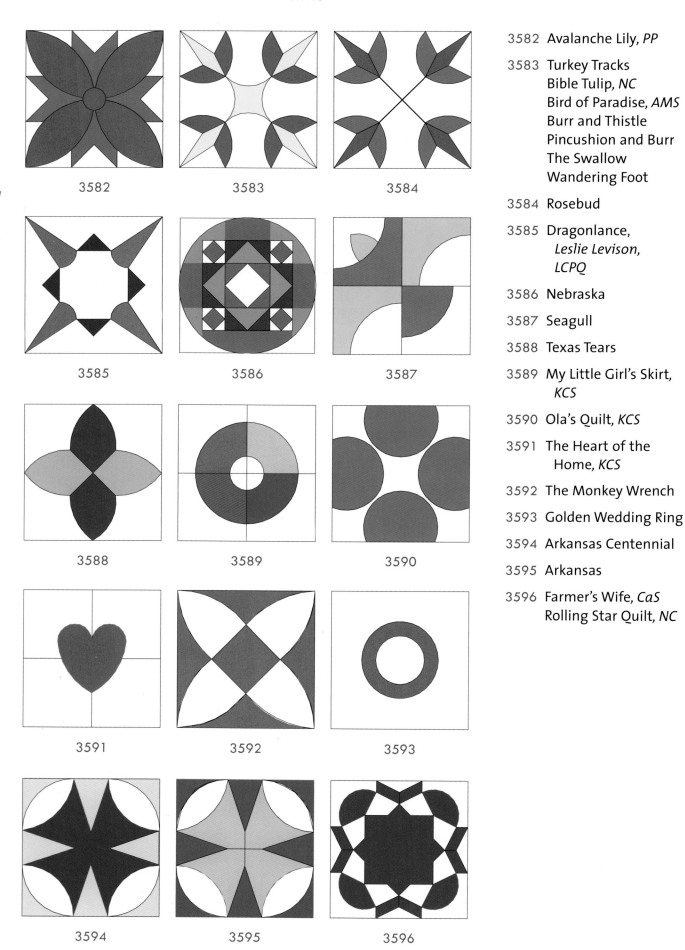

3582   3583   3584

3585   3586   3587

3588   3589   3590

3591   3592   3593

3594   3595   3596

3582 Avalanche Lily, *PP*

3583 Turkey Tracks
Bible Tulip, *NC*
Bird of Paradise, *AMS*
Burr and Thistle
Pincushion and Burr
The Swallow
Wandering Foot

3584 Rosebud

3585 Dragonlance,
Leslie Levison,
LCPQ

3586 Nebraska

3587 Seagull

3588 Texas Tears

3589 My Little Girl's Skirt,
KCS

3590 Ola's Quilt, *KCS*

3591 The Heart of the
Home, *KCS*

3592 The Monkey Wrench

3593 Golden Wedding Ring

3594 Arkansas Centennial

3595 Arkansas

3596 Farmer's Wife, *CaS*
Rolling Star Quilt, *NC*

3597 Wagon Wheels, *KCS*
    Old Fashioned Wagon
     Wheels

3598 Fan and Ring,
    Margaret Dewey, KCS

3599 Pointed Ovals, *KCS*
    Love's Chain, *NC*

3600 The Quilter's Fan, *KCS*

3601 Around the World, *KCS*

3602 Lost Paradise, *KCS*

3603 The Full Moon, *KCS*

3604 The Broken Stone, *KCS*

3605 Friendship Knot, *KCS*

3606 Hands All Around, *KCS*

3607 Drunkard's Trail, *KCS*
    Rainbow Quilt

3608 The Four Winds, *KCS*

3609 Orange Peel Variation,
    PQ

3610 Hearts and Flowers

3611 Arab Tent
    Chimney Swallow

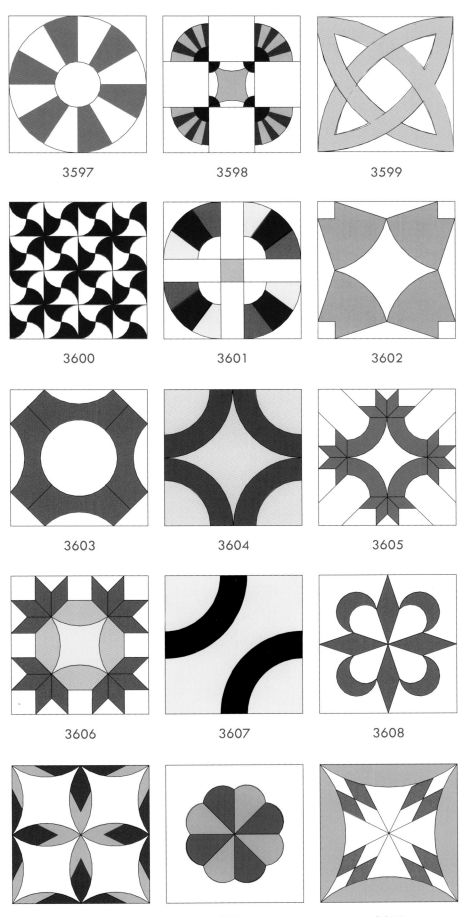

3597   3598   3599

3600   3601   3602

3603   3604   3605

3606   3607   3608

3609   3610   3611

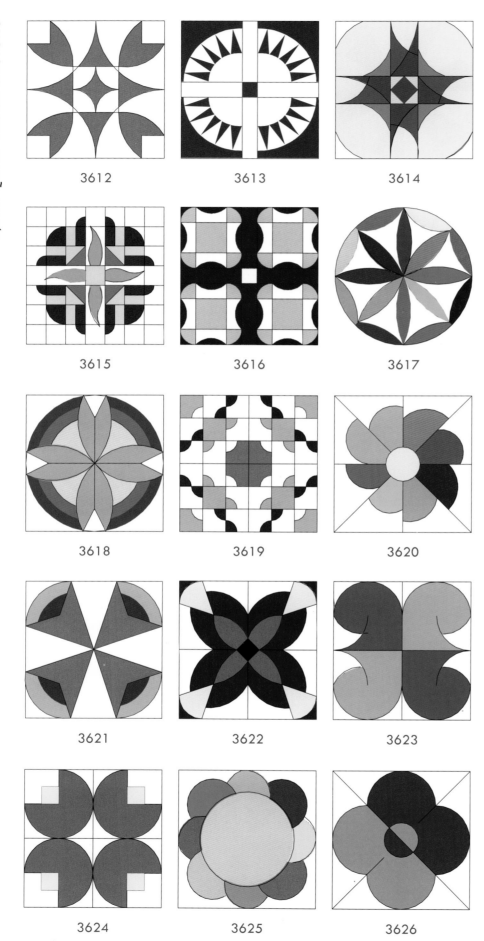

3612
3613
3614
3615
3616
3617
3618
3619
3620
3621
3622
3623
3624
3625
3626

3612 Bleeding Heart
Violet Blossoms, *NC*

3613 Circular Saw
Circle Bar Quilt
Melodie's Baby
Bunting Quilt

3614 Westfalen Waltz,
Jan Cook, QN, 1990

3615 Wild Lily

3616 Medieval Spirits,
*Karen Fitzgerald, SSQ,
1982*

3617 Joseph's Coat
(continuous design),
KCS

3618 The Rainbow

3619 Drunkard's Path
Variation

3620 Whirligig
Whirling Pinwheel, *KCS*

3621 Grandmother's Tulip,
KCS

3622 America's Pride, *LW,
OCS*

3623 Thirteenth Summer

3624 Alice's Tulips, *QN*

3625 Rolling Stone, *KCS*

3626 Rose and Trellis, *LW,
OCS*

3627 Pieced Sunflower
Single Sunflower
Sunflower

3628 Aster

3629 Sunburst

3630 Mariner's Compass

3631 Mariner's Compass

3632 Mariner's Compass
Sunburst
Sunrise, *GD*

3633 Starry Compass,
Paula Libby, LCPQ

3634 Mariner's Compass

3635 Compass

3636 Sunrise

3637 Georgetown Circle

3638 Sylvia's Choice

3639 Sundials,
Gayle Ropp, QT

3640 Sunburst

3641 Without Constraint,
PAG

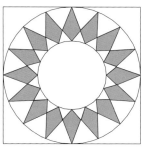

3627

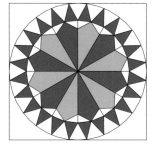

3628

3629

3630

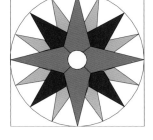

3631

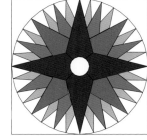

3632

3633

3634

3635

3636

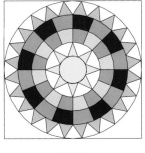

3637

3638

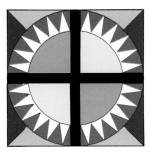

3639

3640

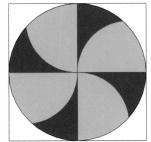

3641

5,500 QUILT BLOCK DESIGNS

3642

3643

3644

3645

3646

3647

3648

3649

3650

3651

3652

3653

3654

3655

3656

3642 The Wishing Star, *HaM, SSQ, 1986*

3643 Sunburst Star

3644 Farmer's Delight
Triple Sunflower

3645 Devil's Puzzle

3646 Suspension Bridge

3647 The Wheel of Fortune, *HH*

3648 Car Wheels
Harvest Sun
(two colors)

3649 Rolling Pinwheel

3650 Irish Chain

3651 Fortune's Wheel

3652 Star of the West, *LAC*

3653 Rainbow, *LAC*

3654 Slashed Star, *LAC*
Mariner's Compass
Sunrise Pattern

3655 Sunset Star
New York (full circle)

3656 Tic-Tac-Toe, *QN, 1975*

3657 Through the Looking
Glass, *HaM, SSQ*

3658 Rosebud Quilt, *KCS*

3659 Tulip Pattern, *KCS*

3660 The Tulip Quilt, *KCS*

3661 Sunset Quilt Block,
QW, 1985

3662 Joseph's Coat

3663 Cog Wheels

3664 Oil Fields of Oklahoma,
KCS

3665 Honey Bee, *KCS*

3666 Jinx Star, *KCS*

3667 Missouri Morning Star,
KCS

3668 Rising Sun, *KCS*

3669 Friendship Quilt, *KCS*
Block and Ring

3670 Strawberry
Friendship Ring
Full Blown Tulip
Oriental Star
Pilot's Wheel

3671 Mace Head, *NC*

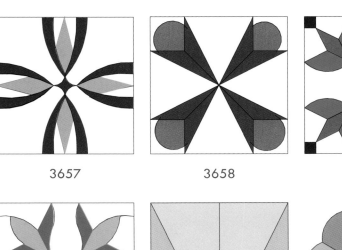

3657

3659

3660

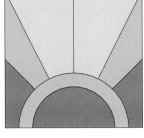

3661

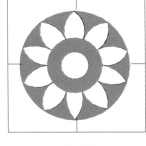

3663

3664

3665

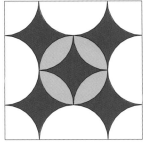

3666

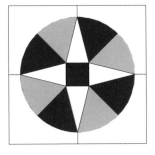

3667

3668

3669

3670

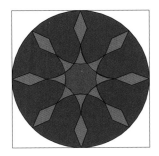

3671

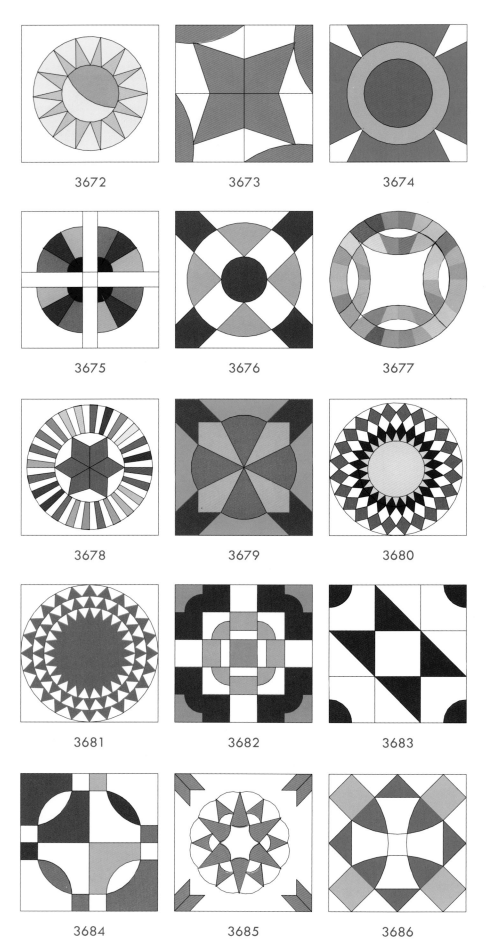

3672

3673

3674

3675

3676

3677

3678

3679

3680

3681

3682

3683

3684

3685

3686

3672 Moon in Eclipse, *1800s*

3673 Twist and Turn, *LW, OCS*

3674 Name Unknown, *QW, 1987*

3675 Color Wheels

3676 Wagon Wheels

3677 Double Wedding Ring

3678 Lincoln Quilt, *1865*

3679 Whirling Stars

3680 Sunburst

3681 Sawtooth Circle

3682 Savannah Squares

3683 Wishing Well

3684 Cactus Rose

3685 Album Quilt

3686 Lady of the Lake

3687 The Name Is Hesper, *KCS*

3688 The Moon Is New, *KCS*

3689 Quilter's Fan, *KCS*

3690 Ice Cream Cone, *KCS*

3691 Ice Cream Cone, *KCS*

3692 Lost Paradise, *KCS*

3693 Circular Flying Geese, *Judy Mathieson*

3694 Circular Flying Geese Variation

3695 Pathfinder

3696 Yellow Point

3697 Flywheel
Circle Saw, *KCS*
Oklahoma Star
Rising Sun, *LAC*
Wagon Wheel, *HH*
Wheel of Life, *HAS*

3698 Cogwheel

3699 Star and Planets

3700 Southern Pride

3701 Bride's Prize

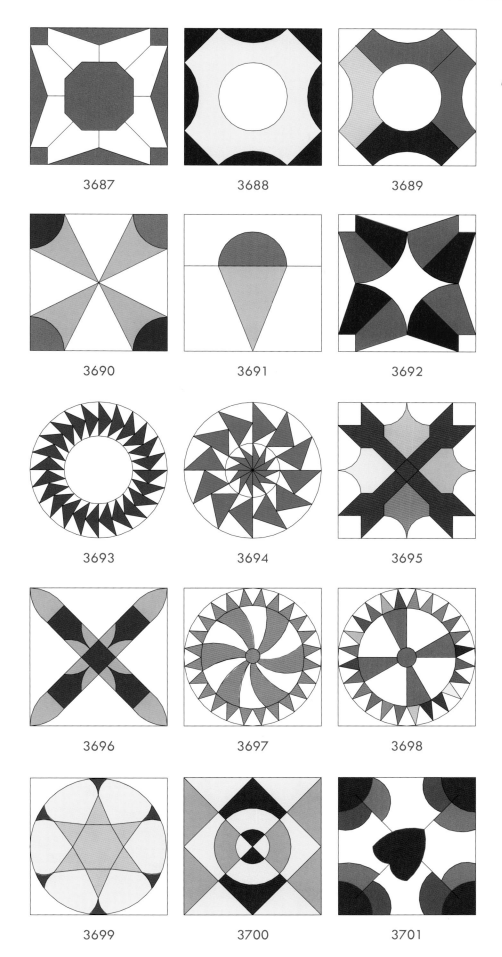

3687   3688   3689

3690   3691   3692

3693   3694   3695

3696   3697   3698

3699   3700   3701

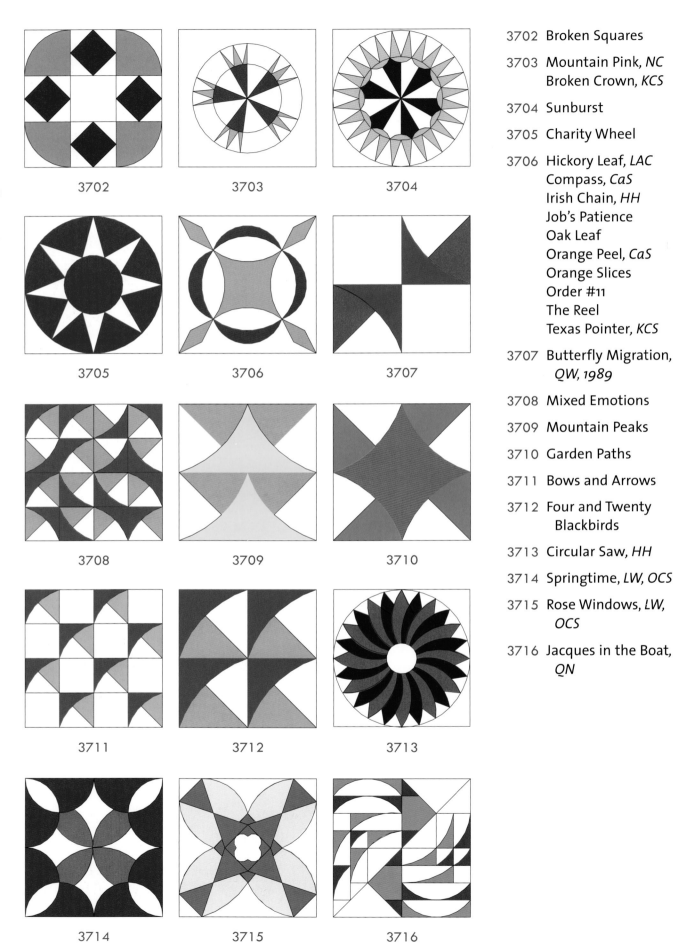

3702 Broken Squares

3703 Mountain Pink, *NC*
Broken Crown, *KCS*

3704 Sunburst

3705 Charity Wheel

3706 Hickory Leaf, *LAC*
Compass, *CaS*
Irish Chain, *HH*
Job's Patience
Oak Leaf
Orange Peel, *CaS*
Orange Slices
Order #11
The Reel
Texas Pointer, *KCS*

3707 Butterfly Migration,
QW, 1989

3708 Mixed Emotions

3709 Mountain Peaks

3710 Garden Paths

3711 Bows and Arrows

3712 Four and Twenty
Blackbirds

3713 Circular Saw, *HH*

3714 Springtime, *LW, OCS*

3715 Rose Windows, *LW,
OCS*

3716 Jacques in the Boat,
QN

3717 Pride of the Bride,
     AB, OCS

3718 Borrow and Return,
     Coats & Clark

3719 A Winding Trail, *NC*

3720 Round Table, *CS*

3721 Four Buds, *KCS*

3722 Wedding Ring
     Bouquet
     Formal Elegance

3723 Indian Summer
     Broken Circle
     Sunflower

3724 Wheel of Fortune
     Buggy Wheel
     Sunflower

3725 Fanny's Favorite

3726 White Rose

3727 Flo's Fan
     Rainbow Quilt Design,
     NP

3728 Imperial Fan

3729 Sunrise, Sunset

3730 Grandmother's Fan

3731 Fan Quadrille,
     MoM

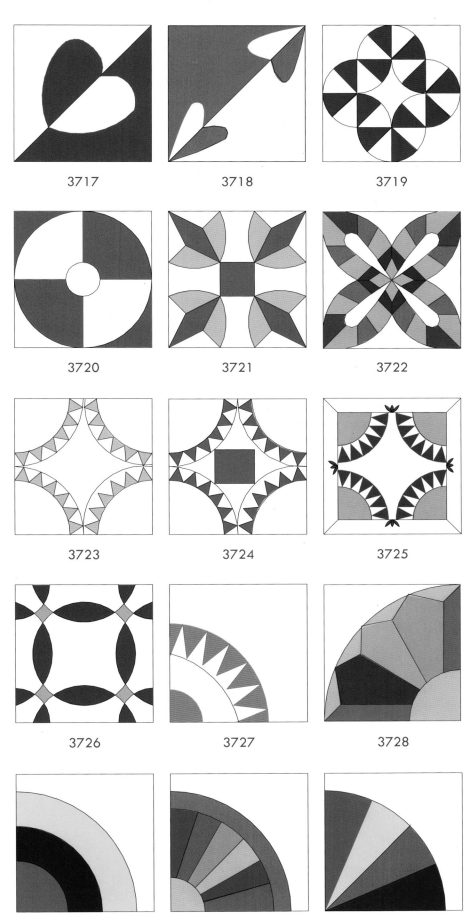

3717

3718

3719

3720

3721

3722

3723

3724

3725

3726

3727

3728

3729

3730

3731

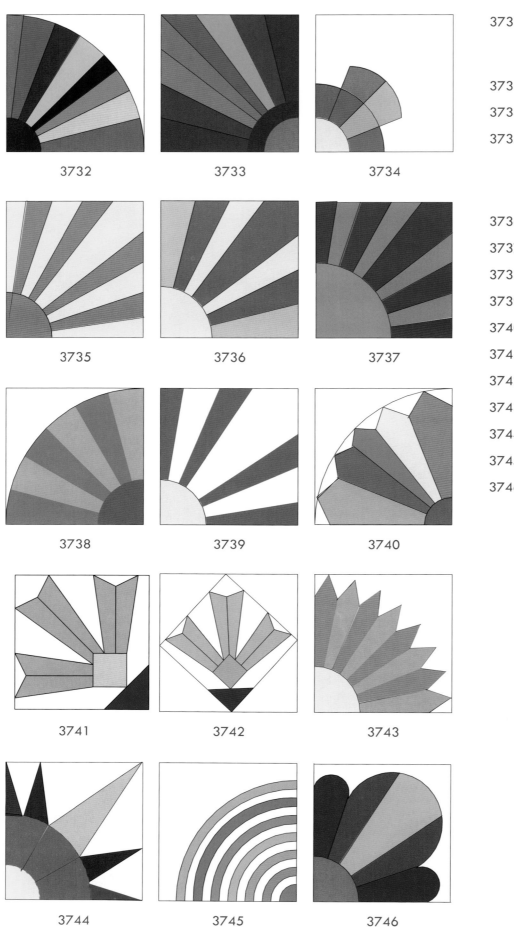

3732 Grandmother's Fan
      Fan Quilt, *KCS*
      Formosa Fan, *NC*

3733 Friendship Fan, *NC*

3734 Unnamed

3735 Kansas Sunshine, *CS,*
      1910
      Sunshine
      Friendship Fan, *CS*

3736 Rebecca's Fan, *KCS*

3737 Friendship Fan, *NM*

3738 Grandmother's Fan

3739 Harvest Sun

3740 Mary's Fan

3741 Floral Bouquet

3742 Floral Bouquet

3743 Eight Point Fan

3744 Rising Sun, *AB*

3745 Caroline's Fan

3746 Grandmother's Scrap
      Quilt, *AB*

3747 Fan Patchwork, *LAC*
A Fan of Many Colors, *KCS*
Grandmother's Fan
Mary's Fan, *HAS*

3748 Japanese Fan, *LW*

3749 Unnamed Fan

3750 Lattice Fan

3751 Fannie's Fan

3752 Japanese Fan
Grandmother's Fan

3753 Fanny's Fan
Grandmother's Fan
Mother's Fan

3754 Flower of Autumn, *KCS*

3755 Fan

3756 Fan, *LAC*

3757 Art Deco Fans

3758 The Pride of East
Kingston, *Nancy
Kiman, SSQ, 1989*

3759 Milady's Fan, *AMS*
Chinese Fan

3760 Victorian Fan

3761 Milady's Fan

3747

3748

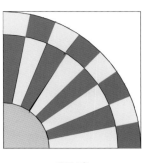

3749

3750

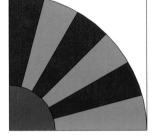

3751

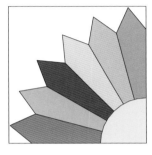

3752

3753

3754

3755

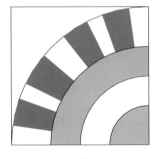

3756

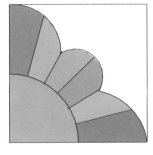

3757

3758

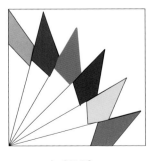

3759

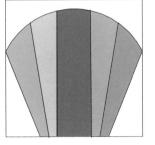

3760

3761

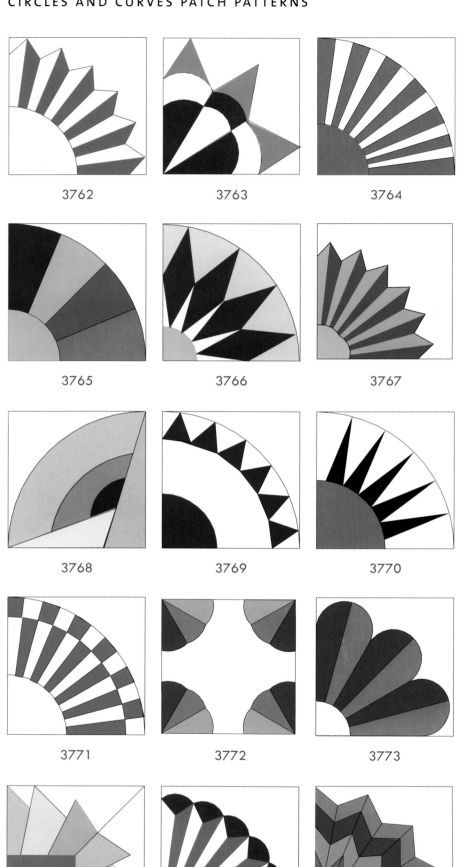

3762

3763

3764

3765

3766

3767

3768

3769

3770

3771

3772

3773

3774

3775

3776

3762 Fancy Fan, *AK*

3763 Flower of the Woods,
     LW

3764 Art Deco Fans

3765 Fan of Friendship,
     AB

3766 Fancy Fan, *AK*
     Diamond Fan

3767 Fan

3768 Fan

3769 Fan

3770 Chinese Fan, *NC*

3771 Fan

3772 Daisy Fan, *AMS, 1942*

3773 Art Deco Fans
     Dresden Fan
     Grandmother's Fan, *AB*

3774 Grandmother's Pride,
     LW
     Empress

3775 No Name

3776 Sunset, *NC*
     Sunset Glow

3777 Fringed Aster, *1943*

3778 Wedding Ring

3779 Circle of Fans,
    TQr, 1992

3780 Broken Circle
    Sunflower

3781 King David's Crown

3782 Kansas Sunflower

3783 Ferris Wheel

3784 Grandma's Favorite,
    1971

3785 Daisy Wheel, *MM*

3786 Carnival, *MM*

3787 Oriole Window, *KCS*
    Circular Saw, *KCS*
    Four Little Fans, *KCS*

3788 Red, White and Blue,
    CoM

3789 Squared Circle, *HM*

3790 Friendship Ring, *LW*

3791 Spinning Wheel

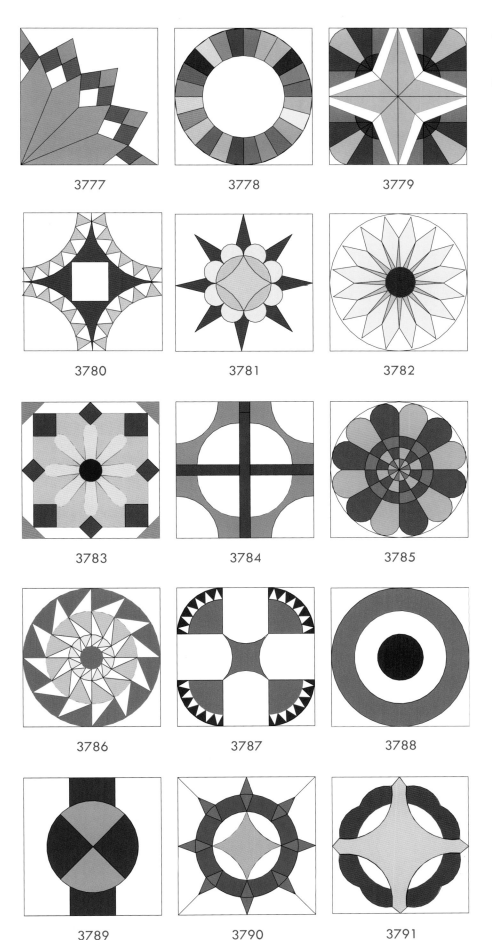

3777

3778

3779

3780

3781

3782

3783

3784

3785

3786

3787

3788

3789

3790

3791

5,500 QUILT BLOCK DESIGNS

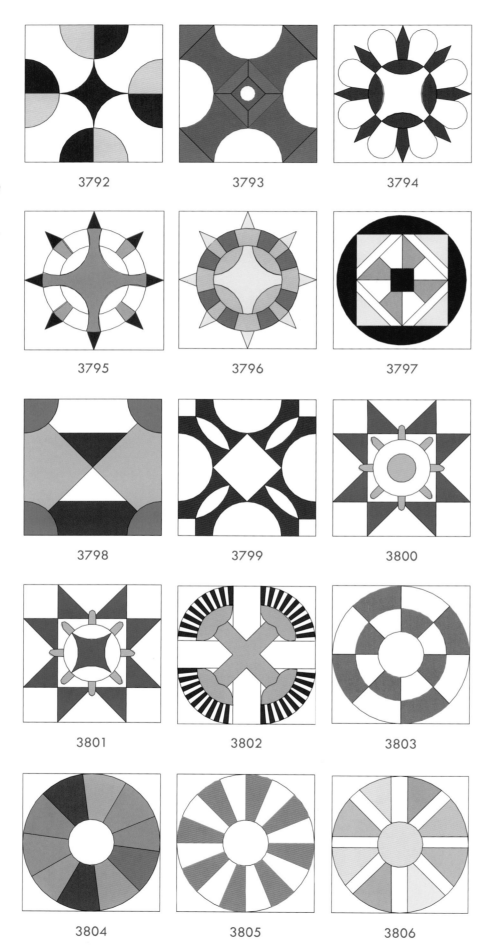

3792

3793

3794

3795

3796

3797

3798

3799

3800

3801

3802

3803

3804

3805

3806

3792 Half Moon Block, *NC*
Moon Block, *NC*

3793 Babe Ruth Diamond, *QN*

3794 The Sunflower, *LAC*

3795 The Pilot's Wheel

3796 Whirling Wheel, *HM*

3797 Old Mill Wheel, *AK*

3798 Hour Glass, *NC*

3799 The Stockade, *CS*

3800 Rose Album, *LAC*

3801 Rose Album

3802 Claws, *NC*

3803 Wheel of Fortune

3804 Baby Aster

3805 Wheel of Fortune

3806 Double Rainbow, *LW*
Ozark Sunflower, *KCS*
Pieced Sunflower, *KCS*

3807 Wheel of Fortune

3808 Chariot Wheel

3809 Windblown Daisy, *NC*

3810 Wheel of Time

3811 Parasol Block, *NC*

3812 Pinwheel Quilt

3813 Feathered Star, *LW*

3814 Southern Star, *HH*

3815 Rhododendron Star,
    QN

3816 Spinning Ball

3817 Whirl Wind, *PP*

3818 Spinning Ball
    Spiral

3819 Noonday
    A Brave Sunflower
    Kansas Sunflower
    Oklahoma Sunburst,
     KCS
    Rising Sun
    Russian Sunflower
    Sunburst

3820 Noxall Quilt Block
    Narcissus

3821 Peeled Orange, *NC*

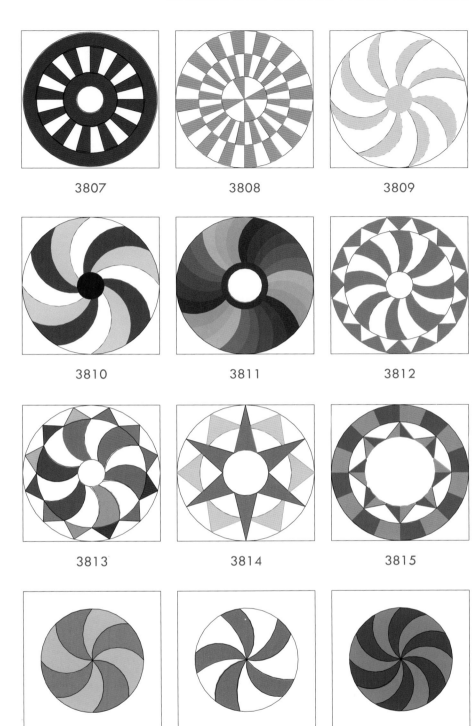

3807   3808   3809

3810   3811   3812

3813   3814   3815

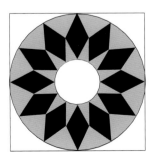 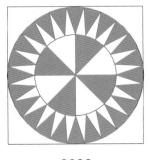 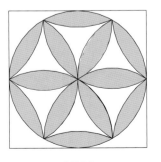

3816   3817   3818

3819   3820   3821

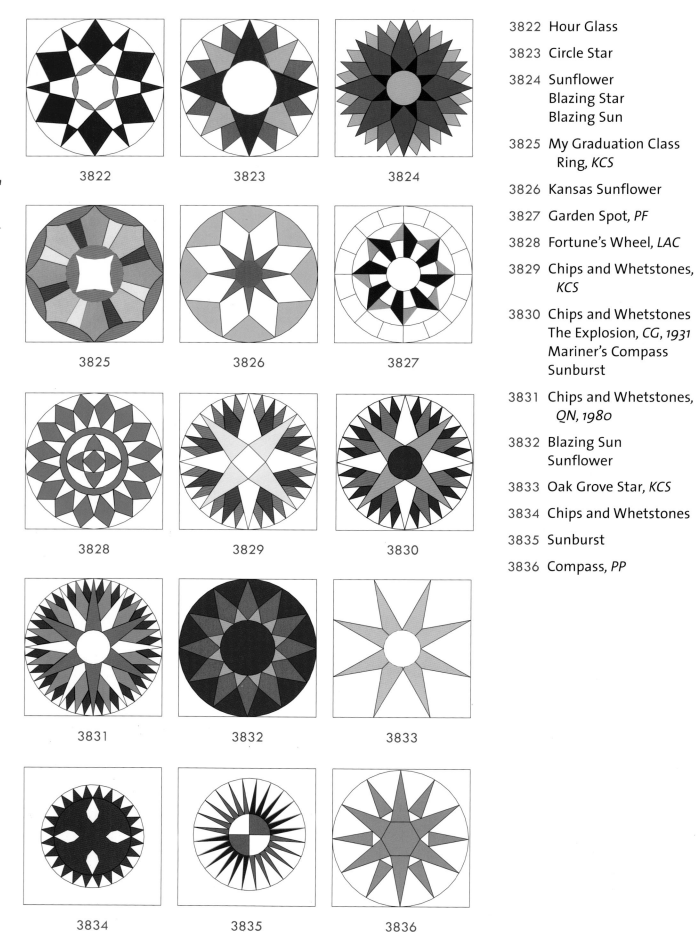

3822 Hour Glass

3823 Circle Star

3824 Sunflower
Blazing Star
Blazing Sun

3825 My Graduation Class
Ring, *KCS*

3826 Kansas Sunflower

3827 Garden Spot, *PF*

3828 Fortune's Wheel, *LAC*

3829 Chips and Whetstones,
KCS

3830 Chips and Whetstones
The Explosion, *CG, 1931*
Mariner's Compass
Sunburst

3831 Chips and Whetstones,
QN, 1980

3832 Blazing Sun
Sunflower

3833 Oak Grove Star, *KCS*

3834 Chips and Whetstones

3835 Sunburst

3836 Compass, *PP*

3837 Sunflower

3838 The Buzz Saw, *KCS*

3839 Indian Paintbrush, *PP*

3840 Car Wheel, *KCS*

3841 Mariner's Compass

3842 Compass Star Quilt

3843 Mariner's Compass

3844 French Star

3845 Cog Wheels, *LAC*
   Harvest Sun
   Pennsylvania Wheel
      Quilt, *HH*
   Topeka, *HH*

3846 Signature

3847 Sunburst, *GC, 1931*

3848 The Sunburst,
   Modern Priscilla

3849 Pyrotechnics, *LAC*

3850 Petal Circle in a
   Square, *KCS*

3851 Pyrotechnics, *LAC*
   Wheel, *FJ*
   Wheel of Fortune

3837

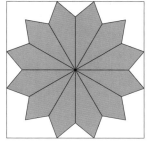

3838

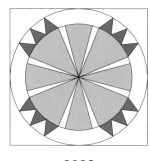

3839

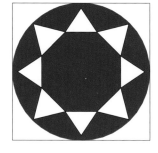

3840

3841

3842

3843

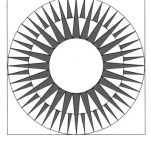

3844

3845

3846

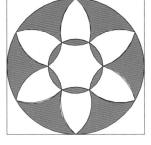

3847

3848

3849

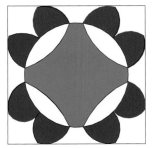

3850

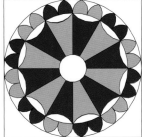

3851

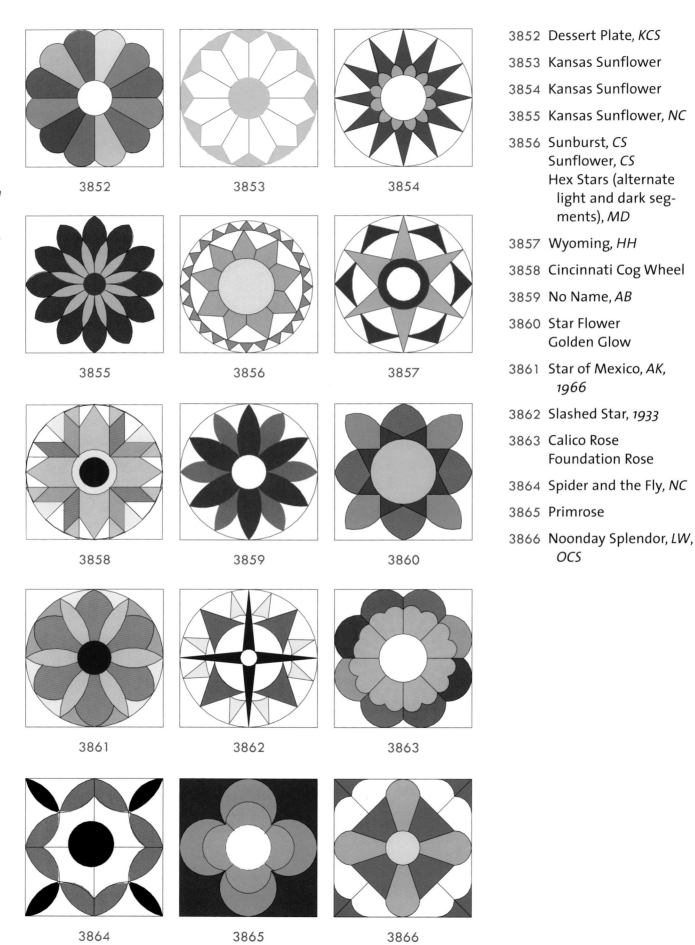

3852

3853

3854

3855

3856

3857

3858

3859

3860

3861

3862

3863

3864

3865

3866

3852 Dessert Plate, *KCS*

3853 Kansas Sunflower

3854 Kansas Sunflower

3855 Kansas Sunflower, *NC*

3856 Sunburst, *CS*
Sunflower, *CS*
Hex Stars (alternate
light and dark seg-
ments), *MD*

3857 Wyoming, *HH*

3858 Cincinnati Cog Wheel

3859 No Name, *AB*

3860 Star Flower
Golden Glow

3861 Star of Mexico, *AK*,
1966

3862 Slashed Star, *1933*

3863 Calico Rose
Foundation Rose

3864 Spider and the Fly, *NC*

3865 Primrose

3866 Noonday Splendor, *LW*,
OCS

3867 Full Blown Rose, *NC*

3868 Airship, *CoM*

3869 Magnolia Blossom

3870 Star of West Virginia, *HH*

3871 Pilot Wheel, *GC*

3872 Orange Peel, *GD*

3873 Noonday Lily, *HAS*

3874 Painted Snowball, *NC*

3875 Wyoming Patch, *LAC*
Texas Sunflower, *CoM*

3876 The Jewel, *AMS*
Hummingbirds, *NC*

3877 No Name

3878 Spool of 1966, *AK*

3879 Dogwood Bloom, *CS*

3880 Fox and Geese, *LAC*

3881 Tulip Wheel

3867

3868

3869

3870

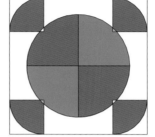

3871

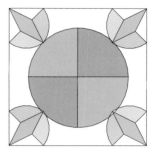

3872

3873

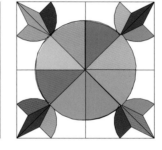

3874

3875

3876

3877

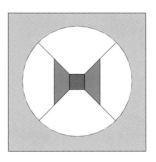

3878

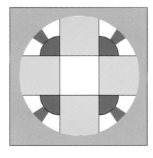

3879

3880

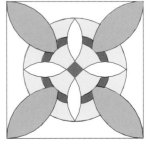

3881

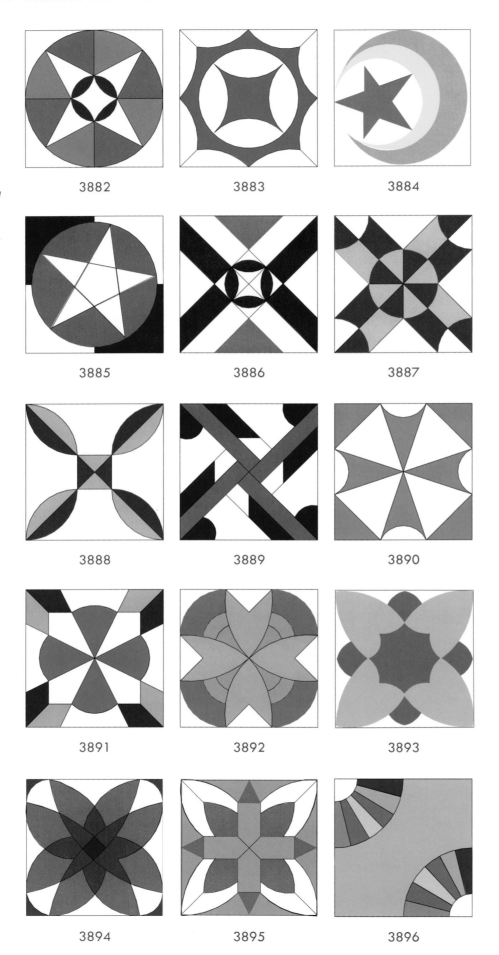

3882

3883

3884

3885

3886

3887

3888

3889

3890

3891

3892

3893

3894

3895

3896

3882 Progressive, *HH*

3883 Caesar's Crown,
 LCPQ
 Grandmother's Quilt,
 AMS

3884 Star and Crescent, *CS*

3885 Union Star, *LAC*
 Moon and Star, *HH*
 The 20th Century Star,
 CS

3886 Herald Square, *NC*

3887 Square and Compass,
 NC

3888 Grandmother's Prize,
 AB, OCS

3889 Peony, *AB, OCS*

3890 Spider Web, *LW*

3891 Unnamed, *LW, OCS*

3892 The Rainbow
 Indian Raid, *NC*

3893 Garden Beauty, *LW,
 OCS*

3894 Double Poppy, *NC*
 Modernized Poppy, *NC*

3895 Flower of Spring, *LW,
 OCS*

3896 Snake Trail
 Railroad Around Rocky
 Mountain, *CoM*
 Rattlesnake, *NC*

3897 Whirling Fans, *AB, OCS*
Double Fans

3898 Rainbow, *AMS*

3899 Snake in the Hollow,
QN
Gypsy Trail

3900 The Sea Shell Quilt,
KCS

3901 The Bleeding Heart,
1898

3902 Mariner's Compass
Mary Strickler's Quilt

3903 Black Eyed Susan

3904 Golden Corn

3905 Alcazar, *NC*
A Young Man's
Invention, *KCS*

3906 Double L

3907 Wheels

3908 Wedding Ring
Bouquet, *AMS*

3909 Corsage Bouquet, *AMS*

3910 Tennessee Circle

3911 King's Crown, *PF*

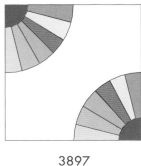
3897

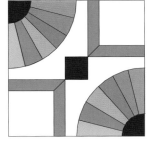
3898

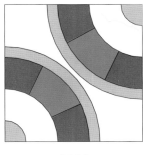
3899

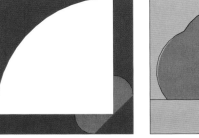
3900

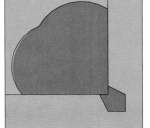
3901

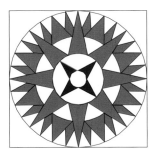
3902

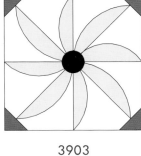
3903

3904

3905

3906

3907

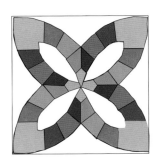
3908

3909

3910

3911

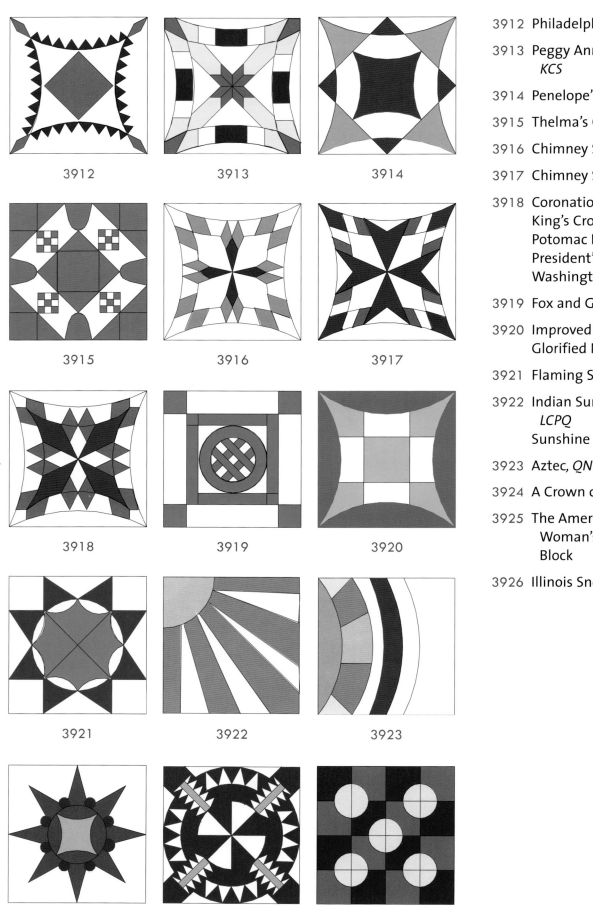

3912

3913

3914

3915

3916

3917

3918

3919

3920

3921

3922

3923

3924

3925

3926

3912 Philadelphia Patch, *LAC*

3913 Peggy Anne's Special, *KCS*

3914 Penelope's Favorite

3915 Thelma's Choice

3916 Chimney Swallows

3917 Chimney Swallows

3918 Coronation
King's Crown
Potomac Pride
President's Quilt
Washington's Quilt

3919 Fox and Geese, *LAC*

3920 Improved Nine Patch
Glorified Nine Patch

3921 Flaming Sun, *PF*

3922 Indian Sunburst, *LCPQ*
Sunshine

3923 Aztec, *QN*

3924 A Crown of Thorns, *KCS*

3925 The American
Woman's Own Quilt
Block

3926 Illinois Snowball

3927 Arkansas Star

3928 Kaleidoscope, *MM*

3929 Butterfly Quadrille

3930 Noonday Sun

3931 Sylvia's Choice

3932 Broken Circle, *CS*
    Sunburst
    Sunflower, *KCS*
    Suspension Bridge, *LAC*

3933 Wheel of Fortune
    Buggy Wheel

3934 Setting Sun
    Indian Summer

3935 A Red, White and Blue
    Quilt, *MD*

3936 Lady Finger, *LHJ*
    Lady Finger and
      Sunflower
    Grandmother's
      Engagement Ring,
      MoM

3937 Sunflower

3938 Jupiter's Moons, *NC*

3939 Saturn's Rings
    Grist Mill

3940 Duke's Dilemma

3941 Bleeding Heart, *PP*

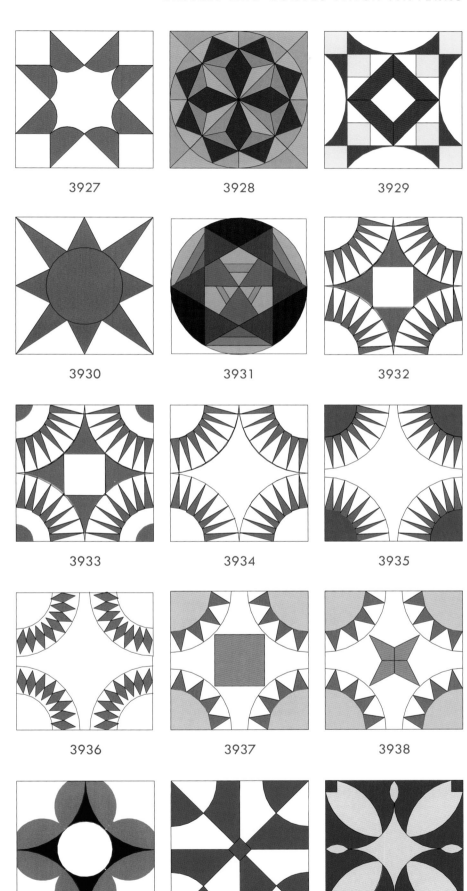

3927   3928   3929

3930   3931   3932

3933   3934   3935

3936   3937   3938

3939   3940   3941

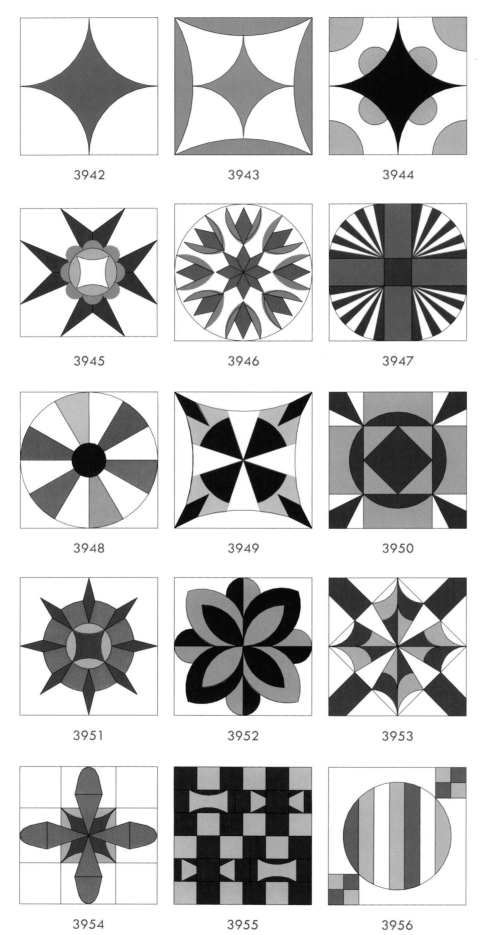

5,500 QUILT BLOCK DESIGNS

3942

3943

3944

3945

3946

3947

3948

3949

3950

3951

3952

3953

3954

3955

3956

3942   Doors and Windows

3943   Elsie's Favorite, *CS*

3944   The Rosebud, *KCS*

3945   North Star

3946   Cottage Tulips

3947   Color Wheel

3948   Color Wheel

3949   Christmas Day, *QW, 1987*

3950   Center Ring, *MLM, SSQ, 1983*

3951   Caesar's Crown

3952   Carolina Favorite

3953   Grandmother's Choice

3954   Paducah Peony

3955   Chain Bridge, *Sharyn Durham, SSQ, 1983*

3956   Candy Drops, *Ursula Michael, SSQ, 1989*

3957 Cameo Quilt (continuous scrap design)

3958 Behold...a Star, *QWO*

3959 Circle Petal in a
Square, *KCS*

3960 Bay Leaf

3961 Autumn Kaleidoscope,
*Norma Robson,
SSQ, 1985*

3962 Apple Cores,
*Dorothy Herbston,
QWO, 1988*

3963 Autumn Spinning Star,
*Dorothy Herbston,
QWO, 1988*

3964 Rattlesnake

3965 Kansas Sunrise

3966 Sunflower
Sunburst

3967 Sunflower

3968 Swallow's Nest

3969 Paragon Quilt Block

3970 Palm Leaf

3971 Papa's Delight, *CS*

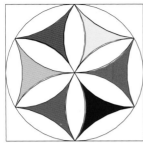
3957

3958

3959

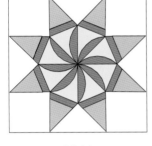
3960

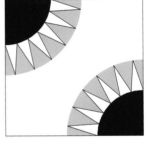
3961

3962

3963

3964

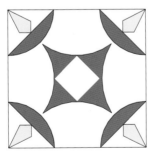
3965

3966

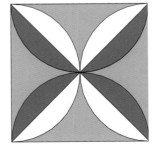
3967

3968

3969

3970

3971

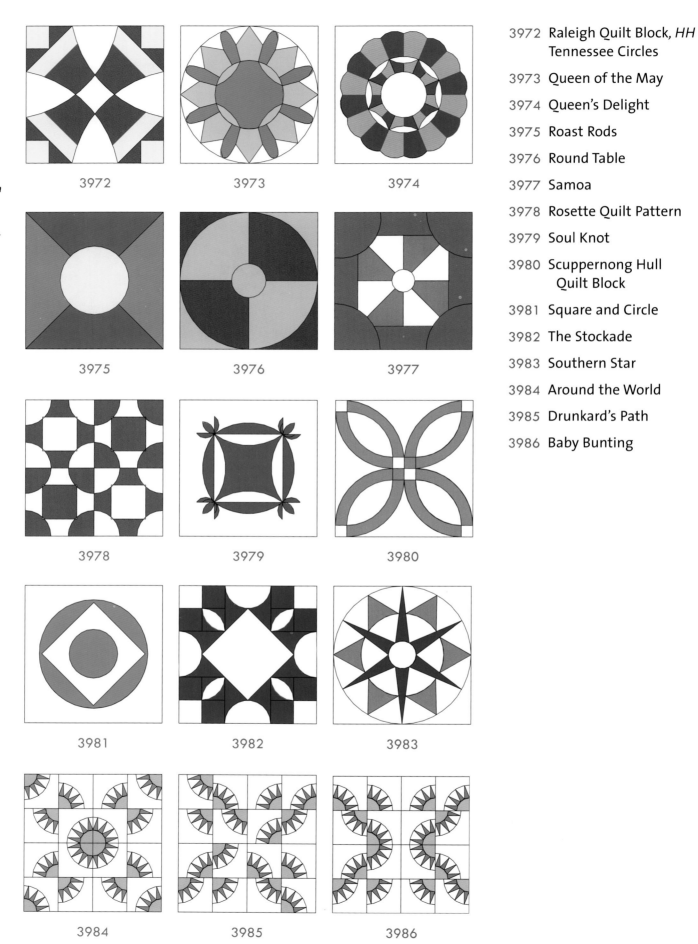

3972   3973   3974

3975   3976   3977

3978   3979   3980

3981   3982   3983

3984   3985   3986

3972 Raleigh Quilt Block, *HH* Tennessee Circles

3973 Queen of the May

3974 Queen's Delight

3975 Roast Rods

3976 Round Table

3977 Samoa

3978 Rosette Quilt Pattern

3979 Soul Knot

3980 Scuppernong Hull Quilt Block

3981 Square and Circle

3982 The Stockade

3983 Southern Star

3984 Around the World

3985 Drunkard's Path

3986 Baby Bunting

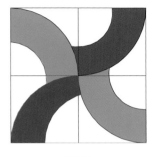

3987

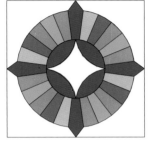

3988

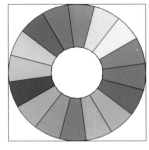

3989

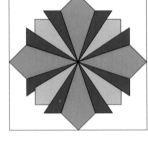

3990

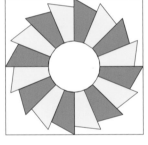

3991

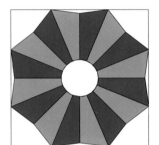

3992

3993

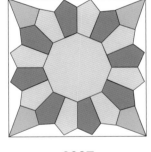

3994

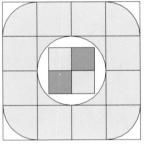

3995

3996

3997

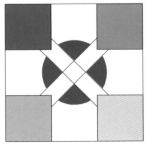

3998

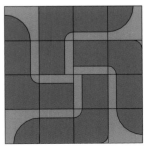

3999

4000

4001

5,500 QUILT BLOCK DESIGNS

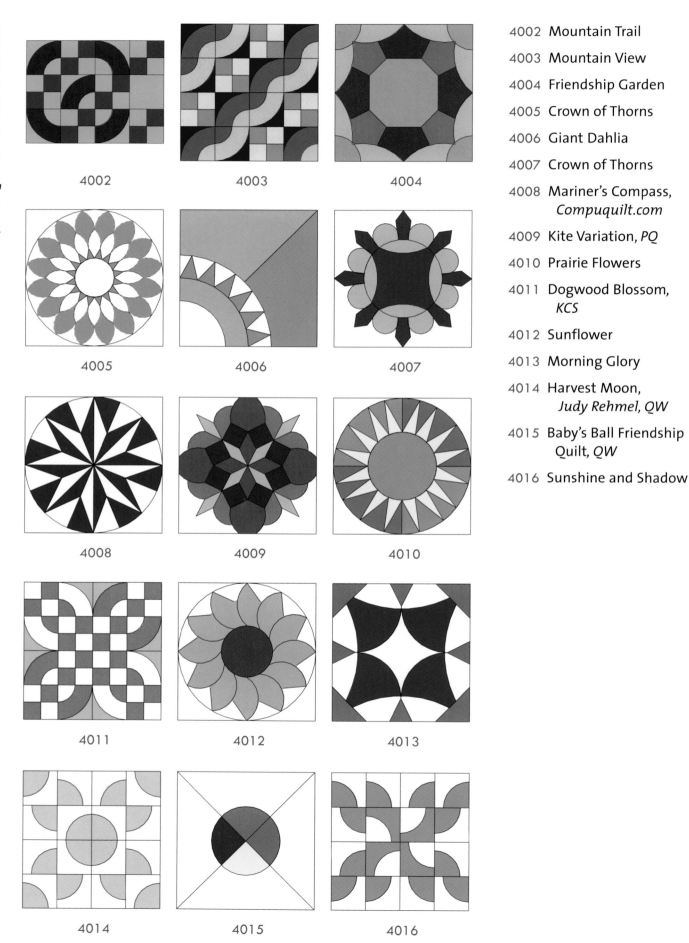

4002

4003

4004

4005

4006

4007

4008

4009

4010

4011

4012

4013

4014

4015

4016

4002 Mountain Trail

4003 Mountain View

4004 Friendship Garden

4005 Crown of Thorns

4006 Giant Dahlia

4007 Crown of Thorns

4008 Mariner's Compass, *Compuquilt.com*

4009 Kite Variation, *PQ*

4010 Prairie Flowers

4011 Dogwood Blossom, *KCS*

4012 Sunflower

4013 Morning Glory

4014 Harvest Moon, *Judy Rehmel, QW*

4015 Baby's Ball Friendship Quilt, *QW*

4016 Sunshine and Shadow

4017 Wishing Well

4018 Baseball

4019 Greek Cross, *LAC*
    Cross Patch
    Maltese Cross, *NC*
    Work-basket, *HH*

4020 An Heirloom Quilt, *OCS*

4021 No Name

4022 Grandmother's Brooch
    of Love

4023 Cross Roads, *HAS*

4024 The Great Circle Quilt,
    AMS

4025 Lost Paradise, *KCS*

4026 Evergreen, *HAS*

4027 Twist, *NC*

4028 Double Pinwheel, *LW*,
    OCS

4029 Hunter's Horns, *AG*

4030 Friendship Circle, *LW*,
    OCS

4031 Round Robin, *CS*

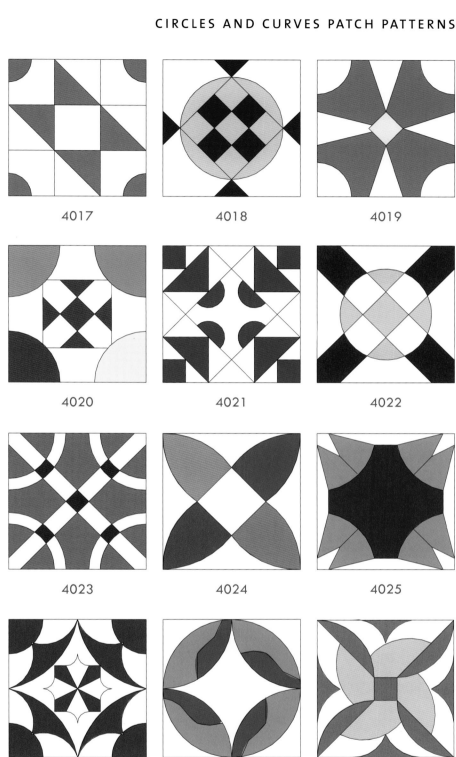

4017

4018

4019

4020

4021

4022

4023

4024

4025

4026

4027

4028

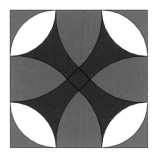

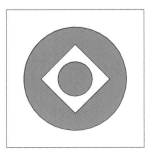

4029

4030

4031

5,500 QUILT BLOCK DESIGNS

4032

4033

4034

4035

4036

4037

4038

4039

4040

4041

4042

4043

4044

4045

4046

4032 Grandma's Fan, *PF*

4033 Queen's Crown

4034 Sunrise, *PF, 1977*

4035 Bluebell, *KCS, 1940*

4036 Letha's Electric Fan, *KCS*

4037 Friendship, *1871*

4038 Rocky Mountain Variation
Rocky Mountain Fan (1/4 of Rocky Mountain Variation)

4039 Rocky Mountain Star, *Gail Garber, SSQ, 1991*

4040 Gemstones

4041 Mountain Pink

4042 Rhododendron Star

4043 Wyoming Quilt Block, *HH*

4044 Wandering Path of the Wilderness, *HH*

4045 Amish Angel, *PQ*

4046 Tea Leaves

4047 Cockleburr, *LAC*

4048 Washington Merry-Go-Round

4049 Violet Blossoms

4050 Butterfly in the Garden

4051 The Snowball, *KCS*

4052 Byrd at the South Pole, *NC*

4053 Perry's Expedition, *NC*

4054 Gothic Windows

4055 Pieced Sunflower, *KCS*

4056 Spring Beauty

4057 Everglades, *NC*

4058 Bay Leaf, *AMS*

4059 Illinois Star

4060 Bride's Quilt, *OCS*
       Heart Quilt, *OCS*

4061 Foundation Rose

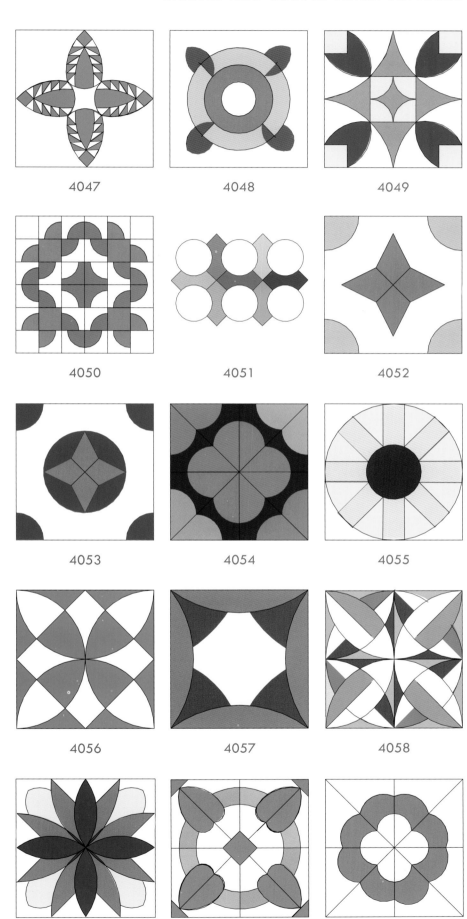

4047   4048   4049

4050   4051   4052

4053   4054   4055

4056   4057   4058

4059   4060   4061

5,500 QUILT BLOCK DESIGNS

4062   4063   4064

4065   4066   4067

4068   4069   4070

4071   4072   4073

4074   4075   4076

4062 Wedgewood Tiles, *NC*

4063 Equivalents,
    *Rebecca Rohrkaste,
    QN*

4064 Chips and Whetstones

4065 Flower Star

4066 Morning Star

4067 Missouri Beauty

4068 Lena's Magic Circles

4069 Good Fortune

4070 Triple Wedding Ring

4071 Shamrock

4072 Airplanes

4073 Priscilla's Prize, *LW, OCS*

4074 Sunset Star, *LW, OCS*

4075 Flower Bed

4076 Flowering Snowball,
    AK

4077 Garden Bloom, *LW, OCS*

4078 Spirit of 1849, *NC*

4079 Sunshine and Shadow

4080 Rolling Stars

4081 Wheel of Fate, *CS*

4082 Circle in a Circle

4083 Delaware

4084 Utah, *HH*

4085 Missouri Trouble, *NC*

4086 Arms to Heaven, *NC*

4087 Star of the Decathlon, *QN*

4088 Quilter's Pride, *AB, OCS*

4089 Anna's Pride, *KCS*

4090 Paducah Peony, *NC*

4091 Sweet Clover

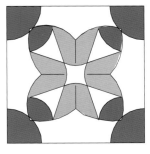
4077

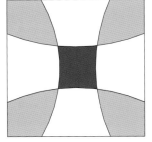
4078

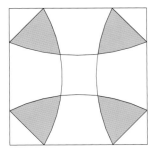
4079

4080

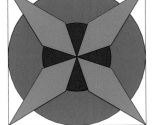
4081

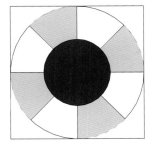
4082

4083

4084

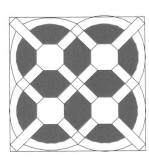
4085

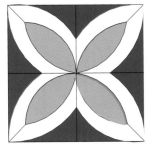
4086

4087

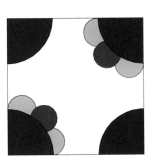
4088

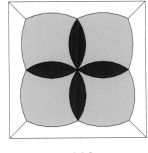
4089

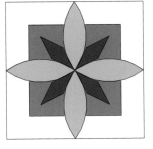
4090

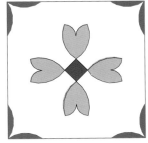
4091

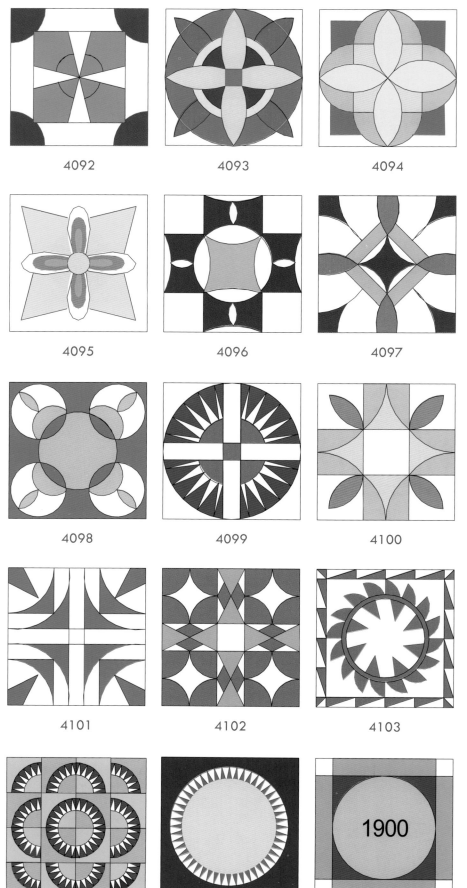

4092

4093

4094

4095

4096

4097

4098

4099

4100

4101

4102

4103

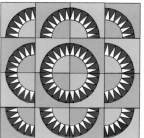

4104

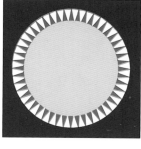

4105

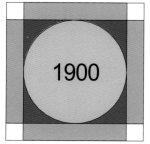

4106

4092 Four Leaf Clover, *NC*

4093 Tulip Wheel, *GD*

4094 Day Lily Garden, *AK*

4095 Points and Petals, *KCS*

4096 Unnamed, *AMS*

4097 Linked Squares, *LW, OCS*

4098 Hero's Crown

4099 Fredonia Cross, *MD*

4100 Morning Star, *NC*

4101 Mayflower, *LW, OCS*

4102 Delaware, *HH*

4103 Circular Saw

4104 Full and Change of the Moon, *late 1800s*

4105 New York Beauty

4106 End of the Century Patchwork, *1899*

4107 Road to California, *CaS*

4108 Pinwheel

4109 Unnamed

4110 Peony, *LW, OCS*

4111 Hearts and Darts, *AK*

4112 Birds in the Air

4113 Moon and Swastika, *NC*

4114 Honolulu, *HH*

4115 Quatrefoils

4116 Crisscross, *LW, OCS*

4117 Penelope's Favorite, *NC*
Penn's Puzzle, *NC*

4118 Posies Round the Square, *NM*
Dandelion Quilt, *QN*
The Posey Quilt, *KCS*
Spice Pinks (with ruffled flowers in the corners), *MD*
Sweetheart Garden (with rosebuds in the corners), *NC*

4119 Squares and Crosses, *NC*

4120 Dahlia, *AMS*

4121 Sunburst
Sunrise

4107   4108   4109

4110   4111   4112

4113   4114   4115

4116   4117   4118

4119   4120   4121

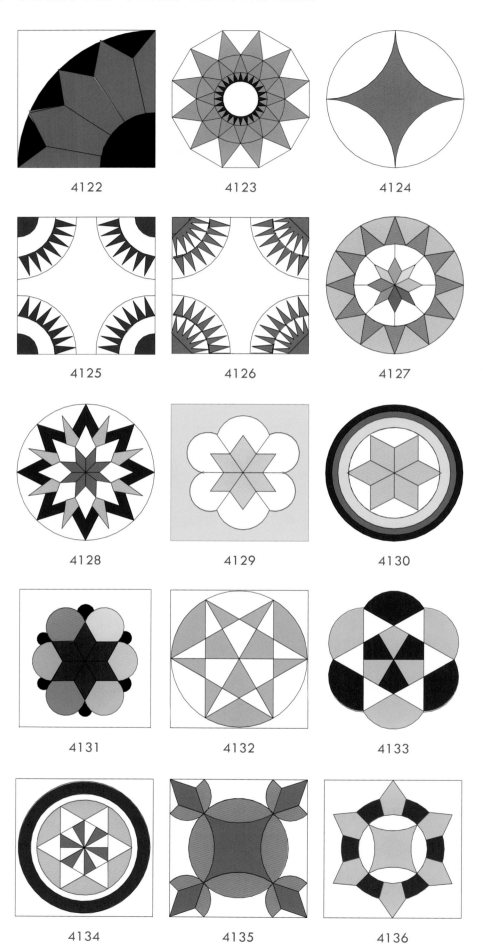

4122 Imperial Fan, *KCS*

4123 Man in the Moon, *AMS*

4124 Cathedral Window

4125 Crown of Thorns
New York Beauty, *MoM*
Rocky Mountain, *PP*
Rocky Mountain Road
Split Rail

4126 Spice Pink, *QN*

4127 Party Plate Quilt, *WB*,
1943

4128 Texas Star

4129 Buttercup, *PP*

4130 Rainbow Star Quilt,
HAS

4131 Star and Planets

4132 Savannah Beautiful
Star, *LAC*
Southern Plantation,
NC
Sylvia's Choice, *CS*

4133 Savannah Beautiful
Star

4134 Ohio Star, *AK*

4135 Devil's Footprints, *NC*
Milwaukee's Own, *LAC*
Mississippi Oak Leaves,
NC

4136 Caesar's Crown
Grecian Star
Whirling Wheel

4137 Indian Wedding Ring
    Pickle Dish
    Sweetwater Quilt

4138 Double Wedding Ring
    Around the World, *CaS*
    Double Wedding
     Bands, *MoM*
    Endless Chain
    King Tut, *CaS*
    The Rainbow
    Rainbow Wedding Ring
    Wedding Ring
    Wedding Ring Chain, *GD*

4139 A New Wedding Ring,
    NM, 1930

4140 Whig's Defeat
    Democrat's Fancy
    Fanny's Favorite
    Grandmother's
     Engagement Ring,
     MoM
    The Lady Finger, *LHJ,*
     1912
    The Lotus, *LHJ*
    Lotus Blossom
    Missouri Beauty
    Richmond Beauty

4141 Flight of the Wild
    Goose

4142 Star of Diamonds
    The Star, *HH*

4143 Dahlia
    Sunburst

4144 Star Chain, *KCS*

4145 The Sunflower, *LAC*
    Chinese Star, *GC*
    Queen of the May, *CS*

4146 A Quilt Pattern

4147 Grandmother's
    Favorite

4148 Hands All Around, *PF*
    Caesar's Crown
    Friendship Ring
    Grecian Star

4137   4138   4139

4140   4141   4142

4143   4144   4145

4146

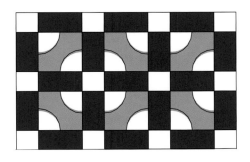

4147

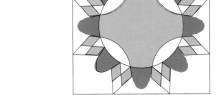

4148

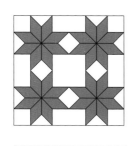

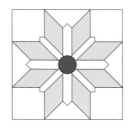
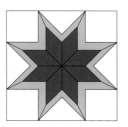
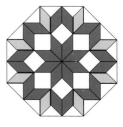

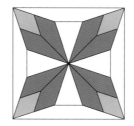
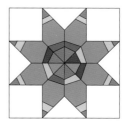

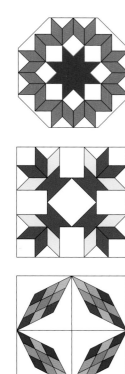
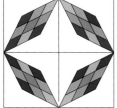

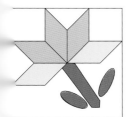

OCTAGONS, DIAMONDS, AND EIGHT POINT STARS

PATCH

PATTERNS

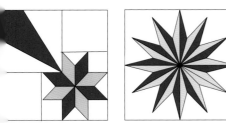

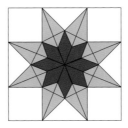

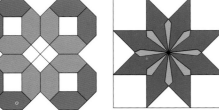

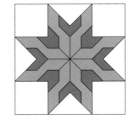
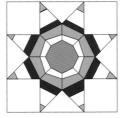

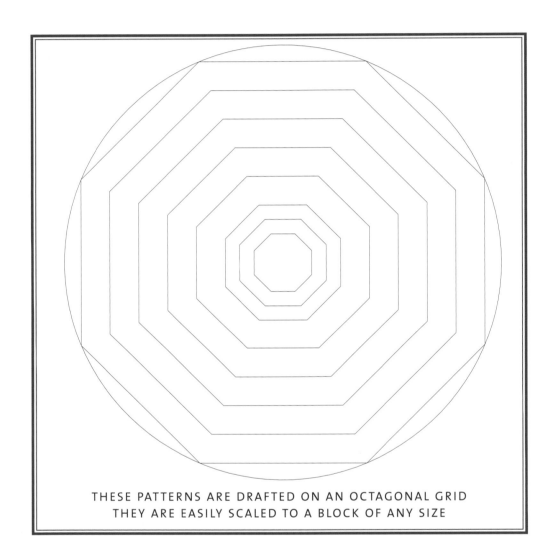

THESE PATTERNS ARE DRAFTED ON AN OCTAGONAL GRID
THEY ARE EASILY SCALED TO A BLOCK OF ANY SIZE

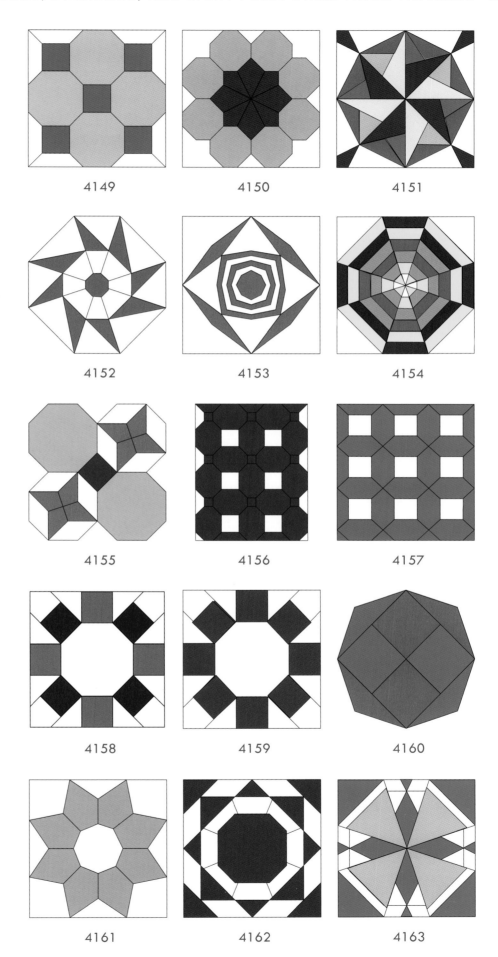

4149   4150   4151

4152   4153   4154

4155   4156   4157

4158   4159   4160

4161   4162   4163

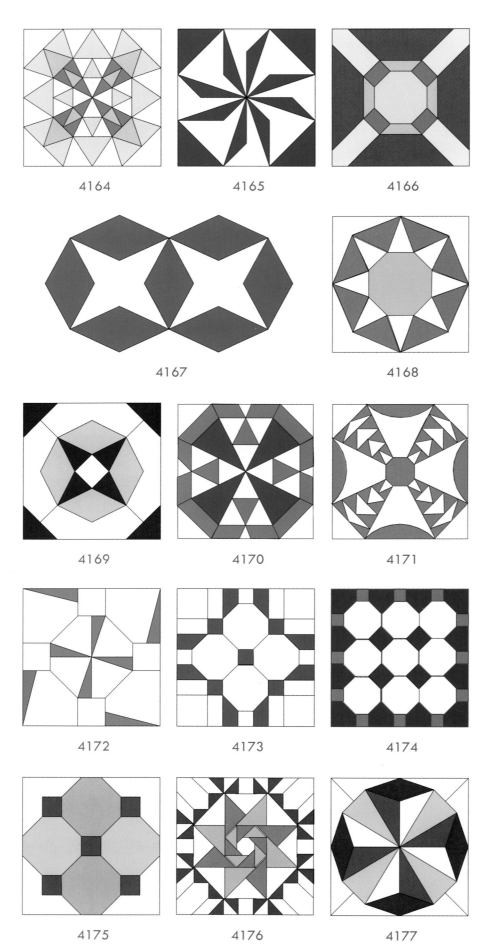

4164

4165

4166

4167

4168

4169

4170

4171

4172

4173

4174

4175

4176

4177

4164 Precious Gems

4165 Star of the East

4166 Imari Plate, *PQ*

4167 Diamond & Star

4168 Rising Sun

4169 Spider Web

4170 Aerial Beacon, *SSQ, 1989*

4171 Dusty Miller

4172 Waterwheels, *NC*

4173 Catalpa Flower, *NC*

4174 Nine Snowballs, *NC*

4175 Meadow Flower, *LW, OCS*

4176 Unfolding Star

4177 Skyscrapers, *QN*

4178 The Sunflower

4179 Chained Star, *LW, OCS*

4180 Rising Star, *LW, OCS*

4181 Ozark Cobblestones

4182 Five Cross, *CS*
Church Windows
Lattice Block, *NC*
Ogden Corners, *WB,*
  1935

4183 Old-Fashioned Quilt
Ozark Tile Pattern, *KCS*

4184 Puzzle Tile, *LAC*
Endless Chain
Mosaic Patchwork #4

4185 Red Cross, *KCS*
A Red, White & Blue
  Color Scheme, *KCS*

4186 Chinese Puzzle, *KCS*
Mosaic Patchwork #3
Tile Patchwork, *LAC*

4187 Octagon, *LAC*
An All Over Pattern of
  Octagons, *KCS*
Job's Trouble, *CS*
Mechanical Blocks
Octagonal, *NC*
Octagons
Ozark Cobblestones
Snowballs, *NC*

4188 Octagon Block, *NC*
Patriot's Quilt
White Mountains, *NC*

4189 Dove in the Window

4190 Wedding Ring Tile, *WB,*
  1941

4191 Bluet Quilt, *NP*
Hummingbird
Periwinkle

4192 Periwinkle

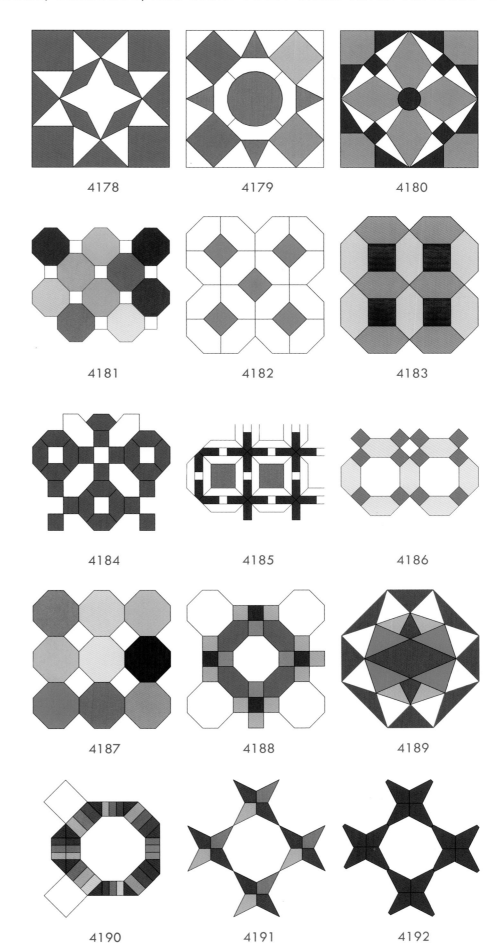

4178   4179   4180

4181   4182   4183

4184   4185   4186

4187   4188   4189

4190   4191   4192

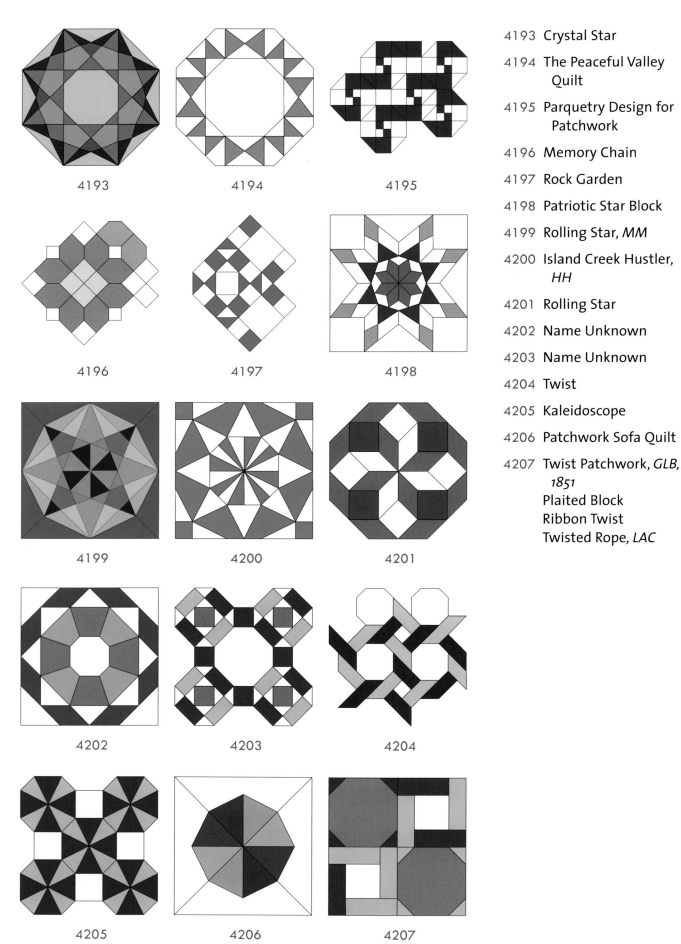

4193   Crystal Star

4194   The Peaceful Valley Quilt

4195   Parquetry Design for Patchwork

4196   Memory Chain

4197   Rock Garden

4198   Patriotic Star Block

4199   Rolling Star, *MM*

4200   Island Creek Hustler, *HH*

4201   Rolling Star

4202   Name Unknown

4203   Name Unknown

4204   Twist

4205   Kaleidoscope

4206   Patchwork Sofa Quilt

4207   Twist Patchwork, *GLB, 1851*
Plaited Block
Ribbon Twist
Twisted Rope, *LAC*

4208 Rolling Stone
Job's Trouble Quilt
    Block
Snowball

4209 Honeycomb Variation

4210 Garden Path

4211 Saw Blades, *QW*
Windmills

4212 Star Dancer,
    Tristan Audrey Mor,
    TQ

4213 Kite String Quilt

4214 Whirling Hexagons

4215 Periwinkle Variation

4216 Periwinkle
    Hummingbird

4217 Hexagon Beauty

4218 Puss in the Corner

4219 Morning Star, *OCS*

4220 Clydescape
Wheel of Fortune

4221 Rock Garden

4222 Memory Chain

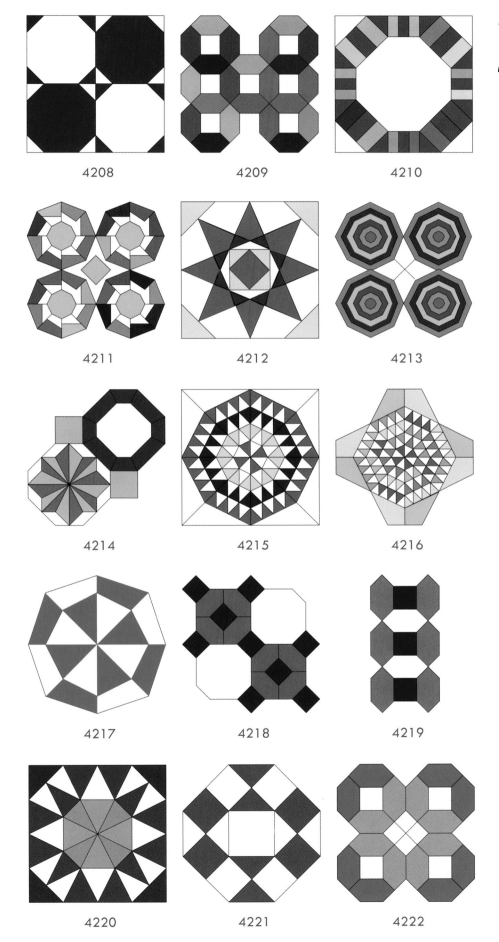

4208   4209   4210

4211   4212   4213

4214   4215   4216

4217   4218   4219

4220   4221   4222

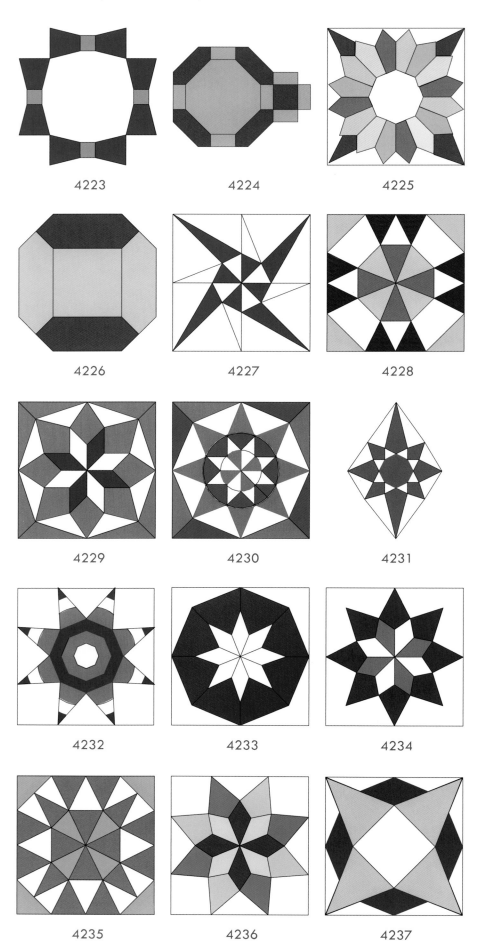

4223 True Lover's Knot, *AMS*

4224 White Mountains, *NC*

4225 Dresden Flower Quilt

4226 Kansas Dugout, *AMS*
Lattice Block, *NC*
Ogden Corners, *WB*

4227 Rolling Star

4228 Octagon Wheel

4229 Pole Star

4230 State of Oklahoma, *HH*

4231 Comet Star

4232 Helena

4233 Tennessee Mountain
Laurel

4234 Enigma, *LAC*
North Star, *NP*
St. Louis Block, *NP*

4235 Grandma's Surprise

4236 Wishing Star, *WB*
New Star
Star of St. Louis, *NC*

4237 Geometrical Star

4238 Godey Design

4239 Wheel of Fortune, *KCS*
  Road to Fortune, *OCS*
  Pinwheel Quilt,
    McCall's

4240 Target, *MoM*

4241 String Quilt

4242 Topsy Turvy

4243 Diamond Head, *NC*

4244 Emerald Block, *NC*

4245 Bull's Eye

4246 Midsummer Night, *NC*

4247 Ladies' Chain, *CS*

4248 Spinning Star

4249 Morning Star

4250 Joseph's Coat

4251 Carousel, *EH*, *LCPQ*

4252 Spring Blooms

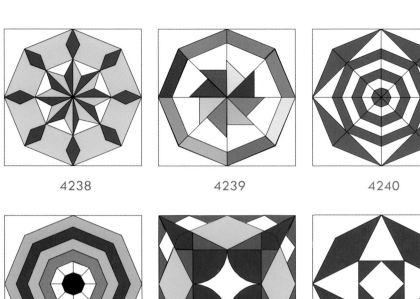

4238   4239   4240

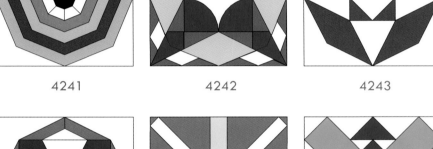

4241   4242   4243

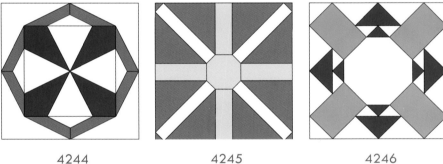

4244   4245   4246

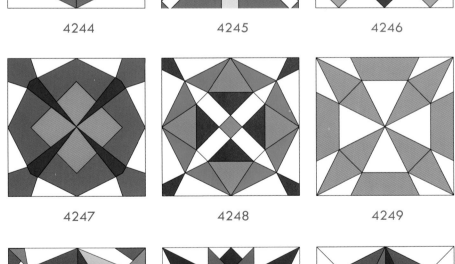

4247   4248   4249

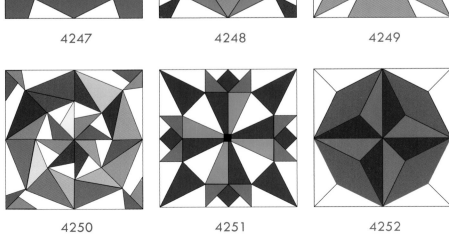

4250   4251   4252

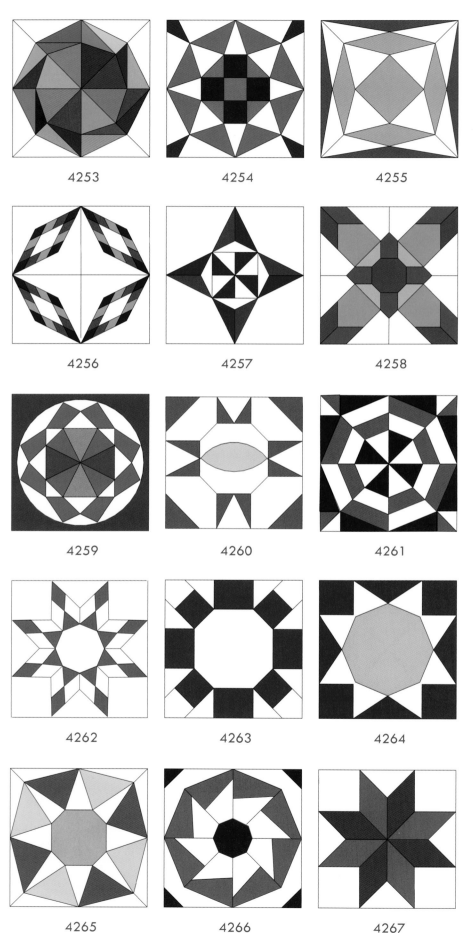

4253   Diamond Circle, *KCS*

4254   Kaleidoscope

4255   Morning Star (6), *SSQ*

4256   No Name, *LW, OCS*

4257   No Name Octagon

4258   Rising Star, *QW, 1991*

4259   Heavenly Bodies,
       Star Quilts

4260   Gemstones

4261   Homecoming, *QN*

4262   LeMoyne Star
       Lemon Star

4263   Mosaic, *GC*
       Venetian Design, *LAC*

4264   Star of Sweden

4265   Rising Sun, *LW*

4266   Friendship Circle, *LW*

4267   Eight Point Star
       Diamond
       Diamond Design, *WW*
       Eastern Star, *McCall's*
       Hanging Diamonds
       Idaho Star, *NC*
       Lemon Star
       Puritan Star
       Star of LeMoyne
       The Star, *KCS*

4268   Star
       Eight Point Star
       Eight Pointed Star, *LAC*
       Shasta Daisy, *LW*
       Simple Star, *CaS*
       The Southern Star, *KCS*
       Star Bed Quilt, *HH*
       Twinkle, Twinkle Little
         Star, *KCS*
       Variable Star

4269   Arrow Star, *KCS*

4270   LeMoyne Star &
         Windmill
       Pin Wheel
       Star of the Milky Way
       Twinkle Star

4271 LeMoyne Star
Lemon Star
The Divided Star
Louisiana Star, *AK, 1965*
North Star, *HAS*
Star of the East

4272 Silver and Gold, *KCS*
Gold and Silver, *NC*
Winter Stars, *NC*

4273 Liberty Star, *KCS*
Star of Bethlehem
Stars of Stripes
Tennessee, *HH*

4274 Patriotic Star, *KCS*
Blazing Star
Blazing Star of Minnesota
Bright Morning Star
Combination Feathered
 Star
Eastern Star
Little Star, *NC*
Morning Star, *KCS*
Quilt of the Century, *CW*
Rising Star, *NP*
Star of the Bluegrass,
 MoM
Star of the East, *CaS*
Sunburst Star

4275 Starry Heavens, *KCS*

4276 Flying Bat, *LAC*
Dove in the Window
Doves, *HAS*
Flying Star, *HAS*
Polaris Star
Witches Star, *NC*

4277 The Spider Web, *KCS*

4278 Wandering Jew, *CS*
The Winding Blades, *KCS*

4279 Olympiad

4280 Christmas Star, *KCS*

4281 Friendship Knot, *KCS*
Starry Crown

4282 Friendship Knot, *LW*
Friendship Wreath

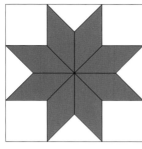
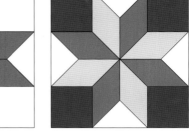

4268   4269   4270

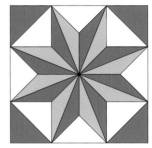

4271   4272   4273

4274   4275   4276

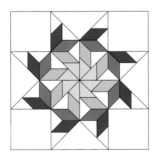

4277   4278   4279

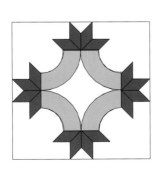

4280   4281   4282

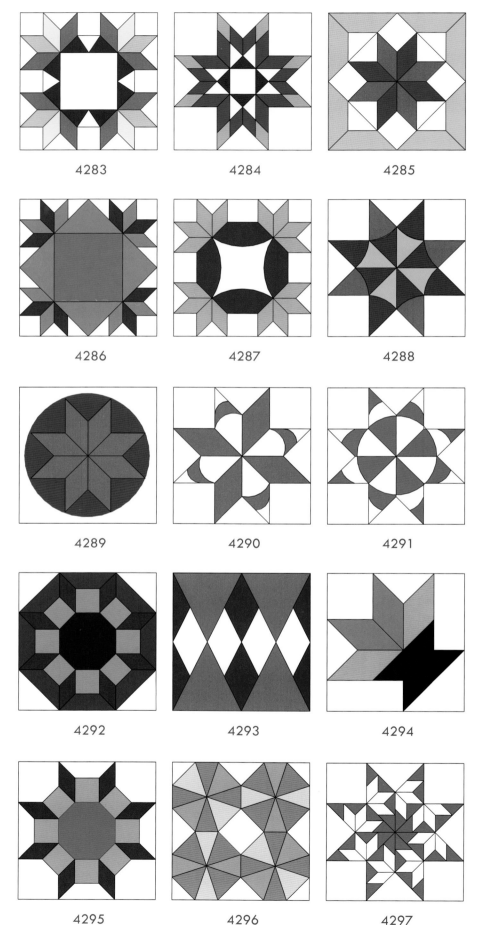

4283

4284

4285

4286

4287

4288

4289

4290

4291

4292

4293

4294

4295

4296

4297

4283 Lotus Star, *VS*

4284 Northumberland Star, *CS*

4285 Brunswick Star, *LW, OCS*

4286 Swallows in the Window, *KCS*

4287 Hands All Around, *LAC*
All Hands Round, *CaS*
Center Table Quilt, *CoM*
Old Fashioned Star Quilt
Wreath of Lilies

4288 Sailor's Joy, *CS*

4289 Log Cabin Star

4290 The King's Crown, *LAC*

4291 King's Star, *NC*

4292 The Castle Wall

4293 Four Diamonds

4294 Texas Cactus

4295 Dogwood, *LBC*

4296 Kaleidoscope

4297 Whirling Star, *KCS*
Circling Swallows
Falling Star
Flying Barn Swallows, *NC*
Flying Swallow, *LAC*
Flying Swallows, *AMS*
Flying Star
The Wreath, *LW*

4298 Diamond Star, *HH*
Diamond Star #2, *CS*

4299 Dove in the Window
Airplanes, *FJ*
Bluebirds for
 Happiness, *MoM*
The Bluebirds
The Dove
Four Birds, *WW*
Four Doves
Four Swallows

4300 Formosa Tea Leaf, *KCS*

4301 Missouri Star, *KCS*
Shining Star
Star and Arrow, *NC*

4302 Love in a Mist, *FJ*

4303 Chips and Whetstones,
 KCS

4304 Royal Diamonds, *KCS*

4305 Star of Hope, *KCS*
Celestial Sphere, *NC*
Twinkling Stars, *LAC*

4306 Connecticut Star, *FJ*

4307 Goldfish, *KCS*
An Airplane Motif, *KCS*
Bass and Trout, *QW*
Dove in the Window
Fish, *CS*
Fish Block
Fish Circle, *LCPQ*
Flying Fish, *KCS*
Starfish, *LCPQ*
Trout and Bass Block, *NC*
Whirligig, *CS*

4308 Pole Star, *HH*

4309 Bouquet in a Fan

4310 Diamond Cluster in a
 Frame

4311 Rolling Star

4312 Hunter's Star
Indian Arrowhead,
 AMS

4298

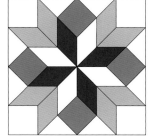

4299

4300

4301

4302

4303

4304

4305

4306

4307

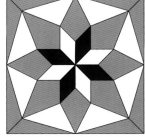

4308

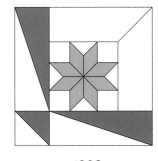

4309

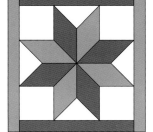

4310

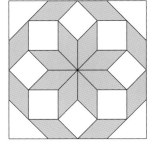

4311

4312

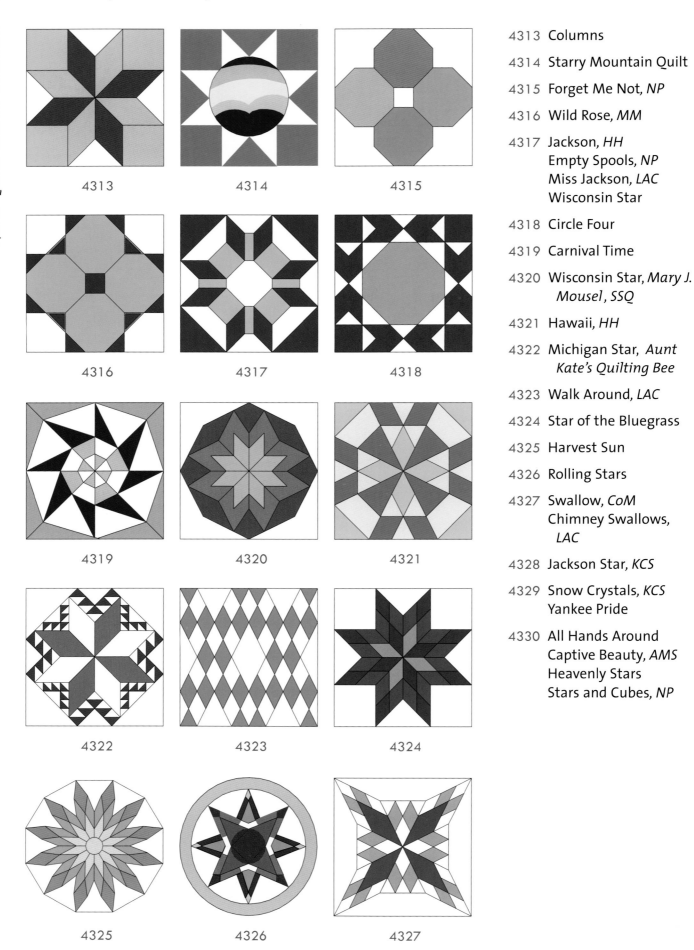

4313

4314

4315

4316

4317

4318

4319

4320

4321

4322

4323

4324

4325

4326

4327

4313 Columns

4314 Starry Mountain Quilt

4315 Forget Me Not, *NP*

4316 Wild Rose, *MM*

4317 Jackson, *HH*
      Empty Spools, *NP*
      Miss Jackson, *LAC*
      Wisconsin Star

4318 Circle Four

4319 Carnival Time

4320 Wisconsin Star, *Mary J.
      Mousel, SSQ*

4321 Hawaii, *HH*

4322 Michigan Star, *Aunt
      Kate's Quilting Bee*

4323 Walk Around, *LAC*

4324 Star of the Bluegrass

4325 Harvest Sun

4326 Rolling Stars

4327 Swallow, *CoM*
      Chimney Swallows,
      LAC

4328 Jackson Star, *KCS*

4329 Snow Crystals, *KCS*
      Yankee Pride

4330 All Hands Around
      Captive Beauty, *AMS*
      Heavenly Stars
      Stars and Cubes, *NP*

4331 The Double Star Quilt
Circle Saw, *KCS*
Dutch Rose, *LAC*
Eccentric Star, *GC*
Morning Star
Octagonal Star, *HH*
Orphan Star, *HAS*
Star and Diamond
Star of the East, *MD*
Triple Star, *HHJ*

4332 Lone Star of Paradise, *KCS*

4333 Dutch Rose
Octagon Star

4334 Carpenter's Wheel
Black Diamond, *CS*
Diadem Star, *HH*
Double Star, *HH*
Knickerbocker Star, *WB*
Lone Star of Paradise
Star of Bethlehem, *CS*
Star Quilt Block
Star Within a Star
Sunflower, *NP*
Twinkling Star, *NP*

4335 Bethlehem Star
Christmas Memory Quilt,
 QN
Jewels in a Frame
Star of Bethlehem, *KCS*
Star of the Magi, *NC*
Winged Star, *KCS*

4336 Rolling Star

4337 Eight Pointed Broken Star

4338 Broken Star

4339 Carpenter's Wheel

4340 Dutch Rose, *CS*
Mother's Choice, *NM, 1918*

4341 Black Diamond, *NM*

4342 The Starbright Quilt
Circle Saw
Star of the East

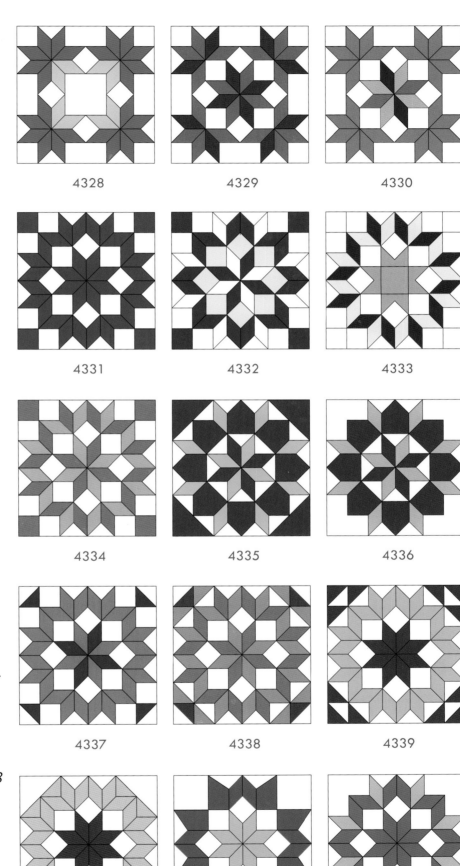

4328   4329   4330
4331   4332   4333
4334   4335   4336
4337   4338   4339
4340   4341   4342

4343

4344

4345

4346

4347

4348

4349

4350

4351

4352

4353

4354

4355

4356

4357

4343 Poinsettias, *QN, 1975*

4344 Rolling Star, *LAC*
Brunswick Star
Chained Star
Cross and Crown
Rolling Stone
Virginia Reel

4345 Victory Star, *CS*

4346 Cubes and Tiles, *NC*
Double Star, *HH*
Star, *OF*
Stars and Cubes, *LAC*
Yankee Pride

4347 A Flash of Diamonds,
KCS

4348 Blazing Star
LeMoyne Star

4349 Star and Chains

4350 Four Stars Patchwork,
LAC
The Four Stars
Old Maid's Patience,
NC

4351 Diamond Wedding
Block, *NC*

4352 The Maple Leaf, *1931*

4353 President's Quilt

4354 Sitka Star

4355 Buckeye Beauty, *NC*
Rockingham's Beauty,
LAC

4356 Star of Many Points,
NC

4357 Blazing Star, *LAC*
Carpenter's Wheel
Variation
Virginia Star
Harvest Star

4358 Columbus Quilt Block

4359 Four Block Star, *AK*

4360 Cleveland Tulip
Carolina Lily
Pineys, *NM*
Tree Quilt Pattern

4361 Missouri Quilt Block,
HH

4362 State of California, *HH*

4363 Virginia's Star

4364 Tennessee Star

4365 Pinwheel Star, *WW*
Modern Star

4366 Aurora Borealis

4367 Missouri

4368 Peony

4369 Tennessee Star

4370 Octagon Star

4371 Octagonal Star

4372 Kaleidoscope Star

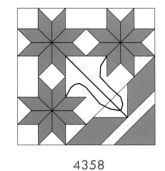

4358

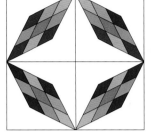

4359

4360

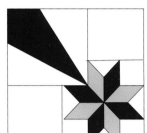

4361

4362

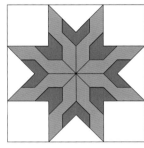

4363

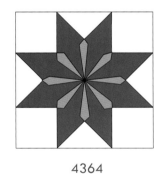

4364

4365

4366

4367

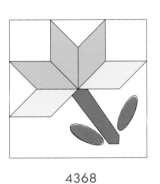

4368

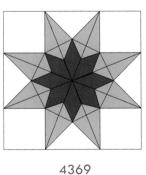

4369

4370

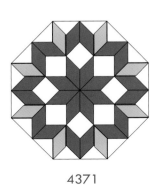

4371

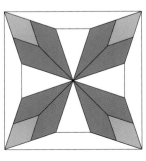

4372

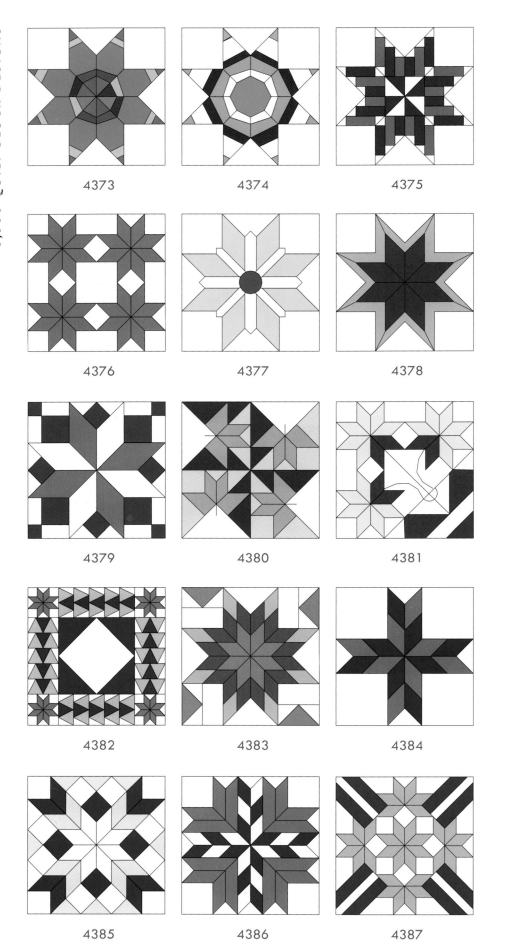

4373

4374

4375

4376

4377

4378

4379

4380

4381

4382

4383

4384

4385

4386

4387

4373 Scrap Star Quilt,
    U Khin, *QW*

4374 Capital Star
    Helena
    Spiderweb Star

4375 Fence Row Star, *HH*
    Log Cabin Star, *HH*

4376 The Four Stars

4377 Gardener's Prize

4378 Double Star

4379 A Three-in-One Quilt,
    KCS

4380 Autumn Breeze,
    Susie Ennis, *QN*

4381 Columbus, Ohio, *HH*

4382 Fox and Geese
    Stars in the Corners

4383 Sunburst and Mill, *NC*

4384 Double Star, *CS*
    Fish Tails, *NP*

4385 Mosaic, *FJ*
    Bursting Star, *NC*
    Moorish Mosaic, *NC*

4386 A Swallow at the
    Window

4387 My Country, *AK*

4388 My Mother's Star

4389 Parallelogram, *KCS*
Design for Light and
Dark, *CoM*

4390 Calico Stars

4391 Star Shower, *NC*

4392 The Triple Star Quilt

4393 Star Net, *NC*

4394 Westward Ho, *NC*

4395 Turtle

4396 Compass, *AMS*
Calico Compass, *NC*

4397 Octagon Star, *CoM*

4398 Octagon Star, *FJ*

4399 Ring Around the Star,
WB

4400 National Star, *PF*
Patty's Star

4401 Kentucky's Twinkling
Star

4402 Little Star

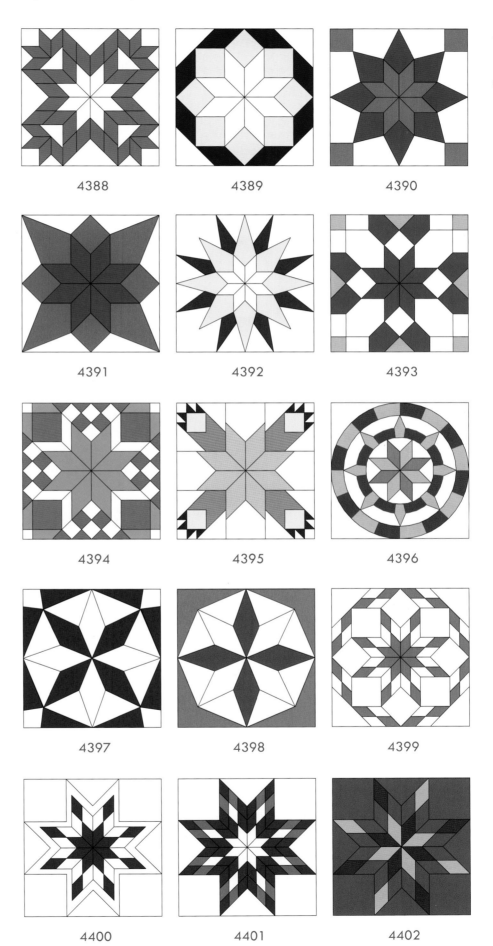

4388   4389   4390

4391   4392   4393

4394   4395   4396

4397   4398   4399

4400   4401   4402

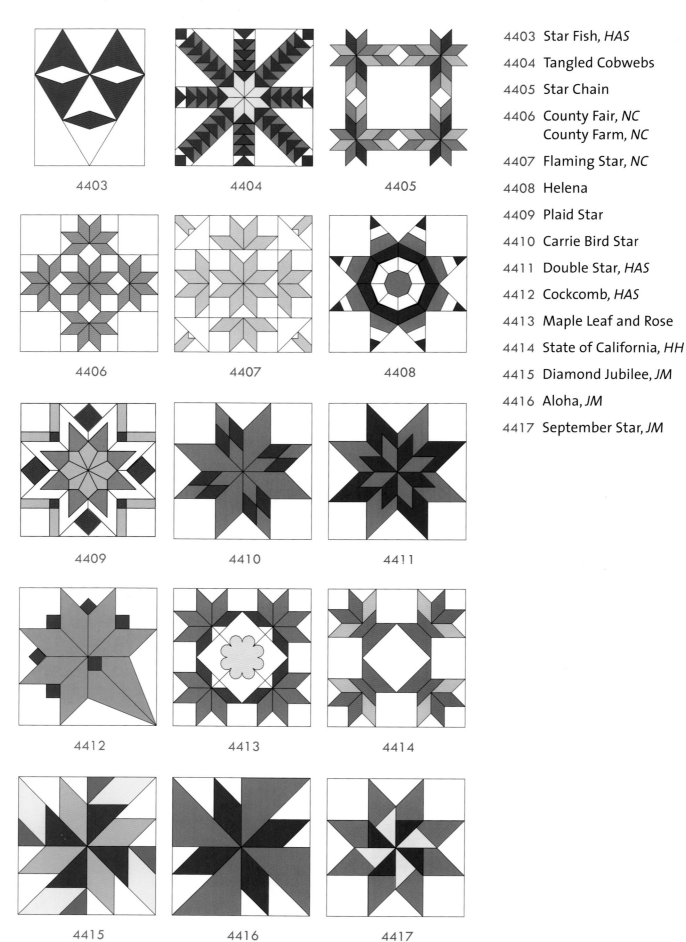

5,500 QUILT BLOCK DESIGNS

4403
4404
4405

4406
4407
4408

4409
4410
4411

4412
4413
4414

4415
4416
4417

4403 Star Fish, *HAS*

4404 Tangled Cobwebs

4405 Star Chain

4406 County Fair, *NC*
County Farm, *NC*

4407 Flaming Star, *NC*

4408 Helena

4409 Plaid Star

4410 Carrie Bird Star

4411 Double Star, *HAS*

4412 Cockcomb, *HAS*

4413 Maple Leaf and Rose

4414 State of California, *HH*

4415 Diamond Jubilee, *JM*

4416 Aloha, *JM*

4417 September Star, *JM*

4418 Writer's Block, *JM*

4419 Eyes of Blue, *JM*

4420 March Winds, *JM*

4421 Motown Sounds, *JM*

4422 Cornucopia

4423 Stained Glass Window

4424 All American Star

4425 Christmas Star, *Ursula Michael, QW, 1988*

4426 Whirling Tulip

4427 Summer Star Flower

4428 Old Maid's Patience

4429 Pinwheel Star

4430 Starburst

4431 Peony

4432 Wandering Diamond

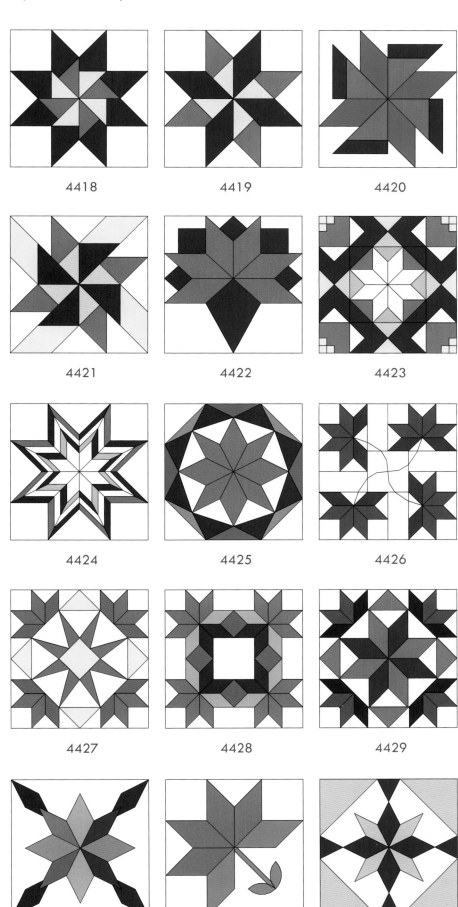

4418   4419   4420

4421   4422   4423

4424   4425   4426

4427   4428   4429

4430   4431   4432

5,500 QUILT BLOCK DESIGNS

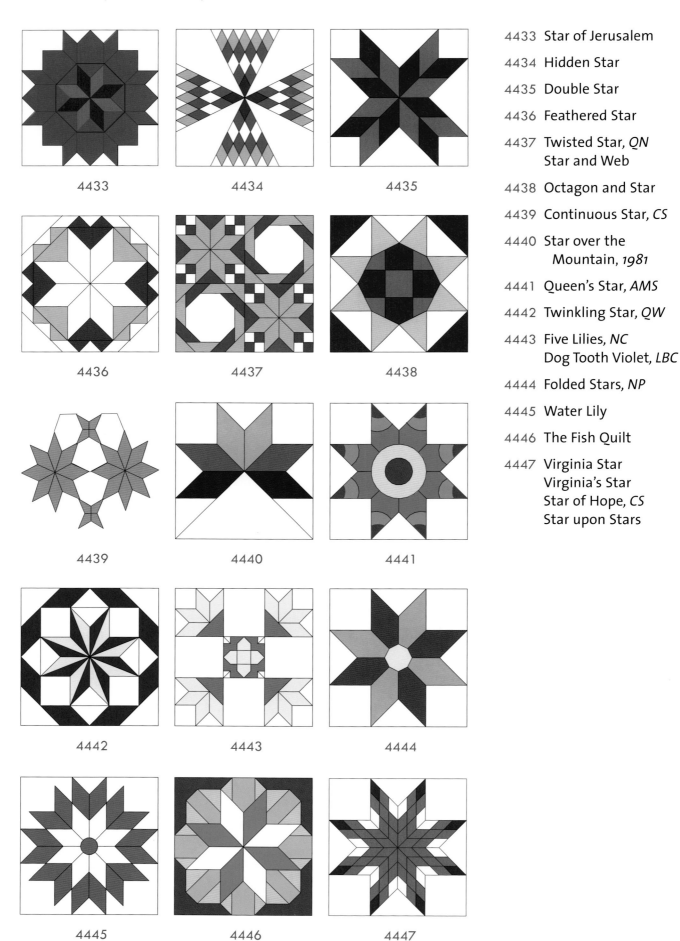

4433

4434

4435

4436

4437

4438

4439

4440

4441

4442

4443

4444

4445

4446

4447

4433 Star of Jerusalem

4434 Hidden Star

4435 Double Star

4436 Feathered Star

4437 Twisted Star, *QN*
Star and Web

4438 Octagon and Star

4439 Continuous Star, *CS*

4440 Star over the
Mountain, *1981*

4441 Queen's Star, *AMS*

4442 Twinkling Star, *QW*

4443 Five Lilies, *NC*
Dog Tooth Violet, *LBC*

4444 Folded Stars, *NP*

4445 Water Lily

4446 The Fish Quilt

4447 Virginia Star
Virginia's Star
Star of Hope, *CS*
Star upon Stars

4448 Star of Alabama,
      MoM

4449 Star Bouquet

4450 Virginia Star

4451 National Star, *PF*
      Patty's Star

4452 Grandmother's Choice

4453 Blazing Star of
      Kentucky

4454 Rising Sun

4455 Aunt Dinah's Star, *HAS*

4456 Star Flowers, *NC*

4457 Star of Bethlehem
      Star of Alabama

4458 Triple Star Flower

4459 Walk Around, *LAC*
      Boston Corners, *NC*
      Country Crossroads
      Double X's, *NC*
      Guide Post, *MoM*
      Web of Diamonds, *NC*

4460 Modern Tulip, *AK*

4461 Diamonds, *LAC*
      Boston Corners, *NC*
      Heritage Quilt

4462 Shadow Trail, *MoM*

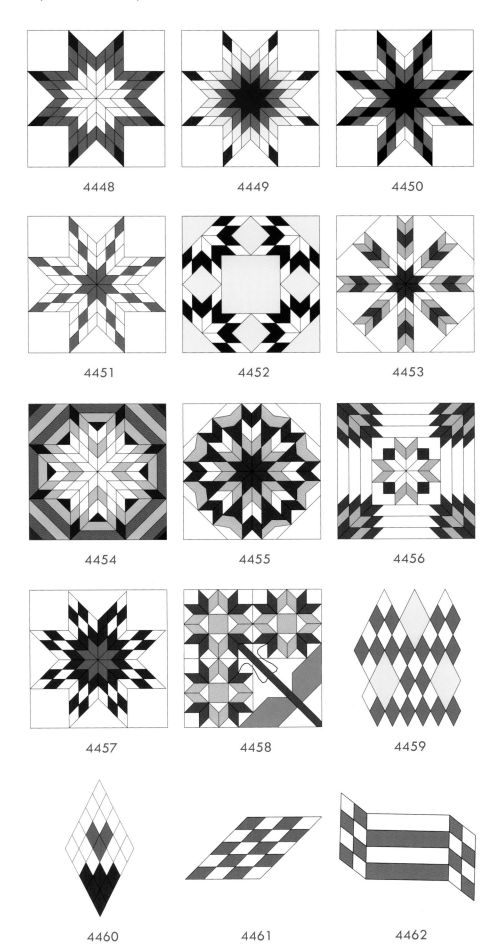

4448   4449   4450

4451   4452   4453

4454   4455   4456

4457   4458   4459

4460   4461   4462

4463

4464

4465

4466

4467

4468

4469

4470

4471

4472

4473

4463 Diamonds, *LAC*

4464 Diamond Design

4465 Springtime in the Ozarks

4466 Diamonds, *NP*
Guide Post
Boson Corners, *NC*
Walk Around

4467 Nine Patch Diamond

4468 Log Cabin Diamond

4469 Evening Star

4470 Star Flower

4471 Lazy Daisy

4472 Stars and Stripes

4473 Tulip Ring, *AK*

4474 Lone Star, *LAC*
An Aesthetic Quilt, *HH*
Blazing Star
Glitter Star
Morning Star, *CaS*
Overall Star Pattern
Pride of Texas, *HAS*
Rainbow Star
Rising Star
Rising Sun
Star of Bethlehem
Star of the East
Star of Stars, *HAS*
Stars upon Star, *LAC*
Sunburst Star, *LW*
(size can be increased
by adding rows of
diamonds; the largest
I saw had 11 inner
rows before branch-
ing into star points
containing 10 rows
each)

4475 Prairie Star
Harvest Star
Harvest Sun
Ship's Wheel

4476 The Lincoln Quilt
(from a quilt pieced
by Abraham Lincoln's
mother), *LBC*

4477 Kaleidoscope Star
(continuous design)

4478 Star and Wreath, *NC*
Pinwheel Star, *LAC*

4474

4475

4476

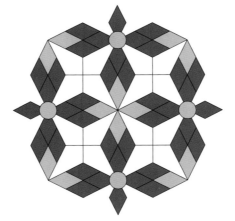

4477

4478

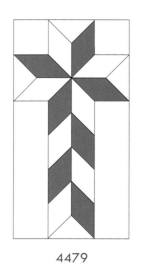

4479

4480

4479 Shooting Star

4480 Candles of Heaven,
Pat Flynn Kyser,
QW, 1989

4481 LeMoyne Star, *QN*

4482 Diamond Star, *NC*

4483 No Name, *AMS*

4484 Prairie Star
Harvest Sun
Ship's Wheel
Stars upon Stars

4481

4482

4483

4484

4485 Thunderbird and Sioux
Star

4486 Prairie Crocus

4487 Broken Star
Blazing Star
Diadem Star
Star of Bethlehem

4488 Pineapple Cactus

4489 Michigan Star,
*Aunt Kate's Quilting
Bee*

4490 Pine Burr

4485

4486

4487

4488

4489

4490

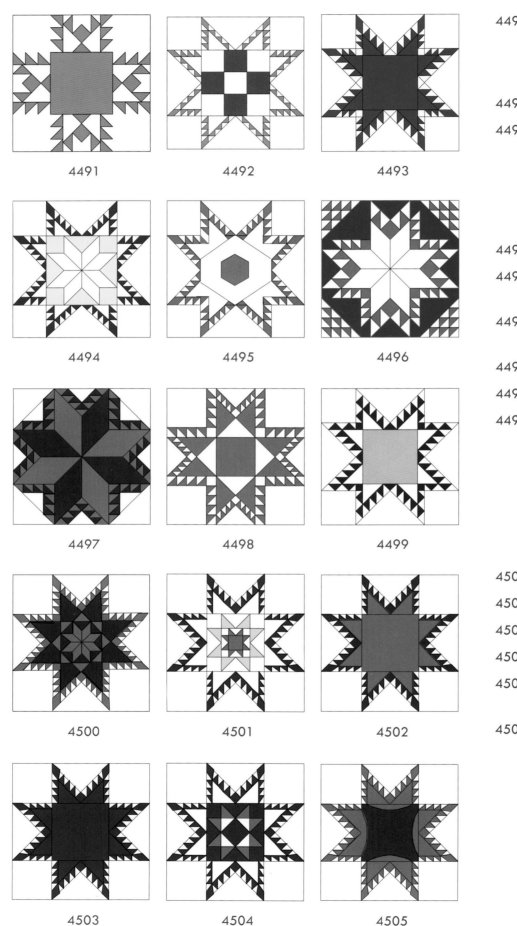

4491   4492   4493

4494   4495   4496

4497   4498   4499

4500   4501   4502

4503   4504   4505

4491   Feather Star
      Saw Tooth
      Star of Bethlehem
      Twinkling Star

4492   California Star, *LAC*

4493   Feather Star
      Blazing Star
      Feathered Star of
        Bethlehem
      Star of Bethlehem
      Star of Chamblie

4494   Feather Edged Star

4495   Radiant Star
      California Star

4496   The Bride's Puzzle in
       Patchwork

4497   Lucinda's Star

4498   Pine Cone

4499   A Very Old Sawtooth,
      KCS
      Diana's Pride
      Dinah's Pride
      Feather Star
      Sawtooth
      Star of Bethlehem
      Twinkling Star, *LAC*

4500   Feather Star

4501   Rising Star

4502   Phoenix Star

4503   Phoenix Star

4504   Feathered Variable
      Star

4505   Feathered Star with
      Reel

4506 Feathered Star

4507 Pierre, *HH*

4508 Radiant Star, *AMS*
Star of Bethlehem
Chestnut Burr, *AMS*

4509 Feathered LeMoyne
Star
Feather Edged Star
Feathered Star

4510 Twinkling Star

4511 Star Diamond, *LHJ*
Triangle Star, *HHJ*

4512 Feathered Star

4513 Feather Star

4514 Sawtooth Star

4515 Feather Star

4516 The Hour Glass, *HHJ*

4517 Joining Star, *LAC*

4518 Morning Star, *NC*

4519 Summer Sun, *NC*

4520 California Star, *AK*

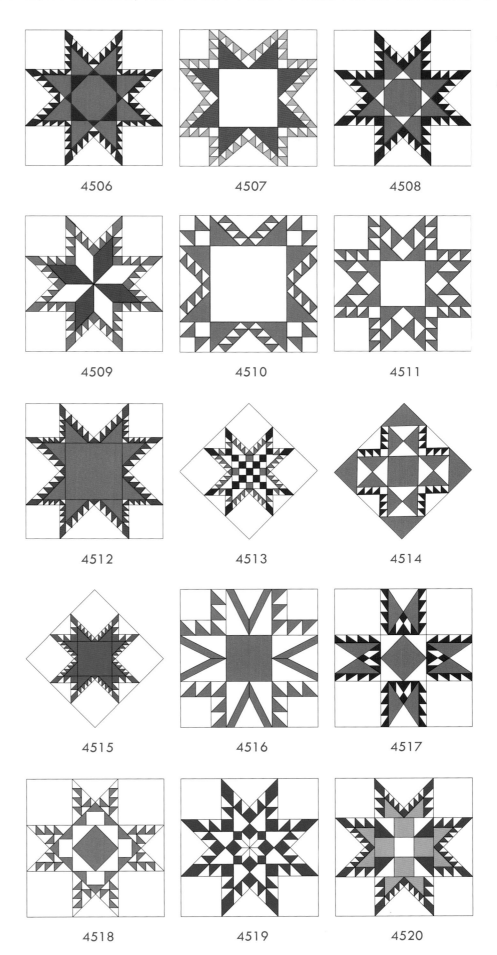

4506 4507 4508

4509 4510 4511

4512 4513 4514

4515 4516 4517

4518 4519 4520

5,500 QUILT BLOCK DESIGNS

4521

4522

4523

4524

4525

4526

4521 Feathered Star

4522 Octagonal Star

4523 Halley's Comet, *NC*

4524 California Star

4525 Pike's Peak, *CS*
      Bride's Fancy, *CS*

4526 Star Spangled Banner

4527 The Mayflower Quilt,
      MD

4528 Philippines, *LAC*

4529 The Double Pineapple

4530 Philadelphia Patch

4527

4528

4529

4530

4531 Philadelphia Patch, *LAC*

4532 Five Pointed Star, *LAC*
  Star in a Square
  Union Star

4533 Union Star
  State of Texas

4534 Star of the West, *LAC*
  Texas (starting at the
    top T-E-X-A-S is
    embroidered in each
    point), *HH*

4535 The American Way,
  RMS, SSQ

4536 New York

4537 Red, White and Blue

4538 Stars and Stripes

4539 Twentieth Century
  Star

4540 Texas Ranger's Badge

4531

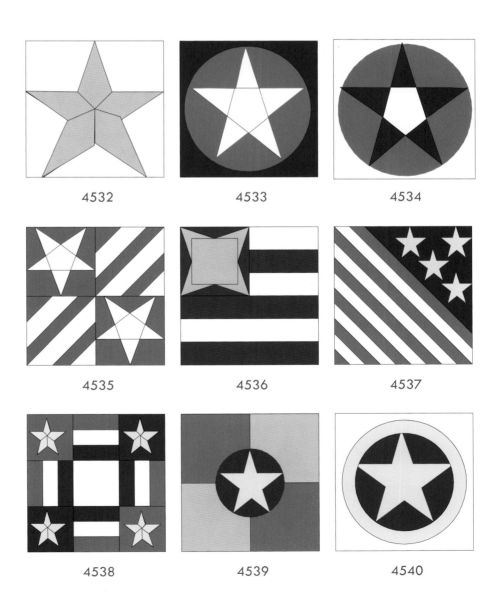

4532   4533   4534

4535   4536   4537

4538   4539   4540

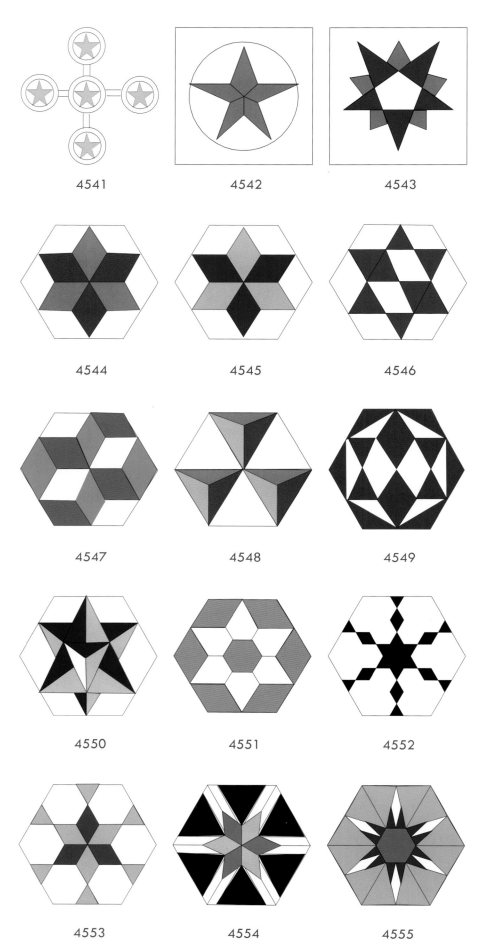

4541

4542

4543

4544

4545

4546

4547

4548

4549

4550

4551

4552

4553

4554

4555

4541 Star of the City of
Indianapolis, *KCS*

4542 Star and Ring

4543 Star upon Star

4544 Eisenhower Star
Jacob's Ladder
Stair Step Quilt

4545 Little Girls' Star, *KCS*
Pennsylvania Hex, *WD*
(set with plain hexagons):
Star Bouquet Quilt, *HAS*
Morning Star

4546 Kentucky

4547 Block Puzzle

4548 Wonder of Egypt

4549 Madison Block

4550 Bezelled Star

4551 Dolly Madison's Star, *HAS*
Dolly Madison Pattern, *KCS*
Desert Flower
Desert Rose
Friendship Hexagon, *NP*
Hexagon Stars, *NP*
Hexagonal Star, *HH*
Solomon's Garden
Star Garden, *KCS*
Texas Star, *LAC*

4552 Trail of Diamonds, *MM*

4553 The Hexagon Star, *KCS*
Brilliant Star, *NP*
Pointing Star, *KCS*

4554 Mother's Prayers, *KCS*

4555 Star of the West

4556 Florida Star

4557 Diamonds and Arrow
     Points
     Favorite, *OF, 1894*

4558 Oklahoma Star
     The Mountain Star

4559 Ozark Diamond
     Ozark Star, *KCS*

4560 Ozark Diamond, *KCS*
     Ma Perkin's Flower
     Garden

4561 Hexagon, *LAC*
     Hexagon Beauty
     An Old Fashioned
     Wheel Quilt
     Spider Web

4562 Crazy Tile
     (continuous design),
     KCS

4563 Boutonniere

4564 Stop Sign

4565 Star Center in French
     Bouquet, *KCS*
     Snow Crystals, *KCS*

4566 Wagon Wheel, *AK*

4567 Twinkling Star,
     MoM

4568 Morning Star, *LW*

4569 Morning Star, *KCS*

4570 Dolly Madison Pattern

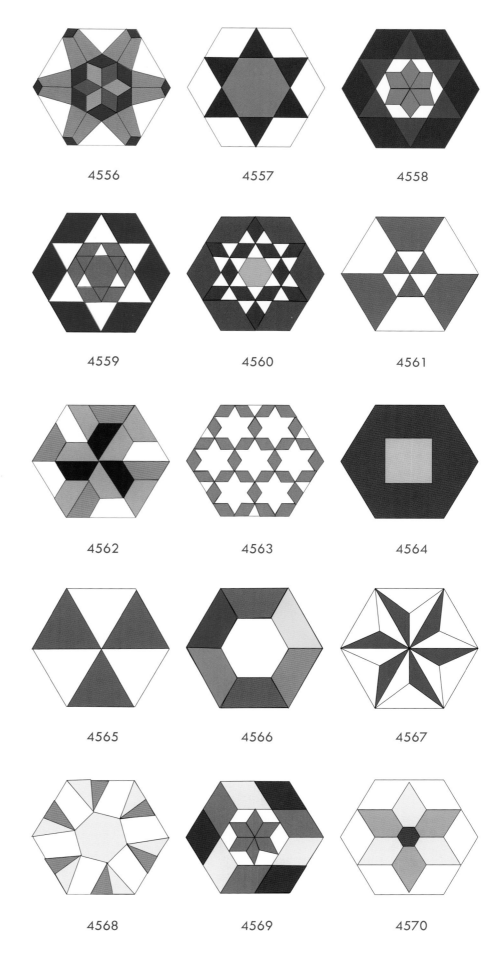

4556   4557   4558

4559   4560   4561

4562   4563   4564

4565   4566   4567

4568   4569   4570

4571

4572

4573

4574

4575

4576

4577

4578

4579

4580

4581

4582

4583

4584

4585

4571 The Pin Wheel

4572 Arrowheads, *KCS*

4573 Double Star, *Fairfield Processing Corp.*

4574 Spider Web, *KCS* A Cobweb Quilt

4575 Trials and Troubles

4576 Hidden Star, *KCS*

4577 Five Patch Beauty, *OCS* Star Studded Beauty, *OCS*

4578 Eastern Star, *OCS*

4579 Oriental Splendor, *HAS* The Smoothing Iron, *PF*

4580 New Hampshire, *HH* Diamond String, *NP* Star Rays, *NP*

4581 Florida, *HH*

4582 Snowflake Quilt, *WB*

4583 Zodiac Stars, *HAS*

4584 Six Pointed Star, *KCS*

4585 Diamond Rows, *FJ*

4586 Hexagons and Flowers, *OCS*

4587 Endless Chain, *OCS*

4588 Pinwheel, *OCS*

4589 Rock Wall, *LCPQ*

4590 Dutch Tile

4591 Grandmother's Flower Basket, *QN, 1980*

4592 Cosmos, *HAS*
Gay Cosmos Quilt, *HAS*

4593 Kansas Sunflower, *QW*

4594 Flower Star
Star and Crescent
Twinkling Star

4595 Sparkling Dew, *NC*

4596 Morning Star, *NC*

4597 Collinsville Rose Star, *QN*

4598 Montana Star, *HH*
Star of Montana, *HH*

4599 Modernistic Star, *AMS*

4600 Unnamed, *OCS*

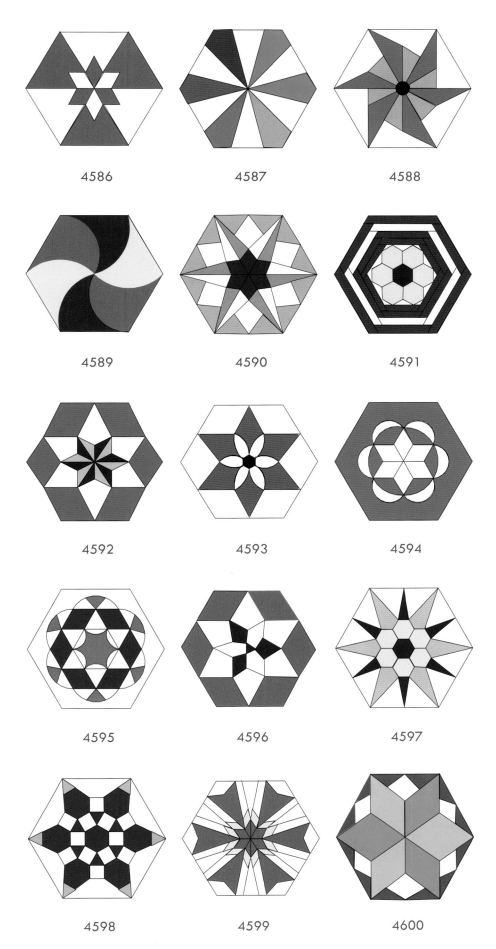

4586   4587   4588

4589   4590   4591

4592   4593   4594

4595   4596   4597

4598   4599   4600

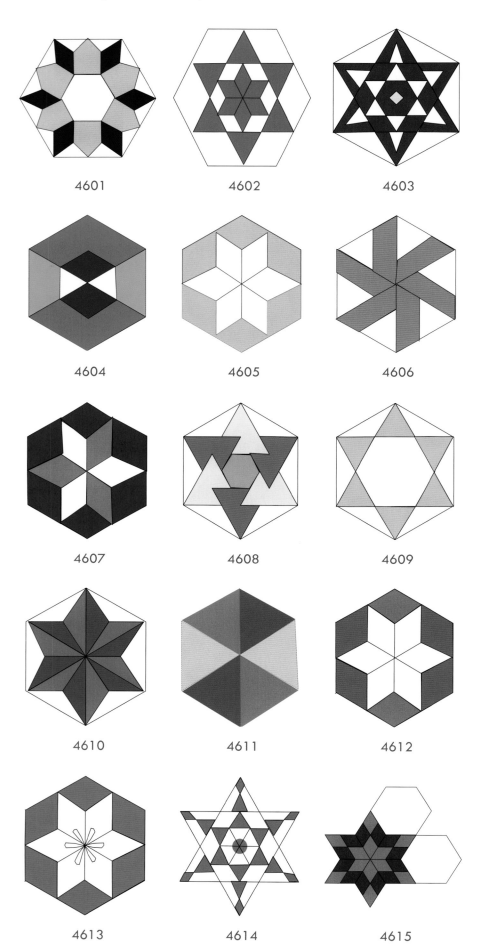

4601   4602   4603

4604   4605   4606

4607   4608   4609

4610   4611   4612

4613   4614   4615

4601 Aunt Martha's Rose

4602 Oklahoma Star

4603 Double Star

4604 Spider Web

4605 Tea Box
      Star Quilt

4606 Texas Trellis
      Maple Leaf
      Whirligig
      Whirling Hexagons
      Whirling Triangles

4607 Hexagonal, *HHJ*
      Hexagonal Star, *CW*
      Rising Star, *CW*

4608 Interlocked Star

4609 Star of Bethlehem
      Diamonds and Arrow
       Points, *KCS*
      A Pattern of Chinese
       Origin, *KCS*
      (set with plain
       hexagons):
      Aunt Etta's Diamond
       Quilt
      Pointing Star

4610 Hexagon Star

4611 Kaleidoscope

4612 Builder's Blocks, *KCS*
      Star and Box Quilt, *KCS*

4613 Dutch Tile, *KCS*
      Arabian Star

4614 Colorado Star

4615 Morning Star

4616 Three Patch, *LW*

4617 Pinwheel Star

4618 Double Link, *NC*

4619 A Six Point Flower
Garden

4620 Ozark Star, *KCS*

4621 The Diamond, *OF, 1896*
Flower Garden Block,
KCS

4622 Dutch Tile, *KCS*
Arabian Star
Star of Bethlehem

4623 Dutch Tile, *KCS*

4624 Jacob's Coat, *AMS*

4625 Unnamed, *OCS*

4626 Hexagon Snowflake,
QN

4627 Stars and Stripes
Forever, *SSQ, 1992*

4628 Blue Flower Garden

4629 Hexagonal

4630 Star and Blocks
The Columbia, *LAC*
Columbia Star

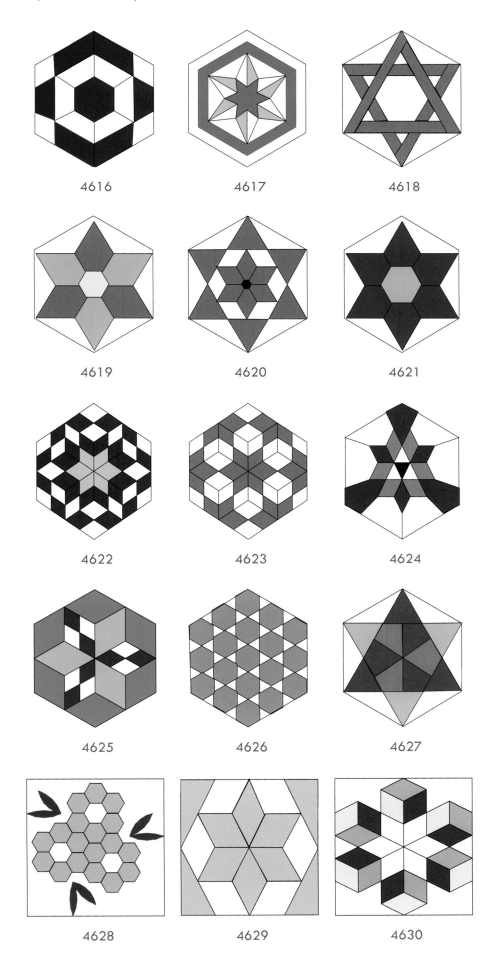

4616

4617

4618

4619

4620

4621

4622

4623

4624

4625

4626

4627

4628

4629

4630

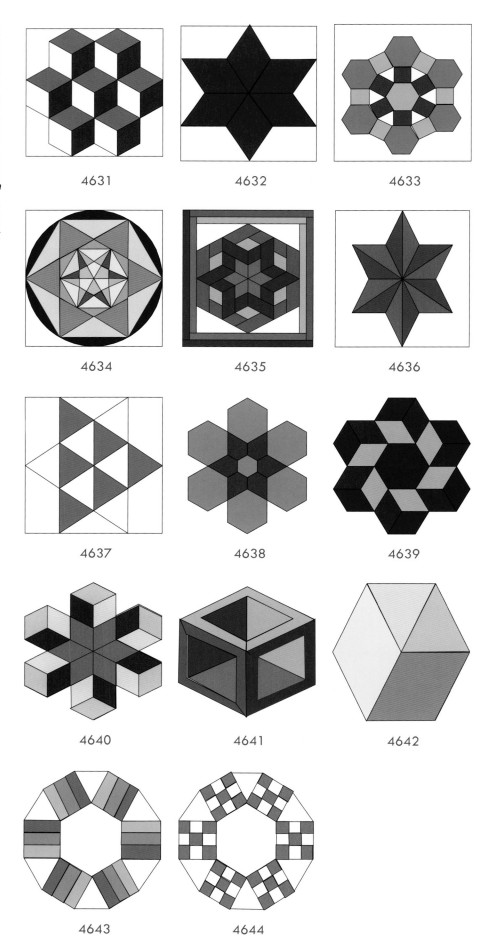

4631

4632

4633

4634

4635

4636

4637

4638

4639

4640

4641

4642

4643

4644

4631 Diamond Cube

4632 Morning Star
Star of Bethlehem

4633 Joseph's Coat, *LW*
Rolling Stone

4634 Roulette Wheel Star,
*Aunt Kate's Quilting
Bee*

4635 Twinkling Diamond
Log Cabin, *QW, 1993*

4636 Star of the East

4637 Saw Tooth Pattern

4638 On a Clear Night

4639 Spinning Blocks

4640 Star and Blocks

4641 See Through Block

4642 Open Top Box

4643 Wedding Tile
Faithful Circle, *AMS*

4644 Jack's Chain
Rosalia's Flower
Garden, *KCS*

4645 Ferris Wheel
Block Patchwork, *LAC*
Merry-Go-Round
(continuous design)
Morning Glory
Venetian Quilt
Wandering Paths

4646 Flower Garden
Aunt Jemima's Flower
Garden
Bride's Bouquet, *TFW*
Country Tile
French Bouquet
French Rose Garden
Grandmother's Flower
Garden
Grandmother's Rose
Garden
The Hexagon
Honeycomb

Martha Washington's
  Rose Garden
Mosaic
Old Fashioned Flower
  Garden
Rainbow Tile
(with dark joining
  rows):
Flower Garden
Garden Walk
Job's Troubles
Martha Washington's
  Flower Garden
Wheel of Life

4647 Mosaic

4648 Hexagon-Scrap Pattern
Century
Friendship Quilt
Hit or Miss
Honeycomb
Mosaic
Poor Boy

4649 Merry-Go-Round
Morning Glory

4650 Snow Crystal

4651 Tumbling Hexagons
Colonial Garden, *GC*
Rose Star One Patch,
  OCS

4652 Texas Star
Lemon Star

4653 Sunburst Star

4654 Cube Work, *LAC*
Diamond Cube, *LAC*
Tea Box, *FJ*

4655 Seven Sisters
Seven Stars, *LAC*
Seven Stars in a
  Cluster

4656 Skyscraper

4657 Orange Peel

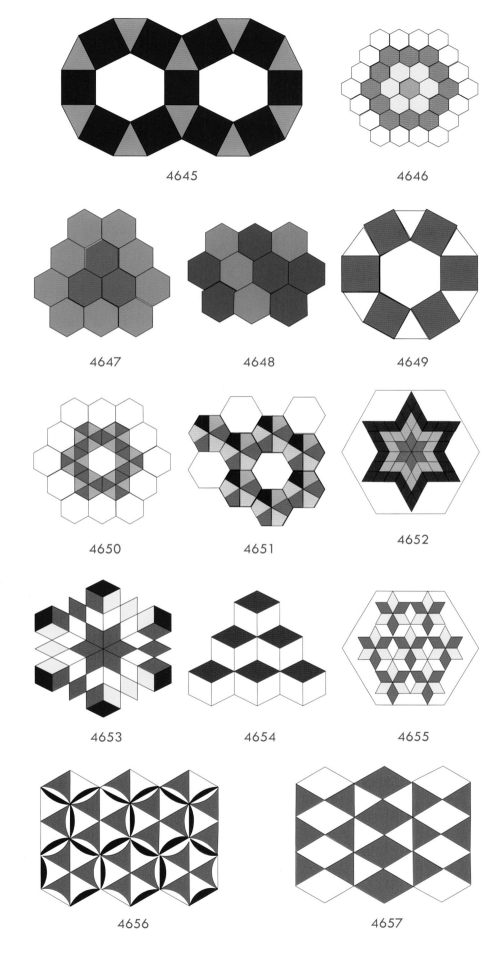

4645

4646

4647

4648

4649

4650

4651

4652

4653

4654

4655

4656

4657

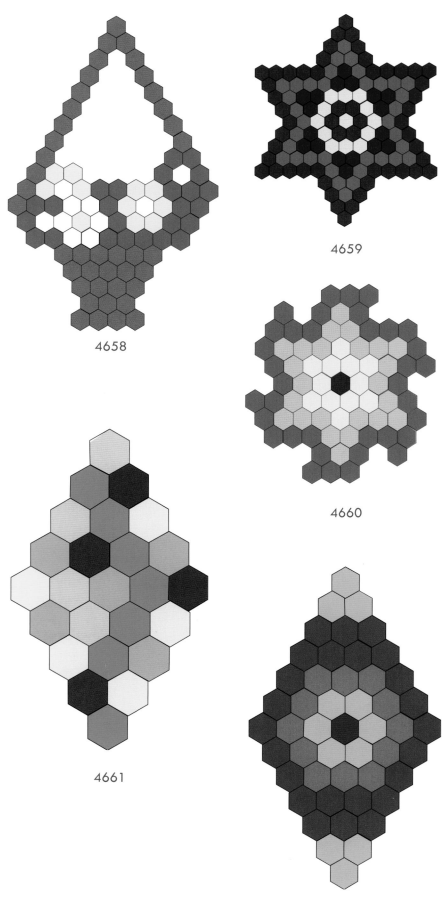

4658

4659

4660

4661

4662

4658 Hexagon Flower
    Basket

4659 Grandmother's Flower
    Garden
    Grandmother's Star
    Garden
    Hexagon Star

4660 Star Hexagon

4661 Rainbow Tile
    Diamond Field

4662 Martha Washington's
    Flower Garden

4663 Whirling Diamonds,
  KCS

4664 Variegated Diamonds,
  LAC

4665 Baby's Blocks
  Block Pattern
  Box Patchwork
  Box Pattern
  Box upon Box, *NP*
  Building Blocks
  Cubework
  Dancing Cubes, *PF*
  Disappearing Blocks,
  MoM
  English T Box
  Godey's 1851
  Golden Cubes, *NC*
  Grandma's Red and
  White
  The Heavenly Steps
  Jacob's Ladder, *WD*,
  1940
  Patience Corners, *LAC*
  Shifting Cubes, *HH*
  Stairs of Illusion
  Stairstep Quilt, *WD*
  Steps to the Altar
  Tumbling Blocks
  Variegated Diamonds

4666 Baby Block
  Box Quilt
  Cube Work
  Pandora's Block
  Pandora's Box
  Tea Box
  Tumbling Blocks

4667 Glory Block, *KCS*
  Glory Design, *WW*
  Old Glory, *NC*

4668 Blazing Star, *NP*
  Lone Star, *NP*
  Lone Star of Texas, *NP*
  The Sunburst, *NP*

4669 Baby Blocks

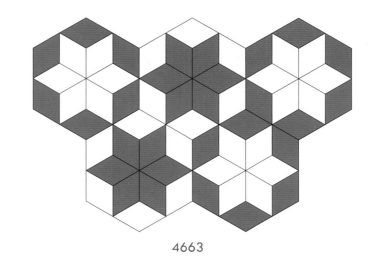

4663

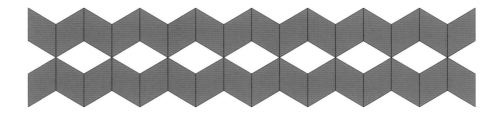

4664

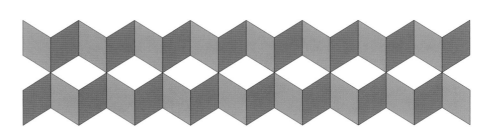

4665

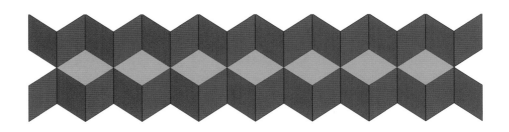

4666

4667　　　　4668　　　　4669

5,500 QUILT BLOCK DESIGNS

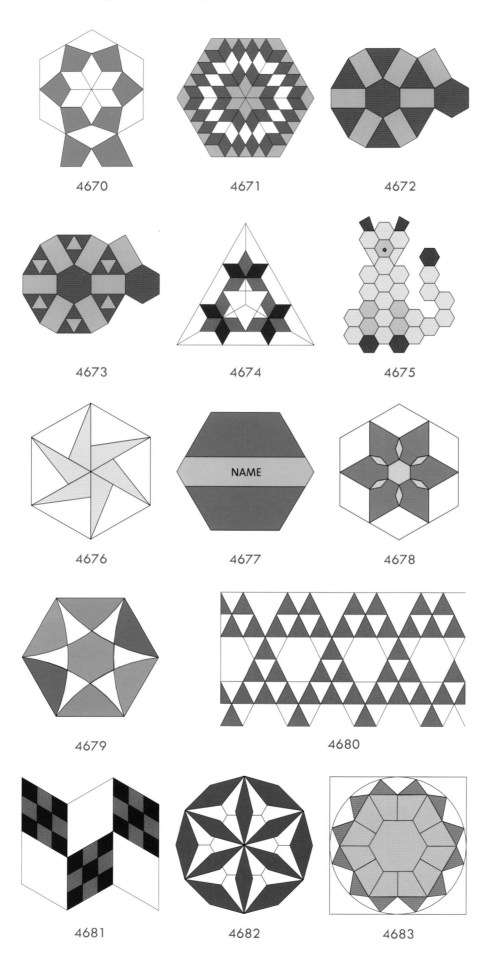

4670

4671

4672

4673

4674

4675

4676

4677

4678

4679

4680

4681

4682

4683

4670 A Pretty Patchwork, *HH*

4671 Columbia Star

4672 Joseph's Coat

4673 Wagon Wheel

4674 Star Flower, *1870*

4675 Hexacat, *Madeline Hawley, QC*

4676 Pinwheel

4677 Friendship Patch

4678 Arrowheads

4679 Star of the Mountains

4680 Tumbling Hexagons

4681 Diamond Nine Patch

4682 Chained Star

4683 Queen of the May

4684 Basket of Berries

4685 North Star

4686 Turning Triangles
Whirling Hexagons

4687 Trials and Troubles

4688 Hexagon and
Diamonds

4689 Basket of Flowers,
Betty Boyink

4690 Grandmother's Star,
1944

4691 The Pyramids, *PF*

4692 Spider Web

4693 A Pretty Patchwork

4694 Windblown Star

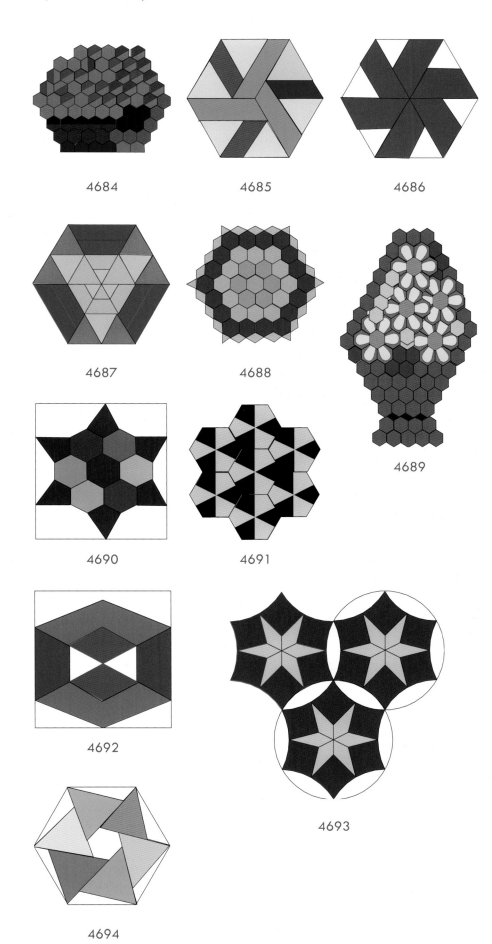

4684

4685

4686

4687

4688

4689

4690

4691

4692

4693

4694

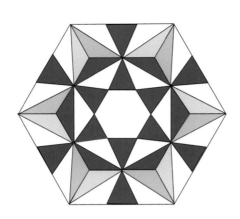

4695

4695 Mosaic,
   Linda Halpin, 1984

4696 Snowflake

4697 A Trip to Egypt
   (a continuous design
   building from the
   center out), *HAS*
   Triangle Mosaic

4698 Rose Star One Patch,
   LW
   Canadian
     Conventional Star
   Colonial Flower
     Garden
   Hexagons

4699 Hexagon Patchwork,
   GLB, 1835
   Honeycomb
   Colonial Bouquet
   Six-Sided Patchwork

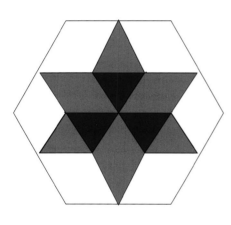

4696

4697

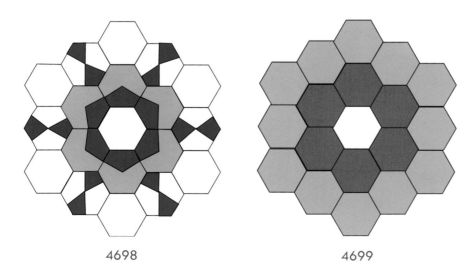

4698   4699

4700 Charm
Endless Chain
Honeycomb Patch
Simplicity's Delight

4701 Ocean Wave

4702 Chevron, *OCS*

4703 Crazy Kite
Charm Packet Odyssey,
Pat Moore, QN

4704 Old Colony Star

4705 Brunswick Star, *LAC*

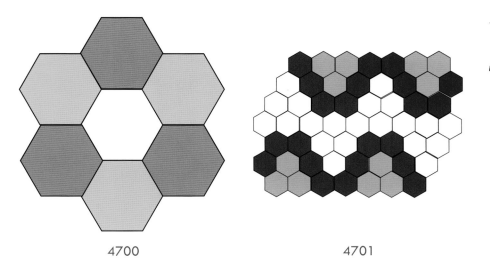

4700

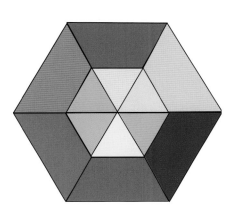

4701

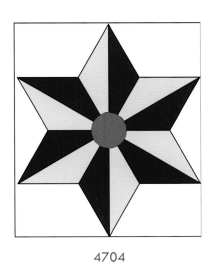

4702

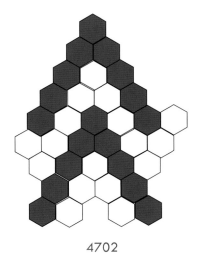

4703

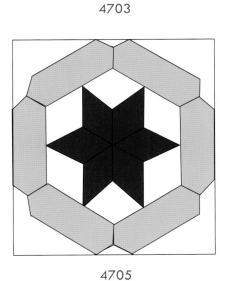

4704

4705

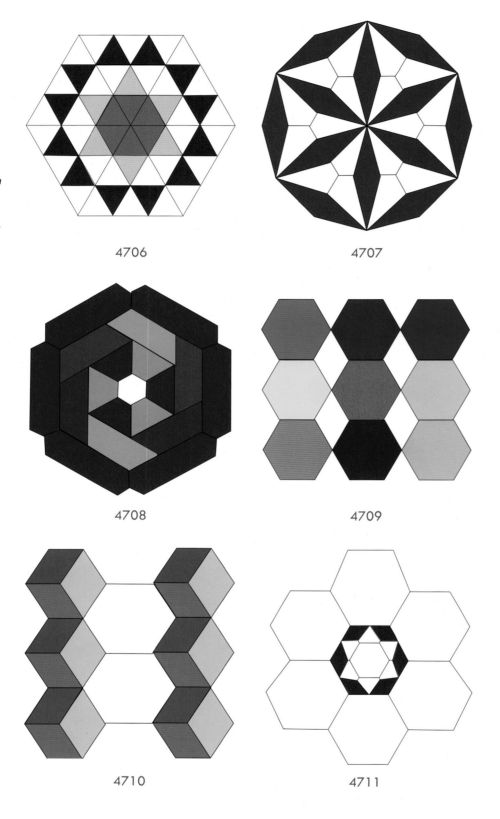

4706

4707

4708

4709

4710

4711

4706 One Thousand
      Pyramids

4707 Chained Star
      Diamond Beauty Quilt
      Poinsettia Quilt, *HAS*

4708 Granddaughter's
      Flower Garden,
      SSQ, 1987

4709 Hexagons and
      Diamonds

4710 Diamond Hexagon, *NP*

4711 Pepper and Salt
      Shakers

4712 Variable Triangles

4713 Octagon, *FJ*

4714 Flower Basket

4715 Windy City

4716 Star of David

4717 Trapezoid

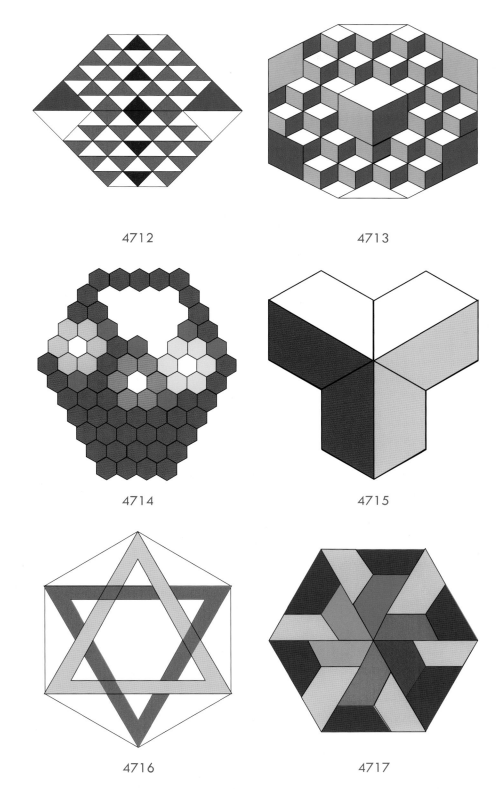

4712

4713

4714

4715

4716

4717

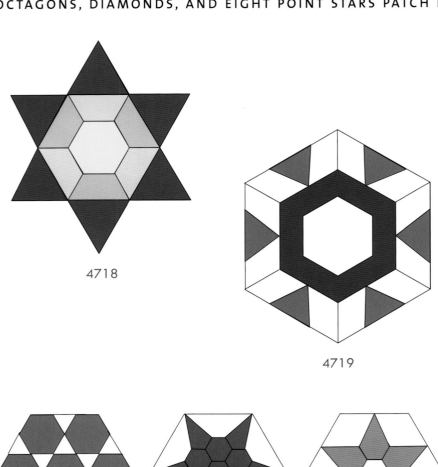

4718

4719

4718 Hexagon Star

4719 Floating Clouds

4720 Pointing Star

4721 Ducks in a Pond

4722 Star Bouquet

4723 Sam's Quilt

4724 Snowflake

4725 Snowflake

4726 Flower Trail

4727 Ocean Wave

4728 Diamond Field

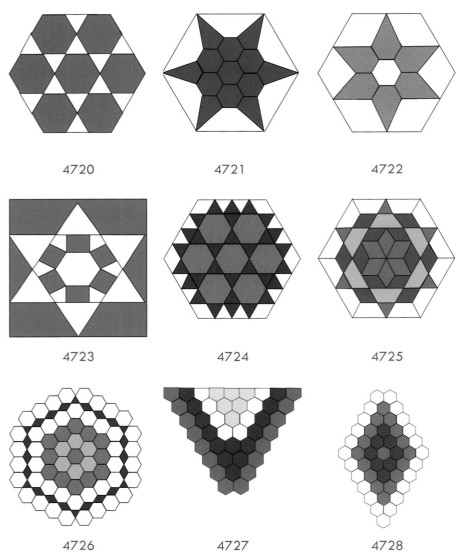

4720

4721

4722

4723

4724

4725

4726

4727

4728

4729 Hexagon Flower Block

4730 Star and Crescent

4731 Star and Planets

4732 Orange Peel Variation

4733 Inspiration

4734 Hexagon and Triangles, *Jenny Beyer*

4735 Starfish Block

4736 Starfish Block

4737 Sam's Quilt, *CS*

4738 Thunderbird

4739 Compass in a Hexagon

4740 Inner City

4741 Flower

4742 Grandmother's Cartwheel

4743 Tile Pattern

5,500 QUILT BLOCK DESIGNS

4729

4730

4731

4732

4733

4734

4735

4736

4737

4738

4739

4740

4741

4742

4743

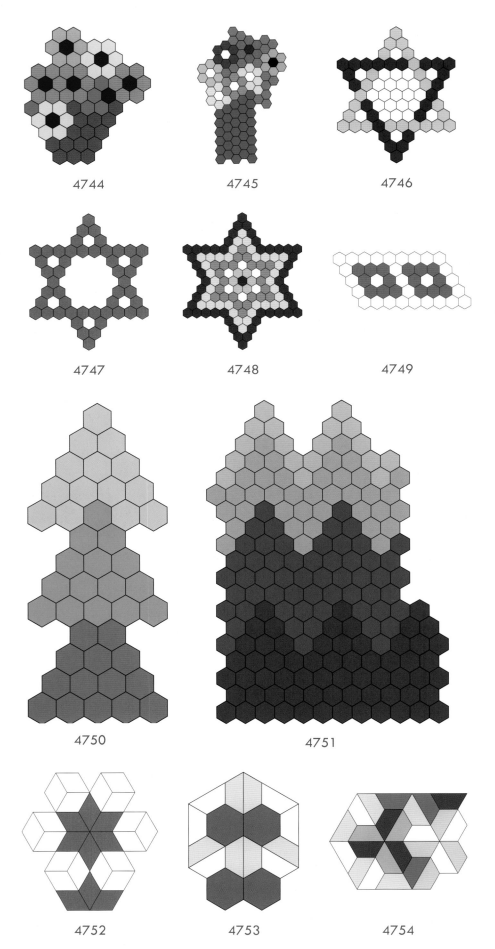

4744

4745

4746

4747

4748

4749

4750

4751

4752

4753

4754

4744 Flowerpot

4745 Vase of Flowers

4746 Interlocked Star

4747 Star of David

4748 Hexagon Star

4749 Diamond Chain

4750 Arrowheads

4751 Hexagon Waves

4752 Tiny Star
Aunt Stella's Pattern
Star and Blocks

4753 Monk's Puzzle, *NC*

4754 Crazy Tile, *KCS*
Ecclesiastical, *LAC*
Right Angle Patchwork

4755 Ecclesiastical

4756 Star and Diamonds, *NC*

4757 The Sirius Star Quilt, *HAS*

4758 Red and White Quilt
Sawtooth
Sawtooth Diamond

4759 Who'd a Thought It
(scrap quilt, continue
adding rows to
desired size)

4760 Chrysanthemum Quilt
Top

4761 Save-All, *AMS*
Save All Chain
Happy Memories

4762 Cow

4755

4756

4757

4758

4759

4760

4761

4762

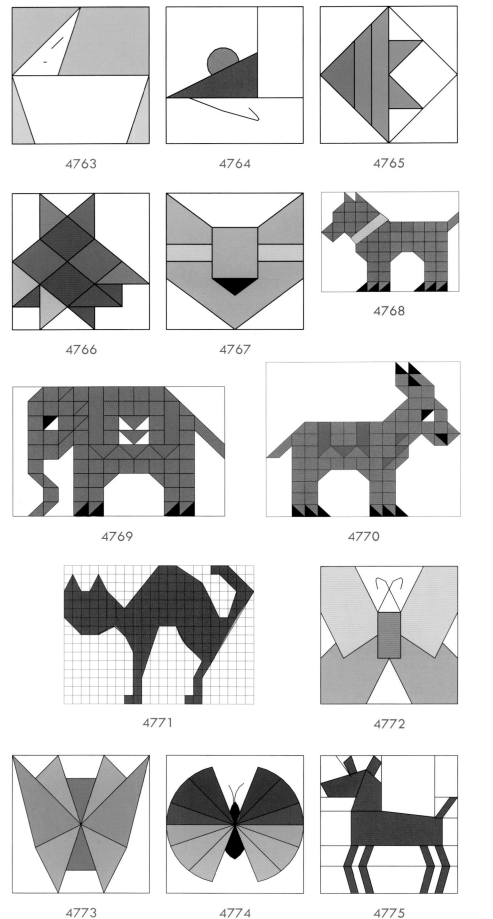

4763

4764

4765

4766

4767

4768

4769

4770

4771

4772

4773

4774

4775

4763 Bunny

4764 Mouse

4765 Fish

4766 Bat

4767 Scrap Cats,
*Linda Platt,
QN, 1979*

4768 The Dog Quilt
A Scottie Quilt for Boys

4769 Ararat

4770 Giddyap

4771 Black Cat Block,
*Susan C. Druding,
qac*

4772 Butterfly

4773 Butterfly

4774 Butterfly

4775 Reindeer

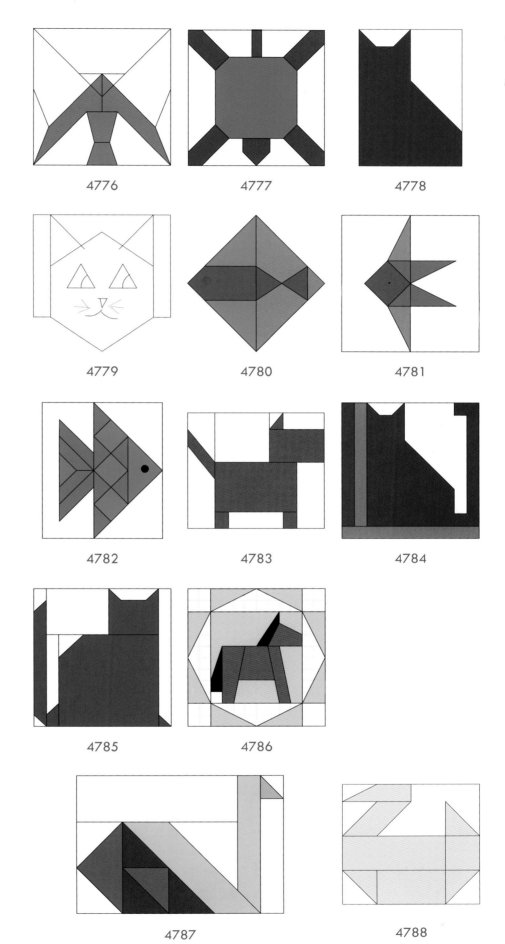

4776   4777   4778
4779   4780   4781
4782   4783   4784
4785   4786
4787   4788

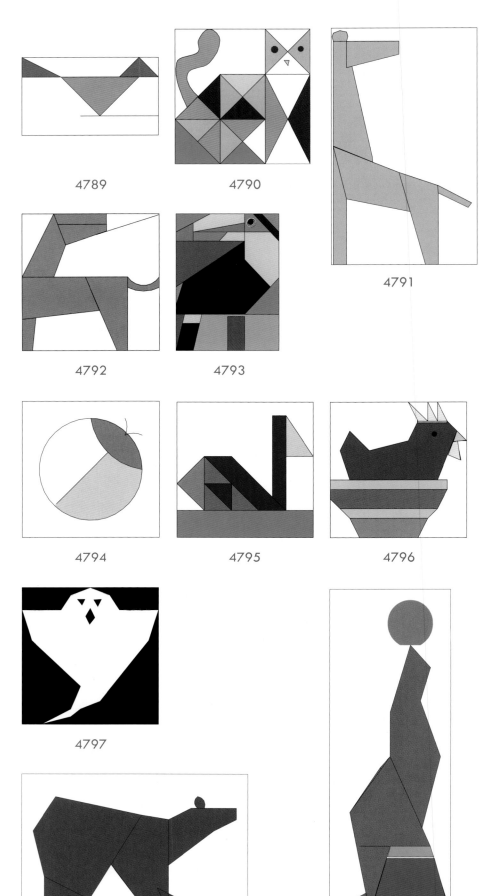

4789

4790

4791

4792

4793

4794

4795

4796

4797

4798

4799

4789 Bird Feeder,
   Doreen Burbank,
   SSQ, 1990

4790 Cat, *QN*

4791 Giraffe,
   Margit Echols, QC

4792 Zebra,
   Margit Echols, QC

4793 Toucan,
   Margaret Rolfe

4794 Lady Bug,
   Aunt Kate's Quilting
   Bee

4795 Duck

4796 Miss Henrietta,
   piecebynumber.com

4797 Ghost,
   piecebynumber.com

4798 Bear

4799 Seal,
   Margit Echols, TQ

4800 Fish

4801 Turkey, *geocities.com/ Heartland/Acres*

4802 Frog

4803 Elephant, *Woman's Home Companion*

4804 Butterfly

4805 Butterfly

4806 Nighttime Butterflies, *RM*

4807 Pieced Butterfly #1408, *CoM*

4808 Duck

4809 Bug

4810 Fowl Weather, *Alice L. Vail, SSQ*

4811 Hippopotamus, *PP*

4812 Reindeer, *PP*

4813 Seal, *PP*

4814 Ostrich, *PP*

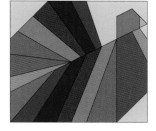
4800

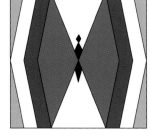
4801

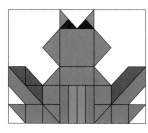
4802

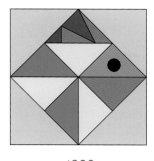
4803

4804

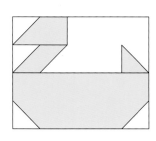
4805

4806

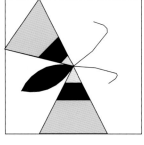
4807

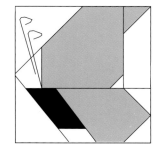
4808

4809

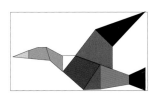
4810

4811

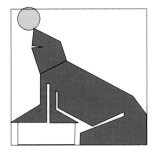
4812

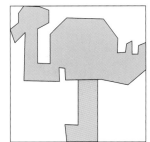
4813

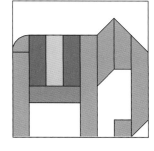
4814

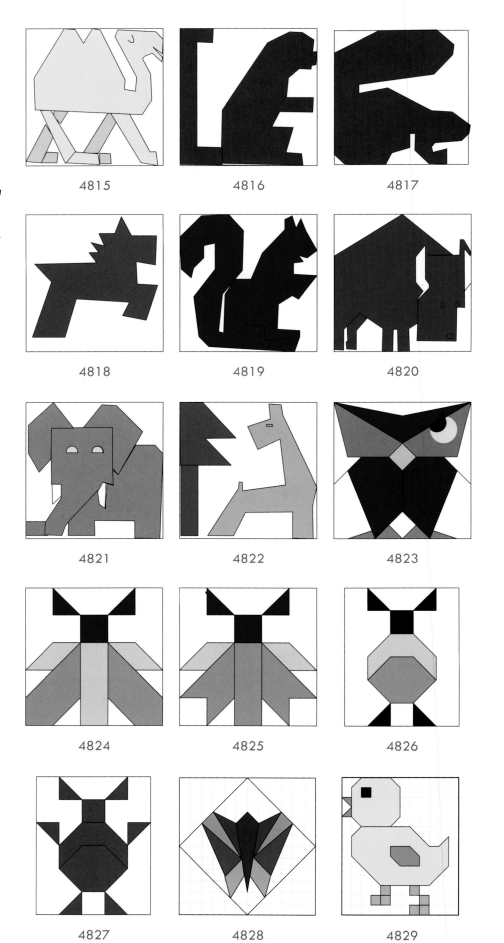

5,500 QUILT BLOCK DESIGNS

4815

4816

4817

4818

4819

4820

4821

4822

4823

4824

4825

4826

4827

4828

4829

4815 Camel, *PP*

4816 Monkey, *PP*

4817 Beaver, *PP*

4818 Zebra, *PP*

4819 Squirrel, *PP*

4820 Buffalo, *PP*

4821 Elephant, *PP*

4822 Giraffe, *PP*

4823 Georgia's Owl,
 GB, 1990

4824 Fly

4825 Fly

4826 Fantasy Bug

4827 Blackbug

4828 Butterfly Squared

4829 Chicken Little

4830 Elephant

4831 Cowboy Boot,
   Susan C. Druding

4832 Perky Pumpkin,
   *Marilyn Busch,
   SSQ, 1985*

4833 Ice Cream Bowl

4834 Ice Cream Bowl, *LAC*

4835 Pumpkin

4836 Chinese Lantern, *CW*

4837 A Japanese Garden,
   KCS

4838 The Bell, *KCS*

4839 Coffee Cups, *KCS*
   The Cup and the
   Saucer, *KCS*

4840 The Ice Cream Cone

4841 Four Vases, *KCS*

4842 The Goblet Quilt, *KCS*
   The Old Fashioned
   Goblet
   Tumbler
   Water Glass

4843 The Soldier Boy, *KCS*
   Soldier at the Window

4844 The Ice Cream Cone

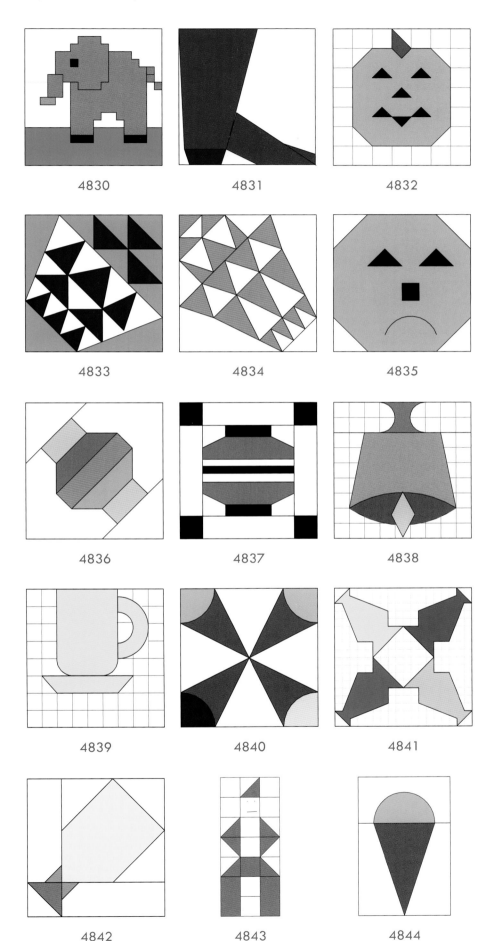

4830

4831

4832

4833

4834

4835

4836

4837

4838

4839

4840

4841

4842

4843

4844

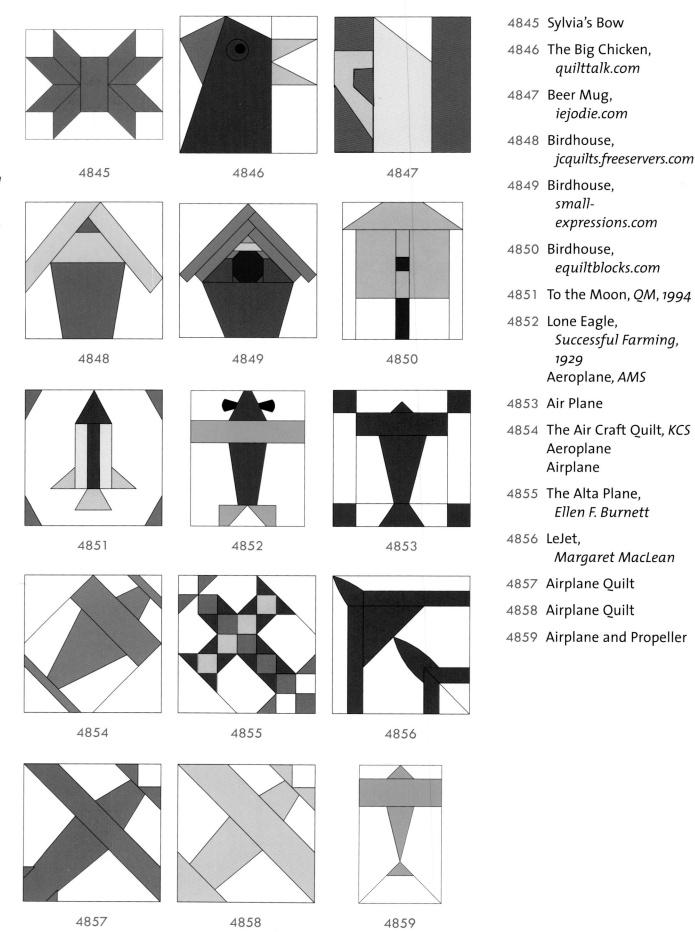

4845

4846

4847

4848

4849

4850

4851

4852

4853

4854

4855

4856

4857

4858

4859

4845 Sylvia's Bow

4846 The Big Chicken,
quilttalk.com

4847 Beer Mug,
iejodie.com

4848 Birdhouse,
jcquilts.freeservers.com

4849 Birdhouse,
small-expressions.com

4850 Birdhouse,
equiltblocks.com

4851 To the Moon, *QM, 1994*

4852 Lone Eagle,
*Successful Farming,
1929*
Aeroplane, *AMS*

4853 Air Plane

4854 The Air Craft Quilt, *KCS*
Aeroplane
Airplane

4855 The Alta Plane,
Ellen F. Burnett

4856 LeJet,
Margaret MacLean

4857 Airplane Quilt

4858 Airplane Quilt

4859 Airplane and Propeller

4860 Lone Eagle Airplane

4861 Aeroplanes

4862 Truck

4863 Truck

4864 Airplane, *NC*

4865 Air Ways

4866 Lindbergh's Night
 Flight

4867 Truck Patch

4868 Boat in a Bottle,
 *Lyn Peare Sandberg,
 QN, 1991*

4869 Baby Food Jar (3"x3"),
 winnowing.com

4870 Wine Bottle (3"x6"),
 geocities.com

4871 Bottle, *qac*

4872 Wine Glass, *qac*

4873 Perfume Block,
 quiltaholics.com

4874 Mason Jar,
 geocities.com

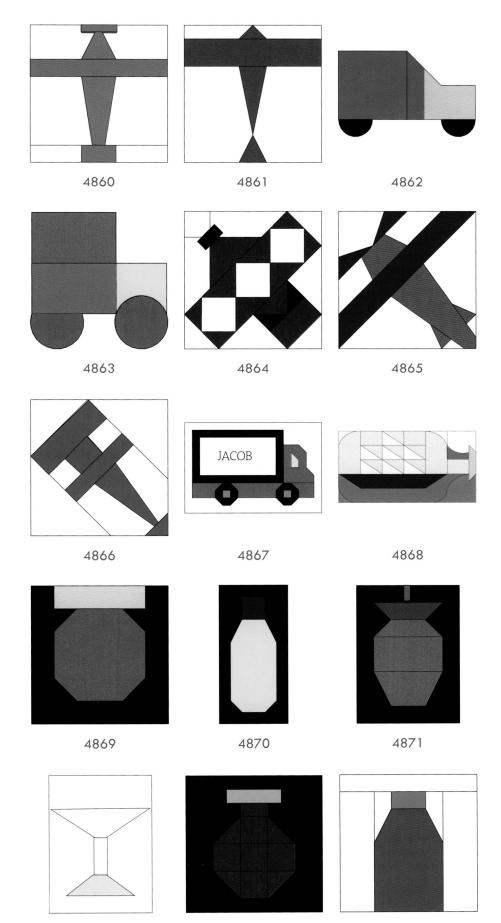

4860 4861 4862

4863 4864 4865

4866 4867 4868

4869 4870 4871

4872 4873 4874

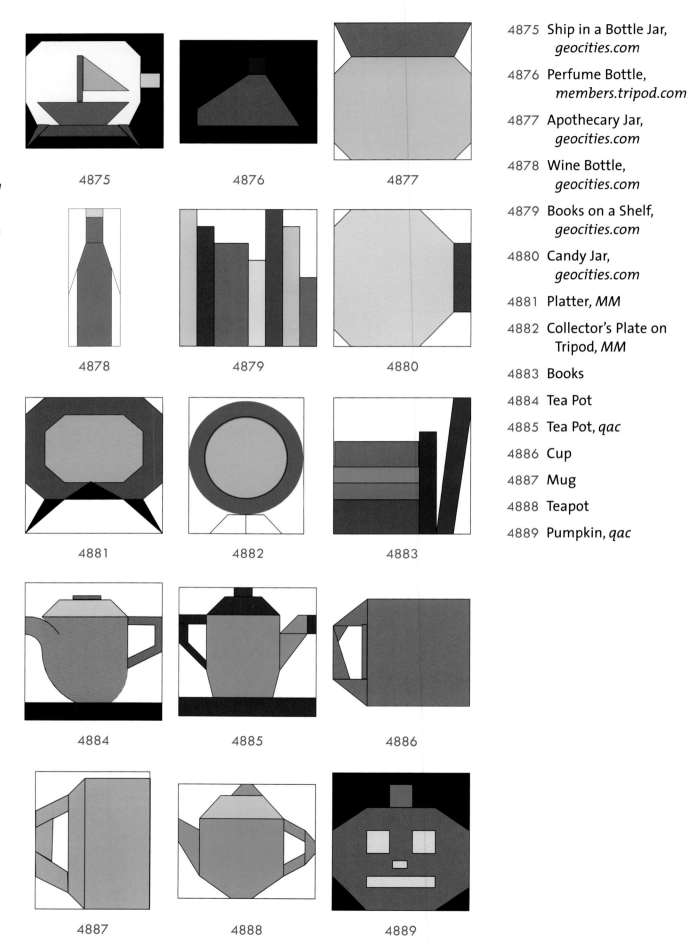

4875

4876

4877

4878

4879

4880

4881

4882

4883

4884

4885

4886

4887

4888

4889

4875 Ship in a Bottle Jar, *geocities.com*

4876 Perfume Bottle, *members.tripod.com*

4877 Apothecary Jar, *geocities.com*

4878 Wine Bottle, *geocities.com*

4879 Books on a Shelf, *geocities.com*

4880 Candy Jar, *geocities.com*

4881 Platter, *MM*

4882 Collector's Plate on Tripod, *MM*

4883 Books

4884 Tea Pot

4885 Tea Pot, *qac*

4886 Cup

4887 Mug

4888 Teapot

4889 Pumpkin, *qac*

4890 Pumpkin, *qac*

4891 Pumpkin, *qac*

4892 Pumpkin, *qac*

4893 Pumpkin, *MM*

4894 Baby Shoe, *qac*

4895 Auntie's Kitties,
   auntie.com/qzine

4896 Candlestick

4897 Telephone,
   *Aunt Kate's Quilting
   Bee*

4898 Harvest Grapes

4899 Japanese Lantern, *KCS*

4900 Crocodile, *PP*

4901 Cup

4902 Workbox
   Kitchen Woodbox

4903 Angel

4904 Lamp, *qac*

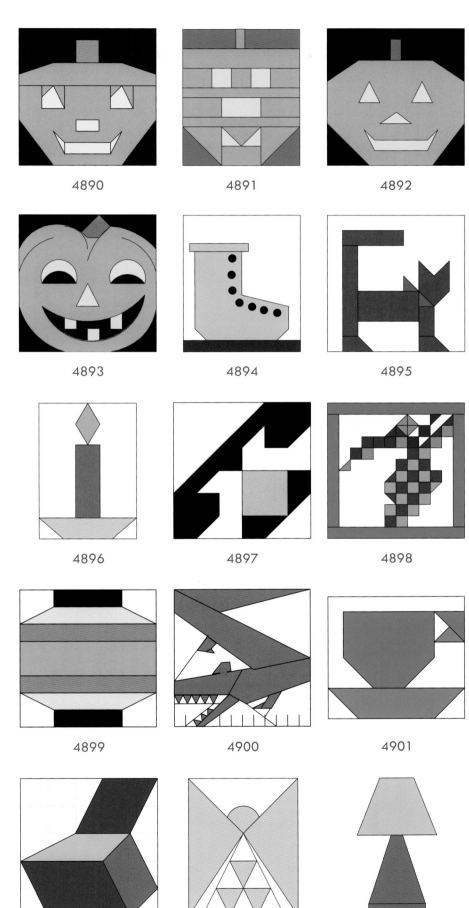

4890   4891   4892

4893   4894   4895

4896   4897   4898

4899   4900   4901

4902   4903   4904

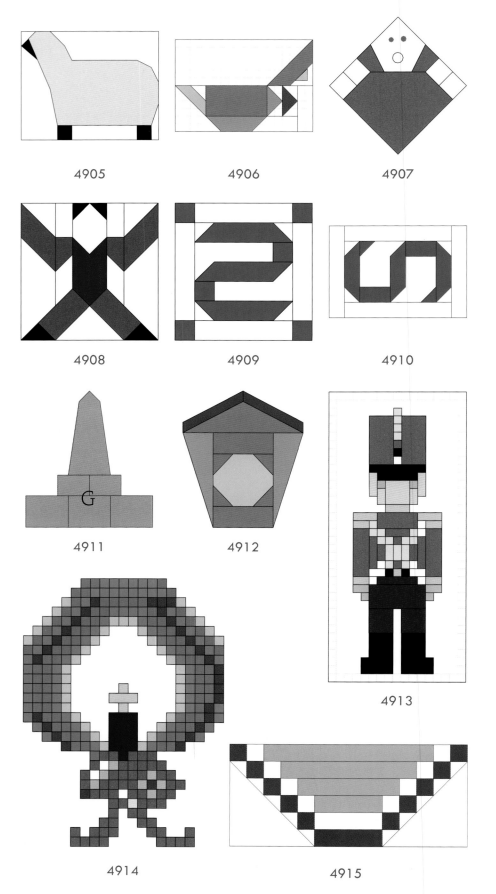

4905

4906

4907

4908

4909

4910

4911

4912

4913

4914

4915

4905 Sheep

4906 Teapot

4907 Baby Dolls

4908 Acrobat

4909 The Mountain Road, *KCS*

4910 The Flowing Ribbon, *KCS*

4911 Garfield's Monument, *LAC*

4912 Birdhouse

4913 Toy Soldier

4914 Christmas Wreath

4915 Watermelon

4916 The Bell, *KCS*

4917 Sunbonnet Sue

4918 Diaper Pins,
    *Rhoda Ochser
    Goldberg,
    Quilting & Patchwork
    Dictionary*

4919 Hobby Horse

4920 Teapot

4921 Blouses, *MM*

4922 Let's Get Pinned, *GB*

4923 Panda Patch

4924 Hobby Horse
    Rocking Horse

4925 Hobby Horse

4926 Bow
    Pieced Ribbon
    Ribbon
    Ribbon Bow

4927 Television Quilt, *QW,*
    1977

4928 Bow Knots, *NC*

4929 Thunderbird

4916

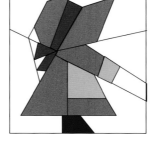
4917

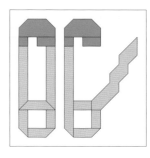
4918

4919

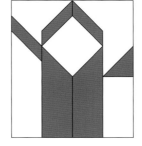
4920

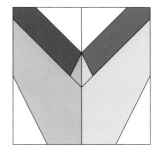
4921

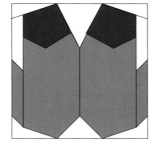
4922

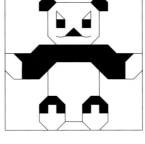
4923

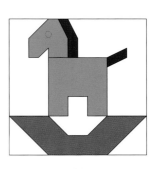
4924

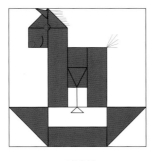
4925

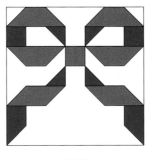
4926

4927

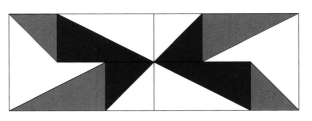
4928

4929

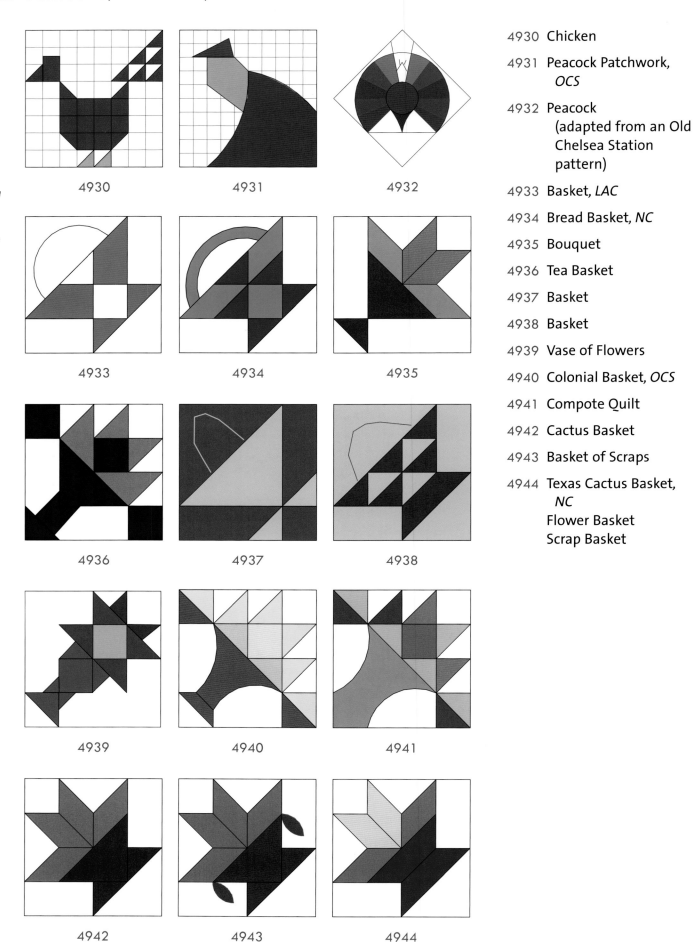

4930

4931

4932

4933

4934

4935

4936

4937

4938

4939

4940

4941

4942

4943

4944

4930 Chicken

4931 Peacock Patchwork, *OCS*

4932 Peacock (adapted from an Old Chelsea Station pattern)

4933 Basket, *LAC*

4934 Bread Basket, *NC*

4935 Bouquet

4936 Tea Basket

4937 Basket

4938 Basket

4939 Vase of Flowers

4940 Colonial Basket, *OCS*

4941 Compote Quilt

4942 Cactus Basket

4943 Basket of Scraps

4944 Texas Cactus Basket, *NC*
       Flower Basket
       Scrap Basket

4945 Cactus Pot

4946 Sugar Bowl, *NC*

4947 Basket, *NP*

4948 Flower Basket, *LAC*
Betty's Basket, *NP*
Basket Quilt

4949 Simple Flower Basket,
NC

4950 Baby Bunting

4951 Strawberry Basket

4952 Basket
Hanging Basket

4953 Flower Basket
Basket of Diamonds
Cactus Basket
Desert Rose
The Disk, *LAC*
Flower Pot
Jersey Tulip
Rainbow Cactus

4954 Grandmother's Basket

4955 A Basket Patch, *HH*

4956 Basket, *1850*

4957 Grandmother's Basket,
KCS

4958 Basket

4959 Flower Basket

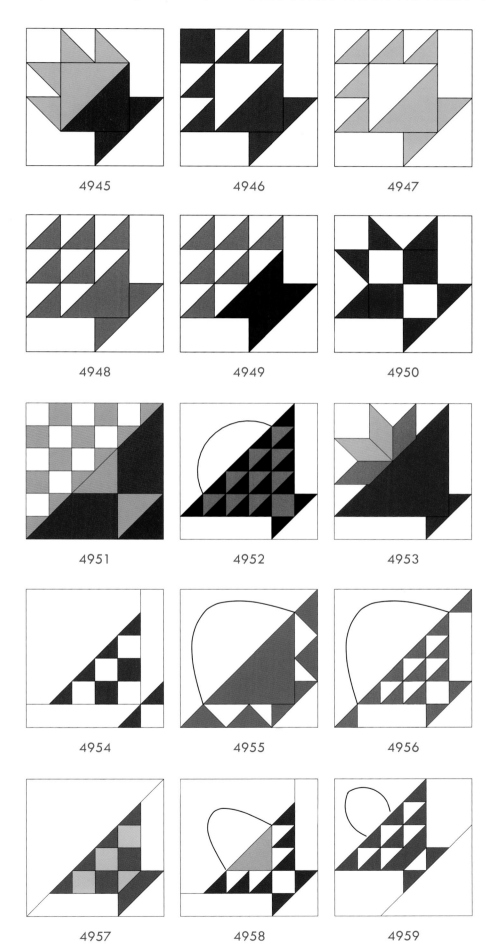

4945   4946   4947

4948   4949   4950

4951   4952   4953

4954   4955   4956

4957   4958   4959

4960

4961

4962

4963

4964

4965

4966

4967

4968

4969

4970

4971

4972

4973

4974

4960 Flower Basket, *HH*

4961 Cherry Basket, *LAC*
Berry Basket
Fruit Basket, *CoM*
Basket, *GC*

4962 Basket of Oranges, *KCS*

4963 Basket Block, *CoM*
Cherry Basket
Flower Basket
Pieced Basket

4964 Baby Basket
Basket Quilt
May Basket, *KCS*

4965 Basket, *CoM*

4966 Basket, *1910*

4967 May Basket, *HH*

4968 The Flower Pot Quilt,
AMS

4969 Basket
Basket of Triangles,
MD
Broken Sugar Bowl
Broken Dish
Fruit Basket
May Basket, *TFW, 1931*

4970 Fruit Basket

4971 Grape Basket, *LAC*
Basket of Chips
May Basket
Picnic Basket, *NP*

4972 Flower Pot

4973 Flower Basket

4974 Little Basket, *HH*
Fruit Basket, *HH*

4975 Basket

4976 Dresden Basket, *GD*
Red Basket

4977 Basket

4978 Basket Quilt, *1899*
The Basket
Cherry Basket
Colonial Basket, *1861*
Flower Basket

4979 Leafy Basket, *LW*

4980 Cake Stand, *LAC*
Basket, *HH*
Fruit Basket

4981 Basket, *1898*

4982 Fruit Basket

4983 Flower Pot, *KCS*

4984 Flower Basket, *CS*
Peach Basket, *NP*

4985 Cake Stand, *NC*
May Basket (colors
reversed), *KCS*

4986 Basket of Chips, *CoM*
Basket of Flowers
Chip Basket, *TFW*
Flower Pot
Anna's Basket

4987 Bea's Basket

4988 Basket, *HH*

4989 Wedding Basket,
QM, 1993

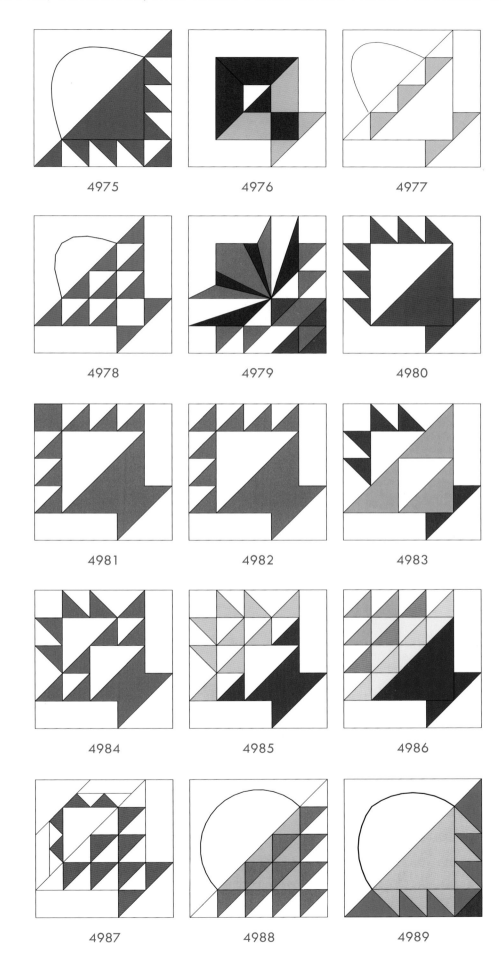

4975   4976   4977

4978   4979   4980

4981   4982   4983

4984   4985   4986

4987   4988   4989

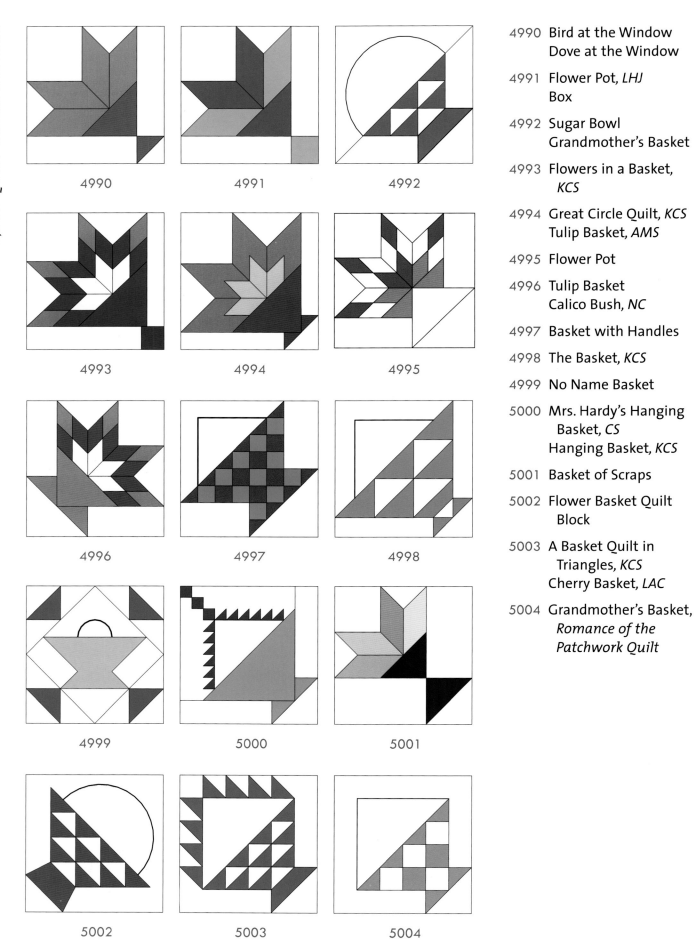

4990 Bird at the Window
  Dove at the Window

4991 Flower Pot, *LHJ*
  Box

4992 Sugar Bowl
  Grandmother's Basket

4993 Flowers in a Basket,
  KCS

4994 Great Circle Quilt, *KCS*
  Tulip Basket, *AMS*

4995 Flower Pot

4996 Tulip Basket
  Calico Bush, *NC*

4997 Basket with Handles

4998 The Basket, *KCS*

4999 No Name Basket

5000 Mrs. Hardy's Hanging
  Basket, *CS*
  Hanging Basket, *KCS*

5001 Basket of Scraps

5002 Flower Basket Quilt
  Block

5003 A Basket Quilt in
  Triangles, *KCS*
  Cherry Basket, *LAC*

5004 Grandmother's Basket,
  *Romance of the
  Patchwork Quilt*

5005 May Basket

5006 Fruit Basket, *NP*

5007 Fruit Basket, *HH*

5008 Nine Patch Basket,
      Connie Litfin, QN

5009 Aunt Em's Basket,
      LCPQ

5010 Cherry Basket, *KCS*

5011 Colonial Basket,
      *Romance of the
      Patchwork Quilt*

5012 Flower Basket, *KCS*
      Basket of Diamonds
      The Disk, *LAC*
      Flower Pot
      Jersey Tulip
      Rainbow Cactus

5013 Flower Pot, *KCS*
      May Basket, *NC*

5014 Cactus Basket Block

5015 Hicks Flower Basket,
      KCS

5016 Basket of Diamonds,
      KCS

5017 Christmas Basket, *QW*,
      1991

5018 Basket of Bright
      Flowers, *KCS*

5019 Tulips in a Vase, *CaS*

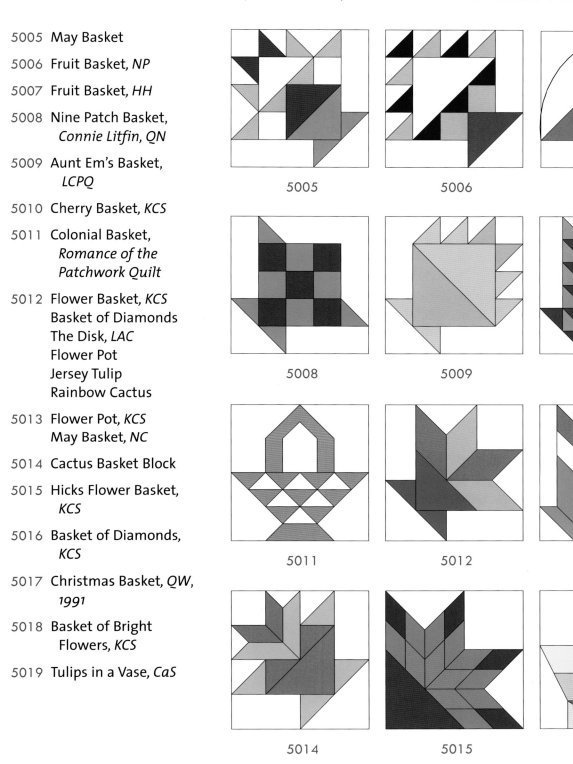

5005   5006   5007

5008   5009   5010

5011   5012   5013

5014   5015   5016

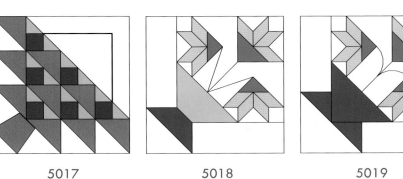

5017   5018   5019

5,500 QUILT BLOCK DESIGNS

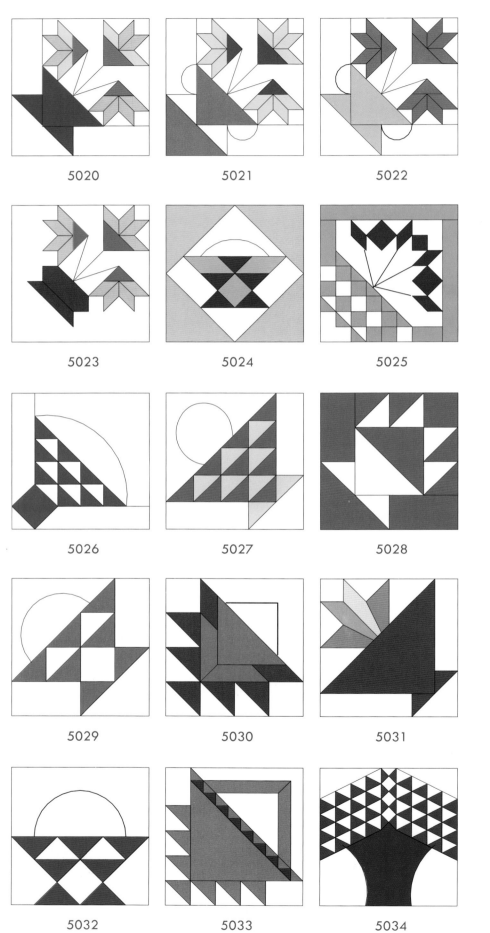

5020
5021
5022

5023
5024
5025

5026
5027
5028

5029
5030
5031

5032
5033
5034

5020 Basket of Lilies, *LAC*

5021 Tulip in a Vase, *LAC*

5022 Royal Japanese Vase,
1890
Royal Dutch Tulip and
Vase
Carolina Lily
Martha's Basket

5023 Pot of Flowers

5024 Bread Basket,
*Romance of the
Patchwork Quilt*

5025 Texas Cactus Basket

5026 Flower Basket, *HH*

5027 Market Basket

5028 Amish Basket

5029 Flower Basket

5030 Martha Washington
Cherry Basket

5031 Flower Pot

5032 Basket Design, *CoM*

5033 Mary's Basket

5034 Tree of Life Basket,
1900

5035 Basket of Lilies

5036 Four Little Baskets, *LAC*
 Four Baskets, *NC*

5037 Postage Stamp Basket

5038 Basket

5039 Japanese Basket

5040 Cherry Basket

5041 Old Fashioned Fruit
 Basket

5042 Basket of Flowers

5043 Flower Pot

5044 Flower Basket, *CaS*

5045 Tulip Basket
 (4 tulips, 2 leaves), *NC*

5046 Basket

5047 Basket of Tulips

5048 Victorian Basket, *QM,*
 1992

5049 Missouri Memories

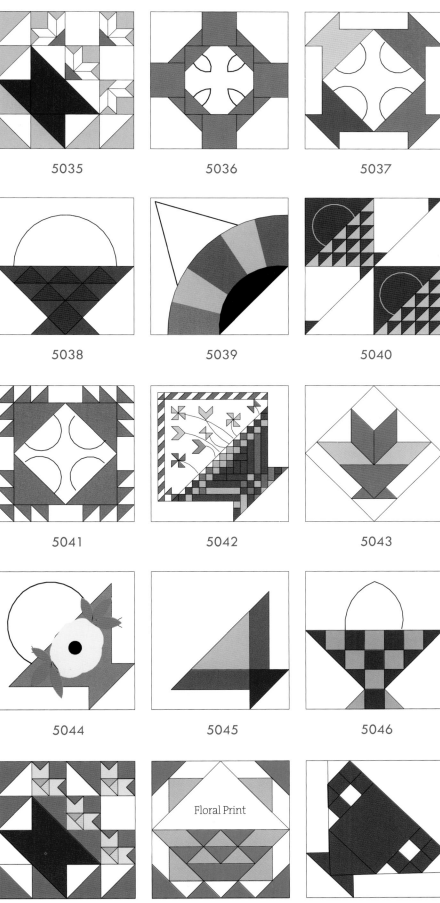

5035   5036   5037

5038   5039   5040

5041   5042   5043

5044   5045   5046

5047   5048   5049

Floral Print

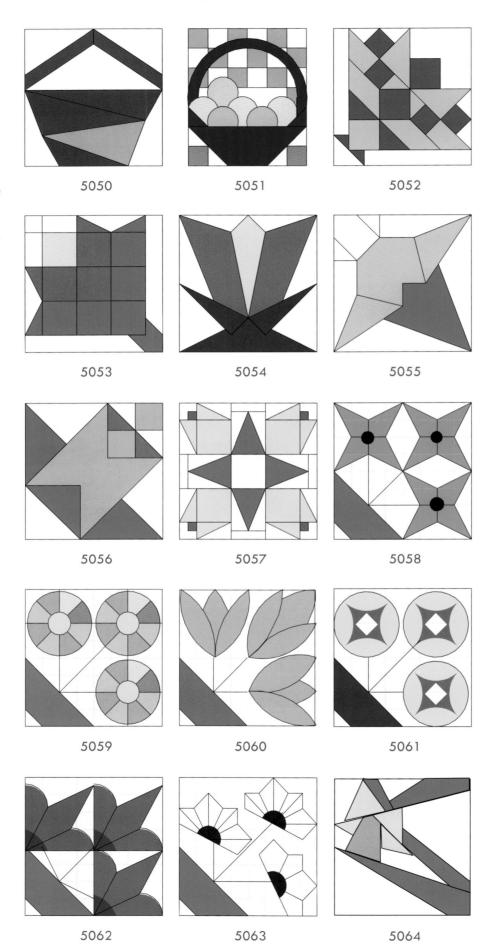

5050   5051   5052

5053   5054   5055

5056   5057   5058

5059   5060   5061

5062   5063   5064

5050 Basket, *his.com/~ queenbee/frugal*

5051 Egg Basket

5052 Flower Basket

5053 Crocus

5054 Tulip Time

5055 Trumpet Flower

5056 Trumpet Flower

5057 Magnolia Bud, *NC* Pink Magnolias, *NC*

5058 Snowdrop (Bowl of Flowers Series), *OCS*

5059 Aster (Bowl of Flowers Series), *OCS*

5060 Tulip (Bowl of Flowers Series), *OCS*

5061 Rose (Bowl of Flowers Series), *OCS*

5062 Lily (Bowl of Flowers Series), *OCS*

5063 Poppy (Bowl of Flowers Series), *OCS*

5064 Daffodils

5065 Tulip, *OCS*

5066 Old Fashioned Garden, *OCS*

5067 Friendship Flowers, *OCS*

5068 Oriental Poppy Modernistic California Poppy

5069 Tennessee Tulip

5070 Crocus, *OCS*

5071 Tulip Garden, *OCS*

5072 Egyptian Lotus Flower

5073 Brown-Eyed Susan

5074 Tulips, *AMS*

5075 Fantasy Flower (8)

5076 Pansy (8)

5077 Stylized Flower

5078 Pieced Tulip

5079 Bud, *his.com*

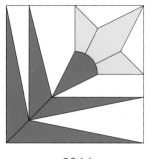

5065

5066

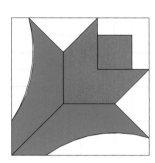

5067

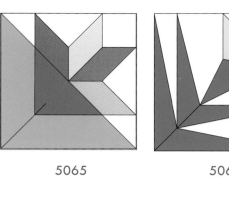

5068

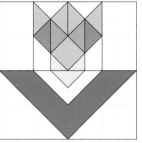

5069

5070

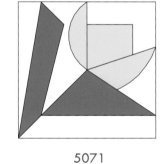

5071

5072

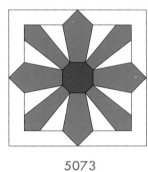

5073

5074

5075

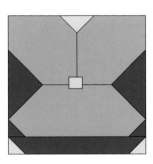

5076

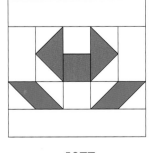

5077

5078

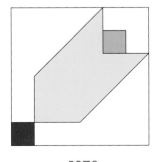

5079

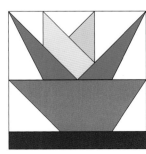

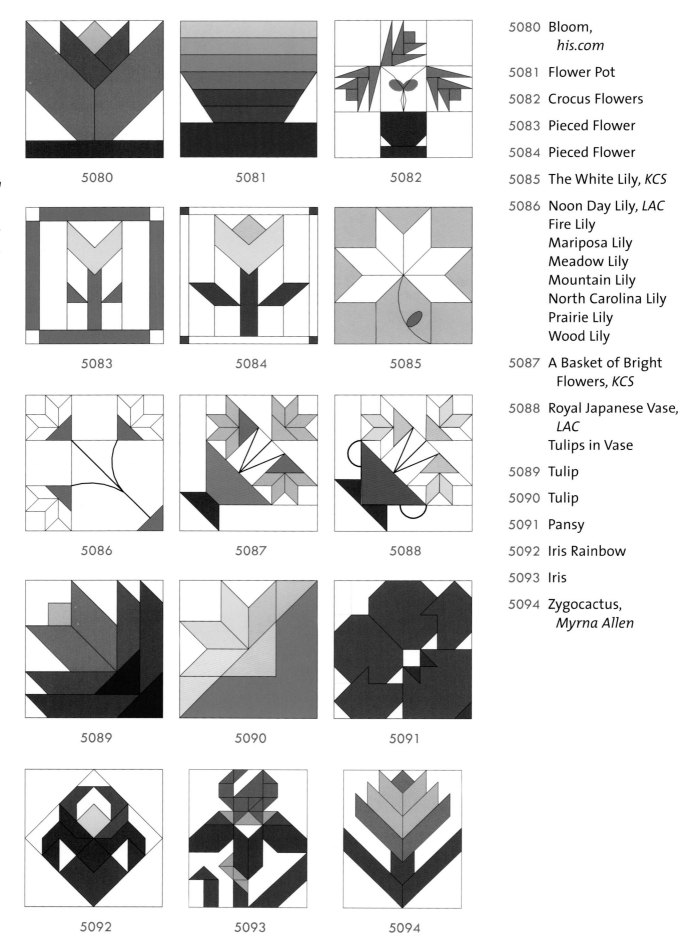

5,500 QUILT BLOCK DESIGNS

5080

5081

5082

5083

5084

5085

5086

5087

5088

5089

5090

5091

5092

5093

5094

5080 Bloom,
   his.com

5081 Flower Pot

5082 Crocus Flowers

5083 Pieced Flower

5084 Pieced Flower

5085 The White Lily, *KCS*

5086 Noon Day Lily, *LAC*
   Fire Lily
   Mariposa Lily
   Meadow Lily
   Mountain Lily
   North Carolina Lily
   Prairie Lily
   Wood Lily

5087 A Basket of Bright
   Flowers, *KCS*

5088 Royal Japanese Vase,
   LAC
   Tulips in Vase

5089 Tulip

5090 Tulip

5091 Pansy

5092 Iris Rainbow

5093 Iris

5094 Zygocactus,
   Myrna Allen

5095 Art Deco Tulip

5096 Modernistic Pansy, *NC* Pansy

5097 Pieced Pansy

5098 Modernistic Pansy

5099 Modernistic California Poppy

5100 Primrose Patch

5101 Modernistic Trumpet Vine (9) Trumpet Vine

5102 Modernistic Rose

5103 Palm Flower

5104 Triple Sunflower

5105 Daisy Block

5106 Star Bouquet

5107 Aunt Martha's Tulips

5108 Lily of the Valley, *QW, 1989*

5109 Evening Flower, *OCS*

5095

5096

5097

5098

5099

5100

5101

5102

5103

5104

5105

5106

5107

5108

5109

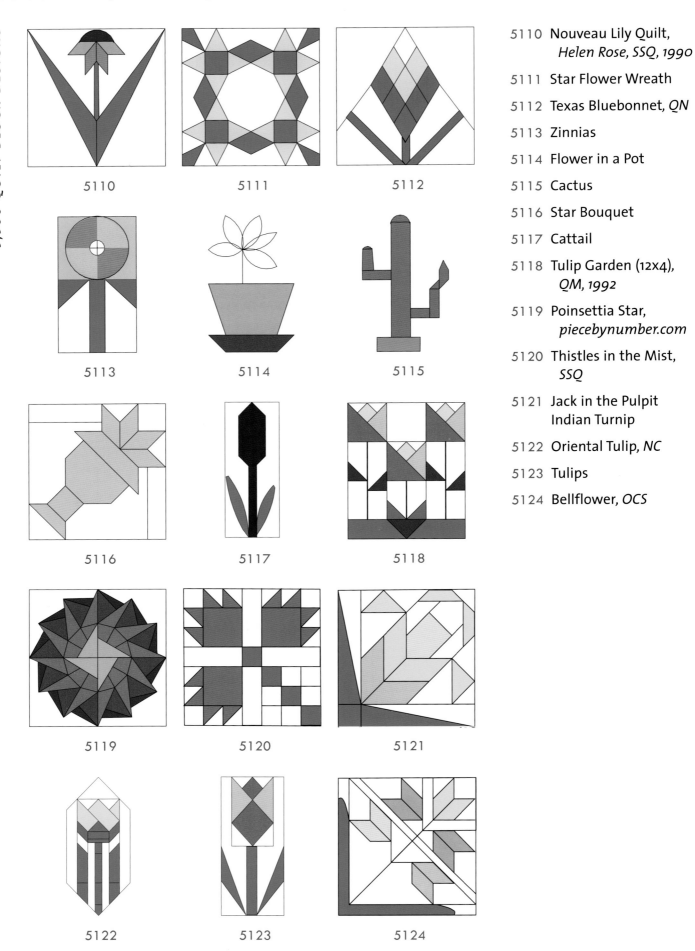

5110

5111

5112

5113

5114

5115

5116

5117

5118

5119

5120

5121

5122

5123

5124

5110 Nouveau Lily Quilt, *Helen Rose, SSQ, 1990*

5111 Star Flower Wreath

5112 Texas Bluebonnet, *QN*

5113 Zinnias

5114 Flower in a Pot

5115 Cactus

5116 Star Bouquet

5117 Cattail

5118 Tulip Garden (12x4), *QM, 1992*

5119 Poinsettia Star, *piecebynumber.com*

5120 Thistles in the Mist, *SSQ*

5121 Jack in the Pulpit Indian Turnip

5122 Oriental Tulip, *NC*

5123 Tulips

5124 Bellflower, *OCS*

5125 Camellia, *QM, 1993*

5126 Baby Rose

5127 Tulip

5128 Tiger Lilies

5129 Peonys

5130 Lily Pool

5131 Tulips

5132 Chrysanthemum

5133 Just Enough Tulips

5134 Diamond Rose,
    Sandra Pierson, QW,
    1983

5135 North Carolina Lily
    The Double Tulip, *MD*

5136 Rose Trellis

5137 Iris Rainbow, *QW, 1980*

5138 Double Tulip

5139 Tulip

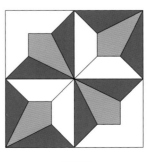

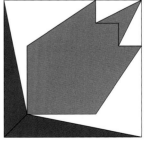

5125 5126 5127

5128 5129 5130

5131 5132 5133

5134 5135 5136

5137 5138 5139

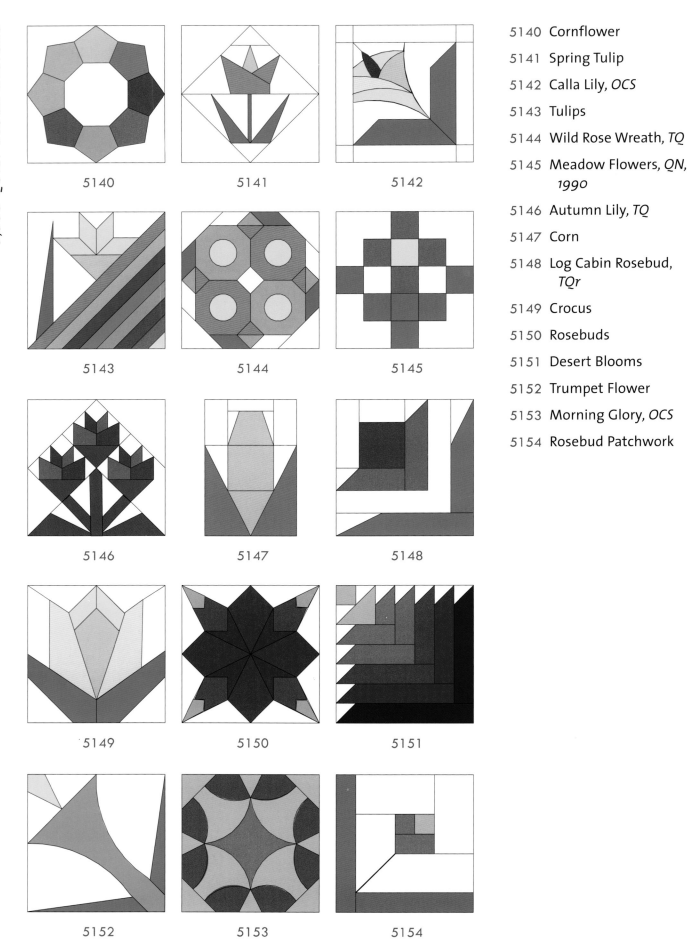

5140   5141   5142

5143   5144   5145

5146   5147   5148

5149   5150   5151

5152   5153   5154

5140 Cornflower

5141 Spring Tulip

5142 Calla Lily, *OCS*

5143 Tulips

5144 Wild Rose Wreath, *TQ*

5145 Meadow Flowers, *QN, 1990*

5146 Autumn Lily, *TQ*

5147 Corn

5148 Log Cabin Rosebud, *TQr*

5149 Crocus

5150 Rosebuds

5151 Desert Blooms

5152 Trumpet Flower

5153 Morning Glory, *OCS*

5154 Rosebud Patchwork

5155 Lily of the Valley

5156 Nosegay, *OCS*

5157 Iris, *OCS*

5158 Acorn

5159 Rose Garden

5160 Oriental Rose, *NC*

5161 Pond Lily, *OCS*

5162 A Lily Quilt
   The Fire Lily
   The Mariposa Lily
   The Mountain Lily
   The Meadow Lily
   The Prairie Lily
   The Tiger Lily
   The Wood Lily

5163 Tulip, *OCS*

5164 My Tulip Garden, *RMS,*
   SSQ, 1989

5165 Conventional Tulip

5166 Pansy Quilt, *HAS*

5167 Shasta Daisy, *LW*

5168 Wild Iris, *PP*

5169 Orange Bud, *AMS*

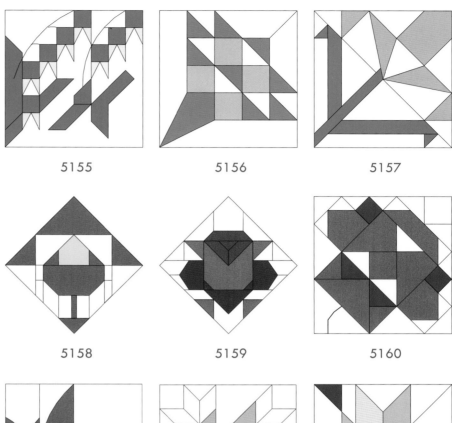

5155

5156

5157

5158

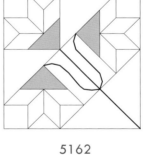

5159

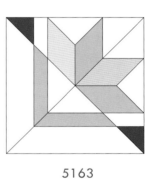

5160

5161

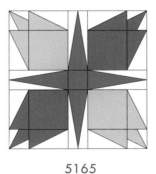

5162

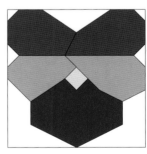

5163

5164

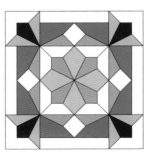

5165

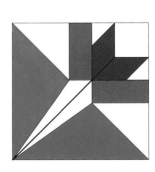

5166

5167

5168

5169

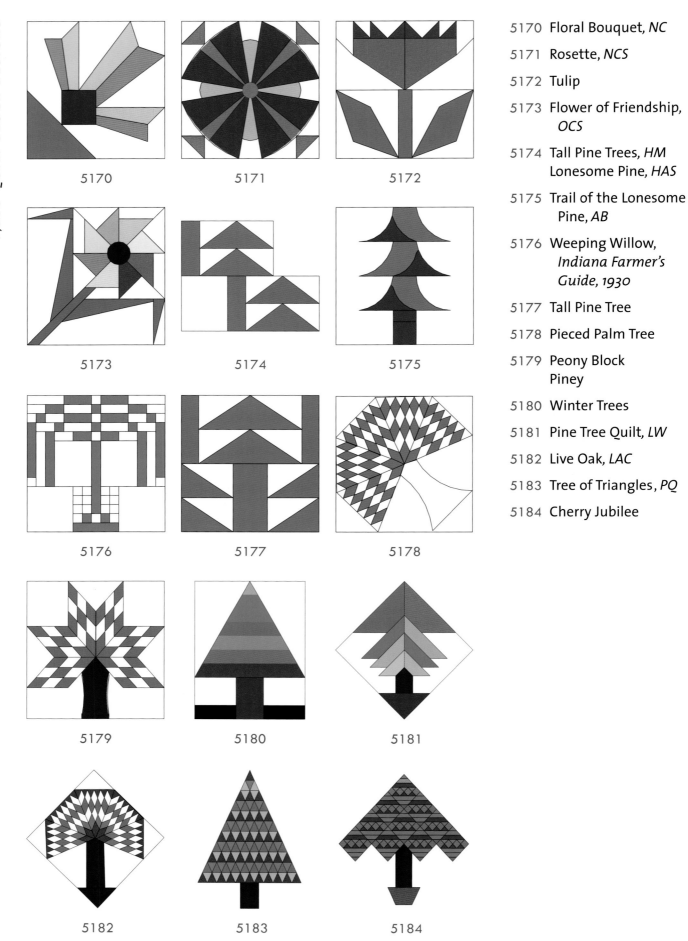

5170   Floral Bouquet, *NC*

5171   Rosette, *NCS*

5172   Tulip

5173   Flower of Friendship, *OCS*

5174   Tall Pine Trees, *HM* Lonesome Pine, *HAS*

5175   Trail of the Lonesome Pine, *AB*

5176   Weeping Willow, *Indiana Farmer's Guide, 1930*

5177   Tall Pine Tree

5178   Pieced Palm Tree

5179   Peony Block Piney

5180   Winter Trees

5181   Pine Tree Quilt, *LW*

5182   Live Oak, *LAC*

5183   Tree of Triangles, *PQ*

5184   Cherry Jubilee

5185 Pines in the Snow, *QT, 1988*
Pine Forest

5186 Pine Tree

5187 Pine Tree

5188 Winter Pines

5189 Pine Tree

5190 Pine Tree
Temperance Tree

5191 Norway Pine
Pine Tree, *OCS*

5192 Pine Tree Quilt Design

5193 Patch Blossom

5194 Christmas Trees

5195 Christmas Tree

5196 Evergreen

5197 North Woods

5198 Pine Tree

5199 Southern Pine

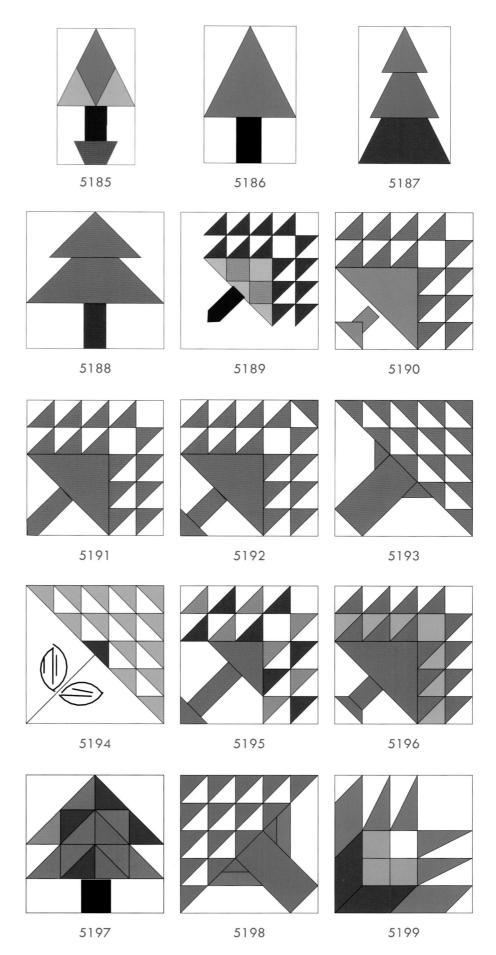

5185   5186   5187

5188   5189   5190

5191   5192   5193

5194   5195   5196

5197   5198   5199

5,500 QUILT BLOCK DESIGNS

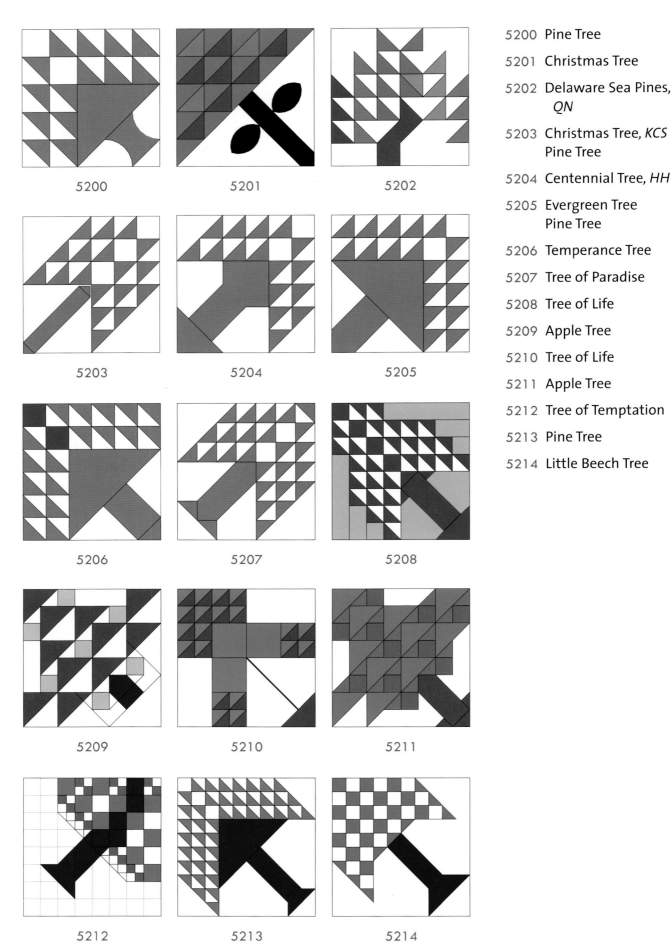

5200	5201	5202
5203	5204	5205
5206	5207	5208
5209	5210	5211
5212	5213	5214

5200 Pine Tree

5201 Christmas Tree

5202 Delaware Sea Pines, *QN*

5203 Christmas Tree, *KCS*
 Pine Tree

5204 Centennial Tree, *HH*

5205 Evergreen Tree
 Pine Tree

5206 Temperance Tree

5207 Tree of Paradise

5208 Tree of Life

5209 Apple Tree

5210 Tree of Life

5211 Apple Tree

5212 Tree of Temptation

5213 Pine Tree

5214 Little Beech Tree

5215 Tree of Paradise

5216 Christmas Tree

5217 Patchwork Pines

5218 The Forest for the Trees

5219 Tree of Life

5220 Scrappy Tree Block #1, *QEQ, 1993*

5221 Scrappy Tree Block #2, *QEQ, 1993*

5222 Scrappy Tree Block #3, *QEQ, 1993*

5223 Arching Tree

5224 Cascade Pride, *QW, 1981*

5225 Pine Tree

5226 Pine Tree Quilt, *OCS*

5227 Temperance Tree, *OF, 1894*
Tree of Paradise

5228 Tree of Paradise

5229 Tree of Paradise

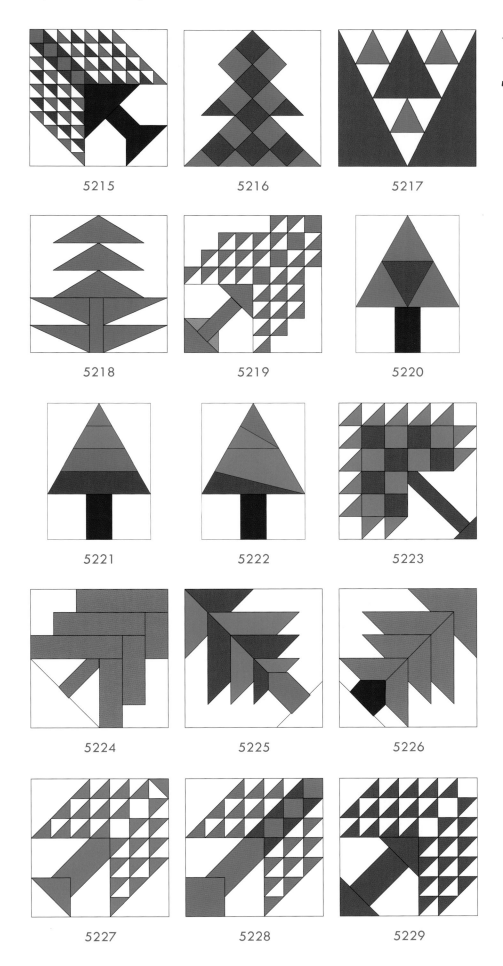

5215

5216

5217

5218

5219

5220

5221

5222

5223

5224

5225

5226

5227

5228

5229

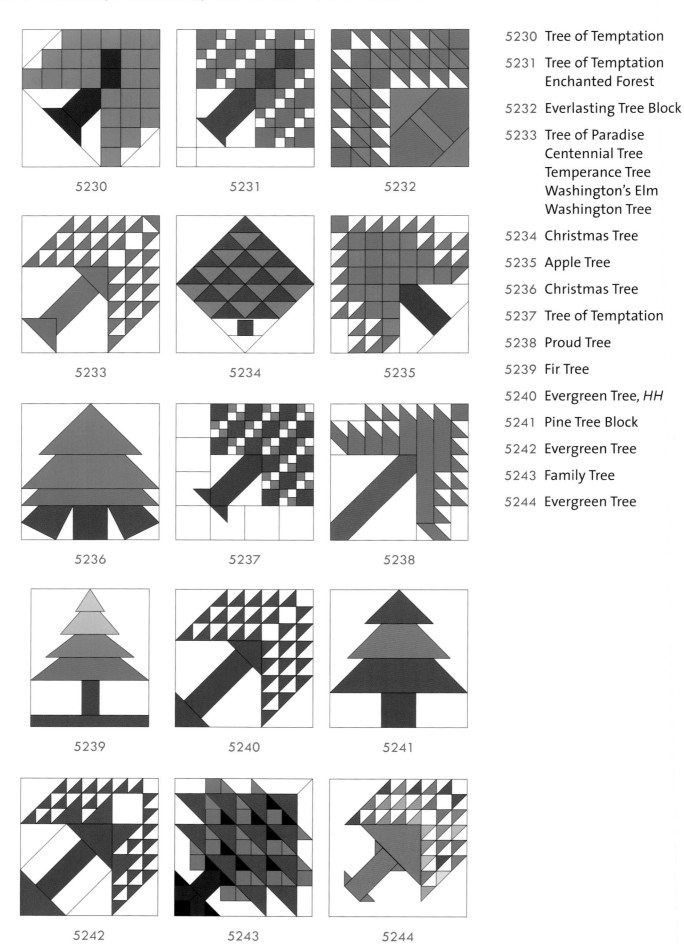

5230

5231

5232

5233

5234

5235

5236

5237

5238

5239

5240

5241

5242

5243

5244

5230 Tree of Temptation

5231 Tree of Temptation
      Enchanted Forest

5232 Everlasting Tree Block

5233 Tree of Paradise
      Centennial Tree
      Temperance Tree
      Washington's Elm
      Washington Tree

5234 Christmas Tree

5235 Apple Tree

5236 Christmas Tree

5237 Tree of Temptation

5238 Proud Tree

5239 Fir Tree

5240 Evergreen Tree, *HH*

5241 Pine Tree Block

5242 Evergreen Tree

5243 Family Tree

5244 Evergreen Tree

5245 Cone Tree

5246 Christmas Tree

5247 Weeping Willow

5248 Temperance Tree

5249 Cherry Tree

5250 Tennessee Pine

5251 Pine Tree

5252 South Jersey Pines

5253 Indiana Redbud

5254 Pine Tree

5255 Pine Tree

5256 Tree of Paradise, *FJ*

5257 Tree of Paradise, *LAC*
      Tree
      Christmas Tree Patch,
        CoM
      The Pine Tree

5258 Tree of Paradise
      Tree of Life

5259 Pine Tree
      Tree of Paradise

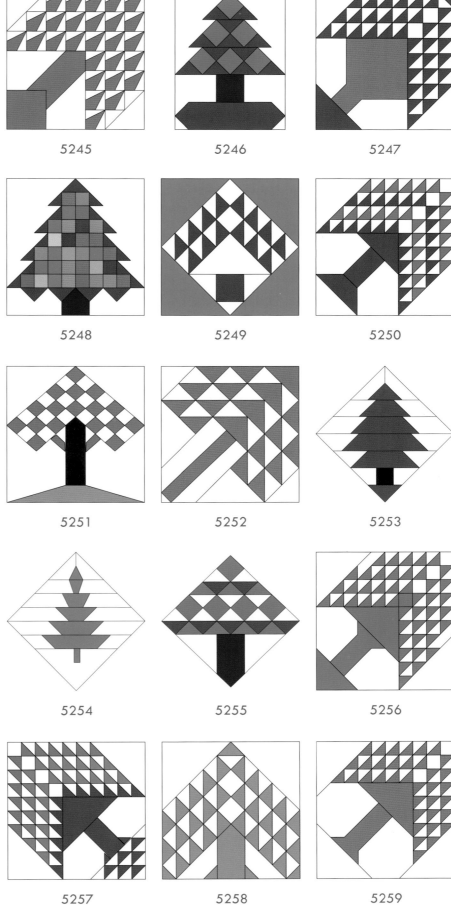

5245 5246 5247

5248 5249 5250

5251 5252 5253

5254 5255 5256

5257 5258 5259

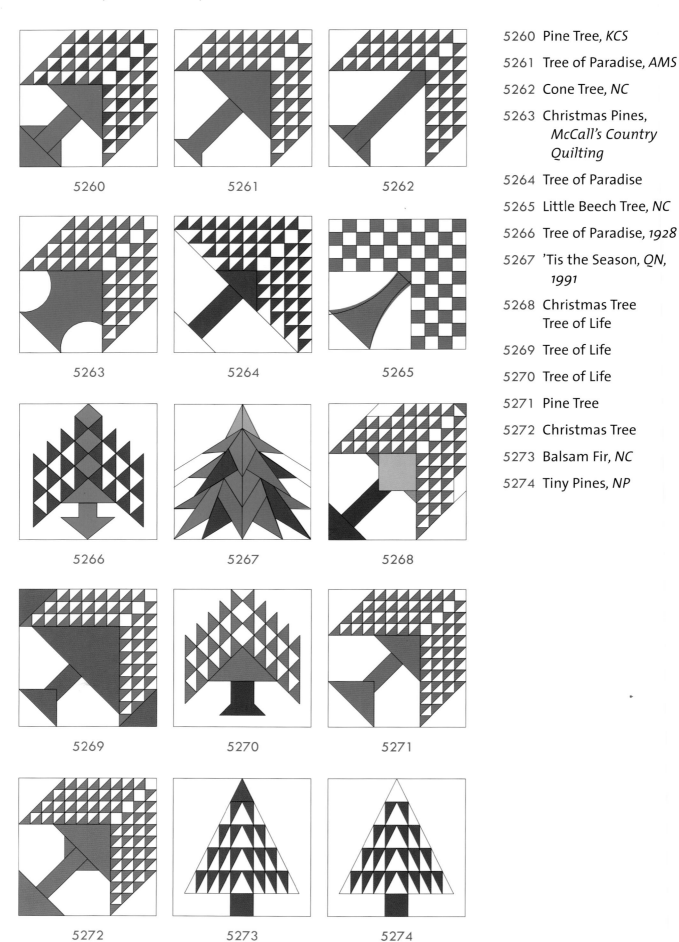

5260	5261	5262
5263	5264	5265
5266	5267	5268
5269	5270	5271
5272	5273	5274

5260 Pine Tree, *KCS*

5261 Tree of Paradise, *AMS*

5262 Cone Tree, *NC*

5263 Christmas Pines, *McCall's Country Quilting*

5264 Tree of Paradise

5265 Little Beech Tree, *NC*

5266 Tree of Paradise, *1928*

5267 'Tis the Season, *QN, 1991*

5268 Christmas Tree Tree of Life

5269 Tree of Life

5270 Tree of Life

5271 Pine Tree

5272 Christmas Tree

5273 Balsam Fir, *NC*

5274 Tiny Pines, *NP*

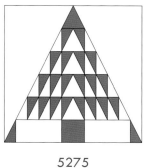

5275

5276

5277

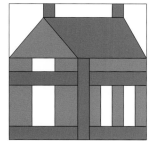

5278

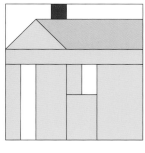

5279

5280

5281

5282

5283

5284

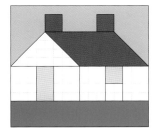

5285

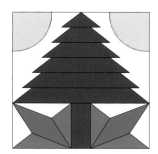

5286

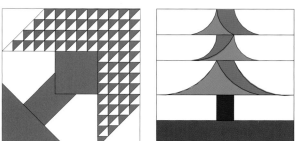

5287

5288

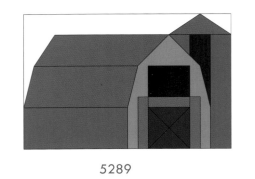

5289

5290

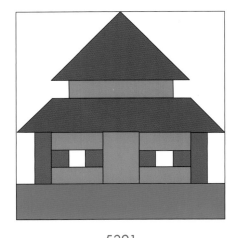

5291

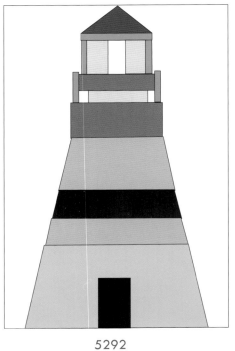

5292

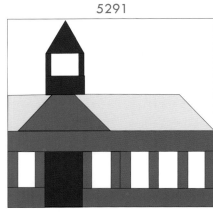

5293

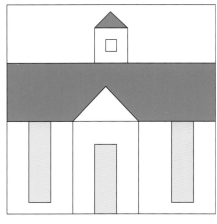

5294

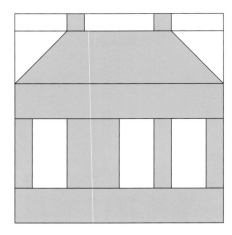

5295

5289 Barn

5290 House Contest Block

5291 The Lighthouse,
his.com/~ queenb

5292 The Train Station,
Debby Kratovil,
his.com/!queenb

5293 Church

5294 Country Church

5295 Pieced Schoolhouse
Block

5296 Village Church, *LAC*

5297 The Old Homestead, *LAC*

5298 Little Red House, *LAC*
House
Lincoln's Cabin Home, *HH*
Log Cabin
Old Home
Old Kentucky Home
Tippecanoe, *HH*

5299 Log Cabin Quilt

5300 Jack's House, *LAC*

5301 Iowa Barns

5302 Honeymoon Cottage (12x16)

5303 House
Back to School

5304 Pioneer Cottage Block

5305 Honeymoon Cottage (13)

5306 Village Schoolhouse, *RM*

5307 Red Barn

5308 Courthouse Square

5309 House on a Hill

5310 Schoolhouse

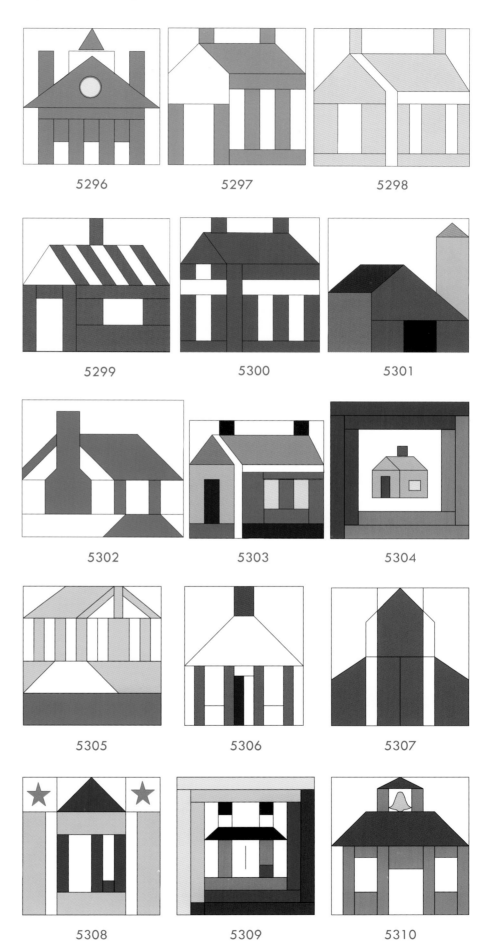

5296   5297   5298

5299   5300   5301

5302   5303   5304

5305   5306   5307

5308   5309   5310

5311

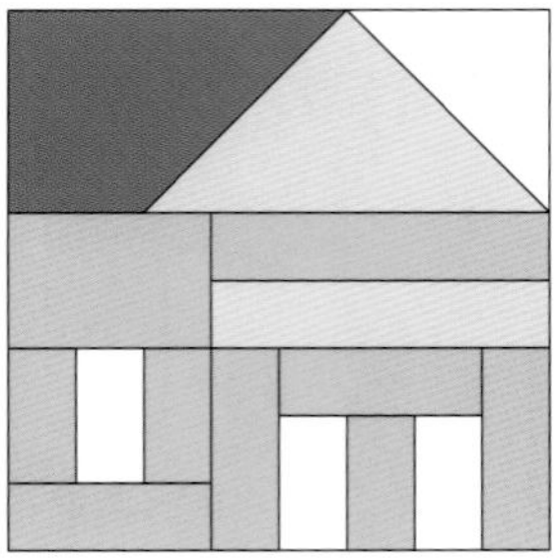

5312

5313

5314

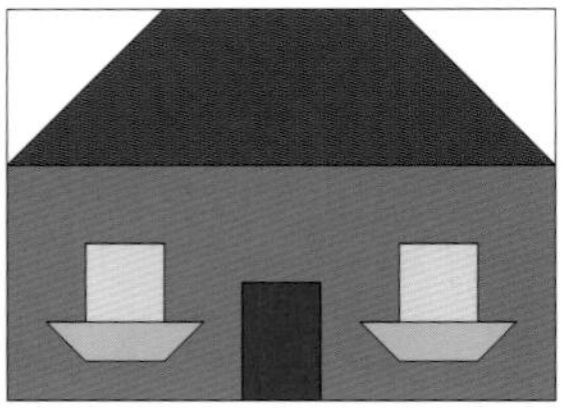

5315

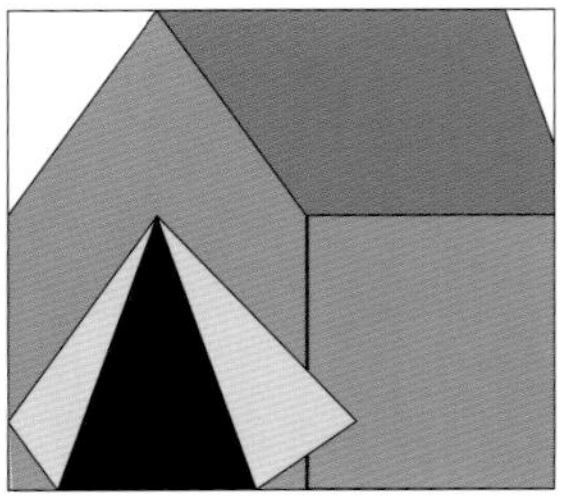

5316

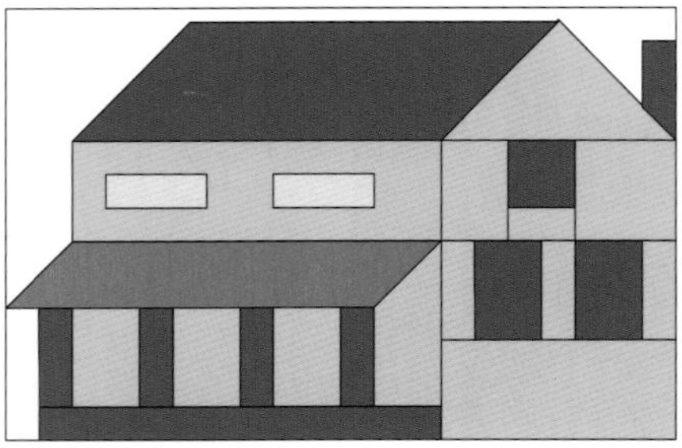

5317

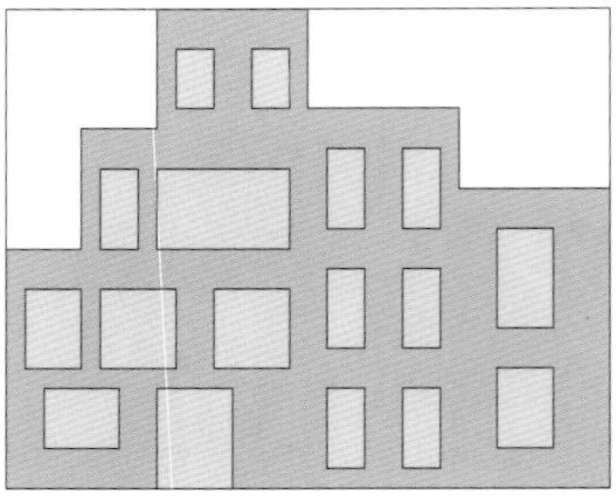

5318

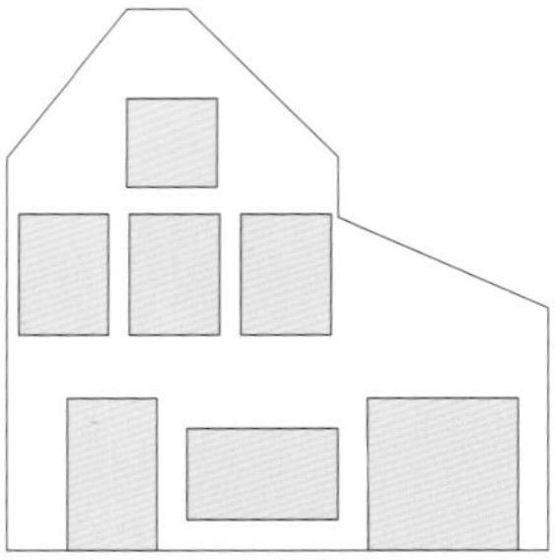

5319

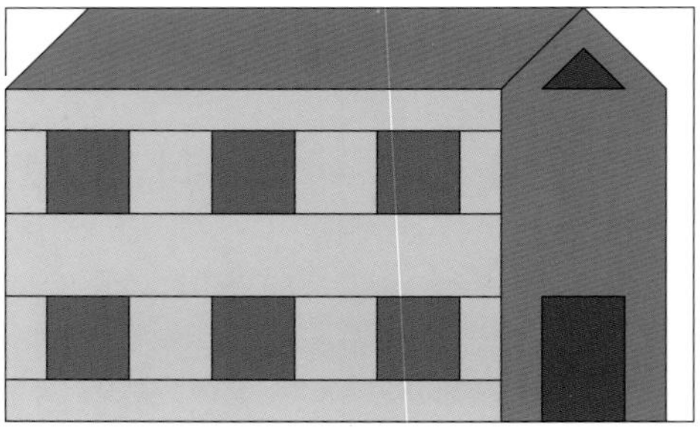

5320

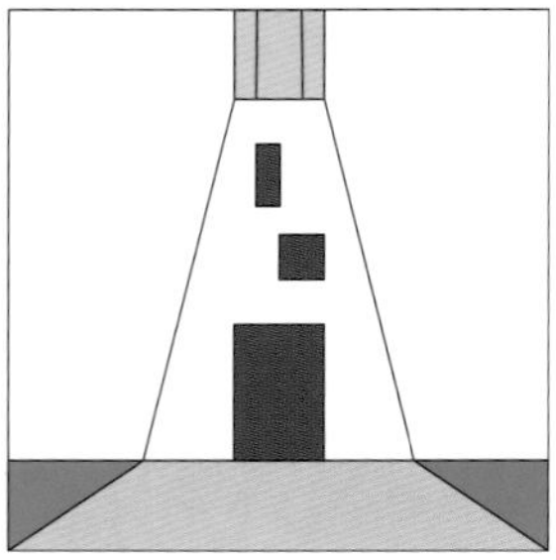

5321

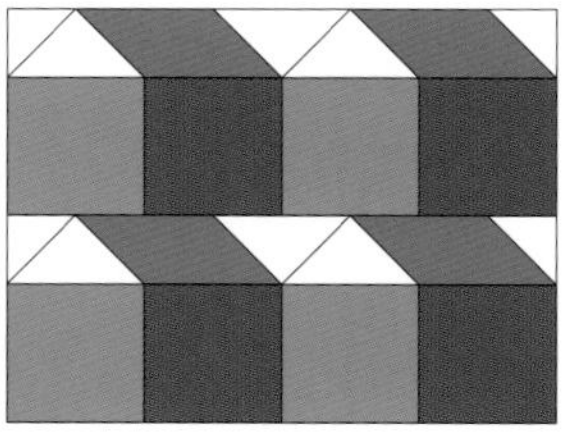

5322

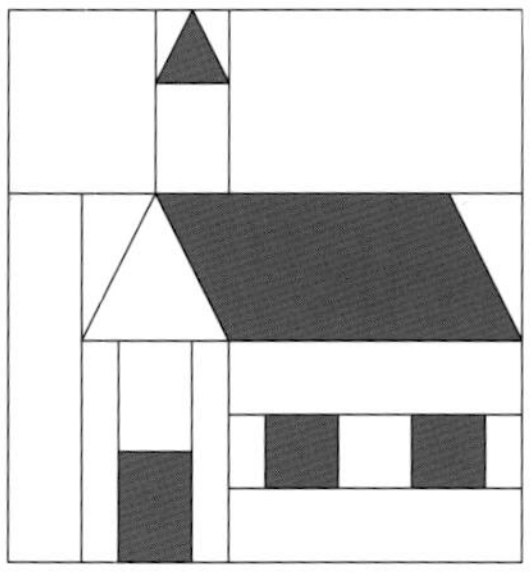

5323

5311 House on a Hill

5312 Home Sweet Home

5313 House with a Chimney

5314 Schoolhouse

5315 House

5316 Home Is Where the House Is, *TQr, 1991*

5317 Home Is Where the Quilt Is , *TQr, 1991*

5318 Apartment

5319 Big House

5320 House

5321 Lighthouse, *quiltmag.com*

5322 Houses

5323 Country Church

5,500 QUILT BLOCK DESIGNS

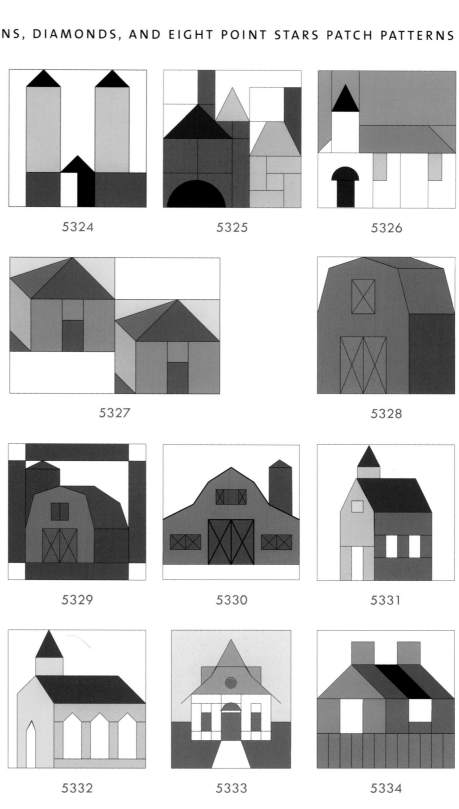

5324

5325

5326

5327

5328

5329

5330

5331

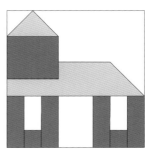

5332

5333

5334

5335

5336

5337

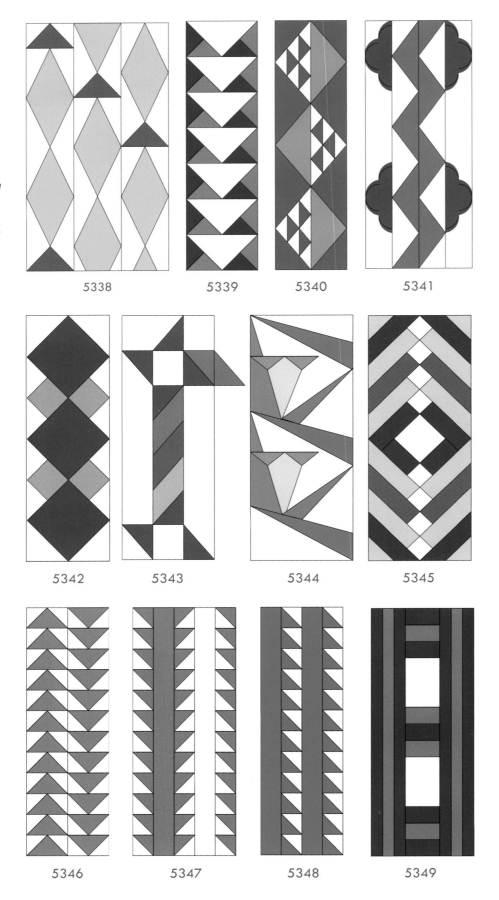

5,500 QUILT BLOCK DESIGNS

5338 Kites in the Air

5339 Flight of Geese

5340 Flying Geese

5341 Desert Storm

5342 Arabesque, *QM, 1994*

5343 Lattice for Maypole Dance

5344 Trumpet Vine

5345 No Name Strippie

5346 Tit for Tat, *AK*

5347 Arrowheads
 Herringbone
 Prickly Path
 The Path of Thorns
 Saw Blades
 Tree Everlasting

5348 Flags

5349 Roman Stripes and Squares

5350 Herringbone

5351 Chevron

5352 Border 1

5353 Border 2

5354 Border 3

5355 Border 4

5356 Border 5

5357 Border 6

5358 Border 7

5359 Tiffany, *QW, 1986*

5360 Coarse Woven
     Fine Woven

5350   5351

5352   5353

5354   5355

5356   5357

5358

5359   5360

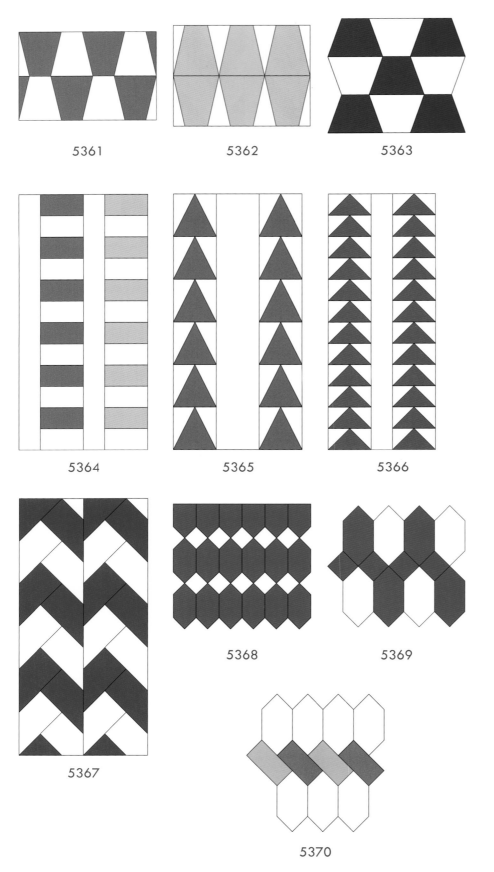

5361   The Tumbler, *LAC*

5362   Tumbler
          Flower Pot, *GD*

5363   Tumbler, *LAC*
          Out of This World, *OCS*

5364   Chinese Coins
          Bars

5365   Wild Goose Chase, *LAC*
          Birds in Flight
          Geese in Flight
          Wild Geese Flying

5366   Wild Goose Chase

5367   Twist and Turn, *LAC*
          Braid
          Pioneer Braid

5368   Fantastic Patchwork,
          LAC
          Quintettes, *NP*
          Stained Glass

5369   Rail Fence, *NC*

5370   Rope, *WW*

5371 Godey's Lady's Book,
1863

5372 Rope Strands, *KCS*

5373 Fenceworm, *PQ*

5374 Rail Fence Quilt, *KCS*

5375 The Mowing Machine,
KCS

5376 Bamboo Spread, *OCS*
Spindles

5377 Triangular Triangles,
LAC
Triangle Quilt, *QW*
Triangular Trees

5378 Flat Iron Patchwork

5379 Sugar Loaf
The Pyramid

5380 Picket Fence, *KCS*
Fine Woven Patchwork,
LAC
Featheredge Stripe
Fence Rail
Streak of Lightning

5381 Picket Fence, *KCS*

5382 Trellis

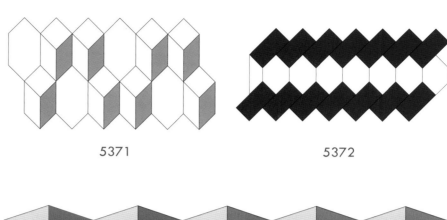

5371

5372

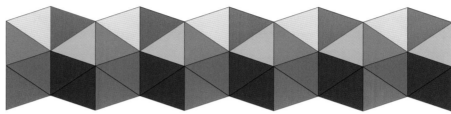

5373

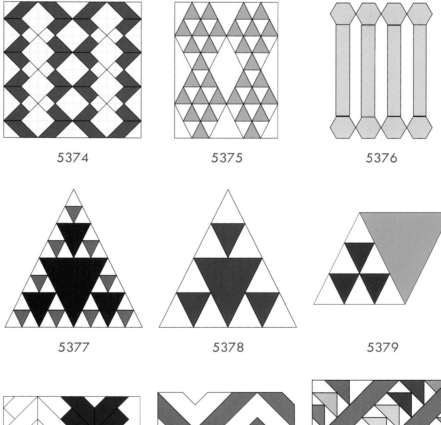

5374

5375

5376

5377

5378

5379

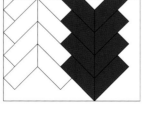

5380

5381

5382

5,500 QUILT BLOCK DESIGNS

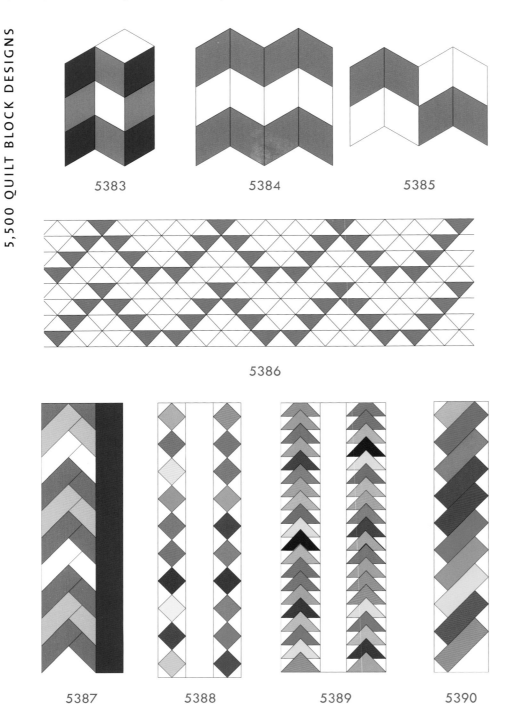

5383

5384

5385

5386

5387

5388

5389

5390

5391 Wild Goose Chase, *KCS*

5383 Building Blocks

5384 Wave, *OCS*
Rail Fence, *OCS*

5385 Butterfly Quilt

5386 Wild Goose Chase, *KCS*

5387 Migrating Geese

5388 Kite's Tail

5389 Nothing Wasted, *FJ,*
1937

5390 Stacked Bricks
Brick Walk

5391 Streak of Lightning

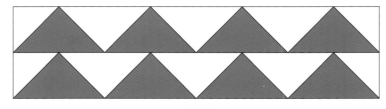

5391

5392 Mountain Memories

5393 Delectable Mountains
          Variation
          Sawtooth

5394 Summer Trees

5395 Border 8

5396 Ribbons 'n Pinwheels,
          QN, 1987

5397 Four Windmills, *NC*

5392

5393

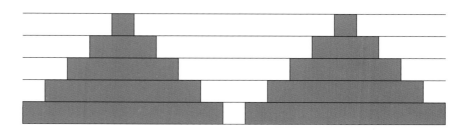

5394

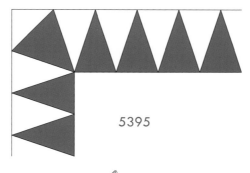

5395

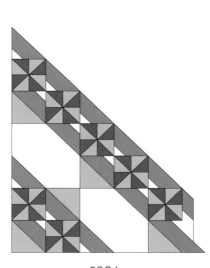

5396

5397

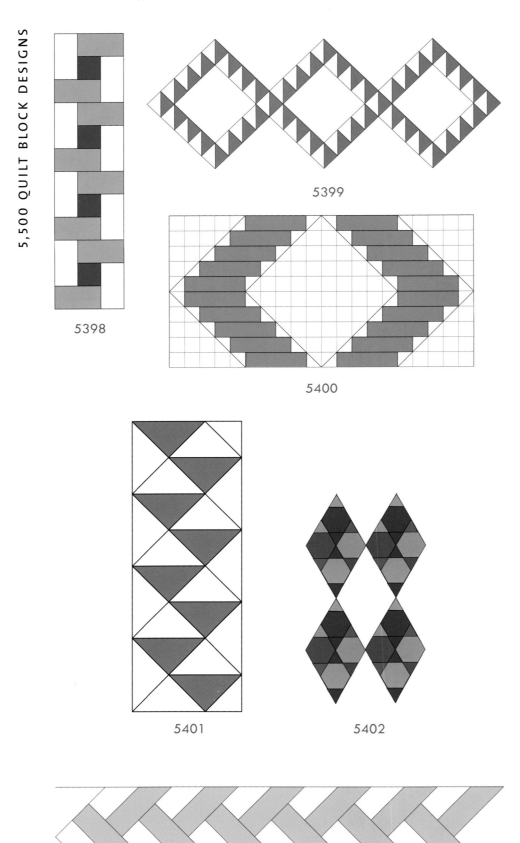

5399

5398

5400

5401

5402

5403

5398 Patience Corners
    Border

5399 Sawtooth Triangles
    Streak of Lightning

5400 Bridal Stairway
    Patchwork Block, *KCS*

5401 Migration

5402 Double Diamonds

5403 Double Braid

5404 Fence Rail

5405 Lover's Knot

5406 Floral Frame, *QN, 1993*

5407 Streak of Lightning

5408 Zig Zag

5409 Pyramids
Thousand Pyramids
Joseph's Coat
Red Shields, *NC*
Triangles

5410 Pyramids

5411 Pyramids

5412 Pyramids

5413 Fence Row Quilt, *KCS*
Dog's Tooth
The Lace Edge Quilt,
KCS
Lightning Streak
Mountains and Valleys
Snake Fence
Zig Zag

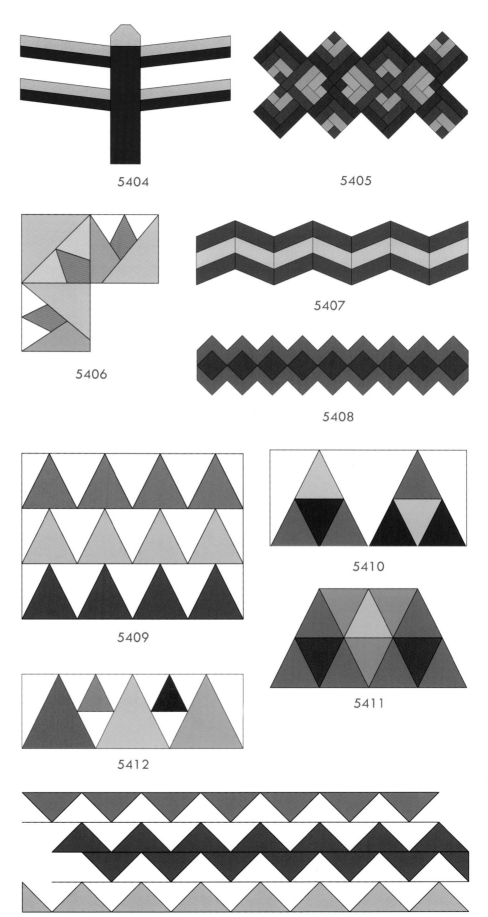

5404

5405

5406

5407

5408

5409

5410

5411

5412

5413

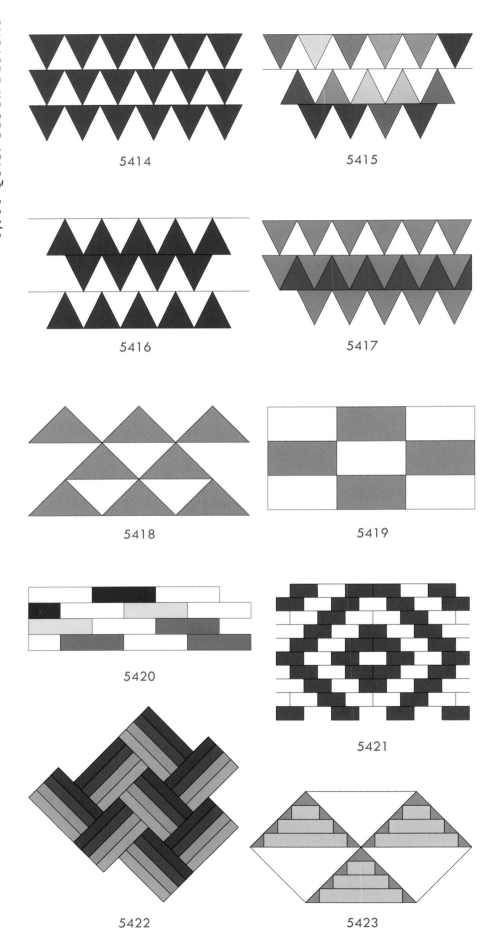

5414

5415

5416

5417

5418

5419

5420

5421

5422

5423

5414 Lightning, *NC*
Dog's Tooth

5415 Lace Edge Quilt
Lightning Strips

5416 Dog's Tooth
Rail Fence
Snake Fence
Streak o' Lightning
Zig Zag

5417 Chained Lightning
Land of the Pharaoh,
 NC
A Thousand Pyramids,
 NC

5418 Ocean Waves, *LAC*
Tents of Armageddon
Thousands of Triangles

5419 Hairpin Catcher
Brickwall

5420 Depression, *KCS*
Brickwall
Brickwork
General Sherman's
 Quilt
Old Garden Wall
Streak of Lightning
Zig Zag

5421 Brickwork Quilt, *LAC*

5422 Orange Pekoe, *NC*

5423 Pyramids, *LAC*
Pieced Pyramids

5424 Box upon Box, *NP*

5425 Diamond Rainbow

5426 Quilter's Rainbow
Charm Quilt

5427 Hawks in Flight, *NC*

5428 Spring and Fall, *NC*

5429 Wavy Navy

5430 Spider Legs

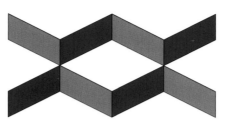

5424

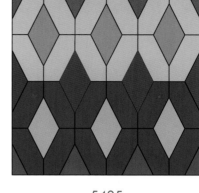

5425

5426

5427

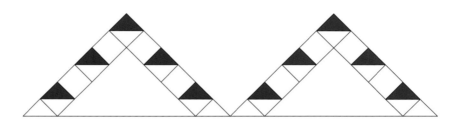

5428

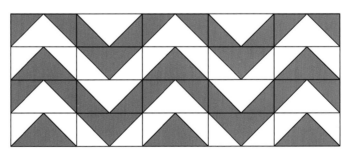

5429

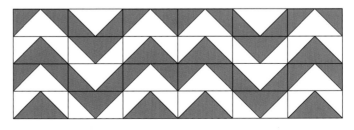

5430

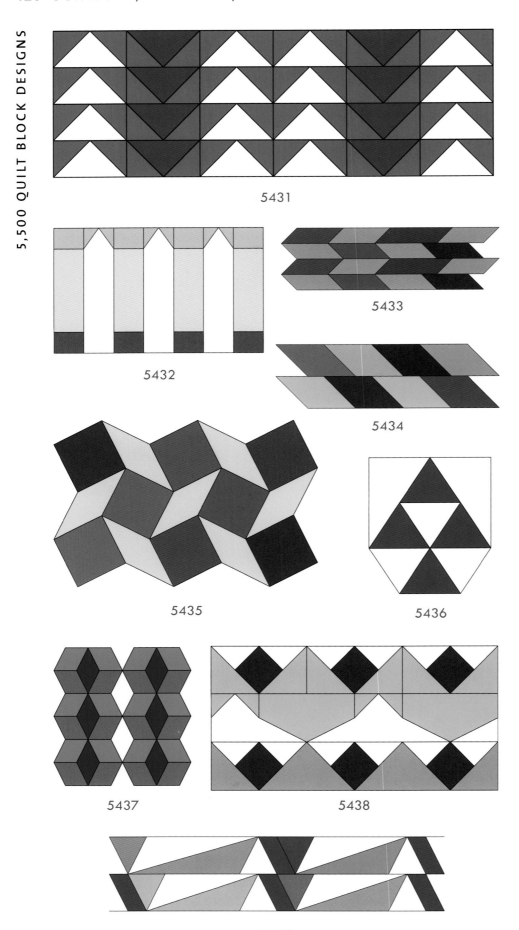

5431

5432

5433

5434

5435

5436

5437

5438

5439

5431 Wild Goose Chase

5432 Picket Fence, *AMS*

5433 Parallelogram Charm Quilt

5434 Diamond Charm Quilt

5435 Magic Squares

5436 Charm, *LAC*

5437 Variegated Diamonds

5438 Hills and Valley

5439 Cumberland Gap, *NC*

5440 Zig Zag Blocks, *GC*

5441 Sawtooth Triangles

5442 Migration

5443 No Name

5444 Clam Shells
Fishscale
Mushroom Shell
Over the Waves
Sea Shell
Sea Shells on the
  Beach, *KCS*
Shell
Shell Chain
Sugar Scoop

5445 Charmed Path, *QM*,
  1992

5446 Goin' Home, *QM*, *1992*

5440

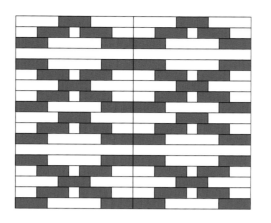

5441

5442

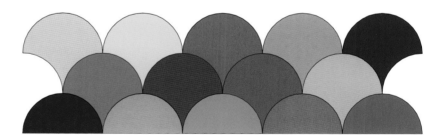

5443

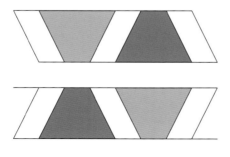

5444

5445

5446

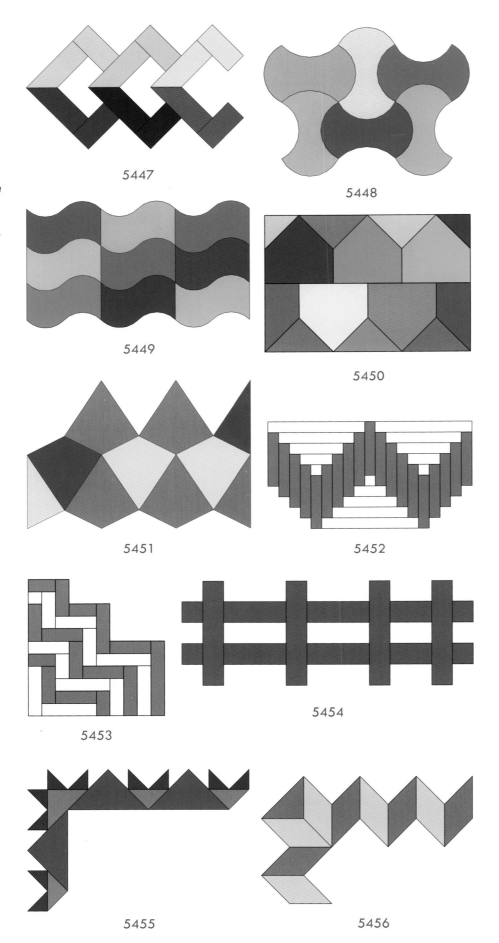

5447

5448

5449

5450

5451

5452

5453

5454

5455

5456

5447 Harvest Chain, *QM*, *1992*

5448 Spool
Always Friends
Axe Blade
Apple Core
Badge of Friendship
Charm
Double Ax
Double Ax Head, *OCS*
Double Bit Axe
Friendship Chain
Friendship Quilt, *KCS*
Jigsaw
Mother's Oddity

5449 Cracker

5450 House

5451 Kite

5452 Coarse Woven
Patchwork, *LAC*

5453 Five Woven Patchwork,
LAC

5454 Rail Fence Border

5455 Border 9

5456 Border 10

5457 Border 11

5458 Border 12

5459 Border 13

5460 Delectable Mountains
     Variation

5461 Delectable Mountains
     Variation

5462 Building Blocks

5463 Delectable Mountains

5464 Rail Fence Wave

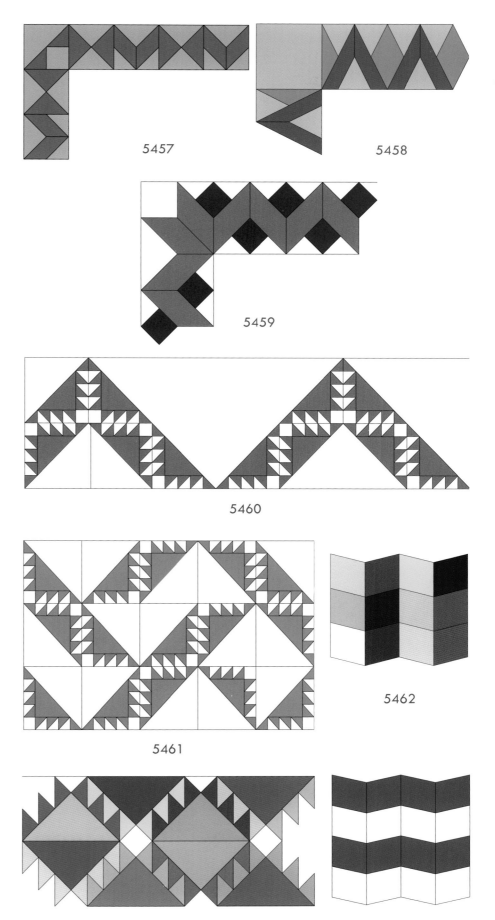

5457

5458

5459

5460

5461

5462

5463

5464

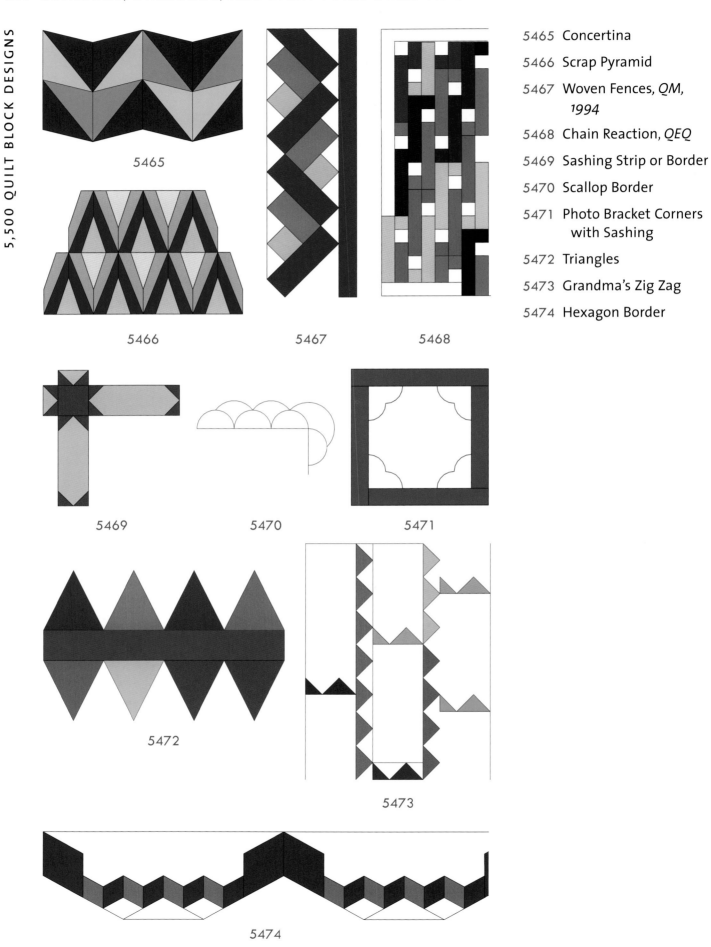

5465

5466

5467

5468

5469

5470

5471

5472

5473

5474

5465 Concertina

5466 Scrap Pyramid

5467 Woven Fences, *QM, 1994*

5468 Chain Reaction, *QEQ*

5469 Sashing Strip or Border

5470 Scallop Border

5471 Photo Bracket Corners with Sashing

5472 Triangles

5473 Grandma's Zig Zag

5474 Hexagon Border

5475 Cupid's Darts, *NC*

5476 Fields and Furrows

5477 Diamond Jubilee

5478 Yo-Yo, *GC, 1932*
    Bed of Roses
    Bon-Bon, *QN*
    Heirloom Pillow
    Pinwheel
    Powder Puff
    Puff
    Puffball
    Rosette
    Suffolk Puffs
    Yorkshire Daisy

5479 Biscuit Quilt, *OF*
    Bun Quilt
    Puffed Squares
    Raised Patchwork
    Swiss Patchwork

5480 Ice Cream Cone

5481 Segmented Diamonds

5482 Honeycomb Quilt

5483 Teepee Town
    Sugar Cone

5484 Crystal Honeycomb

5485 Tea Leaf Strippie

5486 A Floral Strippie

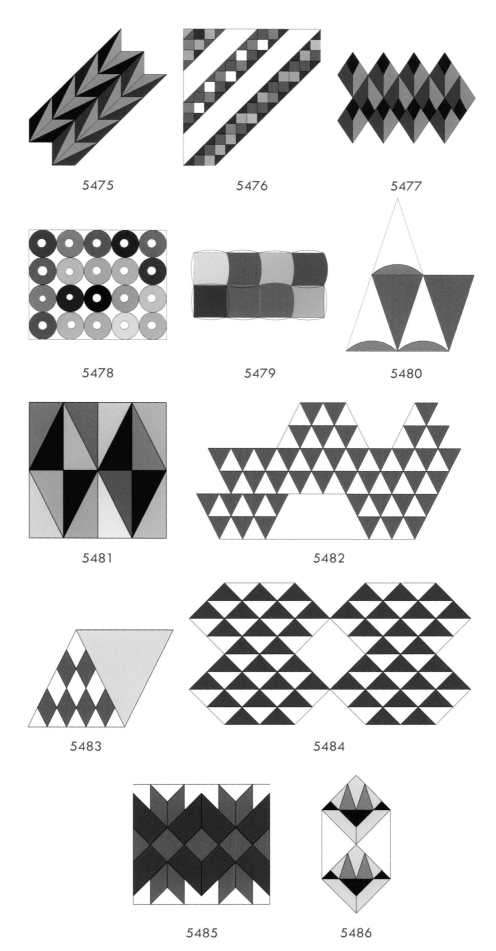

5475   5476   5477

5478   5479   5480

5481   5482

5483   5484

5485   5486

5,500 QUILT BLOCK DESIGNS

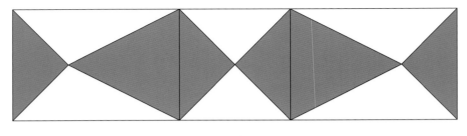

5487

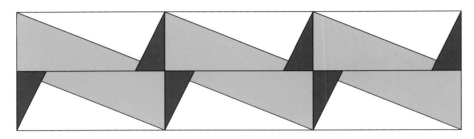

5488

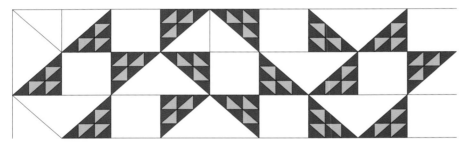

5489

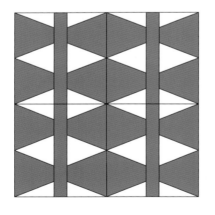

5490

5491

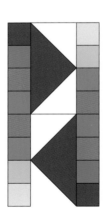

5492

5487 Fish Border

5488 Chaos, *AK, 1973*

5489 Over the Waves

5490 Sylvia's Beige and
     Brown

5491 Unnamed

5492 Marquee

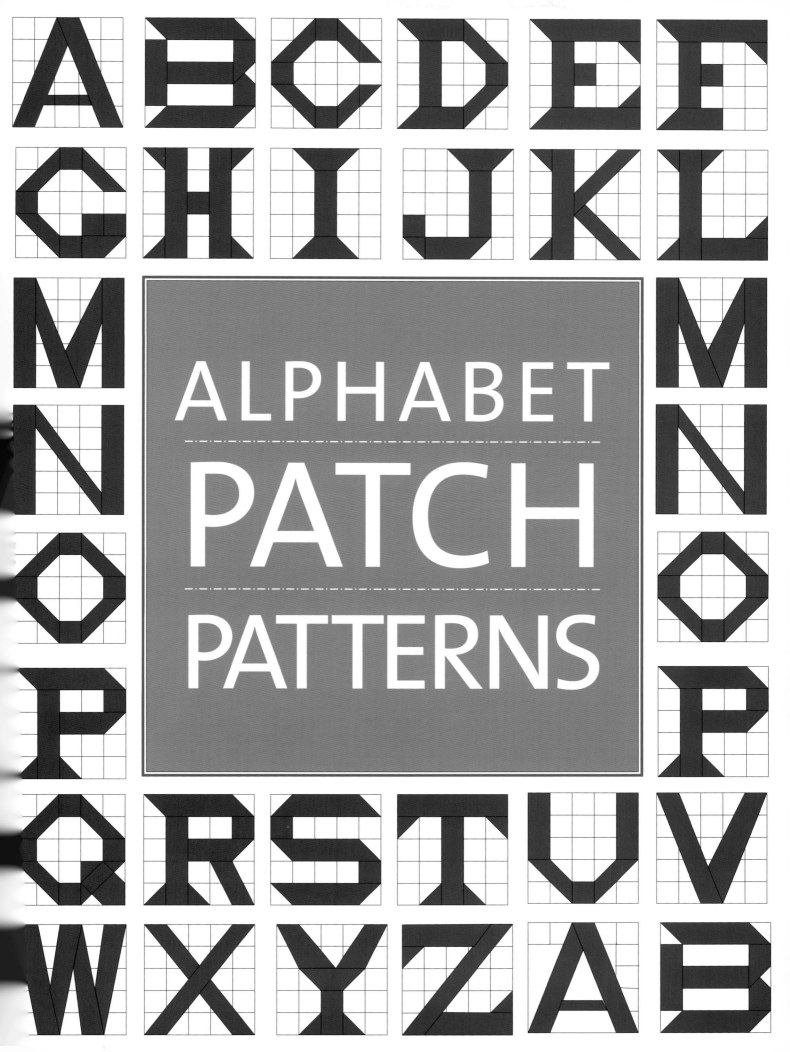

ALPHABET

PATCH

PATTERNS

5 X 5 GRID

THESE PATTERNS ARE DRAFTED ON A GRID 5 X 5 SQUARES
SCALE THESE PATTERNS TO A BLOCK OF ANY SIZE

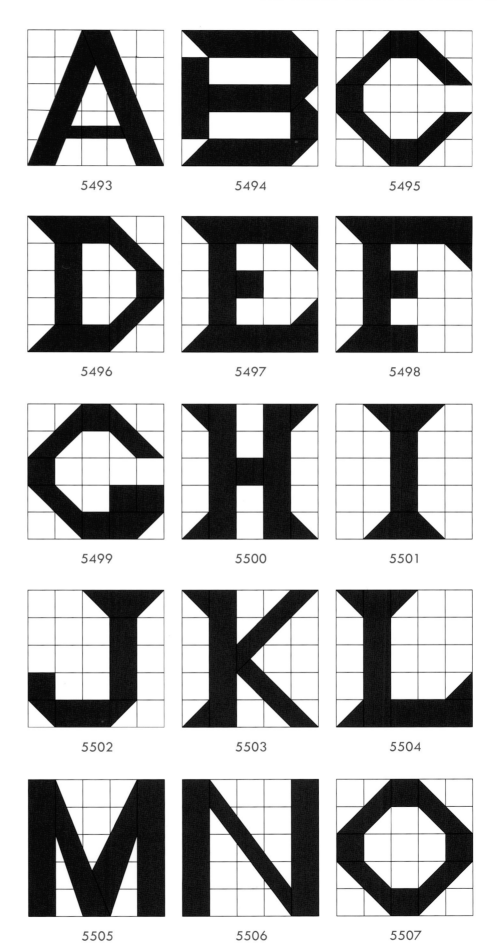

5493   5494   5495

5496   5497   5498

5499   5500   5501

5502   5503   5504

5505   5506   5507

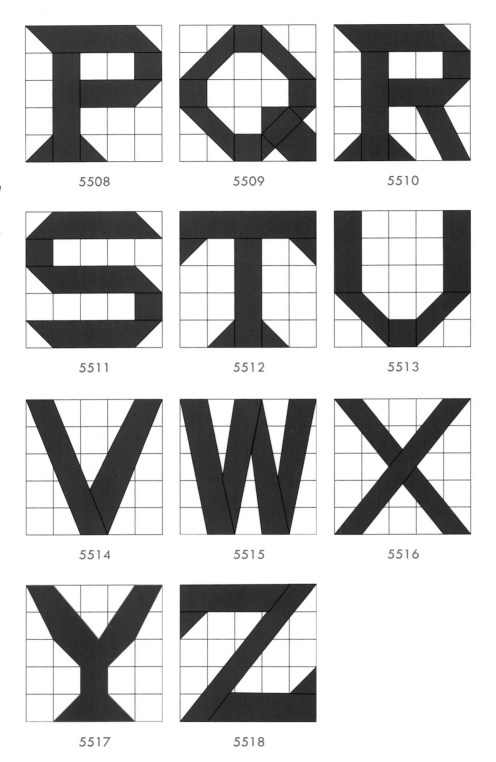

5508

5509

5510

5511

5512

5513

5514

5515

5516

5517

5518

INTERNATIONAL SIGNAL FLAGS

PATCH

PATTERNS

SEMAPHORE QUILTS USE A VARIETY OF PATCH PATTERN GRIDS.
COUNT THE NUMBER OF SQUARES ACROSS OR DOWN TO DETER-
MINE WHICH GRID A DESIGN USES AND SCALE THAT NUMBER TO
A BLOCK OF THE DESIRED SIZE.

5519 A—semaphore

5520 B—semaphore

5521 C—semaphore

5522 D—semaphore

5523 E—semaphore

5524 F—semaphore

5525 G—semaphore

5526 H—semaphore

5527 I—semaphore

5528 J—semaphore

5529 K—semaphore

5530 L—semaphore

5531 M—semaphore

5532 N—semaphore

5533 O—semaphore

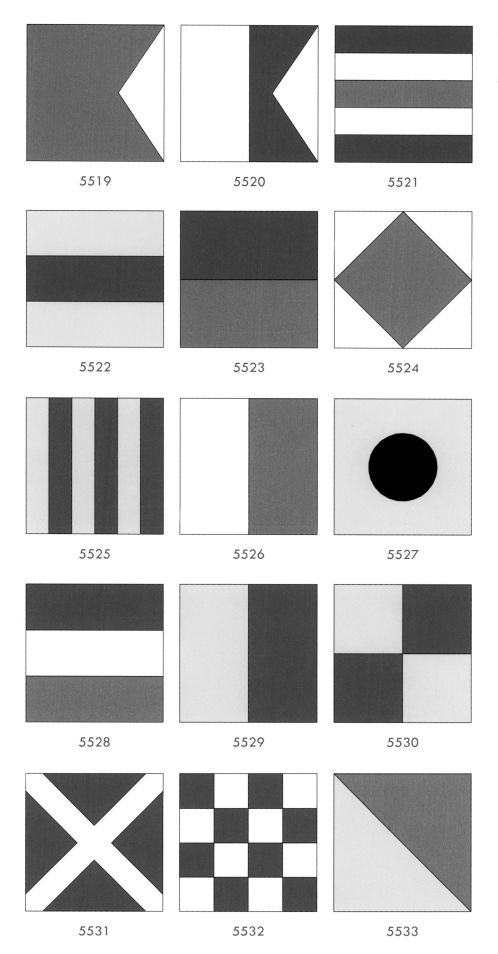

5519

5520

5521

5522

5523

5524

5525

5526

5527

5528

5529

5530

5531

5532

5533

5534

5535

5536

5537

5538

5539

5540

5541

5542

5543

5544

5534 P—semaphore

5535 Q—semaphore

5536 R—semaphore

5537 S—semaphore

5538 T—semaphore

5539 U—semaphore

5540 V—semaphore

5541 W—semaphore

5542 X—semaphore

5543 Y—semaphore

5544 Z—semaphore

Index

5,500 QUILT BLOCK DESIGNS

5,500 QUILT BLOCK DESIGNS

5,500 QUILT BLOCK DESIGNS

5,500 QUILT BLOCK DESIGNS